BRILLIANT BYLINES

A BIOGRAPHICAL ANTHOLOGY
OF NOTABLE NEWSPAPERWOMEN IN AMERICA

D1319513

BARBARA BELFORD

BRILLIANT BYLINES

A Biographical Anthology of Notable Newspaperwomen in America

COLUMBIA UNIVERSITY PRESS
NEW YORK

The articles of newspaperwomen in this book are reprinted by permission of the proprietors of their respective copyrights. Polly Pry: *The Denver Post*; Dorothy Dix: *New York Post* and Doubleday, Doran; Annie Laurie: *San Francisco Examiner*; Anne O'Hare McCormick and Ada Louise Huxtable: *The New York Times*; Emma Bugbee, Dorothy Thompson, Ishbel Ross, Marguerite Higgins, and Judith Crist: © I.H.T. Corporation; Sigrid Schultz: *Chicago Tribune*; Peggy Hull: *The Cincinnati Post*; Doris Fleeson: *New York Daily News*; Mary McGrory: Washington Star/Universal Press Syndicate; Ellen Goodman: © 1979 (83), The Boston Globe Newspaper Co./Washington Post Writers Group; Madeleine Blais: *The Miami Herald*.

PHOTO CREDITS: Jane Grey Swisshelm (Historical Society of Western Pennsylvania); Jennie June (from a photo in *Memories of Jane Cunningham Croly*, G. P. Putnam Sons); Polly Pry (Colorado Historical Society); Ida Bell Wells-Barnett (Moorland-Springarn Research Center, Howard University); Annie Laurie *(San Francisco Examiner)*; Nellie Bly (Courtesy of the New-York Historical Society, New York City); Elizabeth Garver Jordan (from a photograph in *Three Rousing Cheers*, D. Appleton-Century); Anne O'Hare McCormick *(The New York Times)*; Emma Bugbee (Jo-ann Price); Peggy Hull (Courtesy of the Overseas Press Club of America); Sigrid Schultz (Courtesy Ceil Chapman); Dorothy Thompson and Marguerite Higgins (The George Arents Research Library, Syracuse University); Ishbel Ross (Courtesy Pegge Parker); Doris Fleeson (University of Kansas Archives); Mary McGrory (Walter Oates); Ada Louise Huxtable (William G. Hotz Sr., *The Baltimore Sun*); Judith Crist (Tom Victor); Madeleine Blais (Kathy Willens).

Library of Congress Cataloging-in-Publication Data

Belford, Barbara.
Brilliant bylines.

Bibliography: p.
Includes index.
1. Women journalists—United States—Biography.
I. Title. II. Series.
PN4872.B45 1986   070'.92'2 [B]   86-6817
ISBN 0-231-05496-3

Columbia University Press
New York Guildford, Surrey
Copyright © 1986 Barbara Belford
All rights reserved

Printed in the United States of America

c 10 9 8 7 6 5 4 3 2

FOR DEBORAH de FURIA,
my daughter and best friend.

CONTENTS

INTRODUCTION

WHEN I WAS a high school student in the 1950s, writing about weddings and engagements for my hometown newspaper in St. Petersburg, Florida, I dreamed of being another Marguerite Higgins, then the war correspondent for the *New York Herald Tribune*. Her front-page bylines from Korea showed my generation of newspaperwomen that a journalistic life existed beyond the lace and tulle of the society pages.

Twenty years after Maggie Higgins graduated from Columbia University's Graduate School of Journalism, I received my degree from the same school and, like her, went to work on the *Herald Tribune*. I met her only once, when she visited the newsroom on home leave. I expressed my admiration for her accomplishments; she was curtly gracious and departed. For a role model to turn instantly into a mentor was, I realized, an adolescent fantasy. But idols of our youth are ever with us. After I became a professor of journalism at my alma mater, I would often refer to Marguerite Higgins' life and career. Few students knew her name. Her relative obscurity and that of other women journalists, both past and present, was one of the main reasons I decided to write *Brilliant Bylines*.

But rather than write another version of what can already be found on the library shelves—a collection of profiles or a historical narrative of women in journalism—I decided on a biographical anthology that would examine the lives and careers of selected newspaperwomen and include samples of their journalism as well. The anthology section is not intended to be read as "women's journalism," for I do not believe that a truly distinct and separate female journalistic tradition has developed in the United States. To be sure, gender influenced the writing of some stories, notably those on women's issues. But there are few stories herein—or published at any time in a newspaper—that could not have been written in the same context by a man. Women wrote mostly feature stories rather than front-page news in their early days in the profession not because they couldn't handle other assignments but because male editors did not trust them on breaking news stories. No allowances have ever been made for the woman reporter when she is given a chance at covering a front-page story. If she succeeds under pressure, the greatest compliment she can receive from a male editor is that her work is just like a man's.

Men, on the other hand, have never been complimented for writing like a woman, although many have produced stories just as lush as those of the so-called sob sisters whose jeweled prose enlivened newspapers at the turn of the century. One could speculate that Irvin S. Cobb of the *World* coined the much-abused epithet "sob sister" in a fit of jealous pique over women copying his style. Consider his description of Evelyn Nesbit at the Thaw murder trial of 1907: she had "the slim, quick grace of a fawn, a head that sat on her flawless throat as a lily on its stem, eyes that were the color of blue-brown pansies and the size of half dollars, a mouth made of rumpled rose petals." Or Dudley Nichols' depiction of the "pig woman" at the Hall-Mills murder trial of 1926, also in the *World:* "She fell back, perspiration standing out on her broad, aggressive face. The woman seemed made strong again by anger. She was transformed from the pale, dead looking creature brought in three hours before. Her paper-white face had colored, as if with fever, and her lips, which had been bloodless, were almost carmine."

Found on page 106 and page 232 in this book are descriptions of these two famous witnesses as written by Annie Laurie and Ishbel Ross. A comparison shows that in sensational journalism, at least, the men could be as flowery as the women. Moreover, women did not create the florid school of journalism; it was the male editors who bellowed for the purple prose to entice readers and outpace the competition.

The objective of this book, then, is not to examine whether women journalists wrote any differently—or even better or worse—than men. It is to show how the careers of women who became journalists (particularly the nineteenth-century pioneers), and what they wrote were shaped by both personal and economic necessity and by the demands of the newspaper editors of their era. By bringing together examples of work by twenty-four women from different regions and periods, I want to illustrate the important role in the history of American journalism played by women. Many others might just as easily have appeared in these pages, for there were—and are—countless talented women in the field. To limit the scope of this project, however, I have selected only those who made their reputations on daily newspapers. Beyond that, the choices were personal, but each one—living or dead, famous or forgotten—contributed in some way to the profession and to the advancement of women within it.

Throughout, I have attempted to examine the influence of parents, siblings, friends, teachers, husbands, lovers, and mentors. There were many strong-minded nineteenth-century fathers who believed that daughters as well as sons should be educated and who encouraged self-education through reading at a time when women were called on only to exist. Both fathers and mothers fostered independent thinking and supported their daughters who chose journalism over early marriage. But for most of these women, the person who exercised the greatest influence on their career choices and advancement was the mentor. Much to their credit, some male editors such as Horace Greeley of the *New-York Daily Tribune*, Col. John A. Cockerill of the *World*, and L. L. Engelking of the *New York Herald Tribune* recognized talent and initiative, giving women the opportunity to write about something other than food or fashion. And there were female mentors as well. Eliza Nicholson, publisher of the *New Orleans Daily Picayune*, discovered Dorothy Dix; and Helen Rogers Reid, wife of Ogden Reid, editor of the *Herald Tribune*, advanced the careers of Dorothy Thompson and Marguerite Higgins.

As the record shows, there has been progress since Margaret Fuller became the first woman to write regularly for a newspaper 140 years ago. It was not easy for any of the newspaperwomen included here to achieve their professional goals, just as it is not easy in the 1980s for women to move into executive positions on newspapers. Women had to overcome difficult odds not only to find jobs but also to cover stories outside the traditional sphere of women's news. These profiles illustrate that women succeeded because of determination, talent, and a commitment to the profession. They were competitive—even combative—with male colleagues and by having better ideas, taking risks, and never becoming complacent, they proved their worth as individuals—and the value of women in journalism.

While they were breaking down barriers in the newsroom, women witnessed sweeping changes in the journalistic product and process. Over the last century and a half the technology of producing newspapers moved from the pen to the typewriter and from the typewriter to the video display terminal. Unlike the reporter of the 1980s, the early nineteenth-century journalist did not have a taxi or a telephone or a radio to speed up news gathering, or often even a typewriter in the newsroom. Typewriters were not mass-produced until 1874. Telephones were not in general use until the early 1880s, and newspapers were not quick to have them installed. Marconi's wireless, invented in 1895, was not used for news gathering until 1899 when the young inventor reported on the International Yacht Races for the Associated Press.

Reporters relied on the horse and carriage and lots of footwork (reporting was referred to as "legwork") to get to the scene of news events; frequently they were participants rather than observers. Since sources were interviewed in person rather than over the phone, articles were dense with personal description and visual detail. But attribution, documentation, and telling both sides of the story were frequently ignored in favor of stylish writing. Stories emphasizing style over substance were acceptable until World War I when modern news writing started developing.

There were changes too in the background and education of newspaper reporters. Although nineteenth-century newspapermen were considered better educated than their female counterparts, some self-educated newspaperwomen, as these profiles reveal, were widely read, particularly in the classics and history. Many were teachers, and some had the advantages of growing up with extensive libraries that they had read through at an early age. The pride of most journalists at the time, however, was the general knowledge acquired on the job covering a variety of stories and learning to be an instant expert on just about everything. Standards have changed over the years and today's newspaperwoman is expected to have a college degree in the humanities, economics, or political science; many also have advanced degrees in journalism, international affairs, or business, even law or medicine. While modern newspaperwomen may have more impressive academic credentials than those who came before them, their predecessors had a familiarity with Greek and Latin, and an appreciation for the Bible and the great works of literature that are rare indeed today.

There are, of course, many "firsts" included in this book: the first women to be literary and architecture critics, the first women correspondents in Washington and abroad, and the first woman to win a Pulitzer Prize. There are those women—from sob sisters and tabloid writers to political and lifestyle columnists—whose writings form a historical chronicle of their times and have influenced or changed events. And there are a few who won no prizes and were not innovators, but whose lives and careers were so adventurous and exciting that they deserve to be rescued from the past. The biographical essays introducing each journalist are based on original research in newspaper and magazine archives, in published histories, biographies and autobiographies, memoirs of other journalists, unpublished academic theses, as well as countless personal interviews with friends, relatives, and co-workers.

In some instances the accompanying article or articles go beyond reportage to reveal more about the author's personality. Nellie Bly's story of her ten days in an insane asylum, for instance, illuminates her humanity and reporter's instincts, just as her life and career explain how she got the story.

And Polly Pry's combative prose for her article to free Alfred Packer, the convicted cannibal, echoes her lusty love of life and justice.

Literary critics often examine the life of a poet or a novelist in relation to his or her work, but few scholars do the same for the journalist working against a deadline to produce what Matthew Arnold termed "literature in a hurry." Newspaper writing is by nature perishable, relying as it does on continuing reports that eventually become a body of information. Articles rarely stand up well between covers twenty years later, and for that reason newspaper anthologies are not published with tidal regularity. A biographical anthology of women journalists, however, is another matter. Since women tended to report the human dilemma rather than the breaking news, many of the selections herein have a timeless quality, a staying power that entertains or educates the reader.

All articles have been reprinted from either the original newspapers or copied from microfilm. In a few instances, obvious misspellings have been corrected for reading clarity. Archaic spellings, capitalization, and punctuation have not been altered. Headlines and subheads have been reproduced in their capital or lowercase style. To tease the reader into a story, early newspaper copy editors exaggerated the most sensational or bizarre aspects of the story, not unlike the headline writers today at the *New York Post*. In some nineteenth-century papers periods were used after each line in a head, and frequently the reporter's name also appeared in the headline, often in addition to a byline. These headlines taken together illustrate some of the changes in newspaper editing from 1845 to 1983.

Many persons have contributed in various ways to this book. I am particularly indebted to those women who agreed to be profiled: Madeleine Blais, Judith Crist, Georgie Anne Geyer, Mildred Gilman, Ellen Goodman, Ada Louise Huxtable, and Mary McGrory. Although any listing cannot be complete, I have been helped in my research by those friends, relatives, and co-workers who knew—or know—the women here and have contributed their reminiscences, letters, and photographs. I have been encouraged by my colleagues at the Columbia Graduate School of Journalism, in particular Dean Osborn Elliott, Associate Dean Donald Johnston, Professors Phillips Davison, Penn Kimball, and Melvin Mencher and John Shearer, head of the photography department; by colleagues at other schools, including Professor Maurine Beasley of the University of Maryland, Professor James Boylan of the University of Massachusetts, and Professor Bruce Porter of Brooklyn College; and by Soma Golden, William Kutik, and Miles M. Merwin, friends who aided with research and proofreading.

Finally, special thanks to William Bernhardt, my editor at the Columbia

University Press, for his patience; to Wade Doares, head librarian of the Columbia University Journalism Library, for advising me since my student days on research methods; and to Zachary Sklar for being a superb editor.

PART I

BYGONE BYLINES

THERE WAS a time in America when women journalists had wonderful *noms de plume*—Polly Pry, Dorothy Dix, Jennie June, Nellie Bly, Annie Laurie. Many of these women went into journalism to write for and about women at a time when editors were trying to capture this largely untapped audience. Although much of today's newspaper advertising is directed toward women and papers now depend on female readership to build circulation, that was not the case in the early nineteenth century. Newspapers then concentrated on what men wanted to know, and that meant page after page of tightly printed columns mostly about politics and business. A stray column cautiously captioned "For the Ladies" might intrude into this gray, masculine reading matter, but generally those women who read at all preferred books.

The change in women's reading habits that began in the last half of the nineteenth century was the result of public education; women of all classes, not just the Margaret Fullers who were taught by Harvard-educated fathers, were learning to read along with their brothers. Editors were willing to experiment with publishing women's points of view in their papers, but they didn't want females underfoot in the newsroom. Some women were allowed correspondent status, though, working as freelancers and being paid according to space rates—that is, a set amount for every inch of copy published. They wrote tidbits about food and domestic life, often on lavender notepaper from their boudoir desks, and respectability decreed that they hide behind pseudonyms.

But there were others—adventurous, independent, assertive women who
often were family breadwinners—who were not content to sell a column a
month; they wanted a desk of their own in the newsroom and a paycheck
every week. If they had legible handwriting, could spell, and were accurate,
they might be given a chance, but those who persevered and succeeded had,
in addition, the ability to anticipate the needs of newspaper readers in a time
of social and economic change. In 1860, for example, Jennie June (Jane
Cunningham Croly) became the first woman to work and write daily from
the newsroom and the first to cover women's news and everything that today
is called lifestyle. She had more than mere intuition about what women
wanted to find in a newspaper's columns; she was also persuasive enough to
sell her ideas to editors. Although Nellie Bly was best known for her stunts,
she became a star reporter because she was in tune with a spirit of reform
that was sweeping the country in the latter part of the nineteenth century,
and because she had the good instinct to devote her attention to new causes
and issues.

The center of American journalism in the late nineteenth century was
Park Row, informally called Newspaper Row, in lower Manhattan, the location of all of New York City's fourteen newspapers and the foreign-lan-
guage press. Its heyday started with Joseph Pulitzer's purchase of the *Morning World* in 1883 and continued until the death of that paper in 1931. But
long before Pulitzer's arrival from St. Louis, Horace Greeley, the legendary
editor of the *Tribune* and a feminist of sorts, had been the first to recognize
the abilities of women journalists. In 1844 he hired Margaret Fuller as the
nation's first literary critic, later sending her to Europe to be the first woman
foreign correspondent. In 1850 he also hired Jane Grey Swisshelm, the first
woman to cover Washington politics.

At least in his willingness to give outstanding women a chance, Pulitzer
followed in Greeley's footsteps. It was to the Pulitzer Building that ambitious
reporters like Nellie Bly, Polly Pry, and Elizabeth Jordan first went to look
for a job. During a span of twelve years, Pulitzer increased the *World*'s circulation from 19,530 to 298,599, launched campaigns for the erection of
the Statue of Liberty and the nomination of Grover Cleveland for President,
and generally humbled all competitors. Other editors were content to wait
for news to happen, but Pulitzer made it happen. His undercover crusades
exposed villainy and outrageous social conditions; stunts, such as Nellie Bly's
trip around the world, captured the imagination of readers and boosted circulation.

While Pulitzer was sending his stunt girls up in the air in balloons and
down to the river in diving bells, William Randolph Hearst out in San
Francisco was perfecting a new personality: the sob sister. As exemplified by

Annie Laurie (Winifred Black) and Dorothy Dix (Elizabeth Meriwether Gilmer), the sob sisters developed a cathartic style that involved the reader in pity, fear, and remorse. The news event did not count so much as the writer's reaction to it. Invariably, headlines proclaimed: "Annie Laurie Tells . . ." or "Dorothy Dix Examines . . ." The sob sisters were highly merchandised, their stories carrying large bylines or personal signatures and, after the turn of the century, often a photograph. With images of their favorite writers engraved in their minds, readers knew that Dorothy Dix would give them the view of the wise aunt with a heart of gold and that Annie Laurie would report a tragedy that would make them sad but still offer hope.

In 1895, when Hearst arrived on Park Row to take over the ailing *Journal*, a paper its critics said was "published by fools for fools," he knew what he wanted and he had the unlimited funds to buy the best talent away from the competition. Pulitzer, moreover, was in ill health and nearly blind. Trying to run the *World* from European vacation spots, he was fostering a newsroom atmosphere described in Allen Churchill's *Park Row* as "a witch's brew of suspicion, jealousy, and hatred—a maelstrom of office politics that drove at least two editors to drink, one to suicide, a fourth to insanity and another to banking."

The competition that ensued between Pulitzer and Hearst gave rise to the term "yellow journalism" and provided plenty of color to one of the most colorful eras on Park Row. Pulitzer would stage an amazing stunt; Hearst would do one better. They both went in for sensationalism, often putting their female reporters in dangerous situations to titillate readers and increase circulation. While Pulitzer's frailties forced him to be an absentee publisher, Hearst was right there in the newsroom making sure that editors produced a lively, shocking paper. If he read a dull edition, he would often grumble, "This is like reading the telephone book." And it was the intrepid woman reporter who frequently made the difference between dull and lively.

Although nineteenth-century newspaperwomen all had plenty of spunk, they were surprisingly diverse. Nellie Bly and Elizabeth Jordan, for example, were born within four days of each other in May 1865 and were *World* reporters at the same time, but they represented quite different journalistic careers. Among the pioneer journalists, Nellie Bly's name is perhaps the best known, while only specialists have ever heard of Elizabeth Jordan. In 1890 when Jordan arrived in New York from the Midwest to find a job, she was much like some novice reporters today: middle class, well dressed, and well educated, with some journalistic experience and some family connections. A letter of introduction to the *World*'s managing editor paved the way to her job. Once in the newsroom, though, Jordan demonstrated her versatility as a reporter and writer and later as an editor, moving easily to other influential positions on magazines, in book publishing and the fledgling film industry. Unlike Nellie Bly, she did not tire of journalism but adapted herself to changes within the profession. Although Nelly Bly-style stunts would continue to be promoted on some papers until the late 1920s, editors were now intrigued with the circulation-building prospects of women writing sympathetic, saccharine prose, a journalistic genre that would later unfortunately be labeled the work of "sob sisters."

During the new century's sensational trials, the most infamous being the Thaw and Hall-Mills cases, the sob sisters distinguished themselves not only as reporters but often as interpreters of justice. Look at any newspaper microfilm from these times, and you will see that men were assigned the lead news story, with women writing the feature sidebars, which were often sympathetic to the women involved in the trials, though their sins might be scarlet. The sob sisters sought to find that "secret"—not necessarily the "truth"—which only a woman could extract from the combination of testimony, gesture, and appearance—a subtle transference of private insight from defendant or witness to reporter, which created an emotional bond with readers. From the point of view of publishers eager for increased circulation and its attendant profits, good murders were devoutly to be wished for, particularly if they involved love, sex, jealousy, honor, money, greed, and the lifestyles of the very rich.

The 1907 Thaw trial had all these ingredients. To avenge his wife's honor, the defendant, Harry K. Thaw, Pittsburgh heir and playboy, shot Stanford White, architect for New York society, at the roof garden of the old Madison Square Garden, one of White's famous designs. But it was the defendant's wife, twenty-one-year-old Evelyn Nesbit Thaw, a former Gibson girl and Florodora dancer, who made the story such a sensation. The sob sisters covered this trial as if it were the trial of modern society, which at the beginning of the twentieth century it seemed to be. Not until the still unsolved Halls-Mills case, in which a New Jersey minister and his mistress were murdered, came to trial in 1926 would any courtroom drama compete with Evelyn Nesbit taking the stand.

In the courtroom for these two "trials of the century" was Dorothy Dix, an insightful, motherly woman who had attracted Hearst's attention with her advice columns in the *New Orleans Daily Picayune*. She was forty-six when she wrote about Evelyn Nesbit's vulnerability and sixty-five when she sympathized with the plight of the betrayed wife, Mrs. Frances Noel Hall. During the Hall-Mills trial, Dorothy Dix wrote one of journalism's memorable "it was" leads: "It was a dark and dreary day. The rain beat a devil's tattoo on the windows, and the wind ran shrieking like a soul in mortal agony around the corners of the court house."

Covering a spectacular trial was indeed a choice and glamorous assignment. But most women in journalism started with more mundane stories. Usually they began writing women's news, moving later to feature writing as sob sisters if they displayed talent and initiative. Some were able to sidestep the stunt and sob assignments, never posing as someone else or covering courtroom drama. But these exceptions were usually women with a specialty like politics or foreign affairs, or those crusaders who could write as they pleased since they owned a newspaper—journalists like Jane Grey Swisshelm and Ida Wells-Barnett. Among those who were able to fulfill their career goals immediately was Polly Pry, perhaps the first woman journalist to use techniques such as document searches to buttress her stories, earning her a reputation as one of the first investigative reporters. Early on, Jane Grey Swisshelm established herself as a champion of the abolitionist cause, and Ida Wells-Barnett, the most notable black woman journalist of the late nineteenth century, conducted a one-woman crusade against lynching. Both had started their own newspapers as outlets for their opinions.

Historically, freelancing was—and still remains—a backdoor for gaining entry to a newspaper job. Initially, it gave literate women extra money and a sense of satisfaction when their verse and advice were published anonymously in "notes and comment" columns. Once encouraged, women came to the great, forbidding newspaper offices, hoping to be hired, but more often they were politely sent home with the promise of publication of their next letter. When they ventured beyond offering women's news to editors, however, and took risks to explore and understand the world at large, gathering exclusive eyewitness reports and interviews, then they had the clout to ask for fulltime jobs or correspondent status. Anne O'Hare McCormick and Peggy Hull are examples of women who established reputations as freelancers at home and abroad, attracting the attention of newspapers only after they had proved themselves to be astute reporters of the contemporary scene. McCormick was a gracious lady who traveled with her husband after World War I and discovered a talent for interpreting postwar Europe. Hull, on the other hand, was a restless adventurer, ready to go to Shanghai or Siberia or wherever there was a war to cover.

For many of the twelve newspaperwomen in Part I, journalism was something they happened to stumble into. Although most were born in the East and had some formal education or tutoring at home, their experiences growing up were quite different. Seven, however, shared a crucial turning point in their lives that influenced their entry into journalism: the early death of a father or of both parents. Jane Grey Swisshelm lost her father at age seven; Nellie Bly and Emma Bugbee each lost hers at age twelve. Annie Laurie was orphaned at fifteen and Ida Wells-Barnett at sixteen. Margaret Fuller and Jennie June were twenty-five when their fathers died. As a result, these women either had to contribute to the support of a widowed mother and/or siblings or work to support themselves. Still others would later face similar responsibilities: Elizabeth Jordan worked nights writing short stories to send money to her parents after they lost everything in the crash of 1893. For many years Dorothy Dix and Jennie June supported invalid husbands. Anne O'Hare McCormick's father deserted the family; to support themselves and a younger sister, Anne and her mother found work at the same Catholic newspaper. Only Polly Pry and Peggy Hull avoided such family commitments.

All these women with bygone bylines found a job the same way any reporter does today. To be sure, they had talent and were willing to work hard, and some were just lucky, but persistence—not taking "no" for an answer— was the common quality that defined their commitment. Work dominated their lives, overshadowing nonworking relationships and taking precedence over roles as wives and mothers. The only documented happy marriages were those of Anne O'Hare McCormick and Ida Wells-Barnett—and perhaps the nine-year, May–December marriage of Nellie Bly and Robert Seaman, and the liaison of Margaret Fuller and the Marchese d'Ossoli. Jane Grey Swisshelm deserted her husband; Annie Laurie, Polly Pry, and Peggy Hull divorced, remarried, and were widowed. Elizabeth Jordan and Emma Bugbee never married. Margaret Fuller, Jane Grey Swisshelm, Jennie June, Ida Wells-Barnett, and Annie Laurie had children, but motherhood never seemed to interfere with their careers. And except for the relatively short careers of Margaret Fuller and Nellie Bly, all dedicated their lives to journalism, working well past middle age and even into old age.

One is attracted to such women precisely because they demanded more from life than most people of their era. Although they are grouped together as bygone bylines, their careers and often innovative journalistic contributions have made it easier for newspaperwomen of the twentieth century to enter the profession—and to excel.

1

Margaret Fuller

(1810–1850)

WHEN MARGARET FULLER left her genteel and intellectual New England home to become a New York journalist, she stepped through the looking glass; not the one of Lewis Carroll, but of Virginia Woolf, who once noted: "Women have served all these centuries as looking glasses possessing the magic and delicious power of reflecting the figure of man at twice its natural size." And in coming out on the other side, the first woman to work regularly on a newspaper not only jolted the sensibilities of nineteenth-century male editors, but also became a role model for generations of newswomen.

She was never destined to be a drawing-room decoration like the ladies of her era. Her early education, directed by an authoritarian father, turned her into a Cambridge prodigy intellectually aware beyond her years. She rowed around Walden pond with Henry David Thoreau and did needlepoint sitting on the floor of Ralph Waldo Emerson's home. Her finely honed mind was of that kind that can live by itself, and all she read and heard was filtered into talk. Conversation, not the written word, was her natural medium.

Nonetheless, she was a tireless writer and thinker. It was her book *Women in the Nineteenth Century* (1845) that first brought her national attention. If Horace Greeley, editor of the *New-York Daily Tribune*, had not agreed to publish this landmark manifesto in the history of American feminism,[1] criticizing the neglect of woman's intelligence, Fuller might have languished at her desk penning scholarly essays. In addition, Greeley invited the thirty-four-year-old author to be his literary critic, the first of either sex to write criticism for a paper. She would spend but twenty months in this position before leaving for Europe as the first woman foreign correspondent for any paper.

Much has been written about Margaret Fuller: there are numerous biographies and anthologies and in 1983 two of a projected four-volume set of her letters. Attention has been paid to her criticism and dispatches on cultural and political events in England, France, and Italy, and on her intellectual relationships with Emerson, Thoreau, Nathaniel Hawthorne, and A. Bronson Alcott. What is not so well known is that she was, in between her columns of criticism, a general-assignment reporter, producing occasional articles on such issues as prostitution, the blind, women in prisons and asylums. The articles, extensions of her literary style, were actually editorials: Fuller's observations of conditions and recommendations for change.

By the time she started her journalism career, Fuller had been the editor of the Transcendentalist quarterly, *The Dial*, translated *Eckermann's Conversations with Goethe*, and written *Woman in the Nineteenth Century*. She was known also for her "Conversations with Women," which she conducted in private homes from 1839 to 1844, bringing education to upper-class matrons and young women who would have withered intellectually without Fuller's inspired tutelage on topics from mythology and art to women's rights.

Fearing for those women who were "trampled in the mud to gratify the brute appetites of men," she wrote in a *Tribune* article on September 30, 1845, entitled "The Wrongs of American Women, the Duty of American Women":

Were the destiny of woman thus exactly marked out, did she invariably retain the shelter of a parent's or guardian's roof till she married, did marriage give her a sure home and a protector, were she never liable to be made a widow, or, if so, sure of finding immediate protection from a brother or new husband, so that she might never be forced to stand alone one moment, and were her mind given for this world only, with no faculties capable of eternal growth and infinite improvement, we would still demand of her a far wider and more generous culture than is proposed by those who so anxiously define her sphere.

[1] *Woman in the Nineteenth Century* created quite a stir when it was published. It was the first such book in America to advocate equal education and to reject gender roles, and the first in English since Mary Wollstonecraft, the mother-in-law of the poet Shelley, published in England in 1792 A *Vindication of the Rights of Women*. Wollstonecraft's daughter, Mary Shelley, would later write a different kind of book: *Frankenstein*.

Margaret Fuller never had difficulty defining her sphere. "Very early," she once said, "I knew that the only object in life was to grow . . . I am determined on distinction." And thus she molded herself not only to compete intellectually but to surpass those bookish Harvard boys who hung around her house. She survived largely because of an enormous ego and unwavering self-confidence. "I now know all the people worth knowing in America," she once brashly announced, "and I find no intellect comparable to my own." As literary critic, she had no qualms about taking genius to task, and competed in this field with Edgar Allan Poe, her more famous contemporary.

In fact, she found many of America's new authors wanting when she wrote: "It does not follow because many books are written by persons born in America that there exists an American literature." She found Henry Wadsworth Longfellow's verse "imitative and artificial" and predicted wrongly that "his verse is stereotyped; his thoughts sound no depth; and posterity will not remember him." She dismissed the work of James Russell Lowell as "absolutely wanting in the true spirit and tone of poesy." Later Lowell would get his revenge by caricaturing her in his *Fable for Critics* as one "the whole of whose being is a capital I."

An early admirer, Poe, termed her criticism "piquant, vivid, terse, bold, luminous . . . everything a style need be." After Poe received not quite a rave review on his *Tales*, he sniffed that there were three classes of human beings: "Men, women and Margaret Fuller." (Fuller had criticized his word use: "he had with him many books, but rarely *employed* them . . . the results have, in truth, the whole *air* of intuition." The review ended, "Even the failures are those of an intellect of strong fiber and well-chosen aim.") Emerson, her first literary mentor, rightly observed that Fuller had a rather "mountainous ME," but he praised her style: "She poured a stream of amber over the endless store of private anecdotes, of bosom histories, which her wonderful persuasion drew forth, and transfigured them into fine fables."

To be sure, her literary criticism was rich, and she had a particular appreciation for the classics. Here was a writer who read before she was two and had mastered Latin at six. As a child she had read through her father's library, finishing Shakespeare, Cervantes, Moliere, and the German writers. In a letter she outlined her typical day at age fifteen:

I rise a little before five, walk an hour, and then practice the piano, till seven, when we breakfast. Next I read French—Sismondi's Literature of the South of Europe—till eight, then two or three lectures in Brown's Philosophy. About half-past nine I go to Mr. Perkin's school and study Greek till twelve, when, the school being dismissed, I recite, go home, and practice till dinner, at two. Sometimes if the conver-

Margaret Fuller

sation is very agreeable, I lounge for a half an hour over dessert, though rarely so lavish of time.

In the afternoon her studies continued, ending only when she turned to write in her journal before retiring at eleven. Even for someone of Fuller's ability, it was a stressful agenda that resulted in migraine headaches that she suffered from all her life. According to her, she had "special illusions, nightmare, and somnambulism, which at the time prevented the harmonious development of my bodily powers and checked my growth, while, later they induced continuous headaches and nervous afflictions of all kinds."

Sarah (she dropped this name as a teen-ager) Margaret Fuller was born in Cambridgeport, Massachusetts, on May 23, 1810, the eldest of nine children. Her father, Timothy Fuller, was a Harvard graduate of 1801 and a lawyer and politician who served eight years in Congress (1817–1825). Her mother, Margaret (Crane) Fuller, had been a schoolteacher before her marriage. Deprived of a normal childhood, Margaret grew up, in her own words, "bright and ugly." Her only formal education was a short stay at the Prescott Seminary for Young Ladies in Groton, Massachusetts, where she was intellectually advanced but socially awkward. Her emotional life was limited to flirtations with younger Harvard students and at least one incipient lesbian attachment to a visiting English woman who whetted her interest in European culture.

When Fuller was twenty-five, her father died and she had to find work to support her mother and eight siblings. She first taught in Bronson Alcott's Temple School in Boston and in 1837 went to Hiram Fuller Greene's School in Providence, Rhode Island, where she taught for two years earning $1,000 a year, a magnificent salary for a woman at that time. With a light course load, she had free time for her own studies and the translating of *Conversations with Goethe*. At this time she also heard the novelist John Neal speak on "the destiny and vocation of women in America," issues she would later address in *Woman in the Nineteenth Century*.

Returning to Boston in 1839, she decided to earn a living writing articles and tutoring, and became associated with the Transcendentalists led by Emerson and Thoreau. Fuller joined the group in debates on the innate goodness of man and the importance of intuition and insight over logic and reason. Emerson has described his first meeting with her:

I still remember the first half-hour of Margaret's conversation. She was then twenty-six years old. She had a face and frame that would indicate fullness and tenacity of life. She was rather under the middle height: her complexion was fair, with strong, fair hair. She was then, as always, carefully and becomingly dressed. For the rest, her appearance had nothing prepossessing. Her extreme plainness, a trick of incessantly opening and shutting her eyelids, the nasal tones of her voice all repelled, and I said to myself, "We shall never get far."

When Emerson and others decided to publish a quarterly magazine called *The Dial* they chose Margaret Fuller to edit it (without pay). One *Dial* article she wrote, "The Great Lawsuit, Man versus Men, Woman versus Women," was expanded into *Woman in the Nineteenth Century*. This book, highly critical of the constraints that kept women as second-class citizens, contains such insights as: "Male and Female represent the two sides of the great radical dualism. But in fact they are perpetually passing into one another. Fluid hardens to solid, solid rushes to fluid. There is no wholly masculine man, no purely feminine woman." Included among the rallying cries of this treatise, which helped lay the foundation for the Seneca Falls convention on women's rights in 1848, is: "Let them be sea captains, if you will!" Greeley would tease her about this exclamation, and one day refused to open the door for a "prospective sea captain."

Like most of the men who were intimates, mentors, or admirers, Greeley was fascinated with a woman who had digested the world of literature and language and could express herself so eloquently. He was also impressed by her work in *The Dial* and her first book, *Summer on the Lakes* (1844), an account of a trip to Illinois and Wisconsin. During her travels, with an eye for description and detail, she interviewed American Indians, the poor, and immigrants from Germany and Ireland. Greeley asked her to be the *Tribune*'s first literary critic. It was a bold move for Fuller to leave the security of New England for New York, a city termed "vulgar" by her Transcendentalist friends, and accept Greeley's job offer. Emerson declared that journalism might be "honorable" but was not satisfactory to him. Her decision to start a new career at age thirty-four as a literary critic and journalist was a turning point.

Immediately, Greeley stepped into Emerson's role as mentor and surrogate father. Fuller lived with the Greeleys at their Turtle Bay estate on the East River and wrote at home. By 1844 there had been numerous woman correspondents who wrote occasional essays and letters for space rates, but Fuller was the first to write regularly for any paper. She knew little about newspapers as a business and took no interest in the newsroom activities on Nassau Street. A deadline meant nothing to her. She wrote when the muse moved her and in the absence of the "black jailer" or the "vulture with iron talons," names she gave her migraines. This casual approach to journalism exasperated the hard-bitten Greeley, who could write two columns to her one. He began to wonder about hiring a critic who couldn't turn out copy on time. He described her working habits in *Recollections of a Busy Life*:

She could write only when in the vein, and this needed often to be waited for through several days, while the occasion sometimes required an immediate utterance. The new book must be reviewed before other journals had thoroughly dissected and discussed it, else the ablest critique would command no general attention, and perhaps be, by the greater number, unread. That the writer should wait the flow in inspiration, or at least the recurrence of elasticity of spirits and relative health of body, will not seem unreasonable to the general reader; but to an inveterate hack-horse of the daily press, accustomed to write at any time, on any subject, and with a rapidity limited only by the physical ability to form the requisite pen-strokes, the notion of waiting for a brighter day, or a happier frame of mind, appears fantastic and absurd. Hence, while I realized that her contributions evinced rare intellectual wealth and force, I did not value them as I should have done had they been written more fluently and promptly. They often seemed to make their appearance "a day after the fair."

Fuller's attitude toward daily journalism was certainly a handicap. In fact, she was even contemptuous of the medium, once writing to a friend, "What a vulgarity there seems in this writing for the multitudes." She also realized that her pen was often a heavy oar: "I really loathe my pen at present; it is so unnatural for me to keep at it so in the summer." Her familiarity with German no doubt contributed to a convoluted and verbose style. Greeley observed that her attempts "to commit her thoughts to paper seemed to induce a singular embarrassment and hesitation . . . But, one characteristic of her writings I feel bound to commend—their absolute truthfulness."

During the early months at the Greeleys she fell in love with James Nathan, a German Jewish immigrant, who was a wholesale clothier with an interest in music and literature. Together they read poetry in the garden or played lieder on guitar. Here, at last, was someone who was not intimidated by her intellect. The relationship, however, was maintained in secrecy to prevent criticism of her for being involved with a Jew. Eventually, Nathan's mother objected to the match and sent him off to Europe.

Fuller planned to follow him, but first had to finish *Papers on Literature and Art* (1846), a collection of her critical articles. On August 1, 1846, after twenty months as critic and general reporter, she sailed for Europe. She sent Greeley "letters," as news correspondence was called then, on such literary personalities as Milton, Shelley, Carlyle, and George Sand, and in doing so became the first woman foreign correspondent. Her name was known abroad and through Emerson she had introductions to intellectual circles. If Margaret Fuller is remembered today at all, it is for her meeting with Thomas Carlyle in London in 1846. "I accept the universe," she told the Scottish historian. To which Carlyle retorted in an aside, "By Gad, she'd better." Later, after reading her writings, Carlyle conceded that her prose was unique among women of their generation, rare even for men. Europe could boast of George Sand and Madame de Staël, but Margaret Fuller was certainly the best America could offer as an example of womanly genius.

In London, she reached another turning point. After learning that Nathan had married a German girl, Fuller met Giuseppe Mazzini, the exiled patriot who was trying to foment an Italian revolution. Mazzini's fervor was compelling to her: here was a longed-for cause. At his suggestion she left for Rome, arriving shortly before her thirty-seventh birthday. On April 4, 1847, as she admired St. Peter's Square, she was picked up by the Marchese Giovanni Angelo d'Ossoli, a member of the minor nobility with the Papal Court. Uncultivated by Fuller's standards and ten years her junior, Ossoli involved her in the revolutionary cause and they became lovers. Her liaison again was secret, this time to avoid criticism that Ossoli was intellectually inferior. A son, Angelo, was born on September 5, 1848, in Rieti. Some biographers believe the two were wed in 1849 in Florence, but the alleged marriage has never been adequately documented. It is doubtful that a priest would have married two revolutionaries, one a Catholic, the other a Protestant. Still, she felt married and took Ossoli's name. It is under this "married" name that her works are catalogued in libraries.

Her reporting as both a foreign correspondent on European politics and a war correspondent was prophetic. At home, Greeley promoted the revolutionary cause, sponsoring pro-Italy rallies and raising money. When Mazzini's government took over in February 1849, Fuller left her son in the care of a nurse and joined Ossoli at the city walls while the French laid siege to Rome. Through Ossoli she was asked to take charge of the government's military hospital. When the Republic was overthrown later in the month, they escaped to Rieti to claim their child and then to Florence where they found themselves a "scandal" in the English-speaking community. Elizabeth Barrett Browning, whose poems Fuller had previously described as having "many blemishes of overstrained and constrained thought and expression," was hostile initially, but soon relented and invited her into the literary circle. When Greeley learned of her questionable marital status, he was morally outraged and dropped her columns. Ossoli's family, moreover, had disinherited him.

Greeley's rejection was doubly felt since Fuller had counted on him to publish her history of the revolution, and on the five dollars paid for each *Tribune* column to support her family. With no income and their movements curtailed by police surveillance, they booked passage for America on the *Elizabeth*. On the evening of July 19, 1850, in the midst of rain and gale-force winds, the ship was swept onto a sandbar off Fire Island, just east of New York Harbor, only a few hundred feet from shore. After twelve hours, the ship's cargo of Carrara marble broke through the hold and the *Elizabeth* went down, taking with it half the passengers, including the Ossoli family. Only the child's body was recovered. The manuscript on the ill-fated revolution of 1849, which Fuller had called her finest writing, was never found. Some survivors claimed that she could have saved herself, but chose, instead, to perish in a grand suicidal gesture within sight of land. A drawing from the time shows her huddled beneath a swaying mast, clutching Ossoli and Angelo into the billows of her nightgown.

Ironically, Fuller had been fond of a shipwreck quote that she used several times. It ends *Woman in the Nineteenth Century* and in many ways describes Margaret Fuller's own life:

I stand in the sunny noon of life. Objects no longer glitter in the dews of morning, neither are yet softened by the shadows of evening. Every spot is seen, every chasm revealed. Climbing the dusty hill, some fair effigies that once stood for symbols of human destiny have been broken; those I still have with me show defects in this broad light. Yet enough is left, even by experience, to point distinctly to the glories of that destiny: faint but not to be mistaken streaks of the future day. I can say with the bard, "Though many have suffered shipwreck, still beat the noble hearts."

Margaret Fuller Ossoli's criticism and foreign dispatches are available in several anthologies. This daily journalism story details her visit to the Bloomingdale Asylum for the insane, an interesting contrast to Nellie Bly's report on Blackwell's Island, on page 124. There are no sources, no quotes. She was a visitor, an observer, noting the conditions, the people, and philosophizing on insanity. The front-page story had the force of an editorial rather than a news feature. Margaret Fuller signed all her *Tribune* journalism with an asterisk (*).

ST. VALENTINE'S DAY—BLOOMINGDALE ASYLUM FOR THE INSANE

New-York Daily Tribune, February 22, 1845

This merry season of light jokes and lighter love-tokens in which Cupid presents the feathered end of the dart, as if he meant to tickle before he wounded the captive, has always had a great charm for me. When but a child, I saw Allston's picture of the "Lady reading a valentine," and the mild womanliness of the picture, so remote from passion no less than vanity, so capable of tenderness, so chastely timid in its self-possession, has given a color to the gayest thoughts connected with the day. Even the ruff of Allston's Lady, whose clear starch is made to express all rosebud thoughts of girlish retirement, the soft unfledged hopes which never yet were tempted from the nest, to Sam Weller's Valentine is indeed a broad step, but one which we can take without material change of mood.

But of all the thoughts and pictures suggested by the day, none can surpass in interest those furnished by the way in which we celebrated it last week.

The Bloomingdale Asylum for the Insane is conducted on the most wise and liberal plan known at the present day. Its superintendent, Dr. Earle, has had ample opportunity to observe the best modes of managing this class of disease both here and in Europe, and he is one able, by refined sympathies and intellectual discernment, to apply the best that is known and to discover more.

Under his care the beautifully situated establishment at Bloomingdale loses every sign of the hospital and prison, not long since thought to be inseparable from such a place. It is a house of refuge where those too deeply wounded or disturbed in body or spirit to keep up that semblance or degree of sanity which the general conduct of affairs in the world at large demands may be soothed by gentle care, intelligent sympathy, and a judicious attention to their physical welfare, into health, or, at least, into tranquility.

Dr. Earle, in addition to modes of turning the attention from causes of morbid irritation, and promoting brighter and juster thought, which he uses in common with other institutions, has this winter delivered a course of lectures to the patients. We were present at one of these some weeks since. The subjects touched upon were, often, of a nature to demand as close attention as an audience of regular students (not college students, but real students) can be induced to give. The large assembly present were almost uniformly silent, to appearance interested, and showed a power of decorum and self-government often wanting among those who esteem themselves in healthful mastery of their morals and manners. We saw, with great satisfaction, generous thoughts and solid pursuits offered as well as light amusements for the choice of the sick in mind. For it is our experience that such sickness arises as often from want of concentration as any other cause. One of the noblest youths that ever trod this soil was wont to say "he was never tired, if he could only see far enough." He is now gone where his view may be less bounded, but we, who stay behind, may take the hint that mania, no less than the commonest forms of prejudice, bespeaks a mind which does not see far enough to connect partial impressions. No doubt in many cases, dissipation of thought, after attention is once distorted into some morbid direction, may be the first method of cure, but we are glad to see others provided for those who are ready for them.

St. Valentine's Eve had been appointed for one of the dancing-parties at the Institution, and a few friends from "the world's people" invited to be present.

At an early hour the company assembled in the well-lighted hall, still gracefully wreathed with its Christmas evergreens; the music struck up and the company entered.

And these are the people who, half a century ago, would have been chained in solitary cells, screaming out their anguish, til silenced by threats or blows, lost, forsaken, hopeless, a blight to earth, a libel upon heaven.

Now they are many of them happy, all interested. Even those who are troublesome and subject to violent excitement in every-day scenes, show here that the power of self-control is not lost, only lessened. Give them an impulse strong enough, favorable circumstances, and they will begin to use it again. They regulate their steps to music; they restrain their impatient impulses from respect to themselves and others. The power which shall yet shape order from all disorder and turn ashes to beauty, as violets spring up from green graves, hath them also in its keeping.

The party were well-dressed, with care and taste. The dancing was better than usual, because there was less of affectation and ennui. The party was more entertaining, because native traits came out more clear from the disguise of vanity and tact.

There was the blue-stocking lady, a mature bell and bel-esprit. Her condescending graces, her rounded compliments, her girlish, yea, "highly intellectual" vivacity, expressed no less in her head-dress than her manner, were just that touch above the common with which the illustrator of Dickens has thought fit to heighten the charms of Mrs. Leo Hunter.

There was the traveled Englishman, *au fait* to every thing beneath the moon and beyond. With his clipped and glib phrases, his bundle of conventionalities carried so neatly under his arm, and his "My dear sir," in the perfection of cockney dignity, what more could the most select dinner party furnish us in the way of distinguished strangerhood?

There was the hoydenish young girl, and the decourous elegant lady smoothing down "the wild little thing." There was the sarcastic observer on the folly of the rest; in that, the greatest fool of all, unbeloved and unannealed. In contrast to this were characters altogether lovely, full of all sweet affection, whose bells, if jangled out of tune, still retained their true tone.

One of the best things on the evening was a dance improvised by two elderly women. They asked the privilege of the floor, and, a suitable measure being played, performed this dance in a style lively, characteristic, yet moderate enough. It was true dancing, like peasant dancing.

An old man sang comic songs in the style of various nations and characters, with a dramatic expression that would have commanded applause "on any stage."

And all was done decently, and in order, each biding his time. Slight symptoms of impatience here and there were easily smoothed by the approach of this, truly a "good physician," the touch of whose hand seemed to possess a talismanic power to soothe. We doubt not that all went to their beds exhilarated, free from irritation, and more attuned to concord than before. Good bishop Valentine, thy feast was well kept, and not without the usual jokes and flings at old bachelors, the exchange of sugar-plums, mottos and repartees.

This is the second festival I have kept with those whom society has placed, not outside her pale, indeed, but outside the hearing of her benison. Christmas I passed in a prison! There too, I saw marks of the miraculous power of Love, when guided by a pure faith in the goodness of its source, and intelligence as to the design of the creative intelligence. I saw enough of its power, impeded as it was by the ignorance of those who, eighteen hundred years after the coming of Christ, will believe more in fear and force. I saw enough, I say, of this power to convince me, if I needed conviction, that it is indeed omnipotent, as he and it was.

A companion, of that delicate nature by which a scar is left as a wound, was saddened by the sense how very little our partialities, undue emotions, and manias need to be exaggerated to entitle us to rank among madmen. I cannot view it so. Rather let the sense that, with all our faults and follies, there is still a sound spot, a presentiment of eventual health in the inmost nature, embolden us to hope—to *know* it is the same with all. A great thinker has spoken of the Greek, for highest praise as "a self-renovating character." But we are all Greeks, if we will but think so. For the mentally or morally insane, there is no irreparable ill if the principle of life can but be aroused. And it can never be finally benumbed, except by our own will.

One of the famous pictures at Munich is of a mad house. The painter has represented the moral obliquities of society exaggerated into madness; that is to say, self-indulgence has, in each instance, destroyed the power to forbear the ill or to discern the good. A celebrated writer has added a little book, to be used while looking at the picture, and drawn inferences of universal interest.

Such would we draw; such as this! Let no one dare to call another mad who is not himself willing to rank in the same class for every perversion and fault of judgment. Let no one dare aid in punishing another as criminal who is not willing to suffer the penalty due to his own offences.

Yet, while owning that we are all mad, all criminal, let us not despair, but rather believe that the Ruler of all never could permit such wide-spread ill but to good ends. It is permited to give us a field to redeem it—

——"to transmute, bereave
Of an ill influence and a good receive."

It flows inevitably from the emancipation of our wills, the development of individuality in us. These aims accomplished, all shall yet be well; and it is ours to learn *how* that good time may be hastened.

We know no sign of the times more encouraging than the increasing nobleness and wisdom of view as to the government of asylums for the insane and of prisons. Whatever is learnt as to these forms of society is learnt for all. There is nothing that can be said of such government that must not be said, also, of the government of families, schools, and states. But we have much to say on this subject, and shall revert to it again, and often, though, perhaps, not with so pleasing a theme as this of St. Valentine's Eve.   *

2

Jane Grey Swisshelm
(1815-1884)

IN 1850 WASHINGTON was the place for a journalist to watch the pro-slavery and abolitionist forces draw up their battle lines. Daniel Webster, seeking a presidential nomination, was supporting the Fugitive Slave Law, which called on northerners to turn in runaway slaves. In Pittsburgh, Jane Grey Swisshelm, a frail but feisty editor, was publishing the *Saturday Visiter*, one of the country's leading liberal papers. A nationally known crusader and feminist, she wrote to Horace Greeley, editor of the *New-York Daily Tribune*, and asked to be his correspondent in Washington, a place she described as one of the most "infamous slave marts in the land."

Greeley was aware of the *Visiter*'s reputation, so he hired Swisshelm without hesitation to be the first woman Washington correspondent. She arrived in the capital to represent both the *Tribune* and the *Visiter* only to learn that women were barred from the Senate Press Gallery. "The place would be very unpleasant for a lady," warned Vice President Millard Fillmore. Nonsense, Swisshelm said. She demanded—and won—equal rights for women reporters. Then she took up her pen to blister Webster's pro-slavery views. There was a rumor circulating around Washington that Webster had fathered eight inter-racial children. This was exactly the kind of damaging story she wanted, and without substantiating the slur she immediately dispatched an item to the *Visiter*, noting that in Washington lived "a family of eight mulattoes, bearing the image and superscription of the great New England statesman, who paid the rent and grocery bills of their mother as regularly as he did those of his wife."

The accusation was widely reprinted in other weeklies, and Swisshelm, realizing that she had endangered her position on the *Tribune*, immediately left the capital. In her last *Tribune* letter of May 24, 1850,[1] she explained that a serious illness made it necessary for her to return home. She consoled herself later, however, with the knowledge that she was responsible for Webster's defeat for the 1852 Whig nomination.

It was irresponsible journalism, but a minor footnote to a career that included starting four newspapers, helping to secure property rights for married women in Pennsylvania, employing women typesetters, and accurately predicting that union wage demands would kill newspapers. Everything Jane Grey Swisshelm did—from working in an office to Civil War nursing—attracted attention and controversy.

Her writing was witty and insightful, but often venomous, or as one critic put it: "At times her pen seemed dipped in gall, and every word went to the quick like a barbed arrow." A gentler reviewer wrote: she "dips her pen in liquid gold, and sands her paper with the down of butterfly wings." For a nineteenth-century woman she was amazingly candid about her personal life, particularly her boring marriage to a tyrannical husband. In her autobiography, *Half a Century*,[2] an early *Feminine Mystique*, she wrote on her decision to leave her husband: "I have voluntarily assumed the legal guilt of breaking my marriage contract, do cheerfully accept the legal penalty—a life of celibacy—bringing no charge against him who was my husband, save that he was not much better than the average man."

Like Virginia Woolf, Swisshelm wanted a room of her own. For twenty years, she noted, she had lived "without the legal right to be alone one hour." As a feminist, she preferred her own individual efforts in securing equal rights for women to the suffrage movement. Early in the 1840s she joined the campaign for the abolition of slavery and worked twenty years for the cause until Lincoln issued the Emancipation Proclamation in 1863. As a full-time

[1] The Webster slander was never printed in the *Tribune*, although Greeley wrote an editorial censuring the article. Swisshelm refers to this in her last *Tribune* letter, published on May 28, 1850: "I accept your reproof as the rebuke of a friend, and admit the great probability of my doing wrong in any given circumstance." She later exonerates the *Tribune*: "The *Commercial*'s statement that my Webster letter appeared in the *Tribune* must be a willful falsehood. The article was written for the *Visiter*, and first appeared there. I have seen it copied into perhaps a hundred papers, and every one in an editorial notice, stated this fact, so the *Commercial* could not easily be mistaken."

[2] A nineteenth-century Pennsylvania law gave a husband the right to open and read his wife's letters. Swisshelm burned all her correspondence and her childhood diary, and wrote her autobiography largely from memory.

career woman and one of the first to work with men in an office, she realized that most women were still born to a "woman's sphere."

At a time when *Godey's Lady's Book*, the first important woman's magazine, wrote advice for the genteel, urban woman, only Swisshelm, who had
grown up in rural Pennsylvania, wrote for the needs of the country woman.
Her "Letters to Country Girls," published in the *Visiter* in 1849 and 1850,
and in 1853 collected in book form, are classic, common-sense advice columns. She advocated carpets: "I would not live in a house that had to be
scrubbed. It is a senseless useless drudgery." She advocated equal education:
"If parents would give their daughters the same mental training they do their
sons they could not be converted into slaves so handily . . . ignorance, folly
and levity are more or less essential to the character of a slave."

Swisshelm was a maverick, an idealist and, in later life, an eccentric. At
age forty-five, she was described in *Harper's Monthly* as a "large-eyed lively
little woman, with a masculine and unhandsome breadth and heighth of
forehead." Her office was described as "not large enough to swing a cat
comfortable in," and she would sometimes greet visitors while seated on the
floor sewing together a carpet.

As a teenager she overheard someone call her "pretty," and she ran to the
mirror to inspect her face. In her autobiography, she recalled thinking: "Pretty
face, the worms will eat you. All the prettiest girls I know are silly, but you
shall never make a fool of men. Helen's beauty ruined Troy. Cleopatra was
a wretch. So if you are pretty, I will be master, remember that." She grew
up pretty and petite, only five feet tall, with blue eyes and brown hair, looking much like the singer Jenny Lind. As it turned out, her pen—not her
beauty—made a fool of men.

Her early life was typically rural American. Wilkinsburg, near Pittsburgh,
was an awakening frontier town when she was born Jane Grey Cannon on
December 6, 1815. Of the seven children born to her Scottish-Irish parents
Thomas and Marcy (Scott) Cannon only Jane and her younger sister, Elizabeth, survived to adulthood. Reading the Bible at three, she grew up in a
strict Presbyterian atmosphere that stressed obedience, self-denial, and guilt
for going astray.

Her father, a merchant, died when she was seven, and Jane helped support the family by teaching lace making. She was so small that she sat on
the knees of her young lady pupils to provide them a better view of the in-
tricate stitches. Her only formal education was six weeks at the Edgeworth
Boarding School in Braddock's Field, Pennsylvania. Although largely self-
taught, she had a quick mind and a remarkable memory. At fourteen she
was teaching school and developing another talent: painting.[3]

[3] Only one painting still exists—a self-portrait done about 1837, in the collection of the Historical Society of Western Pennsylvania, and reprinted in this book.

Religion was the overpowering influence in this family of three women. Innocent and sexually repressed, she fell in love at nineteen with James Swisshelm, a tall, dark, lumbering man from a leading Methodist family. She called him her "dark knight," and despite her mother's warnings that religious differences would mar the marriage she became his wife on November 18, 1836. Indeed religion was a problem: her husband tried to turn her into a Methodist preacher, and her mother-in-law, with whom they were living, welcomed her as little more than a servant. She had married a mamma's boy and had no rights or dignity as a wife. In a short while the bride went home to her mother and hoped that Swisshelm would change his attitude. Eventually a strange compromise was settled on: her husband would live in the house with his mother and she would live in a small house behind the wagon hut and take care of the wagon maker.

Under this arrangement her husband occasionally visited her, bringing meager supplies doled out under the watchful eye of his mother. Jane's dashing knight turned out to be not only a crashing bore, but a greedy bully as well. To forget her troubles, she spent time painting and reading, totally losing herself in creative sublimation. As a result, she neglected her household duties and later wrote about her guilt:

My conscience began to trouble me. Housekeeping was "women's sphere," although I had never then heard the words, for no woman had gotten out of it, to be hounded back; but I knew my place, and scorned to leave it. I tried to think I could paint without neglect of duty. It did not occur to me that painting was a duty for a married woman! Had the passion seized me before marriage, no other love could have come between me and art; but I felt that it was too late, as my life was already devoted to another object—housekeeping . . . I put away my brushes; resolutely crucified my divine gift, and while it hung writhing on the cross, spent my best years and powers cooking cabbage . . . It was not only my art-love which must be sacrificed to my duty as a wife, but my literary tastes must go with it . . . An uncultivated husband could not be the superior of a cultivated wife. I knew from the first that his education had been limited, but thought the defect would be easily remedied as he had good abilities, but I discovered he had no love for books . . . I must be the mate of the man I had chosen; and if he would not come to my level, I must go to his. So I gave up study, and for years did not read one page in any book save the Bible.

Just as her health was beginning to fail from nervous tension, her husband decided in 1838 to move to Louisville to start a new business. With her mother-in-law left behind, she harbored hopes that her marriage would become more intimate. Her husband, however, had little talent for earning a living, and soon she was supporting them both by making corsets for the hourglass figures of Southern belles. Still, her two-year stay in Kentucky stirred new thoughts and emotions, for there she saw firsthand the cruelties of slavery, evoking in her an instant and deep hatred. An attempt to start a school for black children was abandoned when neighbors threatened to burn her

Jane Grey Swisshelm

home but she started making notes about conditions in a slave state, which she would use later in her abolitionist columns and lectures.

It was 1839 and Jane Swisshelm was twenty-four. She had settled for a mundane domestic life, working, keeping house, and outraging her Southern neighbors with her criticisms of slavery. Then her mother, dying of cancer, sent for her to come to Pittsburgh. Fearing that the lucrative corset business would fail with a prolonged absence, her husband refused to let her make the trip. She went anyway and nursed her mother for a year, and was shocked when her husband sued his mother-in-law's estate for her services.

After her mother's death, Swisshelm did not return to Louisville, deciding instead to find some contentment as a teacher at Butler Seminary in Butler, Pennsylvania. During this time she wrote her first newspaper articles—a series attacking capital punishment—which were published anonymously in a local newspaper. Two years later she returned to her husband, and they moved to his family's farm near Pittsburgh. It was a quiet, bucolic place that she called Swissvale. There she took her first serious step in journalism, contributing stories and rhymes under the pen name "Jennie Deans" to the *Dollar Newspaper* and *Neal's Saturday Gazette* in Philadelphia. Later she wrote her first stories on slavery and women's rights for the *Spirit of Liberty*, an abolitionist weekly in Pittsburgh. Surprisingly, her husband insisted she use her real name as a byline, an unusual attitude in a time when women's names appeared in print, if at all, only when they married and died. Her byline first appeared in 1844 under an antislavery article in the *Spirit of Liberty*. When that paper failed, she moved her views and her byline, Jane G. Swisshelm, to the *Pittsburgh Commercial Journal*.

For the next decade the *Journal's* editor, Robert M. Riddle, would become her mentor, surrogate father, and fantasy lover. Following the failure of another abolitionist paper, the *Albatross*, Swisshelm decided to use the inheritance from her mother to finance her own paper,[4] and asked Riddle to print it. Although at first he tried to discourage her, it appears that without too much discussion Riddle relented and invited her to share his small office. She was joined in this effort by several Republican politicians, and the first issue of the *Saturday Visiter* (she insisted on the spelling in Samuel Johnson's dictionary) was published on January 20, 1848. She was the editor, reporter, and proofreader. The reality of being an editor, however, had

---

[4] Swisshelm had sold her mother's house, and her husband wanted the proceeds turned over to him. Rather than argue with him, she set out to change the law with a series on a married woman's right to hold property. Also fighting for the same cause were Lucretia Mott and Mary A. Grew of Philadelphia. In 1848 the Pennsylvania legislature passed a law allowing married women to own property, at which time Swisshelm was verbally denounced by an angry lawyer who held her responsible and warned: "You will live to rue the day when you opened such a Pandora's box in your native state, and cast such an apple of discord into every family in it."

never occurred to her. She was used to writing at home; now she had to be in an office, responsible not only for editing but also production and circulation.

For that time, it was a scandal for a woman to work in an office with a man—particularly a man she described in her autobiography as "handsome with fine physique and fascinating manners, a man of the world." As she had turned to the Bible to console her in her marriage, so she now looked through it pages once again and decided: "I am going forward. 'Speak unto the children of Israel that they go forward' [a slogan that would run under the masthead of both *Visiters*]. The crimson waves of scandal, the white foam of gossip, shall part before me and heap themselves up as walls on either hand." Her husband did not protest the arrangement, sensing perhaps that she would make a success of this venture as she had the corset trade.

For ten years Swisshelm and Riddle worked side by side, with the shutters open for passersby to observe them—and wonder. Discussing this time in her autobiography, she was circumspect about her feelings for Riddle, but it seems clear that theirs was a platonic relationship built on intellectual respect and journalistic camaraderie. She did write down one charming anecdote: "He [Riddle] turned one day, examined me critically, and exclaimed: 'Why do you wear those hideous caps? You seem to have good hair. Mrs. Riddle says she knows you have, and she and some ladies were wondering only yesterday, why you make yourself such a fright.' " In reply to this veiled compliment, Swisshelm told him that the net scarf tied under her chin kept the cold away from her tonsils: "He turned away with a sigh, and did not suspect that my tonsils had no such protection outside the office, where I must meet a great many gentlemen and make it apparent that I wanted of them votes!"

The *Visiter* attracted immediate attention. That a new abolitionist paper had been launched was not notable, but that the editor was a woman certainly was. A pro-slavery Kentucky editor, George D. Prentiss, wrote that "she is a man all but the pantaloons." Other editors reprinted the ditty calling out, "that woman shall not have *my* pantaloons." The attacks amused Swisshelm and she published the following poem in the *Visiter*:

> Perhaps you have been busy
> Horsewhipping Sal or Lizzy
> Stealing some poor man's baby.
> Selling its mother, may-be.
> You say—and you are witty—
> That I—and tis a pity—
> Of manhood lack but dress;
> But you lack manliness,

A body clean and new,
A soul within it, too.
Nature must change her plan
Ere you can be a man.

In response, one editor tartly commented: "Brother George, beware of sister Jane." And another: "Prentiss has found his match."

Over the next four years the *Visiter* would prosper, raising its circulation from three readers to 6,000. The paper attacked slave catchers and the Fugitive Slave Law. It supported the suffrage cause, but Swisshelm refused to affiliate with any of the movement's organizations. Her crusade for women's rights did not center on the right to vote, but on the need for property rights for married women, and the right for divorced women to have custody of minor children and married women to enter into contracts. On other issues, she advocated temperance, believing, though, that it was useless to try to reform a drunkard. She criticized the fashions of the day, complaining that corsets interfered with breathing and metal hoop skirts injured children. She took on the Catholic church in Pittsburgh when she opposed a proposition to use tax revenues to support parochial schools. As was the custom, the *Visiter*'s articles were widely reprinted. Without wire services or syndicated material or copyright restrictions, editors freely picked up stories from other publications. After her short stay as Washington correspondent for the *Tribune*, Swisshelm assessed the financial state of the *Visiter* and decided in 1852 to merge it with Riddle's *Journal*.

In 1851 she had become a mother for the first time, giving birth to a daughter, Mary Henrietta (nicknamed Nettie). But by 1857 relations with her husband had become intolerable, and she gave up on her marriage and her newspaper, and took her child out west to seek a quiet life in St. Cloud, Minnesota, with her sister. At the time Minnesota was torn by the abolitionist cause; some backed slavery, while others fought for abolition. She had romantic notions of living in a log cabin and rearing her daughter, until she realized the dangers from unfriendly Indian tribes. Her husband had divorced her on grounds of desertion, and had remarried. She had no child support from him and few funds of her own. When the owner of a defunct newspaper suggested that she revive and edit it, she agreed on the condition that the formerly Democratic paper would express her views. She named the paper the *St. Cloud Visiter*, retaining the quaint spelling of the *Saturday Visiter*. Her facilities were limited, and she had only a small selection of type and paper. (It was more than 600 miles to the nearest foundry or paper mill.)

In the first edition on December 10, 1857, she set forth her views: "the Bible, and the Constitution of the United states are anti-slavery; and human chattledom is unconstitutional in any association professing to receive either as fundamental law." On women's rights she wrote: "Paying taxes is as unwomanly as voting; and is a privilege which should be exclusively confined to 'white male citizens, of this and other countries.' " The paper was a bold venture for Minnesota, a hard-line Democratic stronghold led by General Sylvanus B. Lowry, a Tennessee-born landowner who lived, according to Swisshelm, in "semi-barbaric splendor" in a Mississippi-bank house where he kept slaves.

Lowry offered financial support for the new newspaper, provided it supported James Buchanan for President. Swisshelm agreed, and Lowry, a man of considerable charm and power, thought he had swung the paper's editorial policy over to the Democrats. On February 18, 1858, Swisshelm started a dangerous game—in effect, double-crossing her benefactor by telling her readers that the *Visiter* had decided to support the administration. She listed her reasons: the Constitution, she declared, had become the "Magna Carta of a southern gentleman's right to whip women, rob mothers of their children, and sell upon the auction block the souls for whom the Lord of Glory assumed humanity and laid down his life upon the cross . . . We believe the Democratic party is likely to succeed in reducing all the poor and friendless of this country to a state of slavery."

Enraged by this endorsement, Lowry selected James G. Shepley, a Democratic attorney, to give a speech criticizing women. Shepley divided women into four classes: the coquette, the flirt, the old maid, and the strong-minded woman in politics, for whom he had only scorn. The next issue of the *Visiter* reviewed the speech, noting that Shepley had omitted one class of women: "the large-thick-skinned, coarse, sensual-featured, loud-mouthed double-fisted dames, whose entrance into a room appears to take one's breath, whose conversational tones are audible at the furthest side of the next square, whose guffahs resound across a mile wide river, and who talk with an energy which makes the saliva fly like—showers of melted pearls. . . . Her triumphs consist in card-table successes, displays of cheap finery, and in catching marriageable husbands for herself and her poor relations."

Shepley saw in this caricature a description of his wife. To stifle Swisshelm, Lowry and Shepley decided to take the law into their own hands. A vigilante group broke into the *Visiter* office, destroyed the press, threw its type into the street and the Mississippi River, and left the following note:

The citizens of St. Cloud have determined to abate the nuisance of which you have made the "Visiter" a striking specimen.

They have decided that it is fit only for the inmates of Brothels, and you seem to have had some experience of the tastes of such persons.

You will never have the opportunity to repeat the offence in this town, without paying a more serious penalty than you do now.

This attack on freedom of the press prompted Swisshelm to speak for the first time in public, an experience she described as "the revelation of a talent hidden in a napkin." So stirring was her plea that in a grand gesture of frontier spirit local businessmen voted to buy new equipment for the paper and to allow her to publish her views.

Lowry brought a $10,000 libel suit against the *Visiter* to stop Swisshelm from printing any more details on the destruction of her presses. To save her backers from taking any financial loss, she promised never to print anything in the *Visiter*, and kept that promise by folding the paper and starting the *St. Cloud Democrat* on August 5, 1858. She immediately reprinted the libelous article, but Lowry had met his match and took no further action. She announced the publication of her third newspaper with the pledge to "discuss any subject we have a mind . . . If these fellows destroy our office again, as they now threaten to do, we will go down to Hennepin County; and publish the St. Cloud Democrat there."

Subsequently Lowry ran for lieutenant governor and Swisshelm went on lecture tours denouncing him and advocating her favorite causes: women and politics and slavery. Lowry was defeated, had a nervous breakdown, and in 1862 was committed to a sanitarium, and the Republican Party took over Minnesota until the New Deal seventy years later.

In 1862 when there was a Sioux uprising in the state, and many white settlers were massacred, Swisshelm immediately embarked on a crusade against the "lazy, impudent beggars." She traveled to Washington and at a public address cried out: "Make peace with the devil and all his hosts sooner than with those red-jawed tigers whose fangs are dripping with the blood of the innocents. . . . Our people will hunt them, shoot them, set traps for them, put out poisoned bait for them—kill them by any means we would use to exterminate panthers!" She sought out President Lincoln to ask him for strong federal action against the Indians. Unable to see him, she renewed acquaintances with old political friends and was offered a clerk's post in the War Department. The government was experimenting with woman employees, and she was offered $50 a month—more than she had ever made in journalism.

She would later meet President Lincoln and his wife at a reception and change her opinion of the man she felt had not been tough-minded enough on the issues of slavery and the Indians. In her autobiography she noted the meeting, commenting on Lincoln's "sad, earnest, honest face . . . irresistible in its plea for confidence."

At this time Jane Grey Swisshelm was ready for new challenges. Since 1858 she had been both editor and printer for the *Democrat*, in addition to printing such outside jobs as legal notices and tax lists. She had learned to set type when she could not afford to pay union wages, and had trained her female assistants in the craft. In 1863 she sold the *Democrat* to her nephew but continued for the next three years to write letters to the paper on Washington politics. She spent the time before her job started caring for Civil War wounded at nearby Washington hospitals where she swept through the wards, complaining, improving, and writing letters to Greeley's *Tribune* asking readers to send her lemons and limes to combat hospital gangrene. When she found lice in the beds, she promptly reported it and was dismissed for not keeping a hospital "secret." In her office job, she also found the need for reform: jobs were patronage appointments and women did not receive equal pay for equal work.

Using money from her clerk's paycheck, she started her fourth paper, *The Reconstructionist*, on December 21, 1865. She was outspoken against President Andrew Johnson's policy of conciliation toward slave holders; after continued attacks on government policy, Johnson had her fired from the clerk's job. Without funds she had to fold the paper in March of 1866, facing an impoverished old age and no employment options. Then she learned that she had a claim to part of her late husband's estate at Swissvale. She brought suit and won the property, where she settled to write her autobiography and reform articles for the *New York Independent*.

At her death on July 22, 1884, at age sixty-eight, she was hailed as a philanthropist and a foe of slavery. In 1935 when *Crusader and Feminist*, a collection of her Minnesota journalism was reviewed, the *New York Times* noted: "Mrs. Swisshelm was a born journalist, and the stuff she wrote, not withstanding her strong personal bias, still has vitality, appeal, interest, a graphic quality like that of an old print. And also, more important, she was a knight crusader to whom all newspaper women should doff their hats, for she fought their battles for them long before they were born and helped to open for them the doors of the future."

The following letter to the *Tribune* telling of her success in securing a press seat, and an article on War Department office workers show how visual and detailed Swisshelm's reporting and writing were. Some of the descriptions of her co-workers are beautifully etched, with some of the stylistic trappings of New Journalism.

MRS. SWISSHELM'S LETTERS . . . NO. IV
The Senate Gallery—Woman's Behavior— Col. Benton—Mr. Clay—The Collision in the Senate and some thoughts thereon.

The New-York Daily Tribune, April 22, 1850

Irving House, Washington, Thursday, April 18.

Dear Mr. Greeley: I do hope you have a very large stock of patience on hand, or if not, that you will send on and import some. I have sat here today in my nice, quiet little room, and inflicted letters on every one likely to bear it patiently—have written some thirty pages, and feel like finishing off with a few more to you. You know what a miserable, contemptible, paltry excuse for a gallery there is in the U.S. Senate—a thing like a berth on a canal boat, hung up near the top, about six feet wide, and partitioned into two rows of seats with no way of getting into them but by walking over people who are already there, and who are always sure to be too rude either to move forward to a vacant seat or stand up to allow others to pass. I never was in it but twice, and once I witnessed a scene there, between the wives of honorable members, that would be disgraceful to a Western huckster woman. I saw the wife of a Senator refuse to rise and permit the wife of a member of the House to pass to a vacant seat on the ladies' row, and thus compelled her to crowd through the solid mass of men that always block up the seat. I saw ladies walk over the seats and step over the back of them, to get out or in, while men and women refused to move an inch. I would rather force my way through a crowded horse-market and sit on the auctioneer's block, than go into the gallery again. Brought up in the woods, I know nothing about refinement, but there is rather more rudeness in the Senate gallery than suits my ideas of "pot-luck." The chamber is a disgrace to the nation, and it would be almost impossible to frequent the gallery and remain civilized. One would most necessarily grow savage, and, as I have already a decided tendency in that direction, I was afraid when I went home that they would banish me to the other side of the Rocky Mountains. So I determined, like the poor lover when his lady-love threw him into the swill-barrel, "I'll never go there any more." But I could not thus resign all purpose of seeing the American Senate, and so sought an introduction to Mr. FILL-MORE, made a formal application for a reporter's desk, and it was granted at once, *The Republic* reporters very kindly resigning one of their desks to my use. Yesterday I occupied it for the first time, and thus had a fine opportunity of seeing the FOOTE and BENTON affray. Mrs. Southworth the author of "Retribution," and my dear friend, went with me, and today I have two ladies of this city by the invitation of the gentlemanly reporter, Mr. Andrews, simply to sustain the precedent. So much for a fit of ill-temper! It has established woman's right to sit as a reporter in our legislative halls. I should not have thought of it, if they had not made me angry, and I do really believe, Mr. Greeley, that it is a sin to be good-tempered. One cares for nobody, and can work so fast when one gets in a bad temper, that is, if they do not get too frightfully angry, as Col. BENTON did yesterday. Oh, I was sorry to see it! Some people here who know him well, say I was wrong in thinking him calm all day, and that he was highly excited. He appeared to me in good working order, with spirit enough to fear nothing and calmness enough to know what he was doing. He fought like a lion at bay to defeat the scheme of sending the California bill to FOOTE's Committee, and I did love the noble old man—love to look at him and hear his stentorian vote ringing out its plain, common-sense truths. His eloquence during all the afternoon was far more than a match for even Mr. CLAY. A false position rendered him comparatively petty. When he rose and accused Mr. BENTON of delaying the taking up of the California bill, by delaying the appointment of the Committee and opposing its reference to that Committee, he looked as though he were conscious of the subterfuge. BENTON had urged so plainly the taking up of the bill immediately, so that they might be able to act upon it this week, before next Monday, when the deputation should leave, and no important business could be done for the two weeks of their absence. To this Mr. CLAY's objection, of the House not being ready to act, sounded puerile, and HENRY CLAY did not look like the great statesman in making it. Benton's reply to his charge of delaying the measure was as straight a home-thrust as I ever witnessed in a passage of arms. The Honorable Senator's good will to California, and his charges against those who sought its untrammeled admission, were like the great Emperor's love of Peace. He was a very great friend to peace, yet was always at war, because, he said, the countries into which he marched his armies *"would resist."* The Honorable Senator was for peace, but when he thrust his offensive measures upon them they would resist. It is a thousand pities his powerful intellect was not better balanced. I still doubt whether he would have struck Mr. FOOTE, if that gentleman had turned and waited for him to come up, without making any show of resistance. He was still in the lobby—which in my last I called a "passage"—when Mr. FOOTE started and ran, or, as he afterward explained it "*advanced* toward the Speaker's desk, as the Honorable Senator *advanced* after me." I hope you New Yorkers will remember this new way of advancing, and when you see a gentleman cutting a figure that Western folks call "cutting stick"—looking over his shoulders and a police officer bringing up the rear—just remember the gentleman is advancing toward a certain point, with an honorable gentleman advancing after him. This is the new fashioned way of advancing, but I do not believe Mr. FOOTE is a physical coward. He is of a very nervous organization and cannot act coolly without some time to think. Then he might have as much courage as would be compatible with a physical fight. The best and bravest of animal courage is moral cowardice. Your late *glorious* war has added largely to the national stock of this same cowardice, and I do not think the nation has any right to judge either of these gentlemen harshly. Editors will aim their thunder at, and orators will gasconade over this insult to the American Senate and the American people: but in my humble opinion, "the bite suits the cup" admirably. The American people are very well represented by Messrs. FOOTE and BENTON. The latter, who is a giant, would no more have acted the coward and the bully by striking Mr. FOOTE, who is small and weak, than this nation did by striking poor little shriveled up Mexico. If Mr. FOOTE acted like an assassin, he had a most illustrious example, in the official conduct of the very people who will now judge him—the great American Nation, whose indignant daughter I am. This Nation has taken many opportunities to declare her love of animal courage, her admiration of brute force. She worships guns, bayonets and epaulette, and I can see no reason why she should not be represented with pistols and Bowie knives. "Like father like child." "Shall the thing formed say unto him that formed it, 'Why has thou made me thus?' or shall the creature be greater than the Creator?" The American people created the American Senate, and I can see no reason why it should be any better than they. If they resign the weapons of moral warfare, give up debate, and resort to firearms to settle disputes, why should not the Senate do likewise? "Is the servant greater than his lord?" Col. BENTON's fists and Gen. FOOTE's pistol are a neat little pocket comment on the beautiful military spirit that has kindled and fostered in our Nation; and the people, the dear and dignified and sovereign people, had better scratch their wise heads and think a while before they say much about "this disgraceful affair."   JANE G. SWISSHELM.

MRS. JANE G. SWISSHELM
ON FEMALE CLERKS
A STRANGE PICTURE OF WASHINGTON.
Pieces of Painted Impertinence.
Eyebrows of Black Lead or Lampblack.
CONGRESS IN FAULT,
Evils that Should be Remedied.

St. Cloud (Minnesota) Democrat, December 21, 1865

Washington is, perhaps, the very worst place in the country in which to make any great pioneer movement in reference to woman's social position. It is, to all intents and purposes, a Southern city, and the centre of snobism. Here is the focus of that system of education South which makes all labor degrading, and of our common school education North, which teaches that manual labor is at most to be regarded as a means of reaching the Presidential chair. As our boys and men are all expecting to be Presidents, so our girls and women must all hold themselves in readiness to preside in the White House; and in no city in the world can honest industry be more at a discount than in this capital of the government of the people. Perhaps two-thirds of all important places in the departments are held by southern men, or men who, by long residence here, have become thoroughly Southernized. If the free labor system, for men, in the rebel States, meets its principal obstacle in the ignorance of the employers, what must be the difficulties thrown in the way of the free-labor system for women, by men whose entire habit of thought regards the sex as slaves, drawing room divinities, or toys? Of the clerks employed here, there is not one in twenty who can go into a room where women are employed, and transact any business with one of them without in some way reminding her of her womanhood. They are "sorry to trouble the ladies," or they "hope the ladies are quite well," or "it is a pity to have ladies shut up in offices in such fine weather," or "it is bad for ladies to come out in such unpleasant weather." In some way the ladies are to be deferred to or encouraged, and their shortcomings excused because they *are* ladies. The idea of treating them as copyists and clerks, simply this and nothing more, is beyond the mental caliber of almost any man with whom they are brought into personal relations, while the "ladies," in their dependent position, feeling no assurance of continued employment on any settled principle, naturally resort to personal favoritism as a means of getting bread.

There is a radical error in the manner of appointing women. It is not every man who is fit for any pioneer movement, and to expect that all women or even a majority, are fitted for this advance post on the picket line of civilization, is expecting superhuman perfection of the feminine half of humanity. Yet such is the system, or want of system, on which this grand experiment has been inconsiderately tried. To get an appointment no qualifications are required, except influential friends: and something near one-third of all the appointments are from the District or its immediate vicinity, and, of course, are women of the Southern idea that a woman's personal charms and decorations are her stock in trade—women who have as little idea of themselves as competitors for bread in the world's labor market, as have the men with whom they are associated of them in such a relation. Of the Northern women appointed, it is not always those whom the work wants who get the places.

Some honorable Senator or Representative has a female friend without visible means of support. He gets her a place, and she makes her appearance, perhaps a little piece of painted impertinence, who might have been stowed away in the catacombs in the days of the Pharaohs for all one can tell of her age, but who studiously assumes the airs of a miss of sixteen. Her wrinkles are filled out with pipe clay or some other kind of light-colored mud; her eyebrows are made of black lead or lampblack, or something in that line, her hair is dyed until it is dead enough to satisfy any respectable undertaker of the propriety of burial; and one wonders that she does not add a setting of green leaves to the magenta-colored roses on her thin cheeks. She comes tripping in on the toes of her infinitesimal gaiters, gets off her things, and displays a head which reminds one of a drop chandelier trimmed for a ball and undergoing the process of dusting, while her pins, chains, bracelets, frills, and other fixtures would set up a tin box peddler in trade. She establishes herself at her table, opens her basket, gets out her beads, and goes to counting and stringing: "one, two three, four, and then a large one: one, two, three, four, and a knot;" for you see, she is a philanthropist, and kindly instructs the lady at the next table in the mysteries of this becoming and lady-like employment. The superintendent gets fidgety, and brings this interesting toiler in life's workshop a piece of writing to copy. The lady looks injured, and as the superintendent is, of course, a Southern gentleman, who has been selected for that place with special reference to his amiability, he feels like a "horrid wretch." The dainty little hands take up the pen, and the dainty little brain keeps on, "one, two, three, four, and a large one—one, two, three, four, and a loop." "Loop?" Yes. Beg pardon! I said "knot," but is a "loop" which comes after the second four.

The writing finished, it is sent off by a messenger, and presently a clerk appears with it in his hand. He looks weary, has found a mistake, and is directed to the little bead-monger, who drops her hands in her lap and her head on her left shoulder, cocks her right eye at him like a canary making prognostications about the weather, says something silly, and the poor man begins to scratch his head. The conference lasts some time. The man retires baffled and swearing "not loud but deep," the other ladies exchange glances and smiles, or perhaps see nothing wrong, while not one begins to comprehend the "deep damnation" of the whole affair, or to know that then and there every woman in the room "felt flat" and richly deserved so to feel.

Another, pure as New England frost, "bright as a button," active as a bee, does as much work in the month and does it as well as any man in the department, but her book is wanted for reference. She wants to surprise some friend with a pair of socks for a new baby; and while her book is gone, whips out her knitting and goes nimbly to work. Some clerk comes into the room, goes out and reports that the women in that room do nothing but knit.

Still another comes sailing in at 9½ o'clock, gets off her wraps; sinks into her chair with the air of a willow wand cracked in the middle; languidly asks someone to call a servant; sends said servant, with her compliments, to the head of the bureau for the loan of his morning paper; reads it leisurely, with a running comment, loud enough to be heard all over that room and in the one adjoining, on the houses to rent, the late appointments and removals; tells who built the house for sale on such a street and who lived in it at such a time; gives an inventory of their furniture and history of their family in its lateral and collateral branches; finds who is dead and who married, and does as much for their genealogical trees; begins writing at 10½, but keeps up the stream of small talk until some other lady is through with her morning paper; when she reads that, gets several new texts, and goes on with the commentary until 2 or 2½ o'clock, when, being quite worn out with her day's labor, she gracefully retires. Of course, she is one of those favored mortals who can trace some root of their family tree back to some one of those excellent women who came to the Old Dominion, originally, as exchange for tobacco, and whose descendants wear the title of "F.F.V." with such proud satisfaction. Of course she is one of those Government employees who shrug their high shouldered dignity, and elevate their aristocratic noses at sight of "Lincoln's rabble," i.e. Union soldiers, and are shocked at the immoralities introduced by strangers, i.e. Northern people, into Washington, which has been transformed by these vandals, that a native born gentleman can no longer sell his own baby when it gets old enough, in order to gratify his lady friend with a drive behind a pair of fast horses. As she is "a law unto herself," and her fine lady airs make her monarch of all she surveys, is it a wonder that other women imitate her, and that a very few such do much to disorganize the working force of a department?

There is yet another class of appointees—the lady who must see the clerk for whom she is recording or copying, and who, when he comes, strikes a St. Agnes attitude, folds her hands meekly, draws her lips to a "prunes, prism, and potato" pucker, turns up her eyes like a duck in a thunder storm, or a juvenile bovine in the act of becoming veal, makes a pun and an impression, or several puns and as many impressions, grows witty, tells the unfortunate man that she dreamed last night she was married *to him*, is self-satisfied and subsides in a simper, while there is no one with the nerve or authority to order her out of the room and see that she never returns.

In the same bureau, where you find the assortment described, and that is most of them, there is perhaps a majority of female clerks with whose dullness and demeanor it would be difficult to find fault—women working like horses, scarcely taking time for lunch, making books of records second to none, and copies of important papers with wonderful rapidity and correctness; some of them doing the same kind of work, and as much of it, as men at salaries of $1,200, $1,400, and $1,600 per annum, while they get $820.

At the end of the month all get equal pay. Their chances of promotion are the same, and special favors are for those who have done the least work. What wonder that the experiment is thought by many to be a failure?

It is for the people to say whether influential men shall close their door against honorable women by making these places accessible to women of bad character and no character. Will they pay men double or treble salaries for doing what women can do quite as well, and will do for a compensation so much lower? Will they not sustain heads of departments against that type of Congressional influence which carries corruption of the worst kind into the departments, and makes government offices places of assignation, or excludes honorable women from honorable and suitable employment? The exclusion of women from these places will not improve the morals of the city or the country, while their employment in them, under proper regulations could not fail to exercise a most beneficial influence. There are thousands of women perfectly able and willing to perform the duties of any first or second class clerkship here; thousands who by the war have been deprived of their former means of support, and left with families dependent upon them; and it is mean and cowardly for the government to set the example of driving such from a class of *occupations* well suited to their capacity, as the shortest way of *disposing* of abuses for which government officials are responsible.

Washington, Nov. 13, 1865. JANE G. SWISSHELM.

3

Jane Cunningham Croly
"Jennie June"
(1829–1901)

F OR FORTY YEARS, Jane Cunningham Croly worked to better the status of women. Her career was one long list of firsts. Known by the pen name Jennie June, she brought women readers to the newspapers, which prior to 1870 were for men only, by creating the first commercial shopping column that named stores. She was the first woman to work daily for a newspaper and the first to teach undergraduate journalism. She originated the women's page, which led to the development of women's departments, now often called lifestyle sections. She presaged the development of syndicates by sending duplicate copies of fashion columns to other papers. She pioneered in the field of "advice" journalism, paving the way for Dorothy Dix, who called her a "newspaper foster mother." And she founded Sororis, the oldest existing women's club, and promoted national and state organizations for women. "A well-rounded club," she said, "was an epitome of the world."

Until 1890 when Nellie Bly captivated the public with her globe-circling stunt, Croly was the best-known woman journalist in America. As the forerunner of today's general assignment reporter, she rushed around New York with her long dress trailing through the mud, visiting stores, reporting on parties, interviewing homemakers. Although she anticipated the needs of twentieth-century women and became a household name, she is virtually forgotten today. Her main interest was fashion, and in a breezy but authoritative style, she told women how to dress. She counseled her readers to ignore foreign fashions and to strive for uniformity, and she campaigned—unsuccessfully—for a standard evening gown. Simplicity and good taste were her mottoes. Discussing fashions for the year 1872, she noted:

It is not in the nature of things to return to the "good old days" of spinning wheels, and irons, and sanded floors, nor does any intelligent man or woman really wish that we could; but every one is glad that a more healthy tone prevails in the community over the fierce passion for dress and display which has been stimulated to the unhealthy height it reached during the past few years.

There is a lull this season caused partly by the want of Parisian excitement, partly by the increasing preponderance of the German element in our midst, and the influence of their simple, sober manners and customs, and completed by our own commercial disasters, and the disgrace into which mere money getters and money spenders have fallen.

A great display of gold and diamonds is rated "bad style," and vulgar ladies belonging to the very best class are even in some instances making a show of simplicity, putting all the cost into the fineness and genuineness of material worn, into jewelry or the trimming of their toilets. Others with less refinement or intelligence, are using laces and stores of a less cherished description.

Taken together, her writings form a history of nineteenth-century American fashion and merchandising. Moreover, she wrote not in reaction to the moment, but with a sense of vision. A product of that vision, her first commercial shopping column ran in the *New York Daily Graphic* of November 8, 1873. It included the following mention: "An excellent glove, fine, soft, well fitting and extremely durable, has been introduced by Lord & Taylor. It is of the 'Trefousse' Paris Manufacture, and has become already a great favorite."

A busy career woman, mother of five, and a sought-after hostess, Croly tempered her feminist writings with an intimate knowledge of how most of her readers really lived. In one column, she observed that a "good wife, good mother and helper in the maintenance of the social order was more important to the race than the practice of any profession." As for the suffrage movement, she believed that the vote would be won through women's economic independence, not through marches and agitation. Writing in *Demorest's Weekly*, she noted that for women "equality carries equal responsibilities; for equal rights in the household, they must take their share in its duties: for equal pay they must give equal work—equal in quality as in quantity; for equal education they must show energy and aptitude and for equal political rights, an intelligence beyond the eternal discussion of the trimming of a dress or bonnet."

The women's angle, however, was only part of her work. Prolific beyond any standard, she wrote editorials, book reviews, criticism, and covered major news events such as the inauguration of the Silver Palace (the first Pullman sleeper) and the maiden voyage of the *Tokio* (the largest steamship of the time). During her forty-year career she worked for the *New York World, New York Daily Graphic*; contributed articles for nine years to the *New York Times*; edited *Madame Demorest's Illustrated Magazine* for twenty-seven years; was editor and part owner of *Godey's Lady's Book*, the first important women's magazine, and founded the *Woman's Cycle*, which later merged with the *Home-Maker* to become the *New Cycle*. The Jennie June byline appeared on freelance and syndicated articles throughout the country.

She frequently objected to having all she did judged as women's work. One of her favorite quips was: "There is no sex in labor, and I want my work taken as the achievement of an individual, with no qualifications, no indulgence, no extenuations simply because I happen to be a woman, working along the same line as a man." She went to the office every day and easily fit into the newsroom atmosphere. Her editor once commented: "Why you go on so naturally and make so little fuss about your work that I sometimes forget you are a woman."

Her success with numerous editors and her loyal readership were due in no small part to her ability to see the changing forces in society. Indeed, she was that most valuable of journalists: the trend spotter. She maintained that a profession for a married woman could be justified only "by the failure or inadequacy" of the husband, a situation she related to her own, with a "large family, small means and a husband who never saw an entirely well day." She believed that some women could work a career into their married life "like yeast into bread in such a way to vitalize the whole and not as an inscription on the graveyard of their hopes." But drawing perhaps from her own experience, she commented on the price frequently paid for a dual-career marriage: "Often both sexes suffer, the wife by losing much of her love and tenderness and spirit of repose" and her husband by losing "the qualities which made the very soul and essence of his manhood." And she was indeed prescient when she warned women who wanted a career for "its apparent superiority, its success, its rewards, its honors . . . its variations from the monotony of every day life" that long years were necessary to make success possible.

Her early life both in England and the United States was typical of the well-bred ladies of her generation. She was born Jane Cunningham on December 19, 1829, in Market Harborough, Leicestershire, the fourth child of Jane (Scott) Cunningham and Joseph Howes Cunningham, a Unitarian minister whose unpopular religious views once led to a stoning of his house.

When she was twelve, the family moved to Poughkeepsie and then to Wappinger's Falls, New York. Under her father's supervision, she was educated at home and read widely in his extensive library. Often she would compose stories and read them aloud for the family's entertainment.

As a young girl she taught school and kept house for her older brother, John, a Congregational minister with a parish in Worcester, Massachusetts. This was a job she enjoyed, and at this time she started collecting kitchen lore that would later become part of the popular *Jennie June's American Cookery Book* (1866). Anticipating the interest in nutrition and well-balanced meals, she advocated eating fresh fruits, salads, and tomatoes. It was her opinion that women had to conquer domestic chores so they could rise above the basic duties of feeding and clothing their families. An accomplished cook, she felt that "cooking a bad meal was a crime and a woman convicted of it should be arraigned for manslaughter."

She explored the women's interests that would make up future stories, and at twenty-five made her first move toward journalism when her father died. To support herself, she started sending articles to various newspapers; the *Tribune* in New York accepted her first, and she signed the story "Jennie June." She had derived the name from a childhood incident: When she was twelve, her minister gave her a poem by Benjamin F. Taylor called "January and June," inscribing it with, "You are the Juniest Jennie I know." In the 1850s she convinced the editor of the *Sunday Times* and *Noah's Weekly Messenger* to publish her column, "Parlor and Side-walk Gossip," which was the first step toward the development of a women's department. In 1856 she started what she called "duplicate correspondence," sending her columns to the *New Orleans Daily Picayune*, the *New Orleans Delta*, the *Richmond Enquirer*, and the *Louisville Journal*.

By all accounts, she was a charmer. Petite, with big blue eyes and brown hair, she wore feminine clothes and had a vivacious energy that drew people quickly into her circle. Shortly after she started her New York career, she met David Goodman Croly, a handsome self-educated Irish immigrant, who was a reporter on the rival *Herald*. They were married on Valentine's Day 1856, and began parallel careers in journalism. After three years in New York they moved to Rockford, Illinois, where her husband founded the short-lived *Rockford Daily News*. Returning to New York in 1860, they worked together on the *World*, where she took charge of the women's page and he was managing editor. Never content with just one project, she also started her association with the popular women's magazines published by William Jennings Demorest and his wife, Ellen Curtis Demorest, the Diana Vreeland of the time.

Marriage to Croly, a conservative reformer with a short-fuse temper and

Jane Cunningham Croly

a trenchant pen, was never dull. He too left his mark on journalism, originating both the Sunday newspaper and the first illustrated daily, the *New York Daily Graphic* (1872). After five years on the *World*, he quarreled with the publisher over his social views, left journalism for good and at age forty-eight became the American leader of the Positivist Movement started by the Frenchman Auguste Comte. (Its followers believed that science could resolve the conflict between truth and religious superstition.) For ten years, until his death in 1889, his considerable, although often misdirected talents would be curtailed by illness. By this time, Jane Croly had borne five children. (One died in infancy, and another, Herbert David Croly, would become famous as a political thinker, author of *The Promise of American Life* (1909), and founder and first editor of the *New Republic*.) With an invalid husband, she became the family's main support.

More responsibility made her even more involved. She managed a busy home on New York's West 14th Street off Washington Square, entertaining such diverse personalities as Louisa May Alcott and Oscar Wilde. Her Sunday evening receptions were described as the nearest thing to the Parisian salon that America had to offer. She followed a hectic, but strict schedule. Every morning she spent three hours at home supervising household duties, and by noon she would be in her office, working frequently until 2 a.m. Charles Forcey, writing in *Crossroads of Liberalism*, notes that her son Herbert resented his mother's recognition and her literary and social agenda which superseded home interests. To be sure, she wrote sincerely on the perils of women neglecting family duties, but for herself work increasingly became the centerpiece of life.

Her articles were always more than listings of fashions or food, for she wrote for "maids and matrons of the country . . . who had never before been so addressed by one of their sex." In an article called "Returning to Town," published in the *Daily Graphic* in September 1873, she pointed out:

There is one cardinal principle in the New York woman's mind, and that is that she must have the one thing that happens to be the rage, or she is not "fit to be seen." This is the pivot upon which her whole being revolves, and which makes her lively, agreeable, or the reverse. Given the belt with oxidized attachments, the Roman sash, the shell ornaments, the walking stick parasol, the set of mink furs, or whatever else happens to be the reigning vogue, and she is happy in the supreme consciousness of having done her duty to herself; but without them, or, worse still, obliged to wear them when they have been superseded by something else, and she is the most unhappy and least understood of created beings.

In 1868, her life took on a new focus, which began quite simply with a visit to the city by Charles Dickens. The all-male New York Press Club planned a dinner for him and refused Croly a ticket—not as a journalist, but as a woman journalist. A meeting of indignant women was hurriedly called in her parlor, where it was decided to form a women's club that would be a forum for education and the exchange of ideas. Croly would later describe that meeting as "the stirring of an intense desire that women should come together—all together—not from one church, or one walk of life, but from all quarters, to take counsel together, and find the causes of failures and separations, of ignorance and wrong doing, and try to discover better ways and more intelligent methods."

Again Croly had selected the right time for change. Women, it seemed, wanted to create a bond of sisterhood, and thus the country's first women's club was begun. It was called Sorosis, a name suggested by a member who knew the Greek word, which means the sweet flavor of many fruits. (As its emblem, the club chose the pineapple.)

The incident of the Dickens dinner was not forgotten, however. To make amends the somewhat chagrined newsmen offered to give a dinner for the new Sorosis members, a formal affair with the women in hoop skirts and white gloves. During the evening, the men, one by one, rose to toast their guests, but not one woman was asked to speak. Another gathering at the Croly residence was called to spin a devious web. A tea was held at which the women made the speeches and the men were ignored. Not to be outdone, the newsmen countered with an invitation to a party where both men and women would pay their own way and sit alternately at the speaker's table, sharing equally in the speeches and responsibilities. This compromise was considered the first mixed banquet, with women seated above the salt.

In the following years the idea of women's clubs caught on, and chapters were formed in other states. As a result, the General Federation of Women's Clubs was organized in 1889, the same year that Croly founded and became the first president of the Women's Press Club of New York. During the century's last decade, Croly devoted much of her time to organizing women's clubs, and started a magazine, *Woman's Cycle*, for the Federation. She also taught journalism at the New Rutgers Institute for Young Ladies in New York, the first woman to teach that subject on the college level. What spare time she had she devoted to writing a 1,172-page *History of the Woman's Club Movement in America*, which was published in 1898. The Library of Congress copy bears this inscription: "Dedication: This book has been a labor of love, and it is lovingly dedicated to the Twentieth Century Woman by one who has seen, and shared in the struggles, hopes and aspirations of the women of the Twentieth century.—J. C. Croly."

During her last years a broken hip that never healed properly curtailed her activities. She went to live in England with her daughter, Vida, and there founded the Society of American Women in London. In addition to her cookbook and women's club history, her columns were collected in book form: *Jennie Juneiana: Talks on Women's Topics* (1864); *For Better or Worse* (1875), which has articles on women's responsibility in marriage; and *Thrown on Her Own Resources* (1891), which provides advice to the working woman. Shortly before her death of a heart ailment in New York on December 23, 1901, at the age of seventy, she had written to a friend: "It seems as if everything has been taken from me but the affection of women, and that manifests itself here [London] as well as at home. God bless them! They have made all the brightness of my life."

An economic recession similar to the one in 1973 swept the country a century earlier, forcing the middle class to economize. In one letter of that time an elitist Jennie June discussed the effect of lowering wages for domestic servants, who she disparages as "ignorant children," and in another reported on nineteenth-century fashions.

THE DOMESTIC QUESTION
What the Panic Has Done At Home—
Its Lessons.

To the Editor of The Daily Graphic

The New York Daily Graphic, November 5, 1873

The financial panic, which has created distrust and alarm throughout the whole country, promises more lasting results in many directions than was foreseen at the beginning. Among other things it has revived domestic grievances and brought the "servant girl" to the front by lowering the rate of wages, few housekeepers and householders being able to pay recent prices, and threatening, according to some, the disruption of our entire domestic system.

I will not say that the absence of system in our domestic arrangement relieves us from all such fears, for it is confusion, want of order, method, and thoroughness on the part of mistresses as well as servants which is at the bottom of all our troubles. But I am quite sure that the necessity for exactness and moderation in expenditure will be a real blessing, and conduce to domestic happiness rather than to domestic misery.

The question of good domestic service is not one of high wages; it is of trained, conscientious work. The rates have been fixed arbitrarily, and have little or nothing to do with willingness, capacity, or proficiency.

"If ladies want to pay sixteen dollars a month, wouldn't I be a vool not to take it?" said a raw German girl the other day, when an indignant housekeeper inquired how she dared to ask such wages when, by her own showing, she did not even know the name of utensils in which she was to cook her dinner!

A few weeks ago a lady went to an intelligence office for a girl to "cook, wash, and iron." "How much do you pay?" asked the keeper. "Fourteen dollars per month," was the reply. "Then you must go somewhere else. We don't keep cheap girls here," was the uncivil answer. Yet it was impossible that in a mixed crowd, such as assemblies in intelligence offices, all could have been deserving of high wages.

Take the experiences of housekeepers, and it is unanimous on this point—

the highest wages have been demanded and generally paid to the poorest and least competent servants.

I would not be understood as wishing to reduce the standard of value of female labor in any department. I only wish to see it graded according to what it is worth. In the present chaotic condition of domestic service the best have to suffer for the faults of the worst, because there is no means of testing the truth of the representations made, and also because the ignorance of girls is such that they do not know what are the qualifications required for positions which they aspire to fill, and are often perfectly unconscious of the extent of their own shortcomings.

In such cases truth and honesty on the part of the servants and willingness and competency on the part of the mistresses would remedy the evil, but in nine cases out of ten there is neither qualification on either side. The girl refuses to acknowledge herself below the standard of requirements, and the mistress is only able to judge by results. She is both unable and unwilling to instruct her.

Another cause of difficulty is the custom among American men of taking upon themselves the responsibility of housekeeping, and the payment of all housekeeping bills, including servants' wages. A desire to relieve their nerves from all trouble is the ostensible reason for this practice, which is pernicious in many respects. In the first place, their wives ought not to be spared "troubles" which it is their business to take upon themselves. In the second place, it is quite impossible for a man to judge accurately of what is done or what is needed in a household in his absence, or to organize it upon any but the most general plan, leaving the details to create a thousand minor "troubles" which no one has the authority to settle. Servants soon learn their cue in these cases, and will pay attention to no one but their "master," while the nominal mistress becomes a mere cipher of much less importance than the cook, if that worthy happens to be able to please her master in the preparation of his favorite dishes.

A point of importance in the consideration of servants' wages is this: What relation do they bear to the other expenses of the family—the table, the allowance for dress of wife and daughter, and the like? I have heard the wife of a rich man say she would be very glad to be sure of a sum every month equal to the wages paid by her husband to his cook. Some men are liberal to servants and mean to stinginess in their provision for other family expenditures, and nearly all force retrenchment at home, in cases of moneyed difficulty, when there is really the least object for it, and in most instances the least opportunity for it.

Extravagant housekeeping—housekeeping which involves high rents, many servants, and large bills,—is never the fault of the wife, where husband and wife are involved in it, because it is he who wants the house which is the prime cause of all. It is the old story told in many ways of the house that Jack built, but neither cat nor rats could have feasted on his malt if he had not built the house.

Table expenses are a small matter compared with the aggregate of rent and wages and fuel and loss by carelessness and the destruction of valuable materials, and it is, therefore, not so much in this one matter that it is necessary to retrench as in the general scale of living. Let every one grade each one of his expenses according to his means, and retrench abroad, when they are obliged to retrench, rather than at home. It is upon their homes and upon family life that most men fall back for comfort and solace in their dark hours, and these they should preserve as much as possible, therefore, from the changes and fluctuations of their wretched systems of business and finance. There are plenty of men who spend five dollars a week upon cigars who will worry their wives to death to effect a saving of twenty-five cents a week upon butter. In such times as these the better policy is to save the large sums, and, if anything, be rather more liberal than usual in the small ones. Move into a smaller house or a "flat;" get rid of your high-priced cook, who cannot make anything without quantities of butter and eggs and milk and sugar, and uplifts her eyebrows at being required to account for the remains of a turkey or a leg of mutton; and get a good maid of all work who is not afraid to make herself "useful." This will cut down on the twenty-five tons of coal, and enable you to burn as much gas as you please in the sitting-room, keep Thanksgiving, and carry THE DAILY GRAPHIC home every night to brighten up the little ones.

There is nothing that makes us feel poverty as utterly as being cut off from small daily comforts and pleasures in the family, and this is generally unnecessary if the larger and more selfish indulgences are sacrificed. A great house and pampered servants are no comfort to children; an hour of "mamma" is worth all of them.

In regard to servants, the Woman's Free Educational and Industrial Society is coming to the rescue. Already their "training school" for girls has sent out over six hundred operatives, book-keepers, and the like, and they are now in treaty for a building, the middle floors of which will be devoted to the industrial school already in operation, the upper part to free dormitories for needy girls and women, the lower part of a "soup kitchen," which will also be a "service" kitchen on the German plan, the kitchen and entire institution serving as a training school for domestics, and the soup and other simple comestibles being neatly served free or for a nominal sum to poor women.

This is the first practical scheme which has been put forth in regard to improving domestic service, and if it is carried out will not only give us trained labor in our kitchens, but it will compel intelligence officers to grade their prices and give some sort of guarantee for their pretensions.

There ought also to be a blind, unquestioned and unquestioning obedience exacted from servants, who are only big, ignorant children after all. Feeling they have, but only rare intellect or imagination; and to expect of them the exercise of the higher reasoning and intellectual faculties is absurd. Human sympathy they can appreciate, but fellowship they only recognize in those who are like themselves.   J. J.

A CHAT WITH THE LADIES
SOMETHING ABOUT THE FASHIONS—
GLOVES—
OPERA TOILETS—STREET COSTUMES—
THE MODE IN COLORS
To the Editor of The Daily Graphic

The New York Daily Graphic, November 8, 1873

Ladies of high fashion in New York are beginning to copy the English custom of remaining in the country until very late in the autumn, so that the "season" in town does not actually commence until near the holidays.

This is particularly the case with those who have country seats, where they can entertain parties of friends, and who spend a part of the summer at the watering-places.

The result is to rob New York of much of the charm and brilliancy during the fall season, and surrender it to its floating population—to birds of passage who spend the winter in hotels and boarding-houses, or only hide a little on their way home from northern summer resorts.

GLOVES

The glove trade is as good a test as any of the presence or absence of the strictly fashionable element.

Quantities of gloves are sold during the fall season, but are purchased in single pairs or couples, very light or very dark, and often of the inferior qualities. Later, about this time, the real trade in gloves begins. Then ladies carry scraps of dress materials, spend hours in matching shades—navy blue, olive, ash gray, brown, and wonderful intermediates, which must be placed together in order to detect the difference. These are selected by the box, for, though few ladies are so extravagant as some gentlemen who wear two new pairs (one day and one evening) every day, in regard to gloves, yet a single pair would be of little use, and indeed, ladies in society do not want to be reduced to their last pair before ordering a fresh supply.

So fine are the shades of color and so accurately are they graded that ladies who are fastidious in this respect would find it advantageous to go to Stewart's and select their gloves and then match them in dress materials.

Gloves were never in better taste than now; they are perfectly plain with the exception of the small gilt stud buttons, which are riveted in so that they cannot come off, and have no contrast in color stitching or mounting. They fit miraculously well, and if of standard make are durable also. They are still worn long upon the arm, three to four buttons being the rule for day wear, four to six for evening.

An excellent glove, fine, soft, well-fitting, and extremely durable, has been introduced by Lord & Taylor. It is of the "Trefousse," Paris, manufacture, and has become already a great favorite.

OPERA TOILETS

The remarkable changes which have taken place in dress will be more generally recognized and appreciated when the infusion of the aristocratic element is more marked in public assemblages. Already opera toilets begin to show an improvement, and before long we may expect to see, in spite of the panic, an ensemble not unworthy of the highest human attainment in musical and dramatic art.

The special change consists in the absence of overskirts, bustle, ruffles, and the like, the graceful length and outline of the single skirt, and the restoration of the plain, rich, unencumbered surfaces. This admits of the use of richer fabrics than it has been the custom of late to put into even the most ceremonious costumes. Moire antique is revived, and velvet will be considered most *distingué* slightly enriched with embroidery of silk and jet and mounted with fine old lace.

The recent over-trimmed and brushed-up costumes had indeed reached the limit of vulgarity. When they have passed away women will look back with surprise, and refuse to believe they could ever have committed the absurdity of wearing them.

The most popular method of trimming trained dresses is upon the front breadths, with diagonal bands or narrow ruffles, and bands alternated, robed in at the sides, and the robing extended round the edge of the skirt at the back.

TRIMMING

There are other rich dresses which are cut in the princesse style, and finished only with a thick piping of the material. These have a girdle and chatelaine attachment, or they are confined at the waist by a belt embroidered with jet and bordered with deep jet fringe, or loops of velvet placed at regular intervals, but irregular in length. Belts with pendant attachments will be remembered as having been worn eight or ten years ago, when the princesse dress was first introduced, and those who have them in reserve will find them sufficiently in accordance with the present style for all practical purposes.

Some charming princesse dresses have been made recently for in-door wear of cashmere, with coat-sleeves slashed or puffed at the top and over the elbows, and square necks cut close and finished with a plaiting. With these the chatelaine belt and pocket is most appropriate.

OPERA STYLES

New theater, opera, and reception costumes are made very showy by the use of beaded trimmings, black and white, and "garniture" laces. The prettiest of these latter are "pearled"—that is, enriched with lovely round pearl beads many times larger than seed pearls. They are used upon pale pink, blue, and water green silks, and are exceedingly effective.

As yet, styles *decoletée* have not made their appearance; balls and receptions have indeed hardly begun, and dresses worn at the opera are either high or completed by a fichu of lace which covers the neck. The quaint, mediaeval simplicity of the high, square neck, slashed coat-sleeves, and trailing skirt win many admirers, however, and has been copied for a distinguished young married lady, in the richest materials.

Black velvet belts with old or polished silver-mountings are the most fashionable for house wear, and not unfrequently have nice silver chains pendant from the chatelaine. To these are attached scent-bottle, small netted purse, note-book, keys, fan, silver fruit-knife, pencil-case, small hand-mirror, and silver whistle, or perfume holder. Besides these there is an engraved pendant attachment, from which the black enamelled watch, brilliantly jewelled, is suspended.

Buttons of steel, gilt, or old silver are now almost universal upon the pretty English cloth jackets worn in the street. They are used in profusion, and are particularly effective upon very dark purple and navy blue cloth. Corwin, 194 Church street, by the way, makes a specialty of these jackets, has them strictly cut, and made by tailors, and is just now offering very desirable styles at exceedingly low prices.

Navy blue is undoubtedly the color of the season. So great is the demand for it that wholesale houses will only sell limited quantities of it, in silk, velvet, or cloth, and then, not unless the buyer will take also several pieces of goods in less salable colors. The general ignorance, or color blindness, or both, is so great, however, that quantities of fabrics in different shades of purple are sold for navy blue, and the mistake is not discovered by either seller or buyer.

A few persons who have not suffered by the great crash are beginning to look out in a guarded way for holiday gifts. Dress materials are down so low that they will be in great demand by those who want "useful" presents for servants and others. R. H. Macy & Co. have already opened full samples of French and German toys and fancy goods, including dolls, dolls' trousseaus, and dolls' houses, of every kind and degree, and even those who cannot purchase will find a pleasure in looking at these details in miniature of grown-up ideals and splendors. All the purchases were made in Europe under Mr. Macy's own supervision, so that ladies may rely on getting the best and the prettiest, as well as the cheapest, at this establishment.   J. J.

4

Leonel Campbell O'Bryan "Polly Pry"
(1857–1938)

DESCRIBED BY John Gunther in his "inside" America stories as "the most lunatic paper in the United States," the *Denver Post* at the turn of the century loved scandal and lurid headlines; it was a broadsheet with a tabloid mentality. Its publishers were Harry Tammen and Frederick G. Bonfils, two rapacious pirates who never let the facts get in the way of a good story. And its indomitable investigative reporter was Polly Pry. A rebel with many causes, she had been able to sidestep the standard sob-sister assignments to do battle with Colorado's scamps and villains. She was at her best attacking those labor, political, and social leaders whom she saw as manipulators.

While reporting a series on prison reform, she visited the Canon City state prison and there met a "tall, solemn, silent fellow." She asked the warden about him and learned that he was Alfred Packer, known even today by every Colorado school child as Packer, the "Man-Eater," the first convicted cannibal. Packer had been hired to guide five prospectors from Provo, Utah, to Colorado during the winter of 1874. The party was trapped in a snowstorm and ran out of food. Only Packer came back. He admitted eating the bodies of his companions, but said that four of them had been killed by the fifth.

Packer claimed to have killed that man in self-defense. He was convicted and sentenced to the gallows; later his term was commuted to forty years.

The story was made to order for the sensational *Post*. Immediately Polly started work on a "Free Packer Campaign." She reasoned that he was guilty of nothing more than cannibalism, long the unwritten law of the seas and permissible under blizzard conditions. The *Post* trotted out the whole story, but the governor refused a pardon. Polly, who knew the value of public documents, went to the parole board and asked to see the list of convicts who had received executive clemency. The paper printed the stories of those pardoned for murder or rape and asked: "Why not Packer?"

Tammen and Bonfils hired W. W. "Plug Hat" Anderson to represent Packer in his appeal and offered the lawyer $1,000 if he succeeded. Anderson however, then went to Packer and demanded more money, persuading the convict to hand over $1,500 he had earned making hair-ropes and bridles in prison over eighteen years. On January 13, 1900, when the publishers learned of the double deal, they fired Anderson, who immediately walked across the street from his office to the newspaper to confront Tammen, Bonfils, and Polly. A fight ensued, and Anderson pulled a pistol, shooting Bonfils twice in the chest and Tammen in the shoulder and wrist. Then, according to Polly's eyewitness account in the *Post*: "The pistol was still aimed at Mr. Tammen when I ran between them and cried out for Anderson to desist, but he tried to shoot over my shoulder at Mr. Tammen, where he lay on the floor . . . Then there was a crowd at the door and Anderson walked out with the smoking revolver in his hand."

For the time it was not an unusual occurrence; disagreements were often settled with a gun. Disgruntled readers would vent their anger over a story and storm the newspaper office. The publishers soon recovered from their wounds. Anderson was tried and after two hung juries was acquitted on a plea of self-defense. Packer was paroled in 1901 after twenty years in prison and became a bodyguard for the publishers. But the two men never felt the same about Polly. It was as if they couldn't forgive or even thank her—a woman—for saving their lives.

The Packer affair notwithstanding, Polly Pry was far from the rough-and-ready pioneer lady of the new West. A personality who commanded attention, she had refinement and great beauty. "Wherever she went, eyes followed Polly Pry," the *Denver Post* noted in her obituary, "for in her prime she was one of the Lillian Russell, Mae West type of dazzling blonds. To beauty, she added a gift of conversation worthy of the French court and a charm of manner designed to captivate all who came within the radius of her personality, and above all she had courage to live life as she pleased." Pictures from the time show Polly wearing the extravagant Worth gowns,

the nineteenth-century's social armor, and "La Belle Epoque" hats fes-
tooned with yards of tulle and lace. She was, wrote Gene Fowler in *Tim-
berline*, the story of the raucous *Denver Post*, "a great and tender character
with courage unbounded."

Leonel Ross Campbell was born November 11, 1857, the eldest of four children of James Nelson Campbell, a Kentucky plantation owner who lost
everything in the Civil War, and Mary Elizabeth (MacKinney) Campbell.
When she was fifteen, she was sent to a private boarding school in St. Louis,
where she grew bored and restless. She met George Anthony, a wealthy Kansas
engineer who was building the Mexican Central Railroad, and one night
put on her first long dress made of black velvet, climbed over the school wall
and eloped with him.

Married life was immediately varied and adventurous. The couple lived
in an opulent private train car, which followed the building of the railroad,
and the young bride entertained financiers, government officials, and train
executives. At one point she was the guest of Mexican President Porfirio Díaz
in his palace, and became acquainted with the intricacies of Latin American
politics.

After five years of life in a moving parlor car, she left Anthony and went
to New York with a letter of introduction to a friend of her father's, Col.
John A. Cockerill, who was the managing editor of Pulitzer's *World*. They
probably met around 1879, shortly before Nellie Bly wheedled her way in
to see Cockerill without an introduction. In *Ladies of the Press*, Ishbel Ross
reports the editor's reaction: "Give you a job? I ought to spank you and send
you home to your husband." He hired her for $6 a week and sent her to
cover a tenement fire. Her story, according to the *Denver Post*, was "a siz-
zling classic which created a standard for descriptive writing." Next she was
sent to Panama to report on the proposed building of the canal by the French.
The stories she filed on the canal carried no byline; the *nom de plume* Polly
Pry originated later in her career.

Polly's time in New York, roughly until 1898, is not documented. All
reports indicate that her time on the *World* was spent mostly in South America,
and Ishbel Ross noted that she wrote some pulp fiction after leaving the *World*.
What is known is that her parents moved to Denver in 1892 for the health
of their two sons and, on a visit there in 1898, Polly met Tammen and Bonfils, who immediately hired her on the basis of her reputation on the *World*.

There is no doubt that she had a talent for description and scene setting.
She often traveled to other cities for the *Post*, and in one story published
January 7, 1900, she goes to New York's Chinatown to report on the death
of a white woman who had stabbed herself after learning that her son by a

Chinese man had died in a fall from a tenement. Here she described her entry into the tenement:

I shuddered as I climbed the broken steps and entered the dark hall where the faint light from the halls above struggled with the thick blackness of the place. Shadowy figures huddled about the lower step, but as I approached they drew back into the darkness, where I could not see them but could hear their breathing and feel their eyes upon me. Above, the wailing cries grew louder and indistinct voices floated down towards me. I stumbled against something on the stairs and hurriedly crossed myself, when I bent down and looked into the bead-like eyes of an old man who crouched there in the gloom, an old man with toothless mouth, scant gray queue and ugly, claw-like fingers. Two flights of crazy stairs and then a narrow hall from which opens innumerable tiny rooms. The air is close, hot, unspeakably vile. At the front end of the hall stands another police officer and behind him is a closed door. All the other doors are open and the place swarms with men and women, with here and there a little child clinging to its mother's dress and staring with frightened eyes at the dread policeman.

Following the Packer parole and the shooting aftermath, Polly launched an investigation into the mine workers. In 1902 she went to Telluride, the stronghold of the Western Federation of Miners and the place where Arthur J. Collins, owner of the Smuggler Union Mine, had been murdered. She interviewed miners and owners, and wrote a story quoting the federation president defending the murder. Later he repudiated the interview, and his union boycotted the *Post*. It was simply good business to offer up Polly as reparation, so Bonfils and Tammen refused to stand behind her.

She left the *Post* shortly thereafter to start her own weekly magazine of comment and opinion. She called it *Polly Pry*, with the motto, "To hold, as 'twer, the Mirror up to Nature." In the first edition of September 5, 1903, she announced that Denver was "just big enough and just lively enough and just naughty enough to need a weekly paper of its own as desperately as a lively boy needs his Saturday night tubbing." She promised to give her readers "something we all need and get mighty little of—and that is a dose of that unpalatable and evanescent bug-a-bear known as the—truth." She went on to note, "It won't make me beloved, but I hope it will do even better—create a demand for Polly Pry."

In starting a Saturday weekly, she had taken her cue from weeklies already published in New York and San Francisco. Hers was a lively publication of some twenty pages with political cartoons, lots of gossip and brutal anecdotes, written in a harrumphing style. Copy from *Polly Pry* was widely reprinted, with 200 other papers in Colorado using items. The gossip column was called "Tell Truth and Shame Devil." A typical entry, from March 26, 1904, shows Polly's arch style:

Leonel Campbell O'Bryan

Dr. Trask, corpulent and suave, has gotten himself into trouble, down at the Springs, for keeping the lingerie of a patient who couldn't pay. What the doctor is going to do with the stuff, only the angels know. Dr. Trask has a private hospital at the Springs, and being of the "ladies' delight" brand of surgeons, has his hands full and his knife out ten hours out of every twelve—he is big, pink and white, wears diamonds on his capacious shirt-front and diamonds on his roomy finger, a silk hat and a frock coat— oh, it's a joy, is Dr. Trask; and should the naughty little widow succeed in getting back all the presents which have been given her by her dear, good friends the grave and reverent seniors at the Springs—Trask may have to pitch his tent on another oasis. On a corner in a hack, the Doctor would be as beauteous and successful as a tarra-rum on the brow of beauty—the public like his sort.

Soon after starting publication, the newsweekly began in-depth coverage of the mining problems in Las Animas County. Mine owners had been using unskilled immigrants as cheap, non-union labor. Union members, in turn, would try to drive off the scabs by intimidation and physical force. "The anarchists and socialists of the entire country are making a desperate effort to establish their headquarters in Colorado," Polly warned. "I was there [Las Animas County] last week, and not a day passed without its murders, killings, assaults." And she continued to hammer away at her promise that the union leaders, not the mine owners, were responsible for the violence.

Her crusade may have resulted in an attempt on her life. As Polly told the story, on January 10, 1904, she had been interviewing applicants for a job. The doorbell of her West Colfax Avenue home had been ringing most of the evening. She wrote that she had received threatening letters about her campaign against the imported labor agitators, and was being cautious about visitors. The doorbell rang again and Polly went to answer it. "I went to the front door and some instinct or fear or apprehension made me step behind it—otherwise I would not be writing this—as I swung it open. I looked around the door, and instantly two shots were fired . . . I saw a long red flame, caught a fleeting glimpse of a big man in dark clothes, and a derby hat; had an instantaneous impression of a dark moustache and a side face marred by a red mark."

The next day, according to the *Denver Post*, all the city rallied to Polly's side. The chief of police announced: "They certainly intended to kill her. We have men out West who would be willing to kill her or any newspaper man for the asking." The governor offered to call out the militia to guard her. The adjutant general declared the attempt the start of a reign of assassination. Newsboys stood guard outside her house.

Her former *Post* colleague, Winifred Black (Annie Laurie), published a special notice announcing that she was a *Polly Pry* contributor and wanted to share in the responsibility for the labor stories. "If there is any shooting to be done," she wrote, "the gentlemen who are handy with guns will find

me at the Polly Pry office every day between 10 o'clock and 5. It is time for
the men and women of Denver who have one spark of American spirit left
in their hearts to stand by Polly Pry and by the fight she is making for American liberty, American free speech and the right to live a fearless American
life."

Some were skeptical about the attempted assassination, particularly rival
papers like the *Rocky Mountain News* and the *Denver Times*, which hinted
that Polly's barbed attacks at society personalities could have triggered the
incident. She scoffed at such speculations and told a reporter: "It is silly to
even think that any society person would want to put me out of the way for
some little thing I had written about them."

Polly stood strong and assured her readers: "I want the public to know that
I am going to keep right on running my magazine and writing what I think
proper. I have not been attacking union labor, but I have been showing up
some of the leaders." But after two years she tired of her publication and
sold it.

In 1910 she married Henry J. O'Bryan, a lawyer and a founder of the
Denver Club. He died in Oregon six years later, just when Polly was set to
leave for Mexico to cover Pancho Villa's revolutionary movement for the
Rocky Mountain News. She went to Mexico nonetheless, and according to
Ishbel Ross's account, got into revolutionary territory to interview Villa un-
der a flag of truce arranged by the American naval forces.

When World War I broke out, Polly was near sixty and too old for Red
Cross service, but she talked to the right people and got herself assigned as
a public relations officer in Greece and Albania. On her return she organized the first Western States' Poppy Day to benefit French war orphans.

For many years after the war she reportedly worked on her memoirs. Ross
noted: "A gentle old lady occasionally wanders into the Denver Public Library nowadays [1935] and digs about among the books in the Western History collection. Her eyes have a mournful beauty, for they have seen un-
canny things. It is difficult for a younger generation to believe that this is
the Polly Pry of legend—wild, beautiful, fearless." But her life story apparently was never finished. It wasn't published, and no manuscript has turned
up in archives.

Her last years were spent quietly in Denver. In 1968, her sister-in-law,
Annette Campbell, recounted for a *Denver Post* reporter her memories of
Polly, whom she first met in 1914: "I always thought Polly had a very masculine mind—that is, she thought as a man—though she was very feminine
. . . she had a personality like I've never known. No one ever talked when
she was in the room—they just listened."

"She always had money," Campbell recalled, "and she could never accept the fact that it might run out. When she'd get a check for $10 or $20, she'd call me and say, 'Get yourself fixed up pretty, and come downtown. We're going to have a party.' A party meant lunch at the old Daniel's & Fisher tearoom or Curtis Street Baur's. She loved nice places and it never mattered if there weren't any groceries the next day."

At the age of eighty her heart began to fail and she entered a Denver hospital where she died on July 16, 1938. The *Denver Post* reported that "a moment before passing, with characteristic energy, she raised herself from the bed and said to the attending nurse, 'I must be up and _____' "

The following story, one of many she wrote for the "Free Packer Campaign," is notable for its use of public documents.

Polly Pry Passes in Scorching Review the Troop of Ravishers Whom Tender-Hearted Governor Thomas Has Seen Fit to Parole. . . .

The Denver Post, January 8, 1900

Is the "Alfred Packer case" closed?

I have been asked that little question a number of times this week, and at the risk of appearing to differ with his excellency, Governor Charles B. Thomas, chief executive of the state, I have said—no!

No, it is not closed; nor will it be closed until the last bit of evidence obtainable is laid before the public.

Otto Mears may be able to convince his friend, Governor Thomas, that it is good to keep an innocent man in a gloomy prison cell in order that his—Otto Mears'—rest may not be disturbed by terrifying dreams!

But how about the five hundred thousand splendid men and women in this state who believe in truth and mercy and justice?

Do they not think as I do that that is carrying friendship too far?

Is it right, is it just, is it merciful to close your ears to an appeal from one in sore straits because your friend is afflicted with a white liver?

Out from behind great stone walls and heavy steel bars there creeps a cry for mercy, for justice! It is a cry that will not down; it has sounded in your ears at long intervals for twenty years! Once it was a wild, fierce sound that carried a thrill of something like fear to the ears of those who heard it. Its plea for justice in those days was couched in language that burned, but as the years have gone by the wild eagle has learned his lesson, his threats are forgotten and the fire in his eyes been quenched by the bitter waters of many disappointments. Today there is a note of finality in the brave voice that will not down, there is a touch of despair, a quiver of hopelessness, and if you listen you will hear "Mercy, mercy" where once it cried loudly "justice, justice!" It comes from a man who has lived a wonderful life, a life full of danger and hardship and great privation; a man who has feared nothing on earth, whose courage is absolute, unquestioned; a man who has given seven years of his life to his country, who has been solider and scout and guide, when to be either meant to take your life in your hand and bravely face the grim destroyer almost every hour of your days; a man who earned a pension as a scout in that wonderful campaign, where Custer and his immortal band met a heroic death and filled a nation's heart with tears. For three years he was one of that marvellous band of government scouts who carried dispatches across the bleak hills and trackless wastes of our wild Northwest.

And all this he did after the alleged crime was committed! And a grateful nation has rewarded him for injuries received there by granting him a pension—a pension of $25 a month. Do you know what he does with that money?

Let me tell you—this man, this soldier-scout, this man who is crying to you for "mercy"—this man locked up behind the terrible prison bars, accused of a horrible butchery for money, this avaricious devil—well—he gives his money away!

No, it is not a joke. I have it from the warden, from prisoners, from a dozen people who know. It is quite true. I know you find it hard to believe—how can it be possible that a man who deliberately murdered five companions for the trifling sums they had with them is charitable? It is absurd, is it not? But absurd as it is—it is true. Warden Hoyt will tell you as he told me: "Packer is the soul of generosity, and apparently cares nothing for money. I don't believe that there has ever been a man in the penitentiary who has applied to him for aid who has not received it. I know because he has to draw his money through me. Scores of poor devils who have served their time and are about to take their plunge back into the world owe it to Packer's generosity that they are enabled to step out of prison respectably clad and with money enough in their pockets to live on for a month or so until they can get work. They are an ungrateful lot. I don't believe one of them has ever written to thank the old man once they were out, but he goes right along helping the next one just the same."

No other man in the penitentiary has such a record.

Yes, it is Packer that I am writing about. Packer the terrible! Packer who has been behind the bars for twenty years. Packer who has a clean record, who has never refused to work, who obeys the rules of the institution, and who, to the extent of his power, helps his fellow unfortunates. No man can do more than that, can he?

When the merciful lawmakers of this state last winter framed and enacted the "parole law" it was with the object of assisting such prisoners as were found worthy and who betrayed a desire to become decent, law-abiding citizens. When a prisoner has served a certain portion of his sentence, has a clean prison record, is not a habitual criminal, has a means of livelihood and proper recommendations, he is eligible for a parole.

Packer was eligible. His prison record was perfect, he has served a twenty-year sentence, he was never in prison before, had sufficient means to live upon, was recommended by the warden of the penitentiary, and, in addition, 150 of the most prominent men in the state, men thoroughly familiar with the case, asked that clemency, mercy, be granted him.

And the unfortunate behind the bars looked out to where the sun lit the mountain side with prismatic splendor, and hoped.

And the people who asked for mercy hoped. They didn't know of the frightened little man who was flashing across the continent like the yellow tail of a comet, hastening to throw himself into the arms of his friend, the governor, and to protect against the release of the horrible creature, the thought of whom made him quake like a jelly fish. And the little man arrived and went up to the beautiful capitol building and climbed upon a table and whispered in the governor's ear for a long, long time, and then he wept upon the governor's immaculate shirt front and went away back to Washington, but he wept for joy.

For the next day the "Packer case" was closed. The parole was refused!

The merits of the case were in no way affected by this decision. Right and justice cannot be juggled out of sight at the will of a man who is afraid of a shadow. But, alas! might is always stronger than right, and as usual might won.

Knowing that the governor has granted a considerable number of pardons and signed many paroles, I have taken particular pains to find out exactly what manner of man finds favor in his eyes, and I herewith present you the entire list, and ask you to look it over and to compare the case of Packer with those herein set down:

PARDONS

4646—Mary Clarkson, Garfield county, one year—Grand larceny. Sentenced Nov. 27, 1898. Pardoned May 9, 1899.

4707—Bessie Galbraith, Pueblo county, five years—Perjury. Sentenced March 6, 1899. Pardoned Nov. 10, 1899.

4706—Hugh Galbraith, Pueblo county, two and one half years—Perjury. Sentenced March 6, 1899. Pardoned Aug. 7, 1899.

4708—Francis Pudney, Pueblo County, five years—Perjury. Sentenced March 6, 1899. Pardoned November 10, 1899.

4334—J. H. Fisher, Weld county, six years—Grand larceny. Sentenced December 9, 1897. Pardoned July 11, 1899.

4465—Ed McBuckley, Larimer county, four and one-half years—Forgery. Sentenced February 5, 1898. Pardoned August 7, 1899.

4373—James Ryan, El Paso county, three years—Forgery. Sentenced September 20, 1897. Pardoned September 1, 1899.

———J. W. Kelly, Arapahoe county, two years—Grand larceny.

———Henry Behr, Arapahoe county, three years—Embezzlement.

————Arthur Francis, El Paso county, two years—Assault.

4652—William Rimmen. Pitkin county, one year—Assault to kill. Sentenced November 30, 1898. Pardoned August 7, 1899.

————John Weathers, life—Murder.

3386—Buck Robe, Weld county, ten years—murder. Sentenced December 19, 1893. Pardoned March 3, 1899.

4625—Robert G. Penton, El Paso county, life—Murder. Sentenced November 4, 1898. Pardoned October 14, 1899.

2886—Alfred Russell, El Paso county, life—Murder. Sentenced April 12, 1892. Pardoned November 10, 1899.

————Nestor Martinez, Las Animas county, sixteen years—Murder. Sentenced November 10, 1897. Pardoned December, 1899.

4709—Thomas Washington, Arapahoe, one year—Rape. Sentenced March 10, 1899. Pardoned April 8, 1899. Served just twenty-nine days.

COMMUTATION OF SENTENCE

————Franklin C. Couton, twelve years—Rape. Commutation to two and one-half years.

PAROLES

4304—Matt Adams, Arapahoe county, five years—Embezzlement. Sentenced June 21, 1897. Paroled August 6, 1899.

2757—Mike Ryan, Arapahoe county, nine years—larceny. Sentenced December 21, 1891. Paroled August 7, 1899.

4281—James McGowan, Las Animas county, four years—Burglary and larceny. Sentenced May 10, 1897. Paroled December 12, 1899.

4495—Jesus Maes, Costilla county, 5.½ years—Arson. Sentenced April 7, 1898. Paroled December 16, 1899.

4243—E. Frank White, Mesa county, 4 years—Larceny. Sentenced March 16, 1897. Paroled Sept. 10, 1899.

4378—John s. Adams, Denver, 3.½ years—Larceny. Sentenced September 29, 1897. Paroled Sept. 4, 1899.

3773—Wiliam Thompson, Conejos county, 8 years—Grand larceny. Sentenced May 21, 1895. Paroled Sept. 7, 1899.

3950—Robert R. Smith, Cripple Creek, 6 years—Grand larceny. Sentenced Jan. 16, 1896. Paroled Sept. 7, 1899.

4485—Felix J. Chastine, Denver, 2 years—Grand larceny. Sentenced March 30, 1897. Paroled Oct. 23, 1899.

3385—William Shaffer, Montezuma county, 14 years—Robbery. Sentenced Dec. 20, 1893. Paroled Oct. 9, 1899.

3260—John Brown, Denver, 14 years—Robbery. Sentenced June 24, 1893. Paroled Sept. 20, 1899.

4597—Charles Campton, Fort Collins, 4 years—Larceny of stock. Sentenced Oct. 3, 1898. Paroled Sept. 26, 1899.

3465—George Stewart, Pueblo, 9 years—burglary. Sentenced March 23, 1894. Paroled Oct. 11, 1899.

4631—Floyd Grimes, Mineral county, 3.½ years—Larceny of stock. Sentenced Nov. 12, 1898. Paroled Oct. 17, 1899.

4492—Larry O'Neil, Bent county, 4 years—Counterfeiting. Sentenced April 13, 1898. Paroled Oct. 24, 1899.

4367—Henry Behr, Denver, 3 years—Embezzlement. Sentenced Sept. 23, 1897. Paroled Oct. 30, 1899.

4257—Frank Hare, Costilla county, 2 years—Larceny of stock. Sentenced June 20, 1897. Paroled Nov. 17, 1899.

4274—J. N. Ostega, Conejos county, 3.½ years—Larceny. Sentenced May 9, 1897. Paroled Nov. 10, 1899.

4552—W. H. Ryan, El Paso county, 5 years—Perjury. Sentenced June 9, 1898. Paroled Nov. 18, 1899.

4202—Charles Miller, Denver, 5 years—Grand larceny. Sentenced Feb. 9, 1897. Paroled Dec. 16, 1899.

4406—George Jewett, Fremont county, 5 years—Burglary. Sentenced Nov. 10, 1897. Paroled Dec. 23, 1899.

4127—E. Williams, Mesa county, 5 years—burglary and larceny. Sentenced Oct. 18, 1896. Paroled Oct. 12, 1899.

4374—Fred L. Rice, El Paso county, 3 years—Forgery. Sentenced Sept. 26, 1897. Paroled Oct. 12, 1899.

4000—Miles B. Burlew, Larimer county, 5 years—Forgery. Sentenced March 25, 1896. Paroled Oct. 10, 1899.

4440—John Condon, El Paso county, 2.½ years—Grand larceny. Sentenced Dec. 29, 1897. Paroled Nov. 23, 1899.

3383—John Henderson, Conejos county, 10 years—Robbery. Sentenced Dec. 17, 1893. Paroled Nov. 23, 1899.

4573—Arthur Kruckeberg, Logan county, 2.½ years—False pretense. Sentenced July 24, 1898. Paroled Sept. 5, 1899.

3896—Frank Rutledge, Weld county, 6 years—Larceny. Sentenced Nov. 13, 1895. Paroled Oct. 5, 1899.

3856—O. C. Wilder, El Paso county, 10 years—Robbery. Sentenced Sept. 22, 1895. Paroled Dec. 7, 1899.

MURDERERS OUT ON PAROLE

4510—Fred Guay, Rio Grande county, 3.½ years—Murder. Sentenced May 2, 1898. Paroled Nov. 24, 1899.

4379—James W. Lecky, Gunnison, 3 years—Murder. Sentenced Oct. 2, 1897. Paroled Oct. 6, 1899.

3020—Olaf Thisselle, Las Animas county, 14 years—Murder. Sentenced Oct. 4, 1892. Paroled Oct. 4, 1899.

4601—Wm. Dean, Pueblo, 2.½ years—Assault to murder. Sentenced Oct. 7, 1898. Paroled Nov. 17, 1899.

2401—Edward Kelly, El Paso county, 26 years—Murder. Sentenced Nov. 28, 1890. Paroled Sept. 5, 1899.

VIOLATORS OF YOUNG GIRLS AND LITTLE CHILDREN OUT ON PAROLE

4501—John Lippse, Boulder, 18 years—RAPE. Sentenced April 23, 1898; paroled Oct. 9, 1899.

3575—Edward C. Brooks, Denver, 10 years—ASSAULT TO RAPE. Sentenced Sept. 30, 1894; paroled Oct. 12, 1899.

4001—Charles Lamont, Larimer county, 8 years—RAPE. Sentenced March 25, 1896; paroled Nov. 26, 1899.

4391—Burr Kendall, El Paso county, 5 years—ASSAULT TO RAPE. Sentenced Oct. 20, 1897; paroled Nov. 23, 1899.

4393—Joe Jachetta, Pueblo, 5 years—ASSAULT TO RAPE. Sentenced Oct. 29, 1897; paroled Nov. 5, 1899.

2630—W. Bloodworth, Rio Binaco county, 20 years—RAPE. Sentenced Sept. 6, 1891; paroled Oct. 23, 1899.

2631—J. H. Bloodworth, Rio Bianco county, 20 years—RAPE. Sentenced Sept. 6, 1891; paroled Oct. 23, 1899.

It is an important array, is is not? Sixteen pardons and forty-one paroles—fifty-seven men whom Packer has watched walk out into the great free world in the past nine months—forty-one of them since the 6th day of August.

There is Nestor Martinez of Las Animas county. You remember that case, don't you? It's only a little more than two years old. It was a stockmen's quarrel, and a frightful butchery took place. Men were brutally murdered and their bodies burned. Afterwards young Martinez was arrested and threw himself on the mercy of the court, confessed his share in the killing, turned state's evidence and helped to find and convict all of his companions. They paid the full penalty of their crimes while he, after a two years' term, receives a full pardon. It was a crime beside which the alleged crime of Packer pales into insignificance.

But there is a powerful uncle in the Southern part of the state, an uncle who, like Otto Mears, has a big following, and who cannot well be refused.

There is Fred Guay, from Rio Grande county. This interesting gentleman was a deputy sheriff and priviledged to carry a pistol. He had a friend by the name of Montroux, an old man, who was in the habit of sleeping off his frequent debauches in Guay's rooms. One day last summer Montroux got on one of his periodical drunks and, meeting his son, a lad of 20, demanded that he assist him to Guay's house. They went, and there, in a moment of anger at the overturning of a piece of furniture, Guay shot the boy, who died that night after testifying that he was unarmed, was innocent of any known offense, and that he did not know why Guay had shot him.

The court sentenced this cold-blooded murderer to three and a half years in the penitentiary—three and a half years for a boy's life—and even that is too much, so our sympathetic governor thinks, as on November 24 he paroled him.

One year's imprisonment for a life—it looks cheap, does it not?

But there is another criminal, worse than a murderer, a criminal for whom there should be neither forgiveness nor mercy, a hideous, revolting, atrocious brute, the thought of whom gives you the horror—the man who outrages young girls and little children. Think what that means you mothers and fathers of little girls. Imagine to yourselves the sufferings of those unfortunate parents whose tender little one has been brutally assaulted. Should there be any mercy for that sort of crime? I here so say—No! A thousand times no!

And yet the great governor of this state, himself a father, has been moved to pity and to pardon and parole, nine of these inhuman monsters. Nine— you will find them on the list.

There is John Lippse, a youth of nineteen—from Boulder. Let me tell you what he did, not fully, for such things cannot be printed, but what I can. He had a friend, a man, and the two of them got hold of a little girl twelve years of age, a frail little child who happened to pass their way. They took her into a secluded place, and finally, left her, half dead, to lie there on the ground for hours before she was found.

They arrested the two men, who admitted their guilt, and they were sentenced to 18 years in the pen. That was in April 1898. In October 1899, a parole is given to Lippse!

One year—mothers and fathers, what do you think of this?

There are others, but I am only going to mention one more case—and I want to say here that if any one doubts the truth of this tale—and it does seem past credence—they can go to the capitol building in the office of the board of charities and corrections. Mr. Stonaker will show them, as he showed me, a full and detailed account of this case, which is of such a nature that it can only be touched upon.

In September, 1891, one William Bloodworth and his son, John H. Bloodworth, were arrested for crimes committed upon the person of the little 8-year-old stepdaughter of William. They were arrested on the 6th, and so clear was their guilt, so prompt their confession, that on the 8th they were sent to Canon City for twenty years each. They lived upon a claim, with no neighbors nearer than a half mile, in a little three-room shack. The child was a year old when Bloodworth married the mother and grew up with the idea that he was her father, and that the 23-year-old son was her brother, and before she was 8 years old these two inhuman fiends had violated that infant.

The testimony would make a wooden man blush with shame. They made no attempt to deny their guilt, nor did they pretend any remorse for their crime. It was an absolutely brutal and revolting assault of a character such as this country knows little about—there were no palliating circumstances.

The case was tried before Judge Rucker and after reading an account of it and the testimony, I called upon that distinguished gentleman, who not alone confirmed all that I had read about the case, but added that, "in the whole of his career he had never known of a more shocking case, nor one where the criminals were entitled to less sympathy."

The tender conscience of your great and good chief executive, balks at a case like Packer's—a case where a man in the throes of starvation kills a maniac in self-defense. Nothing can convince him that such a crime can be sufficiently punished—seventeen years in the penitentiary—it is nothing—for so frightful a crime he should lie in his narrow cell until he rots; but for two men, two human fiends, two brutes who ravish a fragile child, a child they are bound in honor and decency to protect and cherish—for these men the icy heart of your great governor doth drip tears of pity!

Citizens of Colorado, what do you think of it? POLLY PRY

[signature byline]

5

Elizabeth Meriwether Gilmer "Dorothy Dix"
(1861–1951)

DOROTHY DIX saw a world change and, through her sympathetic, pragmatic, and realistic advice, helped to change it. She suffered over the right word, tone, and phrase in her writing, and she suffered over the letters she received in the fifty-five years she wrote her column. "Dear Dorothy Dix . . ." they would begin. They came from men and women, from the bashful and the bold, and she was a true oracle, ready to reply to any question. She believed in virginity: "Free love means what it says." She frowned on exclusive relationships: "A young girl who lets any one boy monopolize her simply shuts the door in the face of good times and her chances of making a better match." She praised flirting: "The come-hither look in the eye, a sort of come-on look if you get what I mean." She advocated cunning: "Few grafts are more profitable than comforting a widower. But remember that fast work is required." A favorite reply was, "Men are a selfish lot." But she was also willing to say that problems were sometimes the women's fault.

From 1896 when her column started in the *New Orleans Daily Picayune* to 1951 when she died at ninety, it is estimated that more than 60 million people around the world read her words of advice. Others had penned advice columns before,[1] but none had her special omniscience: an insight she attributed to her own unhappiness, particularly a marriage that she maintained with quiet desperation for forty-seven years. Although equally famous for sixteen years as a Hearst sob sister, she always preferred her column, putting its demands above her other reporting. Crime stories, she reasoned, only increased circulation; her column helped people—and herself. By dealing with the troubles of others, she could forget her own; the true serenity she sought always came from her work. Being the country's foremost "mother confessor" shaped her reportorial instincts and sharpened her crime stories—for she understood life's passions, and her sympathy for the accused led many defendants to allow her exclusive interviews. "I was on speaking terms with every criminal in America," she once accurately boasted.

There is no doubt that she had an unhappy marriage, that she once had to live frugally, and that she was prone to illness after middle age, but her life was hardly as miserable as she wanted others to believe. She managed her husband much the way she managed her career—efficiently. Her early penny-pinching days gave way to a top salary of $100,000 a year, enabling her to travel and invest in antiques, and her health never incapacitated her. What she never received, perhaps, was the sympathy and compassion that she lavished on her faceless letter writers. Certainly the introduction to *Dorothy Dix—Her Book*, a collection of her sermonettes, is a maudlin plea for attention:

I have had what people call a hard life. I have been through the depths of poverty and sickness. I have known want and struggle and anxiety and despair. I have always had to work beyond the limit of my strength. As I look back upon my life, I see it as a battlefield strewn with the wrecks of dead dreams and broken hopes and shattered illusions—a battle in which I always fought with the odds tremendously against me, and which has left me scarred and bruised and maimed and old before my time.

Dix's early life had a measure of stability and serenity provided largely by her father, William Douglas Meriwether, a gregarious and charismatic member of a prominent Virginia family. Born Elizabeth Meriwether, on November 18, 1861, on the family's 1,500-acre plantation in Woodstock, located on the Kentucky-Tennessee border, she was the eldest of three children. Her mother, Maria (Winston) Meriwether, was in ill health during Elizabeth's

---

[1] The first advice columnist was John Dunton, a London bookseller, who in March 1689 published the *Athenian Mercury*, which was devoted to questions and answers on love and marriage. Dix's column came before the first comic strip, "The Katzenjammer Kids" (1897), and was the longest-running feature continuously written by the original author. Her only competition was Hearst columnist Beatrice Fairfax, whose column started in 1898; Fairfax was known to be Maria Manning, but over time the column was handled by numerous writers. Presently, the advice field belongs to Ann Landers and Dear Abby.

childhood and took little notice of her. The family lost its land in the Civil War and thereafter lived a life of oddly mingled luxury and poverty; peacock was served for dinner on the silver dishes that the family retainer, Mr. Dicks, had buried in a graveyard during the Civil War; dresses were woven from the wool of their own sheep.

Left to occupy herself, Elizabeth learned to ride, hunt, and shoot. She befriended the black servants and read widely in her father's library. "I cut my teeth on the solid meat of good literature," she once recalled. Her mother died while Elizabeth was in her teens, and her father brought home a cousin, Martha Gilmer Chase, who became a strict but sisterly stepmother to the girl before she was sent to the Female Academy in Clarksville, Tennessee, and to Hollins Institute in Virginia. Well-educated at home, she was an intellectual match for the other worldly Southern girls, but with her pigtails and rustic dresses she was considered a quaint country girl. Shyness prevented any pleasure at school, and she left after one semester.

Back home there remained the option of marriage. At twenty-one she hurriedly accepted the proposal of her stepmother's brother, George O. Gilmer, thirty-one, a reticent man with many business schemes and great mood swings. One of his get-rich ideas was a method for distilling turpentine, which did achieve some success, but an ambivalent nature was his constant undoing and his wife frequently had to bail him out financially. Almost immediately, the young bride realized that she was headed for a life of instability; frightened by Gilmer's mental problems, she decided not to have children. Although she vowed to make the marriage work, she collapsed after two years with a nervous breakdown and was taken by her father to Bay Saint Louis, a Mississippi Gulf coast town.

This location for rest and recuperation would change her life. Living nearby was Eliza Nicholson, owner and editor of the *New Orleans Daily Picayune*, who encouraged her to write some sketches about life on the farm. In 1894 Nicholson asked Elizabeth to join the newspaper staff and write obituaries and recipes. She was thirty-three, bewildered by city life, but fascinated with the newsroom. A slight woman scarcely five feet tall, plainly dressed with brown hair piled on top of her head, she was noticed by colleagues mainly because of her vitality and energy and a disposition that embraced everyone. The *Picayune*'s editor, Major Nathaniel Burbank, sensed something different about this "lady reporter," and he and Nicholson decided to give her a column. It was first called "Sunday Salad," then "Dorothy Dix Talks of Women We Know," and then "Dorothy Dix Talks," a title that remained for fifty years. Elizabeth chose her own byline: Dorothy because she thought it had dignity and Dix for Mr. Dicks who had buried the family silver.[2] The

---

[2] When she put together her *nom de plume*, she was unaware of Dorothea Dix, who helped secure the first legislation protecting the rights of mental patients. Dorothy later recalled, "I

first columns, under headlines like "Some New Women Problems" and "Give the Girls a Chance," had a satirical feminist edge.

Determined to master the journalistic style, she read books of synonyms, the dictionary, and papers throughout the country to compare how they played the same stories. She believed that hard writing eventually made easy writing and would put her early columns through several drafts. "Writing is like firing in the dark," she once said. "You never know whether you hit anything or not. And so it is good to hear the bell ring every now and then."

Her real strength, though, was her insight. She saw everything with a fresh eye, but wrote about it with a mature mind. The columns were an immediate success, and letters seeking her advice and sometimes criticizing her ("You're just about as sentimental as a mustard plaster") poured in. Throughout her career she would answer every one personally.

Her marriage was strained by frequent separations, but she tried to maintain the relationship. As she confided to a reporter when she was seventy, divorce was never a consideration: "I felt that I would not be fit to give advice to others unless I could live that advice myself. I could not say to others: 'Be strong!' if I did not myself have the strength to endure. If I turned my back on a hard job, it would ruin any influence for good my work might ever have—and I took my work pretty seriously."

Soon other editors took her work seriously. In 1900 Hearst's *New York Journal* asked to republish some of her columns. She thought her satire too frivolous for larger audiences, but it was just what Hearst wanted. When the *Journal* offered her a staff position, she backed off, using her ailing husband as an excuse, but colleagues thought the real reason was an apprehension about big-city journalism. If she would not come to New York, the paper countered, she could take a special assignment: follow Carrie Nation on her saloon-busting campaign through Kansas. Dix wrote about Carrie as a modern-day Joan of Arc and received her first sensational headline: "A Woman's Picture of the 'Smasher': Dorothy Dix, the well-known writer, tells all about the Hatchet Heroine."

When the *Journal* finally lured her away at the age of forty with a $5,000-a-year salary in 1901, she went to New York and left Gilmer in New Orleans to fuss over his ill-fated business plans. She found a room in a boarding house (Ethel Barrymore, the actress, was another roomer) and walked the city streets, amazed and frightened by the frantic pace and the obvious poverty. She had to turn out three advice columns every week, but since Hearst believed in working his reporters hard, she feared that she might be assigned to cover a murder, a high-priority assignment in the circulation war between Hearst and Pulitzer. That day came all too soon, and she was sent to New

found out about this [the other Dix] when a book appeared under the title of *Dorothea Dix, the Forgotten*. Had I known of it at the time, I would have chosen some other name, of course."

Elizabeth Meriwether Gilmer

Jersey where a woman had murdered her husband's baby from another marriage. This was Dix's first spot-news story and every door was slammed in her face. Not knowing what to do next, she started talking with her carriage driver and found he knew many of the people she needed to interview. Moreover, the driver had taken an amorous interest in her; his help was her first break. She filed a story with detail not only on the crime, but on the community, its attitudes and prejudices, written with insight and understanding. From then on she had a front-row seat at all the sensational murder trials of the period, including the Nan Patterson, Ruth Wheeler, and Harry Thaw cases.

By the end of 1917 she told her editor that if she ever covered another murder it would be his. She left the *Journal* to join the nationwide Wheeler Newspaper Syndicate and returned to New Orleans to concentrate on heart-mending. She produced a column six days a week, with three columns of sermonettes and three columns of questions and answers.

Her commitment to "woman" made Dix an active suffragist. In 1903 she shared a platform with Susan B. Anthony at the National American Woman Suffrage Association convention in New Orleans. She never abandoned the premise that "being a woman has always been the most arduous profession any human being could follow." As a career woman, she particularly emphathized with the working woman. "Woman has been an angel about four centuries too long, and I have tried all that I could do to get her down from the clouds and to make her see that she must take up the responsibilities of everyday life," she told an interviewer in 1906.

After she gave up the courtroom for courting, life in New Orleans was no less hectic. Up at 7 a.m., she would go through the mail looking for interesting letters. She seldom used form letters for answers, although many were written in a similar fashion by her secretaries. Answered letters were burned by her chauffeur to protect correspondents against blackmail if her files were taken. Her greatest pride was never missing a deadline. Three months worth of advance columns were always locked in a safety-deposit box in case she was ill or had to travel. She also found time to write five books—*Mirandy, Mirandy Exhorts, Fables for the Elite, Hearts à la Mode, My Joy Ride Around the World*—in addition to two collections of her columns, *Dorothy Dix— Her Book* and *How to Win and Hold a Husband*.

She left New Orleans for the courtroom limelight only once, in 1926, to cover the Hall-Mills trial. In 1922 Dr. Edward W. Hall, the handsome and socially prominent pastor of the Episcopal Church of St. John the Evangelist in New Brunswick, New Jersey, was found dead under a crabapple tree on a lonely lover's lane, a bullet through his head. Next to him, with three bullets in her head and her throat slit, was Eleanor Mills, a singer in Halls' choir and mother of two, who was the wife of the church janitor. Strewn over the corpses were their love letters. It took four years before the case was tried, with the pastor's widow and her brothers, Henry and Willie Stevens, as defendants.

Dix was nearing sixty-five when the irresistible offer of $1,000 a week came from the *New York Evening Post* and her syndicate to cover the trial. Few people recognized the tiny, plump, silver-haired lady who listened and watched intently. To Dix, Mrs. Hall was the long-suffering wife who had to live with rumors of her husband's infidelity, a woman so familiar to her from the letters she read daily for her column. She decided the three were not guilty and made her opinion clear in her stories, trial by press being a common practice at the time. Her stories mingled fact with advice to the lovelorn, as in this discourse:

I have never seen a more pitiful sight than this poor, proud woman, clinging with desperate hands to the last shred of her belief in a man who has been proved unworthy. . . . If there is ever a lie on which the recording angel drops a tear that blots it out, it is the one that a wife tells to cover up her husband's defections. Millions of women—God bless them and pity them—tell these white lies. They speak of a drunken husband's shiftlessness as the "artistic temperament." They speak of the "reserve" of a cold and unloving husband. And millions of women boast of the devotion of husbands who are tired of them and neglect them, as if they could conjure back the love they yearn for by pretending that the thing they want to be true is true. . . . And so she lied like a lady about her husband.

As the evidence against the defendants unfolded, Dix found it confusing and contradictory. At the summation her experienced eye ranged over the members of the jury and found them "fat, middle-aged, well-fed," leading her to predict a not guilty verdict. She reasoned thusly: "It is the very young and the very old that are hard and uncompromising in their judgment. In the middle ages we know how to make excuses and to give our fellow creatures the benefit of the doubt." And she was correct. The freed Mrs. Hall shook Dorothy's hand in gratitude. The trial reporter had come full circle: she had begun her career in 1901 covering the death of a child in New Jersey and she ended it twenty-seven years later with New Jersey's most famous unsolved murder.

Also ended shortly was her marriage. Gilmer died in a mental institution in 1929. Thereafter in New Orleans Dix lived well in a home overlooking Audubon Park, and entertained frequently, enjoying the production of serving *café brûlot diabolique* in a darkened room, with flames licking a silver serving bowl. She indulged herself with costly antiques, and would point to her Louis XIV bed and quip to guests, "I'll bet I'm the only respectable woman who ever slept in it."

For the next twenty years she devoted herself to her column, dealing with the problems and the changing social and ethical standards of several generations over a period spanning two wars and the Depression. "Girls used to write to ask whether, when a young man called on them, it would be proper to help him on with his overcoat," she once recalled. "Now they want to know what I think about going to Atlantic City for a weekend with a man." As war approached and families and sweethearts were separated, America, more than ever, turned to Dorothy Dix for help. On hasty marriages she advised: "Watch your step, boys, and go slow. You will worry a lot less about the sweetie you left behind you than you would over a wife, and if the girl doesn't love you enough to be faithful to you when you are off serving your country, she wouldn't make the kind of wife you would want."

Such common sense brought her a new generation of readers, those whose mothers and fathers had read her column. One young man wrote to her syndicate, "This old girl makes sense. Are you sure she isn't younger than that picture you're running?" Some of her starkly simple advice would never change—for instance, her definition of love: "Love means caring for somebody more than yourself. It is putting somebody else's pleasure and happiness and well-being above your own. It is sacrificing yourself for another and enjoying doing it. It is the world being all right when someone is with you and all wrong when he or she is absent. It is knowing someone's every fault and blemish and not caring, because it's John's or Mary's. No one can define love; it just is."

Dorothy Dix's version of love was always built on old-fashioned trust and caring. And the new sexual freedom was not to her liking. In 1931 she took a trip to Tahiti, famed then as the "love nest island." It was cluttered with "husbands and wives—the other women's husbands with the other men's wives," she wrote. The hedonism of unlimited leisure, liquor, and love she found unfulfilling for its practitioners, who were "bored to tears, dissatisfied, disconsolate, bickering . . . love is only the dessert of life. The minute you try to live on dessert, you get sick of it and you can get sicker of love than you can of anything else in the world."

When she received an honorary doctorate that same year from Oglethorpe University in Atlanta, Georgia, she urged women students to consider journalism. "I regard journalism as the ideal career for a woman," she said. "What is a newspaper, anyway, but the aggregate gossip of the world." She wrote her own column until April 1949; a year later she was hospitalized with a stroke and at age ninety died in New Orleans on December 16, 1951.

Despite what she perceived as a hard life, Dorothy Dix achieved all the trappings of success. She was a legend in her own time: famous, wealthy, and influential. She was immortalized in one-liners, in plays, and in song lyrics; and Burma Shave signs, those vanished billboards along the high-ways, told motorists: "Love and Whiskers Do Not Mix—Don't Take Our Word, Ask Dorothy Dix." What she understood so much about, though, she never had for herself: love.

Dorothy Dix's coverage of the Hall-Mills trial was praised for its analytical quality, as shown in the following round-up article. Also reprinted here are Dix's "Ten Rules for Happiness," which by reader demand were published frequently.

HALL RIDDLE GRIPS U.S., MISS DIX SAYS
Every One Has a "Solution" and Each Watches Trial for Vindication of Theory
A NATION OF DETECTIVES

By DOROTHY DIX

The New York Evening Post, November 18, 1926

Somerville, N.J.—Why, the eternal interest in a murder trial over which moralists mourn, at which the intelligentsia sneer and about which even we ordinary folk often marvel?

It is because, to the average man and woman, there is nothing so perpetually fascinating, nothing which so intrigues the mind, as a tale of mystery, and a murder trial is a super-detective story translated into reality. It is the unknown and the dramatic raised to the ultimate degree.

That is why ever since the beginning of the Hall-Mills trial there has been a mob around the little court house at Somerville, struggling to get into the court room. That is why more than 5,000,000 words have been telegraphed all over the world concerning it. That is why newspapers the country over have devoted acres of space to it, and wherever in city or hamlet two or three are gathered together discussion of the case waxes fast and furious.

In business houses, on the street corners, in the lobbies of hotels, in drawing rooms, in kitchens, it is practically the sole topic of conversation. For the time being every man, woman and child in the land is turned into a temporary detective, and each individual has his own private solution of the mystery, which he defends with all the logic at his command.

I have been listening in at a certain family hotel in New York, where, after dinner, the whole assemblage of men and women in its big reading room automatically resolve themselves into a Hall-Mills debating society, and at the court house at Somerville where the real murder fans, who get up early and stand in line for hours in order to wedge past the policeman at the door of the court room, kept their precious vantage by not leaving their seats during the noon recess, and while away the time by discussing the case as they munch on their sandwiches and pickles.

In both places theories advanced are as follows:

(A) That Mrs. Frances Noel Hall, mad with jealousy, slew her husband and the young woman who was her rival, and cut the singer's throat because she believed that it was her voice that had attracted him.

The opponents of this theory urge in rebuttal that it is practically a physical impossibility for a woman of Mrs. Hall's age and habits to have had the marksmanship that would have enabled her to fire three bullets within a range of four inches, and that she would not have had the physical strength to have practically severed Mrs. Eleanor Mills' head from her body.

Also that it is highly improbable that anything could drive a woman of Mrs. Hall's temperament to commit such a crime. Mrs. Hall is a woman who is particularly repressed, unemotional, reserved and proud. Moreover, in women of fifty the fires of passion have died down and they are far more apt to forgive an erring husband, as if he were a bad little boy, than they are to slay him. And, lastly, that if Mrs. Hall wished revenge on her husband she had it in her power to take a far more cruel one than taking his life. She could have disgraced him in church, unfrocked him and sent him forth a wanderer on the face of the earth.

(B) That "Jimmie" Mills was the murderer; that he killed to avenge his honor and because the green-eyed monster had taken possession of his soul. And mention is made of the old shoe knife that he used when he was a cobbler.

To which the succinct answer is made: "Have you seen Jimmie Mills?" Jimmie Mills, mild and patient, who stood in deadly fear of his wife and daughter.

(C) That Mrs. Hall and her brothers, Henry and "Willie" Stevens went to De Russey's lane to confront the Rev. Edward Wheeler Hall and Mrs. Mills in order to obtain evidence for a divorce and that they took with them the love letters that were found between the dead couple and that a fight ensued, in which Mr. Hall and Mrs. Mills were killed.

Divorce Motive Fails

But, objects the opposition, there is no evidence that Mrs. Hall wanted a divorce. And she had plenty of evidence to get it on, without going to De Russy's lane for it. And, they say anyway, Henry Stevens has advanced an alibi that he was fifty miles away at Lavallette on that night.

(D) That another woman who was also much interested in the church and who was likewise in love with Mr. Hall, killed them, or perhaps another man who was in love with Mrs. Mills followed them to their rendezvous and murdered them.

But who could they have been? A couple of names are whispered under the breath, but the evidence against them is so meager that the argument languishes for want of support.

(E) That they were killed by the Ku Klux Klan as a punishment for their crime against the church and the wife and husband they betrayed, and that Mrs. Mills was mutilated because she was regarded as the chief sinner.

Klan Gets a Share

Here the argument runs hot. Why accuse the Ku Klux Klan of working this terrible revenge on two people for leading the double life when there were plenty of others around in the community who were also guilty of philandering? And why blame Mrs. Mills more than Mr. Hall? Surely he was more at fault than she, seeing that he was older than she, that he was rich and highly placed in the world, and that she was a poor and humble woman, easily flattered, easily tempted by his love-making. Also, that he was a priest of God, and, therefore, doubly bound to lead a clean life.

(F) That "Willie" is a dual personality, capable of a Dr. Jekyll and Mr. Hyde transformation; at times the gentle, kindly child-man, interested in little-boy games and amusements, that every one in New Brunswick had known for fifty-odd years; at other times a fierce beast, lusting for blood, committing abnormal crimes.

But if this is the case, say the objectors, why is it that in all of his life he has only had this one lapse from his harmless condition, and how is it that he has swung back so completely to normal?

(G) That Mrs. Hall is a female Svengali and "Willie" a masculine Trilby, so to speak. That she possesses hypnotic power over him, and that under her suggestion he committed the crime, but that he has no memory of it whatever. That was why he stood the long grilling at the hands of the police without breaking down.

Fine theory for a novel, say the objectors, but did you ever know it to happen in real life?

(H) That Mr. Hall and Mrs. Mills were killed by thugs and footpads. Near De Russey's land there is a settlement of lawless foreigners and not far away was a roadhouse frequented by desperate criminals. Many of the people who live thereabouts were capable of holding up any unprotected man and woman who might come their way, and of killing them if they made an outcry.

But, say the objectors, why did they cut Mrs. Mills' throat after she was dead? And nobody can answer that, which is the heart of the mystery after all.

And that is why everybody is waiting with baited breath for every turn of a new page of the Hall-Mills murder trial. Each man and woman wants to know how it is going to end, and if his or her own theory was the correct one.

TEN RULES FOR HAPPINESS
By DOROTHY DIX

Happiness is a matter of self-determination, not luck as is popularly supposed. No human being has ever achieved perfect happiness. There is always a cloud somewhere on the horizon, always a fly in the ointment, always a little discordant note somewhere in the harmony, always something we would have different. We can make ourselves happy or miserable as we choose, and here are ten rules which are a helpful guide to creating our own happiness:

First: HAVE A WILL TO HAPPINESS. Seek happiness as intelligently and energetically as you would any other definitely good thing you desire. Fight for it. Don't just weakly succumb to discontent with circumstances or to people who rub you the wrong way and keep you peevish and fretful and that take all the joy out of you, unless there is some great moral obligation that forces you to endure this martyrdom.

Don't live with people who antagonize you if it can possibly be avoided. Seek cheerful companionship. Gratify your little whims and tastes so long as they do not injure others. Cultivate a pleasure in simple things. You can get a lot of pleasure out of an exquisite view, or a gorgeous sunset, or a good dinner, if you will savor it consciously.

Remember that the one individual on earth from whom you can never get away is yourself, and make yourself good company for your own self by thinking cheerful thoughts instead of letting your mind dwell on old sorrows and old wrongs and old grievances. Don't be one of the people who never "get over" the death of one they loved, or who are still glooming over the money they lost many years ago.

Second: LAUGH THINGS OFF. There are so many things in life over which we must either laugh or weep, so many things that are either tragedies or jokes, according to what we make of them. The little peculiarities of those with whom we live can either run us mad or be an endless source of amusement.

You can laugh off Mary's and John's funny little ways, or you can fight over them for forty years. You can smile over the criticisms that your friends make of you and forget them, or you can let them rankle in your heart and fill it with bitterness. There is no disinfectant so effective as a sense of humor. It will take the sting out of the wounds dealt by malice and envy and out of uncharitableness and will heal all of the abrasions that are inflicted on your vanity and self-love.

Third: ENJOY WHAT YOU HAVE NOW. Most people miss all pleasure in what they have because their whole attention is focused on wanting something they haven't got, and so they lose even the happiness they could have. Don't make this mistake. If you have health exult in it. Realize you have something to give three cheers for every minute of the day. If you have youth rejoice in it. Those who are young really don't need anything else. They are on their tiptoes already. If you have a wife or a husband whom you love, and if you have little children, be down on your knees thanking heaven for its best gifts.

It is pitiful to see strong young people throwing away the happiness they might just as well have because they are longing for automobiles or fine clothes or freedom from work or something equally silly that has nothing in the world to do with happiness. And it is still more pitiful to see mothers and fathers getting no pleasure out of their children. Worrying because they are tied down at home with babies, or because little Johnny is noisy, or the money has to be spent on having little Mary's teeth fixed instead of on golf sticks or a new frock.

And lots of foolish people put off being happy to some future time. They are going to be happy when they get rich. They are going to travel when they are old. The husbands and wives are going to enjoy each other after the children are grown up. But you can't postpone being happy. You've got to get the pleasure out of a thing now or never. And so those who have denied themselves every joy for the great splurge they intend to have when they are old find out that they have waited too long. They have lost their capacity for enjoyment.

Fourth: DON'T EXPECT TOO MUCH. Don't think you have the right to the whole earth with a blue ribbon tied around it. Don't think that you are always going to get all of the breaks with no bad luck thrown in. Don't beat upon your breast and howl to high heaven because you have a few failures and disappointments.

Don't cry out that marriage is a failure because it involves hardship and responsibilities and calls for sacrifices. Don't feel that you have been defrauded in marriage because your wife is not a Follies beauty and a wisecracker. Think more of what a good cook she is and how she saves your money and helps you along. Don't dwell on having missed your soul mate because your husband is a commonplace man who prefers Amos 'n' Andy to *Mourning Becomes Electra*. Enjoy the comforts he is able to give you.

Fifth: DON'T ASK TOO MUCH. Don't be greedy. Don't expect to get more than your fair share. There are a lot of people who make themselves unhappy by expecting to be special pets of Providence. They are always asking: "Why should I be poor? Why should misfortune come to me? Why should I lose those I love?" And so on . . .

The happy people are those who accept their common lot and are grateful for small favors. They are contented with little things and with their lot in life. They do not wear themselves out doing the fruitless tasks Nature never intended to be done by them, nor do they embitter themselves with envy of those who have more than they have.

The only successful people are those who have attained their ambition, even if it is only to be the champion checker player in the village. Those who are happy are those who want little but succeed in getting that little.

Sixth: DON'T BORROW TROUBLE. Don't spoil the sunshine of today by dreading the storm that may come next week or next month or next year. Most of the misfortunes that we fear never happen to us, and if they do happen we find out that they are not half so bad as we had anticipated.

When you think about the folly of borrowing trouble, and that the interest we have to pay on it in fears and tears keeps us bankrupt in happiness, it doesn't seem as if anyone could be silly enough to do it. But people do, and women especially are given to making this losing bargain. I know plenty of women with ample income who never indulge themselves in any luxury they would like to have because they are so afraid that they might lose their money and may have to go to the poorhouse.

I know plenty of mothers with healthy children who are miserable all the time for fear their children might possibly catch some disease and die, and other mothers who go into a perfect panic every time their children are out of their sight, for fear they have been kidnaped or run over by an automobile. I know lots of women with faithful and devoted husbands who lie awake at night worrying about losing their husbands' love.

If we suffered only from our real troubles we would be as happy as kings. It is the imaginary ones that keep us in a perpetual state of gloom.

Seventh: THINK OF OTHERS. Someone has said that we all find it easy to bear the sorrows of our friends. That may be cynically true, but it is also altruistically true.

It may be that we can meet the troubles of others with greater fortitude than we can our own, that we can be more philosophical about the Joneses losing their fortune or the Brown girl eloping with the chauffeur than we could if our own money had gone up in a smash and our own daughter had made a *mesalliance.* Possibly we might even get a secret satisfaction in their being taken down a bit and not being quite so high-hat.

But on the other hand it is certain that no selfish person is every happy. No one who is primarily concerned with his own individual happiness and who puts that before anything else in the world is ever happy.

For the self-centered are never satisfied. They never get all they want. They never get just the center of the spotlight. They are always reaching, asking, craving for something that is just beyond their reach. It is only the unselfish, those who give without thought of return, those who spend themselves on others, those who never notice that they have to endure themselves because they are so absorbed in helping others, who ever really attain happiness.

The one and only panacea for personal sorrow is to try to assuage a grief greater than your own. The only road to contentment leads right by the door of those who are less well off than you are. It is not those who are most loved who are the happiest. It is those who love the most.

Eighth: CULTIVATE THE HUMAN RELATIONSHIP. When all is said happiness does not consist in any particular environment or condition of life or any one big thing that happens to us. It lies in the little everyday things that the poorest and the humblest may have as well as the rich and great. And most of all it consists in the congeniality of our home lives and in our having friends that we enjoy.

It rests with every married couple whether they will go down the years hand in hand, loving each other, enjoying each other, or whether they will fight from the altar to the grave. All parents could have loving and dutiful and companionable children if they would give their youngsters the affection and understanding and comradeship they crave. And we could all have friends if we would bind those we know to us with hoops of steel forged out of loyalty and kindness and consideration and attention.

When you hear old people complaining that they are lonely and have no friends you do not need to be told that it is because they have never done anything to win friendship, and so they are deprived of the one thing that is the solace of age.

Ninth: KEEP BUSY. Work. An idle brain is the devil's workshop in which he manufactures all of the thirty-seven varieties of misery, plain and fancy.

Any kind of work is better than no work at all. The real panacea for everything that ails us is employment.

It is the idle neurotic women who fill the doctors' offices. A wife's discovery that her husband misunderstands her and that her true soul mate is another man usually comes after she has reared her children and after her husband has become so rich that she has no tasks to keep her busy. It is the women with nothing to occupy them who are peevish and fretful and who become talebearers and gossipers, and who break up their children's homes by interfering in them. It is the hard-worked women, whether in the home or in business, who are happy and cheerful and who make others happy and cheerful.

Tenth: REMEMBER THAT YOU GET OUT OF LIFE JUST EX-ACTLY WHAT YOU HAVE PUT INTO IT. If you put envy and spite and bitterness into life you will get out of it only a bitter brew. But if you even put a modest amount of cheer and optimism and courage and faith into life you will get out of it the wine of happiness.

(Reprinted from *How To Win and Hold a Husband* by Dorothy Dix, Doubleday, Doran, New York, 1939.)

6

Ida Bell
Wells-Barnett
(1862–1931)

I DA WELLS was a slight school teacher of twenty-two when she seated herself in the ladies car of the Chesapeake & Ohio Railroad for a trip from
Memphis to her school in Woodstock, Tennessee. In 1884, the law stated
that accommodations should be separate but equal. Asked to move to the
smoking car, which was not equal, she refused and was forcibly removed.
She later described the situation: "He [the conductor] tried to drag me out
of my seat, but the moment he caught hold of my arm I fastened my teeth
in the back of his hand . . .   He went forward and got the baggageman and
another man to help him and of course they succeeded in dragging me out.
They were encouraged to do this by the attitude of the white ladies and
gentlemen in the car; some of them even stood on the seats so they could
get a good view and continued applauding the conductor for his brave stand."
Wells left the train herself, returned to Memphis and sued the railroad. The
local court returned a favorable verdict and awarded her $500 in damages.

The headlines in the *Memphis Daily Appeal* of December 25, 1884, told
the story: "A Darky Damsel Obtains a Verdict for Damages Against the
Chesapeake & Ohio Railroad—What It Cost to Put a Colored School Teacher
in a Smoking Car—Verdict for $500." The railroad appealed to the State
Supreme Court, which reversed the ruling, stating: "We think it is evident

that the purpose of the defendant in error was to harass with a view to this suit, and that her persistence was not in good faith to obtain a comfortable seat for the short ride."

Up to this point in her life, Wells, who would go on to awaken not just America's but the world's conscience to the realities of lynching, had naively believed that legal action would win rights for blacks. She wrote of her discouragement in an unpublished diary: "I felt so disappointed because I had hoped for such great things from my suit for my people generally. I have firmly believed all along that the law was on our side and would, when we appealed to it, give us justice. I feel shorn of that belief and utterly discouraged, and just now, if it were possible, would gather my race in my arms and fly away with them."

Her disappointment soon grew to outrage over racial discrimination and lynching. For forty years she was fearless in the fight for civil rights, never hesitating to go to the scene of riots and lynchings to report the details. She was the first to dare to address the most taboo subject in Victorian America: that any sexual contact between white women and black men was considered rape. She was a leader in the formation of women's clubs for blacks, but refrained from participating in the founding of the National Association for the Advancement of Colored People (NAACP) because she thought the leaders were not militant enough. She attacked the cowardly of her race as vigorously as she did whites, and after her newspaper, the *Free Speech*, was sacked, she always kept a pistol in her office and home. It was her motto that if she had to die by violence she would take some of her persecutors with her.

Ida Bell Wells was born a slave to slave parents on July 16, 1862, in Holly Springs, Mississippi, the eldest child in a family of eight, of which only five survived. Her mother, Elizabeth (Bell) Wells, the daughter of a black slave and a father said to be half American Indian, had been taken from her parents at age seven and sold to an owner who beat her, leaving scars that young Ida never forgot. Her father, James Wells, was the acknowledged son of his master, a Mississippi plantation owner. Although a slave, her father received special treatment since his master had no children by his own wife. He met Elizabeth when he was apprenticed to the carpenter for whom she cooked and soon married her. After they were freed, they stayed on in Holly Springs as cook and carpenter. Their daughter Ida's early education was at the local freedman's school, Rust College. In 1878, a yellow fever epidemic killed both parents and three of their children. Though only sixteen, Ida dressed up to pass for eighteen and secured a teaching position in a one-room rural school for $25 a month.

Six years later, when her brothers and sisters were grown, she moved to

Memphis and continued her education during the summer at Fisk University in Nashville. She taught first in a rural school in Woodstock and then in black schools in Memphis. As a teacher she was industrious, but she disliked the sameness of the routine. Contemporaries remembered her as "refined and ladylike," with a "hard-hearted attitude toward suitors." She wrote her first piece of journalism in 1887 for a black church paper, *Living Way*, and in it described her suit against the railroad. During this time she met the Rev. William J. Simmons, president of the National Baptist Convention and a leader of the Negro Press Association. He encouraged her to write for some of the small newspapers that were being published by blacks.

She would later credit Simmons for whatever fame she achieved as a journalist. Her articles, often signed "Iola," were mostly on race relations. She sent articles to the *Gate City Press* in Kansas City, the *Detroit Plaindealer*, and religious publications such as the *American Baptist* and the *Christian Index*. In 1889 she bought a one-third interest in the *Memphis Free Speech and Headlight* and three years later, when she purchased shares to become half-owner, she shortened the paper's name to the *Free Speech*. A story criticizing Memphis' inadequate black schools resulted in the school board refusing to renew her contract in 1891. Thereafter she devoted all of her time to the newspaper.

In less than a year the paper increased its readership from 1,500 to 4,000. As editor, Wells traveled throughout Mississippi, Tennessee, and Arkansas, signing up new subscribers and local correspondents. She also learned about circulation abuses. The news dealers, realizing that blacks who could not read wanted the paper to pass on to those who could read it aloud, were selling copies of the *Police Gazette* to illiterates who requested the *Free Speech*. So she started printing the paper on pink paper; readers could then ask for the color and not be deceived.

In 1892 she covered a news story that changed her life. On March 9 three Memphis men, all friends of hers, were lynched. She denounced the crime, claiming that the incident stemmed from economic rivalry and white resentment over blacks spending their money at a black-owned grocery store instead of patronizing a rival white grocer. She wrote: "There is nothing we can do about the lynching now, as we are outnumbered and without arms . . . There is therefore only one thing left that we can do; save our money and leave a town which will neither protect our lives and property, nor give us a fair trial in the courts, but takes us out and murders us in cold blood when accused by white persons."

The economic boycott was particularly successful against the public transportation system. And, according to Wells, hundreds of blacks did leave Memphis, settling mostly in Oklahoma. "Memphis had never seen such an upheaval among colored people," she would later recall. "Business was practically at a standstill, for the Negro was famous then, as now, for spending his money for fine clothes, furniture, jewelry, and pianos and other musical instruments, to say nothing of good things to eat."

Before the Memphis lynchings, she had planned to take her first trip East, to a Philadelphia conference. She looked forward to meeting there T. Thomas Fortune, editor of the *New York Age*, who had reprinted many of her articles. Shortly before she left she published in the *Free Speech* a stinging editorial:

Eight Negroes lynched since the last issue of the Free Speech. Three were charged with killing white men and five with raping white women. Nobody in this section believes the old thread-bare lie that Negro men assault white women. If southern white men are not careful they will over-reach themselves and a conclusion will be reached which will be very damaging to the moral reputation of their women.

Wells was not an emotional or hysterical writer. She would concentrate on a problem and in a calm, reasonable way work through to a solution. Her lectures could be filled with militant rhetoric, but she never used her power or her journalism to incite blacks to anger or violence.

In her writings and lectures, Wells saw lynchings as an excuse to eliminate those who were acquiring economic status and as a way to save the reputation of white women who willingly enticed and slept with blacks. She was outspoken against the double standard that allowed white men to have affairs and father inter-racial children, but labeled any sexual involvement between a black man and a white woman "rape." Moreover, she could convincingly argue that the crime of rape was unknown during the Civil War when white women were left alone with only black retainers for protection.

When she impugned the morals of white women in her editorial, she touched a sensitive nerve. On May 27, 1892, while she was away in Philadelphia, a mob drove off the paper's business manager. They dumped the type and destroyed the office and left a calling card stating that anyone trying to publish the paper would be killed. With the assistance of Fortune she stayed in New York, writing for the *Age* and traveling around New England talking to black women's clubs. Fortune described her as having "all of a woman's tenderness in all that affects our common humanity, but she has also the courage of the great women of the past who believed that they could still be womanly while being more than ciphers in 'the world's broad field of battle.' "

When the 1893 World's Columbian Exposition in Chicago excluded black participation, she wrote and had distributed thousands of copies of the pamphlet, "The Reason Why the Colored American Is Not in the World's Co-

Ida Bell Wells-Barnett

lumbian Exposition—The Afro-American's Contribution to Columbian Literature." At this exposition she met Ferdinand L. Barnett, an attorney and widower, and founder and editor of the *Chicago Conservator*, who would later become the first black appointed an assistant state's attorney, a position he held for fourteen years. They were married on June 27, 1895, and she adopted the hyphenated-style last name, an early instance of this form. Barnett had two sons from his previous marriage, and the couple added two more sons and two daughters. Living in Chicago, they shared interests in journalism and racial issues, and she wrote frequently for his paper and helped him with his law work. They became one of the most influential black couples of the time. For three years she served as an adult probation officer, the first woman to hold such a post. Although lecturing to both black and white groups continued to be her major focus, she did continue club organizing. The Ida B. Wells Women's Club in Chicago was started in 1893 and the Alpha Suffrage Club, the first black women's group concerned with suffrage, in 1913. She started the Negro Fellowship League, a settlement house and community center.

It was an active life for a mother with small children, and she solved the child-care problem by traveling with her nursing babies. Addressing a suffrage group, she told the audience that she was the only woman in the United States who ever traveled throughout the country with a nursing baby to make political speeches. She once described her desire to travel and lecture while nursing children a "divided duty." She admitted that being a mother had never been as high a priority with her as with other women, but conceded that as her family grew being a good mother became a profession unto itself. Susan B. Anthony, the suffrage leader, once told her that marriage was fine for some, "but not women like you who had a special call for special work."

During her career she made no secret of the fact that she distrusted the role of whites in the black cause, and she was often critical of and in conflict with black leaders whom she saw as accommodating themselves to white groups. In her fight for racial pride she respected only those who were militant, a view in opposition to that of Booker T. Washington, who called for compromise. She allied herself with W. E. B. Du Bois of the National Afro-American Council and served as council secretary until 1902 when Washington's faction took over. She gave an anti-lynching address as the principal speaker at the National Negro Conference of 1910, out of which the NAACP was formed, but stepped away from active participation in the association because the leadership did not represent her views.

Perhaps her most harmonious work with whites was with women, for she saw the suffrage movement as a way to black emancipation. Twice she led her members in parades, first in 1913 on the eve of Woodrow Wilson's inauguration in Washington, and again in 1918 in Chicago when 5,000 women marched through heavy rains to the Republican National Convention to demand a suffrage plank in the platform. She worked closely with Susan B. Anthony and also Jane Addams to successfully block segregated schools in Chicago.

"Tell the world the facts," was Wells-Barnett's rallying call. And that was what she did in an eloquent 100-page, privately printed pamphlet called A *Red Record: Tabulated Statistics and Alleged Causes of Lynching in the United States, 1892–1893–1894,* the only statistical document on lynchings in the United States published since the Emancipation Proclamation. To give credibility to her arguments, she based her pamphlet on statistics compiled by the *Chicago Tribune,* stating that such data "up to the present time has not been disputed . . . the incidents herein reported have been confined to those vouched for by the *Tribune.*" The London edition, *United States Atrocities,* which identified the author as "Ida B. Wells (A coloured Woman of Tennessee)," called for her readers to have churches, missionary societies, YMCAs, temperance societies, "and all Christian and moral forces in connection with your religious and social life, pass resolutions of condemnation and protest every time a lynching takes place, and see that they are sent to the places where these outrages occur." She urged Europeans not "to invest where lawlessness and mob violence hold sway." Her cause was for law and order for everyone. She explained that "these pages are written in no spirit of vindictiveness," and that their plea is "not for the colored people alone, but for all victims of the terrible injustice which puts men and women to death without form of law."

Although she was a pioneer in the early testing of the separate but equal rules in transportation and schools, it was the campaign against lynching that was originally hers. As early as 1893 and 1894 she had traveled through Great Britain, arousing sentiment against lynching and encouraging economic pressure on the South. And in March 1898, following the lynching of a black postmaster, she had gone to the White House to present a protest petition to President William McKinley. Still, it took many years after the appearance of A *Red Record* in 1895 for mob action to abate. According to the Tuskegee Institute, 1952 was the first time in seventy-one years of compilation that no lynchings were reported.

Notable, too, was her coverage of the East St. Louis riot of 1918, when 150 black people were killed and almost a million dollars worth of property destroyed. In 1922 she was in Little Rock, Arkansas, after a riot in Elaine, Arkansas, allegedly started after blacks refused to sell whites their cotton below market price. When she visited rioters imprisoned in Little Rock, it was her first visit to the South since the sacking of the *Free Speech.*

At home in Chicago she was never as politically active as her husband. However, in 1930, the year before she died, Ida Wells-Barnett decided to be the Republican candidate for the state senate, running against two men, and coming in third. With disappointment she wrote in her diary that "few women responded as I had hoped."

She died in Chicago of uremia on March 25, 1931, at the age of sixty-nine. Her hometown dedicated a low-income housing project to her in 1939; her house on Martin Luther King Drive is a registered historic place. Her daughter, Alfreda Barnett Duster, worked forty years editing her mother's posthumous autobiography, *Crusade for Justice* (1970).

The following is one of her columns from the *Age*, which she wrote under the name "Iola."

IOLA'S SOUTHERN FIELD
Save the Pennies—
Outrages of Columbian Day—
Southern Emigration—
News From all Over the Field

The New York Age, November 19, 1892

Everybody is surprised at the result, and everybody is busy explaining the causes which brought about the result. The Republican party gave way to the South and submitted to a solid South when it had power to break its solidity, by reducing representation in Congress, or passing a law which would insure fair national elections by a free ballot and fair count; a Republican administration has stood by and confessed at home and abroad that the State is greater than the Union and it did not dare interfere to save the lives of its own citizens or those of foreign countries who were hanged, burned and shot within the borders of these several States; the Republican party instead of meeting the issue as drawn by the New York *Sun*, and boldly appealing to the country to sustain it in its efforts to protect the citizen—dodged and denied and relegated the Free Elections plank in their own platform—and tried to make the people believe protection and reciprocity of more value than human lives. In so doing they have ignored and alienated the larger part of the intelligent Afro-American vote of every one of the doubtful States—the balance of power in seven States—and this, together with the solid South, which the Republican party has fostered, largely brought about the defeat which is so richly deserved. A party which hasn't the courage of its convictions deserves to be taught a lesson, and I for one, am glad it has received this lesson. I am a Republican, but I was an Afro-American before I was a Republican, and the race cannot suffer more outrage, indignity and cruelty under a Democratic administration, than it has under a Republican administration, without any protest or effort on the part of the administration to stay it.

Let the Afro-American depend on no party, but on himself for his salvation. Let him continue to get education, character and above all, put money in his purse. When he has a dollar in his pocket and many more in the bank, he can move from injustice and oppression and no one to say him nay. When he has money, and plenty of it, parties and races will become his servants. The Afro-American for the next four years should bank every five cent piece which does not have to go for the necessaries of life, and at the end of that time he will be far more independent than any party can make him. The dimes which go for car rides, for cigars, for drinks, for boot-blacks, for foolishness of all sorts, make others rich and keep us poor. A wasteful and spendthrift race or individual is always poor, is always the slave of the man who has money and will never be in position to dictate to par-ties, or demand race rights. Let each one of us try saving a part of every day's earnings, for the next four years and see how much better off we will be.

It almost breaks my heart to have to go back to the four page AGE, even for a time, when I have so long been proud of the eight page, and confident in the belief that the people would support it. But the support we looked for has not come, at least, not to the extent desired. Many have written and promised to renew themselves, and speak a word to a friend in its behalf, but few have kept their promises.

Eight million Afro-Americans without a national organ reaching in all quarters of this country, and representing every phase of race life, are with-out one of the strongest weapons of defense. To sustain such a journal is to sustain themselves and provide a champion to fight their battles. Here again, doctrine of self-help must be practiced. The white journals will not give space to our defence and for lack of race support, our own cannot do so.

The colored people of several Southern cities so far forgot themselves as to permit their children to take part in a side show celebration of "Columbus Day" by the public schools. Of course they were treated to a "separate" place and hour for the exercises in which all school children were to take part. From McMennville, Tenn., comes the report of the most flagrant outrage of self-respect. The white children marched in one gate, and were seated on the northern side of the park—and the exercises proceeded without waiting for the colored children. When they did arrive, prayer was being offered, so the master of ceremonies rushed toward them, drove the colored band, which was gaily playing "Hurrah for the Red, White and Blue" out of its proces-sion and roughly ordered them to go by as they had not come at the ap-pointment time. They were afterward seated at the back of the park, where they could neither see nor hear anything that was said; every speaker had his back to them. They marched there to sing "My country 'Tis of Thee," and were not allowed to do even that. Those teachers and parents might have known what to expect and they knew where they were to sit, yet they went on and placed themselves where they were not wanted. Will we ever learn self-respect?

The Southern Emigration Association of Chicago was organized for the purpose of finding work for and locating the colored people who wanted to leave the South. The association has no funds to pay the fare of those desiring more. It only undertakes to find homes for those who are able to pay their own way. Yet many write for money to get away on, and because they do not receive it, express their belief that the Emigration Association is a humbug. It is an organization to aid those in finding work, who are enterprising enough to get together money to get away from the South.

The people of Atlanta are helping themselves right along in the street car matter. The ministers have taken hold of it. Elder L. Thomas, the pastor of Big Bethel, one of the largest churches in Atlanta and one other have put it to a vote to their congregations whether they would ride in the cars or stay on the ground. Both voted to stay on the ground. The Atlanta *Journal* announces that the street car company lost $700 during the month of October because the colored people refused to ride and now that the white man's pocket is feeling it, this paper condemns the unjust treatment of colored passengers. He never did so before, and if they keep on losing money, the whites will be the first to petition the legislature for the repeal of any such law. Let the good work go on. A colored lady who determined to ride any way was thrown off the cars two weeks ago, her head bruised, arm broken and other injuries inflicted because she would not sit in the colored people's part of the street car. I only hope this action will make others who refuse to unite with their race for a principle determine to stay off the street cars and keep their nickels to themselves.

7

Winifred Black
Bonfils
"Annie Laurie"
(1863–1936)

I T BEGAN with morning mist and drizzle, and then the rains came. Winds puffed rippling whitecaps into mountainous surf and suddenly, without warning, the waters surrounding Galveston met in a surging handclasp: a tidal wave. By nightfall, on September 8, 1900, bodies floated through the streets. In all, 7,000 would die. In Denver, Winifred Black (Annie Laurie) read the first dispatches from Texas and prepared to cover the story. She knew it would be difficult, probably impossible, for a woman to get across to the flooded island. So she tucked her auburn curls under a cap, wore a long duster, carried a pick-ax, and thus disguised as a boy slipped unnoticed onto a police boat to cross the bay, now a netherworld illuminated by funeral pyres.

Annie was the first woman and the first reporter to reach Galveston from the outside. It was another scoop in that grand competition among newspaper reporters: get there first, file it fastest. If she showed singular initiative in getting her eyewitness account to the *San Francisco Examiner*, it was only what was expected of her by "The Chief," William Randolph Hearst. Spunk and cunning she had in abundance, along with other natural talents—an ear for rhythmic phrases, an eye for descriptive detail, and a personal writing style that was, above all else, caring.

Whether the story was a tidal-wave catastrophe or an essay on California's flowers, she could be relied on to add an emotional, bravura touch. Her stories overflowed with anecdotes, rhetorical questions, heart-tugging quotes, alliteration, repetitions, and snappy phrasing. Style over substance was her motto, and she seldom let the facts get in the way of a good description. If she were working today, she would surely be a member in good standing of the soft or so-called "Jell-o journalism" school.

Her approach, however, was perfect for the era. Readers of a new century's newspaper wanted a change from the lock-step parade of dull facts. They wanted to be entertained, to laugh, to cry, to be part of an exciting adventure, and if it happened to be dangerous or naughty, so much the better. Readers cared as much about how Annie got her story and how she felt as they did about the who, what, why, where, and when. Hearst needed just such a reporter, and he would exploit Annie's sympathetic prose style over and over again as he built his empire.

Her most effective writing took the sob approach, and sometimes she would use the cadences and somnolent rhythms of a bedtime story that was meant to be read aloud. Certainly, her story on July 27, 1935, about a little girl who runs away from home, falls asleep on the road, and is run over, was a three-handkerchief *tour de force*:

The little girl and her brother ran away from home the other day. Things were a little dull at home, nobody told any new stories, and nobody sent out for an order of ice cream cones all around.

Everything was flat and commonplace and very, very dull, and the world was so big and so bright outside, like a nice shiny glass ball, the kind they hang on the Christmas tree.

You could see castles and still ponds and blue lakes and tall trees and people riding horseback—if you looked the right way. And motor cars shining in the sun, and long white robes and brooks chattering under the trees and green meadows sprinkled with flowers yellow and blue, and the sea laughing and shining and talking to itself and calling to the world to come on out and play.

And the wind for a playfellow and puppies and kittens and little calves and colts with wobbly knees and long-legs—oh, it was a lovely world, the little girl was sure of that—if you only went down the right road.

Throughout this story, there is an even tone and rhythm. When the little girl dies, Annie tells her readers not to grieve, that the little girl had her dream, her search for the Holy Grail. "Even if she did not find the Lake of Swans or the Road to Camelot," she concluded, "she had the grace and the understanding to look for them and that is something in itself, isn't it?"

Tributes like this were an Annie Laurie specialty. Two of her own sons had died young, and those tragedies undoubtedly influenced her style. She could write about death and dying with such warm softness that the reader was soothed, reassured. And she could carefully fit the style to the personality. Sometimes she had known the person, as was the case with Father Damien, the priest who had treated and lived with the lepers on Molokai Island. Her last story before her death was a tribute to him, published on May 27, 1936, when his body came through San Francisco on the way to his native Belgium. It began:

'Rollin' home through the silver fog to the song of the wild wind. 'Rollin' home by the starlight and by moonlight and by the flooding sunshine of the Pacific—it took a long time to send for you, didn't it? A long, weary time.

In both reporting and writing style, Annie Laurie was probably the most versatile woman journalist of her time. Her career spanned nearly fifty years, and with ease she went from interviews with Presidents and celebrities to undercover assignments as a Salvation Army lass and a cannery worker. She covered the major murder trials, traveled overseas to report on World War I, and in her later years specialized in stories on the evils of narcotics. With such a range, she could be proselytizing one day, pedantic the next, and maudlin the day after.

In addition to her mingling of style and emotion, which even today is engaging, she often depended on quirky devices. Lewis Carroll was one of her favorite authors, and her articles featured anecdotes or quotes from *Alice in Wonderland* or *Through the Looking Glass*. People were frequently small and little, pale-eyed and pale-faced. They had "sentimental chins" and "grinned in fiendish triumph." Sometimes it seemed that any old word that sailed into her mind she would write down on arrival. "Tut, tut" was a favorite, used effectively when she wanted readers to "tut, tut" along with her. A Chinese houseboy was accused of murder (unjustly in Annie's view) and when he was acquitted, she registered approval with "Oof, what a relief!"

"Biff," to indicate a change of action, was a curious choice. A paragraph would begin: "And then all at once, biff," and two paragraphs later: "And all of a sudden, biff again." When in doubt, the "so" lead got her writing about any event:
–"So they didn't find the leaders of the lynching mob down in San Jose Wednesday after all."
–"So Lawrence of Arabia, one of the most romantic figures in English history, was knocked off his motorcycle the other day and fractured his skull."
–"So we are going to have a third Lamson trial, are we?"

For Annie, words were wonderful toys, meant to be played with. If she used the "oof" or the "biff" to get attention, such theatrics were only part

Winifred Black Bonfils

of who she was. In her memoirs, published in *Good Housekeeping* magazine (January–May 1936), she wrote in detail about her early life in Chilton, Wisconsin, where she was born Martha Winifred Sweet on October 14, 1863, the fourth of five children of Benjamin Jeffrey Sweet and Lovisa Loveland (Denslow) Sweet. Her father, an attorney, and a Union Army officer in the Civil War, achieved some fame as commander of Chicago's Camp Douglas military prison, where he stopped a planned Confederate attack. Later he became the first deputy commissioner of internal revenue under President Ulysses S. Grant.

Her father died when she was eleven, and four years later, so did her mother. Her eldest sister, Ada Celeste, who was a federal pension agent in Chicago from 1874 to 1885, took care of the family. Winifred was sent to boarding schools in Illinois and Massachusetts, and had occasion to meet two second cousins who were journalists: Harold Frederick, a London correspondent, and Fannie Forrester, an American writer. But she chose to try her luck on the stage as a member of the Black Crook touring company. She was cast in only minor parts, but her adventures—and misadventures— made interesting letters to her sister, several of which were published in the *Chicago Tribune*.

In 1890, then known as Winifred Sweet, she left the Midwest to search for a younger brother who had run away from home. She fell in love with San Francisco and decided to leave the theater for journalism. Judging from photographs of the time, she was a great beauty, small-waisted and full-bodied in a Worth gown. An angular jaw, however, revealed her determined nature.

She breezed into the *San Francisco Examiner*'s offices and charmed the managing editor, Sam Chamberlain, who was legendary for bellowing at his staff: "Get excited, damn it! Get excited!" He took her aside, offered her a job and instructed her how to write for the masses:

We don't want fine writing in a newspaper. Remember that. There's a gripman on the Powell Street line—he takes his car out at three o'clock in the morning, and while he's waiting for the signals he opens the morning paper. It's still wet from the press and by the light of his grip he reads it. Think of him when you're writing a story. Don't write a single word he can't understand and wouldn't read.

Her first important assignment was a flower show, a significant event in California. She wandered through the displays taking note of every detail, then wrote the story and handed it in. Like every cub reporter before her, she waited up to read it. As she recalled in her memoirs, her heart sank, for the top half had been rewritten: "I could see at a glance that the two or three opening paragraphs told everything that was important about the flower show—

where it was, who was giving it, who offered the prizes, who won them—and I had never given a thought to one of these good plain facts."

But writing on flowers was not what Chamberlain, and later Hearst, had in mind for young Winifred. Across the country, in New York, Elizabeth Cochrane (Nellie Bly) was attracting front-page attention as the nation's daredevil woman reporter. She had feigned insanity to report on conditions at Blackwell's Island; she had worked in the sweat shops and factories to write firsthand about them. Winifred, obviously, was perfectly cast to be her West Coast counterpart. She needed a name, though, one of those alliterative or lyrical *noms de plume*. She chose "Annie Laurie" from a Scottish ballad her mother had sung.

Her first assignment in the tradition of Nellie Bly was to learn how women were treated in the city hospital's emergency room. Chamberlain suggested that Annie stage an accident, so she dressed in threadbare clothes and pretended to faint in front of a carriage. Passersby crowded around her while policemen sadistically prodded her with clubs. The only ambulance was a horse-drawn carriage, and she rode to the hospital lying on a hard, wooden floor. During her examination in the emergency room, attendants made lewd comments. She was given an emetic of mustard and hot water, and immediately released.

Within thirty-six hours the *Examiner* had a sensational story on the street. The exposé resulted not only in the dismissal of certain hospital personnel, but in the establishment of a regular ambulance service. This stunt-undercover story was typical of a Hearst formula that mixed civic reform with sex. Readers were indignant when they read of Annie's experiences, but they were also titillated by the innuendos she described.

As Annie Laurie, she also took up the case of the lepers on Molokai; publicized polygamy among the Mormons in Utah; investigated the juvenile court system in Chicago; interviewed suffragists in England; traveled cross country with William Jennings Bryan's presidential campaign. It is said that she was the first woman to report a prize fight. (She watched from behind a curtained booth and noted in her story: "Men have a world into which women cannot enter.")

And she was the second woman to interview a President. (Anne Royall, the first, wrote up John Quincy Adams.)[1] How Annie cornered publicity-shy Benjamin Harrison in 1892 is one of the most frequently told anecdotes

[1] Anne Royall edited the Washington newspapers, *Paul Pry* and *The Huntress*, in the 1830s. The oft-told story that she cornered John Quincy Adams as he swam naked in the Potomac and sat on his clothes until he answered her questions is apparently apocryphal. Bessie Rowland James, in a recent biography of Anne Royall (*Anne Royall's U.S.A.*, Rutgers University Press, 1972) maintains that Adams was a long-time friend and spoke with her willingly.

about her career. The story goes that President Harrison had allowed only one press representative to travel with him to California; all male reporters had been rebuffed at the train. Annie was dispatched to use her spunk and cunning. When the train stopped, she had a cowboy, a man she described in her memoirs as a "seven-foot giant," clear a path to the first car, where, luck would have it, stood Henry Markham, the governor of California. Annie had recently interviewed him, and he slipped her on the train, hiding her under a dining-car table with a long, white cloth covering her crouched form. The President entered the car and sat down, and out popped Annie, pen and paper in hand for the interview.

When Hearst decided to challenge Joseph Pulitzer on his home turf, he took Annie east with him in 1895 to launch the *New York Journal*. To her, New York was dreary and dingy: she left after two years, stopping off in Denver in 1897 to join the boisterous *Post*, a worthy rival to the *Examiner* and *Journal*. But she never left the Hearst stable and continued to take assignments for its syndicate. On April 18, 1906, she was riding a trolley in Denver when a newsboy came through shouting, "Extra! San Francisco destroyed!" Back at her office there was a one-word telegram from Hearst: "Go."

Her articles on the devastation of her beloved city centered on hope. A skillful public speaker, Annie could also use the press as a pulpit. Here are excerpts from her first dispatch of April 22:

And then I knew that the dreadful story of death and hopeless misery the blackened ruins were trying to tell me was false. San Francisco, the best beloved of the world, is not dead and can never die while one man or woman with the true spirit that made the old San Francisco what it is still lives.
God did smile when he made California, and he's smiling yet at all our foolish little perplexities and anxieties and want of faith and courage. Let's look back at him up through the smoke and cinders, and smile, too—just to see what will happen

As a *Denver Post* reporter, Annie found a different style and a different byline: Winifred Black. (Annie Laurie was reserved for the *Examiner* only.) Space evidently was unlimited, and features rambled on for 2,000 words, quite a change from the average 800 words with Hearst. Now she discoursed with folksy eloquence on pioneers, covered wagons, literary ghouls, ragtime music, and celebrities. Taken together, these articles make interesting reading today as an anecdotal history of the times. But her writing style at this time was less interesting, for she shelved drama and wit for oppressive opinion. In an opus entitled "Why I Don't Go to Church," she concluded: "The church of today does not want sinners. What it wants are pew holders." Surveying the values symbolized by the buttons of wealth, fame, beauty, youth, brains, she decided: "The button of poverty seems to provide the most happiness." Interviewing women voters on election day, she buried a movement with the epitaph "Woman's suffrage is a failure. A dead failure."

In 1907, she was back in New York, at the trial of playboy Harry K. Thaw for the murder of architect Stanford White. She sat with three other feature writers—Dorothy Dix, Ada Patterson, and Nixola Greeley-Smith—all skillful at producing saccharine sympathy favorable to the star witness, showgirl Evelyn Nesbit Thaw, whose testimony brought in an insanity verdict for her husband. A cynical colleague, Irvin S. Cobb of the *World*, observed this gushy quartet and injected a scornful line into his copy about the "sob sisters."[2] This epithet stuck, and for too long it was used to describe any woman reporter. Annie, to her dismay, was often called "the first and greatest sob sister of them all." Seeing herself as an all-round journalist, she once sniffed: "Most of them are sap sisters."

What soon became important, however, was not Thaw's sanity or insanity, but a new century's morality. The trial had everything: the degenerate rich, the exploited poor, chorus girls of Broadway, adolescent artists' models, jaded lifestyles, kinky orgies. The opportunities for writers were unlimited. Compared with the more intellectual writing of Dorothy Dix (Elizabeth Meriwether Gilmer), also a Hearst reporter, Annie's coverage seemed curiously thin. As usual she wrote the feature sidebars, concentrating on Evelyn Nesbit's testimony, and it was clear that she felt Thaw had every reason to defend his wife's honor. Annie's various descriptions of Thaw verged on the gruesome:

> Harry Thaw looked like a man tortured by a thousand devils as he sat in the courtroom to-day. His skin was the greenish white of a man stretched on the operating table under a surgeon's knife. His great dull eyes rolled in his head and all the resolution he could summon could not keep his face from twitching.
>
> Harry Thaw's pale face turned to dull crimson and his heavy eyes flashed when the last juror stood up to be sworn in. Relief, suspense, terror, defiance—whatever emotion it was that mastered him for the instant—he shook every trace of it off his face with a lion-like toss of his heavy head and stared at the juror, calm-eyed and steady-featured again.

His utterly vulnerable wife, on the other hand, touched Annie's generous heart. Nesbit was "frailer, whiter, bigger-eyed and more like a frightened child," and "little, wan, bent, fragile, white-faced, stooping." She spoke "in the sweet voice of an undeveloped, unemotional, half-comprehending child," and she told "the hideous story of her pitiful, stunted, misled, mishapened little life, a life first of pitiful makeshifts and then of open and undeniable poverty."

---

[2] Irvin S. Cobb was a brilliant word merchant. In addition to "sob sister," he also coined and popularized the terms "innocent bystander" and "stuffed shirt."

Shortly before the summing-up to the jury, Annie played all the tremolo notes: "When I listened to Evelyn Nesbit's story, I felt as once I did when I was stumbling across a country bridge on a dark night, and a sudden flash of lightning showed me the black and terrific torrent of cruel water eddying almost under my very feet. We walk so safely on the bridge built for us by loving hands, we sheltered women. How little, oh, how blessed the little we know of the awful torrents that rush below our calm security."

For most of her career she had her own column in the *Examiner:* "Annie Laurie Says." That headline afforded her unlimited freedom to scoff and scold. For instance:

Attention! First class is everything. Stand up! The woman's clubs are beginning again. They are sending out their advertisements for the fall openings. I notice some fine bargains in ideas. A little shop-worn but still usable, and there is a sale in all kinds of fancy notions that really ought to attract a great deal of attention.

The first thing on the programme, the very first thing, is the child-study class.

Annie's conclusion: "This child-culture fad is all fudge."

Throughout her life Annie had two passions: journalism and San Francisco. "I'm not a sob sister or special writer," she wrote. "I'm just a plain, practical, all-round newspaper woman. That's my profession, and that is my pride. I'd rather smell of the printers' ink and hear the presses go round than go to any grand opera in the world." On first seeing San Francisco, she recalled promising: "I am going to climb to the top of every one of those hills and see what is on the other side." She saved San Francisco's street-corner flower stands, stopped speculators from demolishing the Palace of Fine Arts built for the Exposition of 1915, started the city's first community Christmas tree, and raised funds for the "Little Jim" ward at Children's Hospital, named after a crippled newsboy born to a prostitute in the city's prison hospital, who was turned away from Children's Hospital because he was incurable. For this cause, she organized a special Christmas edition of the *Examiner* for December 21, 1895, which sold 130,000 copies and raised $10,000 toward the hospital wing. Little Jim was one of the wing's first patients, and he died there in 1905.

She encouraged women to be journalists, and picked her successor, Adela Rogers St. Johns, who worked fifty years for Hearst, covering like her mentor all the flashy stories, but eventually gaining another kind of fame as a profiler of Hollywood personalities in *Photoplay* magazine. Annie's frequent advice to the novice was a description of herself:

The ideal newspaper woman has the keen zest for life of a child, the cool courage of a man and the subtlety of a woman. A woman has a distinct advantage over a man in reporting, if she has sense enough to balance qualities. Men always are good to women. At least I have found them so, and I've been in some of the toughest places.

Annie Laurie devoted her entire life to "The Chief." She and Louella Parsons, the movie-gossip columnist, were the featured women in Hearst's collection, for he acquired people with the same possessiveness as he collected art and sculpture for his castle, San Simeon. In return, Annie was treated with courtesy and consideration, privy to all Hearst's high-level meetings. She was once called "the highest paid newspaper woman in the country," although her exact salary was never revealed.

Of her own two marriages Annie wrote very little. The first, in 1882, was to *Examiner* colleague Orlow Black; it lasted five years and they had one son. The second, in 1901, was to Charles Alden Bonfils, brother of the co-publisher of the *Denver Post*. She had two children during this marriage, which lasted formally until her death, but was marked by many separations due to their respective newspaper work. Of her children, one son was an invalid, the other died at the age of nine, and a daughter, Winifred, disappointed her mother by marrying and not becoming a journalist. Both marriages were unhappy and marked by the sadness of her sons' early deaths.

Annie was most comfortable writing for newspapers, but she did find time to turn out two commercially published books: *Dope: The Story of the Living Dead* (1928), based on her anti-narcotic campaigns ("The most powerful evil the human race has had to fight"), and *The Little Boy Who Lived on the Hill*, the story of her eldest son, who drowned while swimming at Carmel. She did two vanity books: *My Neighbor Has Gone on a Long Journey and I Did Not Say Good-by* (1917, reprints from the *San Francisco Call*), and *Roses and Rain* (1920, reprints from the *Examiner*). Both are good examples of her musings on the commonplace and deal mostly with San Francisco's visual delights. The *Roses* volume is flyspecked with some arresting metaphors, such as a description of eucalyptus trees under a harvest moon "throwing their ragged shadows on the ground like beggars playing dice against time."

Then there was her marathon writing project. When Hearst's mother, Phoebe Apperson Hearst, died in 1919, "The Chief" gave orders that Annie had to write her obituary. She had only forty minutes to turn out three columns of copy. Later when Hearst asked for a full-length biography, Annie wrote 54,000 words in twelve days for a privately printed volume on parchment. Hearst historians felt it didn't do this complex woman justice, and it has been labeled "inaccurate" and "the work of a sob sister in a hurry."

Everything in the way of human excitement, it seems, came from her work and friends, who had a pet name for her, "Glorianna." Nearly blind and confined to bed with diabetes, she continued working at seventy-two, dictating an average of nine articles a week. Shortly before her death on May 25, 1936, a visitor recalled her gesturing around her San Francisco home and murmuring, "It's all—all Hearst." Her body, by order of the mayor, lay in state at City Hall and thousands passed by to say farewell to Annie Laurie. She was front-page news for three days in the *Examiner*. In a lead editorial, the *Examiner* noted: "It is said that the words of the newspaper writer are writ on the sands, washed away by the next day's tide. That is not true of the works of Annie Laurie. Her pen was devoted to the physical and moral betterment of humanity. She built enduringly with her great talent."

Her last interview was for *Time* magazine, when she summed up her career: "I like newspapers and newspaper people and newspaper standards, and I like newspaper news too, and I'm just foolish enough to say so. I'm proud of being, in a very humble way, a member of the good old newspaper gang— the kindest-hearted, quickest-witted, clearest-eyed, most courageous assemblage of people I have ever had the honor and the good fortune to know."

The following story is the first eyewitness dispatch Annie Laurie sent out of Galveston after the tidal wave.

CORPSE-LADEN WATERS LIT
BY FUNERAL PYRES
Winifred Black Crosses the Dismal Bay
of Death to the Desolate City of Disaster.

By WINIFRED BLACK (ANNIE LAURIE)

San Francisco Examiner, September 15, 1900

GALVESTON, (Texas), Sept. 14.—I begged, cajoled and cried my way through the lines of soldiers with drawn swords who guard the wharf at Texas City and sailed across the bay on a little boat which is making irregular trips to meet the relief trains from Houston.

The engineer who brought our train down from Houston spent the night before groping around in the wrecks on the beach looking for his wife and three children. He found them, dug a rude grave in the sand and set up a little board marked with his name. Then he went to the railroad company and begged them to let him go to work.

The man in front of me on the car had floated all Monday night with his wife and mother on a part of the roof of his little home. He told me that he kissed his wife good-bye at midnight and told her that he could not hold on any longer; but he did hold on, dazed and half conscious, until the day broke and showed him that he was alone on his piece of dried wood. He did not even know when the women that he loved had died.

Every man on the train—there were no women there—had lost some one that he loved in the terrible disaster, and was going across the bay to try and find some trace of his family—all except the four men in my party. They were from outside cities—St. Louis, New Orleans and Kansas City. They had lost a large amount of property and were coming down to see if anything could be saved from the wreck.

They had been sworn in as deputy sheriffs in order to get into Galveston. The city is under martial law, and no human being who cannot account for himself to the complete satisfaction of the officers in charge can hope to get through.

We sat on the deck of the little steamer. The four men from out-of-town cities and I listened to the little boat's wheel ploughing its way through the

calm waters of the bay. The stars shone down like a benediction, but along
the line of the shore there rose a great leaping column of blood-red flame.

"What a terrible fire!" I said. "Some of the large buildings must be burning." A man who was passing the deck behind my chair heard me. He stopped,
put his hand on the bulwark and turned down and looked into my face, his
face like the face of a dead man, but he laughed.

"Buildings?" he said. "Don't you know what is burning over there? It is
my wife and children, such little children; why, the tallest was not as high
as this"—he laid his hand on the bulwark—"and the little one was just learning
to talk.

"She called my name the other day, and now they are burning over there,
they and the mother who bore them. She was such a little, tender, delicate
thing, always so easily frightened, and now she's out there all alone with the
two babies, and they're burning them. If you're looking for sensations, there's
plenty of them to be found over there where that smoke is drifting."

The man laughed again and began again to walk up and down the deck.

"That's right," said the U.S. Marshal of Southern Texas, taking off his
broad hat and letting the starlight shine on his strong face, "that's right. We've
had to do it. We've burned over 1,000 people to-day, and to-morrow we
shall burn as many more.

"Yesterday we stopped burying the bodies at sea; we had to give the men
on the barges whiskey to give them courage to do their work. They carried
out hundreds of the dead at one time, men and women, negroes and white
people, all piled up as high as the barge could stand it, and the men did not
go out far enough to sea, and the bodies have begun drifting back again."

"Look!" said the man who was walking the deck, touching my shoulder
with his shaking hand. "Look there!"

Before I had time to think I did look, and I saw floating in the water the
body of an old, old woman, whose hair was shining in the starlight. A little
further on we saw a group of strange driftwood. We looked closer and found
it to be a mass of wooden slabs with names and dates cut upon them, and
floating on top of them were marble stones, two of them.

The graveyard, which has held the sleeping citizens of Galveston for many,
many years, was giving up its dead. We pulled up at a little wharf in the
hush of the starlight; there were no lights anywhere in the city except a few
scattered lamps shining from a few desolate, half-destroyed houses. We picked
our way up the street. The ground was slimy with the debris of the sea. Great
pools of water stood in the middle of the street.

We climbed over wreckage and picked our way through heaps of rubbish.
The terrible, sickening odor almost overcame us, and it was all that I could
do to shut my teeth and get through the streets somehow.

The soldiers were camping on the wharf front, lying stretched out on the wet sand, the hideous, hideous sand, stained and streaked in the starlight with dark and cruel blotches. They challenged us, but the marshal took us through under his protection. At every street corner there was a guard, and every guard wore a six-shooter strapped around his waist.

"The best men!" said the marshal. "They've all left their own misery and come down here to do police duty. We needed them. They had to shoot twenty-five men yesterday for looting the dead. Not Americans, not one of them. I saw them all—negroes and the poor whites from southern Europe. They cut off the hands of their victims. Every citizen has orders to shoot without notice any one found at such work."

We got to the hotel after some terrible nightmare-fashioned plodding through dim streets like a line of forlorn ghosts in a half-forgotten dream. At the hotel, a big, typical Southern hotel, with a dome and marble rotunda, the marble stained and patched with the sea slime, the clerk told us that he had no rooms. We tried to impress him in some way, but he would not look up from his book, and all he said was "No room" over and over again like a man talking in his sleep.

We hunted the housekeeper and found there was room, and plenty of it, only the clerk was so dazed that he did not know what he was doing. There was room, but no bedding, and no water, and no linen of any sort.

General McKibben, commander in charge of the Texas division, was down stairs in the parlor reading dispatches, with an aide and an orderly or two at his elbow. He was horrified to see me.

"How in the world did you get here?" he said. "I would not let any women belonging to me come into this place of horror for all the money in America. I am an old soldier, madam. I have seen many battlefields, but let me tell you that since I rowed across the bay the other night and helped the man at the boat steer to keep away from the floating bodies of dead women and little children, I have not slept one single instant.

"I have been out on inspection all day, and I find that our first estimate of the number of the dead was very much under the real. Five thousand would never cover the number of people who died here in that terrible storm.

"I saw my men pulling away some rubbish this very morning right at the corner of the principal street. They thought there might be some one dead person there. They took out fourteen women and three little children. We have only just begun to get a faint idea of the hideous extent of this calamity. The little towns along the coast had been almost completely washed out. We hear from them every now and then as some poor, dazed wretch creeps somehow into shelter and tries to tell his pitiful story. We have only just begun our work.

"The people all over America are responding generously to our appeals for help, and I would like to impress it upon them that what we need now is money, money, money and disinfectants. Tell your people to send all the quicklime they can get through. I wish I could see a dozen trainloads of disinfectants landed in this city to-morrow morning. What we must fight now is infection, and we must fight it quick and with determination or it will conquer us."

The men of my party came over and took me from the great damp tomb of a room, where I was trying to write, to the Aziola Club across the street.

There were eighteen or twenty men there, most representative of the city of Galveston, rich, influential citizens. They had all been on police duty or rescue work of some sort. The millionaire at the table next to me wore a pair of workmen's brogans, some kind of patched old trousers and a colored shirt much the worse for wear. He had been directing a gang of workmen who were extricating the dead from the fallen houses all day long.

The man on my right had lain for four hours under a mass of rubbish on Monday and had heard his friends pass by and recognized their voices, but could not groan loud enough for them to hear him. He told us what he was thinking about as he lay there with a man pinned across his chest and two dead men under him. He tried to make his story amusing and we all tried to laugh.

Every man in that room had lost nearly every dollar he had in the world, and two or three of them had lost the nearest and dearest friends they had on earth, but there were no sighs, and there was not one man who spoke in anything but tones of courageous endurance. In the short time I have been here I have met and talked with women who saw every one they loved on earth swept away from them out into the storm.

I have held in my arms a little lisping boy not eight years old, whose chubby face was set and hard when he told me how he watched his mother die. But I have not seen a single tear. The people of Galveston are stunned with the merciful bewilderment which nature always sends at such a time of sorrow.

8

Elizabeth Cochrane
Seaman
"Nellie Bly"
(1865–1922)

IN 1890 a wisp of a woman went around the world and beat the fictional eighty-day record of Phileas Fogg. It was a stunt worthy of the circulation-crazed *New York World* and it made Nellie Bly's name part of American folklore. As a journalist, though, her most important legacy was a personal approach to undercover reporting, a style that future muckrakers and Watergate-influenced reporters would later refine with objectivity. When she feigned insanity to get admitted to a public asylum and report firsthand on conditions, she, more than anyone else, established a widely imitated though often controversial school of journalism.[1] Whether she was posing as a servant, shoplifter, or shopgirl, she brought to her work the varying talents of an actress, detective, social worker, and journalist. Invariably she wrote first-person stories that cast her as the starring character in a drama where she was tormented, taunted, or tricked. Wherever she went, into tenements,

---

[1] The Pulitzer Prize board denied awards in 1982 to the *Los Angeles Herald-Examiner* partially because the paper's reporter claimed to be an illegal alien and took a job in a garment-industry sweatshop and in 1979 to the *Chicago Sun-Times*, which set up a saloon business and paid bribes to city officials.

factories, hospitals, or jails, she found conditions that needed reforming, as most social conditions of the time did.

As the century drew to a close, the *World* was New York's fastest-growing newspaper and its owner, Joseph Pulitzer, demanded circulation-building stories that exploited the underclass. For eight years this slight, five-foot-three brunette with cool, calculating gray eyes and a shy but stubborn personality wrote the stories that grabbed the headlines. She exposed the bad and interviewed the famous: Buffalo Bill, prize fighter John L. Sullivan, anarchist Emma Goldman, and the wives of the Presidents. In 1890, at the height of her fame, she was only twenty-five years old and earning the astonishing salary of $25,000. Motivated as much by a desire to be recognized as to be respected, Nellie became a national Barbie Doll. Clothes, games, and toys were named after her following her triumphant return from around the world.

Nellie Bly was as brash as they come, a competitive over-achiever. But to her credit she never tried for a job just because she thought the editor would be interested in a woman reporter. She had ideas, and her ability to package her reporting projects was in large part the reason for her swift success. When she arrived in New York after working on the *Pittsburgh Dispatch*, she had a few good stories to her credit, $100 in her purse, and a plan to knock on every editor's door until she got a job. She went first to Park Row and the building with the golden dome, hoping to see the *World*'s managing editor, Col. John A. Cockerill. She waited three hours, ignoring the copyboys who tried to shoo her home and badgering everyone who entered the building to help her get in. Finally, one reporter, impressed by her brashness, slipped her inside and pointed her toward an office where Cockerill was talking with Pulitzer. Nellie first told them how she had been robbed of her last $100 and then she whipped out a list of story ideas. One suggested that she pretend to be mad to get inside Blackwell's Island (now Roosevelt Island).

Indeed, this was a different approach. Social issues hadn't been completely ignored by the press (Margaret Fuller had written essays about mental institutions in the 1840s), but no reporter had ever tried to get inside as a patient. Of course, Nellie had to convince doctors that she was actually insane, and she had a plan ready. She spent hours in front of the mirror in her drab boarding house perfecting her act: long vacant stares, painful grimaces. Then she went to a flophouse for women and there in the hallway staged an Ophelia-like mad act. Medical experts and judges examined her and pronounced the reporter insane. When Cockerill and Pulitzer agreed to this assignment, they had also agreed to use the paper's influence to get Nellie out of bedlam after ten days.

During these ten days, she was not physically beaten or raped, but she was subjected to such indignities as cold baths, callous nurses, harassment, inedible food, and hospital intrigue. Her two-part series, which ran in the Sunday editions of October 9 and 16, 1887, totaled seventeen columns. Nellie, of course, was the featured character, but she surrounded herself with a full supporting cast, all identified and all quoted. The exposé prompted an investigation, with Nellie testifying before a grand jury. Although the jury found little proof for her charges—nurses contradicted her, patients named disappeared, and a touring group found the asylum a model of order and cleanliness—they ended up believing her story. As a result, the city voted $3 million to improve the facility.

With her first assignment, she had front-page space and subsequently the right to think up her own story ideas. She spent two years specializing in reform articles, which frequently followed the same pattern: she would apply for a job or get herself imprisoned and write about her experiences. She worked at an employment agency that exploited immigrant girls. She interviewed prospective husbands at a matrimonial agency that fronted for swindlers. She wrote sympathetic stories about factory girls who worked twelve-hour days, earning less than 50 cents a week. Her assignments as well as her writing followed a set structure. In a story on February 24, 1889, about her experiences in jail to observe how women were treated (she framed a theft with a friend to get in), she stated the purpose of her undercover work in the lead and followed with a chronological listing of her experiences. At the end she summarized her conclusions and offered some solutions:

I have come to several conclusions. First—That a regular woman-searcher should be employed in station-houses.
Second—That the male officers should be given no opportunity of squinting through a peephole at women who are being searched.
Third—That innocent women who fall into the hands of the police are not necessarily badly treated.
Fourth—That the male and female prisoners should not be kept within earshot of each other.
Fifth—That if all the turnkeys were as fine as those I encountered no woman could ever fill their places, because women are never so kind to their unfortunate sisters as men are. Women grow harder from daily contact with crime, so that no sympathy is left in them. Men generally do not.
Sixth—That detectives are very human and liable to err, and I do not think they should be given the sole custody of a female prisoner.

Nellie was a very private person, a loner. She did not mingle with her colleagues or hang around the cityroom swapping stories. Her desk was right in the newsroom, not stuck in an obscure corner like those of women reporters on the other papers. Frequently she looked startling, coming to work in a rustic bonnet and gingham dress or whatever disguise she needed for her undercover work. She obviously loved her impersonations and would stand side by side with a poor girl washing bottles while urging her to try to get an education. Many of Nellie's stories could have been reported with conventional techniques, but then the drama of her performance, which editors depended on to sell papers, would have been missing.

In one of her finest roles she pretended to be the wife of a man with a small patent-medicine factory. Her target was Edward R. Phelps, an Albany lobbyist. She convinced Phelps that her husband wanted to block the passage of a bill to protect the public from phony medicines. Phelps took the bait and ticked off how much Nellie should pay him to bribe certain legislators to vote against the bill. When she was through, she had the names of Albany's corruptible politicians. Later she testified at the trial that found Phelps guilty. Her lead was overly cute for the seriousness of the story, published on April 1, 1888, but, then, the *World* strove to entertain:

For I'm a Pirate King!
I'm in the lobby ring!
Oh, what an uproarious
Jolly and glorious
Biz for a pirate king.

I was a lobbyist last week. I went up to Albany to catch a professional briber in the act. I did so. The briber, lobbyist and boodler whom I caught was Mr. Ed Phelps. I pretended I wanted to have him help me kill a certain bill. Mr. Phelps was cautious at first and looked carefully into my record. He satisfied himself carefully that I was honest and talked very freely for a king.

She followed up the lobbyist story with the entrapment of a masher, a foreman of a livery stable who drove through Central Park picking up lonely country girls. Her costume was a flowered cotton dress, a straw hat, and a long shawl draped over her shoulders. She sat on a park bench, waited until he drove by, then caught his eye and lowered her eyes demurely. He opened the door of the carriage and she got in. They galloped off to a roadhouse where her victim drank and talked about how he helped girls earn a living, which Nellie interpreted as recruiting prostitutes. In all her undercover stories she had an innate sense of timing; she never overplayed an act. She took control of this situation by convincing the man that she had many friends who would miss her and report her disappearance to the police. He drove her back to the park.

Nellie's independent, competitive personality developed at an early age. She was born Elizabeth Cochran on May 5, 1865,[2] in Cochran Mills, Pennsylvania, a town named after her father, Michael, a self-made man who

---

[2] Biographers usually give 1867 as her birth date. Her death certificate gives her age as fifty-six, which suggests a birth date of 1865. Nellie added a final "e" to her last name.

Elizabeth Cochrane Seaman

had worked his way up from laborer to mill owner, and later to associate judge. Her mother, Mary Jane (Kennedy) Cochran, was her father's second wife, and Elizabeth was the youngest of three children in a combined family of ten, including five older brothers. To deal with this home environment, she quickly acquired spunk. She was educated at home by her father until he died when she was twelve. Three years later she was sent to an Indiana, Pennsylvania, boarding school for a year. The family moved to Pittsburgh, and at nineteen she decided she had to find a job to support herself. An editorial in the local paper, the *Pittsburgh Dispatch*, caught her eye. Called "What Girls Are Good For," it criticized women who wanted a career outside the home. She wrote an indignant anonymous reply to the editor, George A. Madden. Intrigued by her logic and writing style, Madden put an advertisement in the *Dispatch* asking the author to get in touch with him, never suspecting the writer was a woman.

On the first job interview she brought a list of ideas that would take her into the slums, prisons, and sweatshops of Pittsburgh. An exception among nineteenth-century editors, Madden thought it would be profitable to have a woman reporter. For her first story, she decided to write in favor of divorce, a controversial topic at the time. She signed this story "Nellie Bly," a *nom de plume* selected by Madden when he heard a copyboy whistling the popular Stephen Foster song.[3] Letters swamped Madden's desk. Nellie became the paper's first woman reporter and thereafter picked her own assignments. After a hard-hitting exposé on sweatshop conditions, the city's business elite pounded on Madden's door, threatening to pull out their advertising. The financial pressure against the paper was intense; reluctantly, Madden took her off investigative stories and put her to work writing women's and cultural news. At first she enjoyed the glamour of going to the theater, but soon soft news bored her. When Madden wouldn't let her return to undercover stories, she took a leave of absence and went to Mexico with her mother.

She found as many ills in that agrarian society as she had in Pittsburgh's industrial one. Her letters printed in the *Dispatch* drew stark contrasts between the lives of the rich and the poor, exposed political corruption, and returned to her favorite theme: the need for reform. In one article she noted that Mexicans are "worse off by the thousands of times than were the slaves in the United States." Her negative observations were reprinted in other papers and the Mexican government ordered her out of the country. But the controversy had enhanced her stature, and Madden asked her back, offering to raise her salary from $5 to $15 a week. Nellie was never a person of strong

---

[3] Written in 1850, this popular song was "Nelly Bly, Nelly Bly, bring de broom along." Nellie probably changed the spelling of the first name, as she had earlier altered her surname.

loyalty or appreciation, and the fact that he had launched her as Nellie Bly mattered little to her. She turned him down.

During her first years at the *World*, when she was concentrating on re-form stories, she spent all her time either under cover on assignments or writing books based on her adventures. Whatever social life she might have had, it was hidden from her co-workers. Her only known escort during this time was James Metcalfe, a writer who later became a founder of *Life* magazine. Nellie was a restless person, and she soon grew tired of undercover stories. One night, according to some accounts, she woke up suddenly with an idea for something spectacular: she would duplicate the 80-day, round-the-world journey of Jules Verne's fictional hero, Phileas Fogg, but she would beat his record.

Nellie went to see the ailing Pulitzer, who directed his newspaper from a yacht in New York Harbor, far from city noise. He listened intently, as he always did to her ideas, nodding and hesitating. Finally he suggested that it was really an assignment for a man. She said she would go anyway; she would race his candidate. So Pulitzer gave in. Preparations were hurried and se-cret. In four days she assembled a wardrobe: a blue broadcloth dress, a checked camel's hair coat with a matching fore-and-aft deerstalker's hat (later made famous by Sherlock Holmes), and in one small satchel she carried a warm-weather outfit of yellow muslin, accessories, toilet articles, a bathrobe, and writing materials. On November 14, 1889, Nellie sailed on the *Augusta Victoria* from Jersey City, New Jersey. The *World*, not to appear too frivo-lous, noted the news value of her trip:

There is an important commercial aspect to her trip. Here, in New York, it was possible to buy a ticket for every part of the trip and Miss Bly has in her pocket the billets which will be taken by the several companies into whose care as a passenger she will entrust herself. Her trip when ended will be a record of how far in this last quarter of the century the facilities for travel and communication have advanced. She will call on no extra help. No chartered locomotives or special boat will wait for her with steam to make extra fast time. She will take her luck as a first-class passen-ger, using the facilities which are demanded by travelers.

Her route was through London, Paris (with only one detour to visit Jules Verne in Amiens, France), Italy, the Suez, Ceylon, Singapore, Hong Kong, Yokohama, and San Francisco. An attempt to share the spotlight was made by *Cosmopolitan*, which dispatched Elizabeth Bisland in the opposite direc-tion.[4] But this journey was totally overshadowed by Nellie and her tales. Everywhere she went there was much to criticize: the heat and the dirt, the

[4] Elizabeth Bisland, born in 1863, received her early training on the *New Orleans Times-Dem-ocrat*. She was an editor on *Cosmopolitan* when she was sent to race against Nellie. She lost by four days, completing the trip in seventy-six days. Her delays were caused primarily by miss-ing two ship connections.

insects and the beggars, the mashers and the bandits. As usual Nellie focused on each country's weaknesses, but she also wrote about the trains, harbors, mountains, temples, and animals.

Back home the Nellie Bly mania mounted. A circular chart tracing her progress was published every day. Readers followed the trip with checkers, pennies, or dice, placing bets on when she would reach a given place. Often she didn't have time to cable stories, and disgruntled male colleagues were kept busy turning out substitute and supplemental copy to fill the front page.

She arrived home on January 25, 1890, some 30,000 miles behind her, in 72 days, 6 hours, 11 minutes. Cannons boomed from the Battery to Brooklyn. As a symbol of the exotic places visited, she brought back a monkey that sat on her shoulder during whistle-stops from San Francisco to New York. "Father Time Outdone!" read the *World*'s headline. The paper noted that her feat marked the end of the stagecoach era and the dawn of the "new age of lightning travel." [5]

There was a pre-ticker-tape parade down Broadway. Her arrival generated as much excitement as the astronauts' missions did in the 1960s. Nellie was a celebrity, at last. She confronted her image everywhere: a poster depicted her holding a parasol while walking a tightrope over a globe. She gave testimonials for Pears soap; a famous race horse was named after her; and she was the topic of jokes, cartoons, and jingles.

There was little she could think of to match her globe-circling stunt, and more and more she sought assignments outside New York. While she was in the Midwest covering a drought, she met Robert L. Seaman, a millionaire hardware manufacturer. He was seventy-two; she was twenty-eight, and on April 5, 1895, Nellie married him after a four-day courtship. Behind her back she was called a golddigger. Her hasty decision, though, was perhaps the perfect answer: she could leave journalism at her peak, with the protection of a longed-for father figure and the privileges of social and financial power. [6] Announcing her wedding, the *World* told its readers: "Few young

[5] In 1936, Dorothy Kilgallen (dubbed the modern Nellie Bly) representing the *New York Journal*, Leo Kiernan of the *New York Times* and H. R. Ekins of the *New York World-Telegram* repeated the race. Ekins won in 18 days, 14 hours, and 56 minutes. Again there was great reader interest, and other city papers in Los Angeles and Washington had their reporters circling the city and the District of Columbia. Not to be outdone, the *New York Sun* sent three reporters to circle Central Park using public transportation. Mabel Greene, using a horse and buggy, won in 50 minutes.

[6] According to a letter dated 1890, but obviously written later, and available in the Smith College manuscript collection, Nellie felt that she had been financially and personally exploited by the *World* after her trip around the world. In the letter, addressed to a Mr. Carpenter, Nellie complains that the paper never thanked her for increasing its circulation and never paid her a bonus. She wrote: "I have a standing invitation from *The World* to go back but it is needless to add that in face of their shabby treatment of me I shall never do so."

women have had more worldly experience than Miss Bly and few are more capable of enjoying the pleasure of a millionaire's existence."

She wintered in a four-story brownstone at 15 West 37th Street and summered on a Catskills farm. There were trips to Paris to buy the latest fashions and dine on the finest food. For nine years the couple lived the good life, and then in 1904 Seaman died. Without children to care for, Nellie enthusiastically took charge of her husband's business, which made everything from milk cans to coal scuttles. With some success she expanded—and, of course, reformed—the American Steel Barrel Company into the largest company of its kind. In a short time, however, she found herself in the midst of employee disputes and lawsuits that would diminish her fortune.

Her name now appeared not in front-page bylines but in news stories about her court battles. Attempting to salvage some of her capital, she transferred property to Austrian ownership, only to lose everything when the United States entered World War I. She was interned in Vienna when war broke out in 1917 and did not return to the United States until 1919. Eventually she was forced to look for work. Out of respect for her reputation, her friend Arthur Brisbane, editor of Hearst's *Evening Journal*, gave her a job. There was a new generation of newspaperwomen on Park Row, and the undercover first-person accounts that had made her famous had no place in the "yellow journalism" era of the 1920s. She worked in a private room, quietly writing about abandoned children and unwed mothers. Her face was often covered with a chenille-dotted veil, and she maintained the same aloofness toward her colleagues that she had as a famous reporter.

She did have one last chance to play the actress-journalist role. Gordon Hamby, one of the many murderers exploited by the press of the era, was to be executed at Sing Sing prison. Pretending that she was campaigning against capital punishment, Nellie convinced authorities to let her witness the execution. She interviewed Hamby and won his friendship. Before his death on January 30, 1920, he left her his Ouija board and a note: "A slight remembrance [all I have at this time] for your infinite kindness and friendship." Her lead for the execution story was vintage Nellie Bly:

Horrible! Horrible! Horrible!
Hamby is dead. The law has been carried out—presumably the law is satisfied . . . Through my mind flitted the thought that one time this young boy going to the death chair had been welcomed by some fond mother. He had been a baby, lo, loved and cherished. And this is the end.

Nellie died of pneumonia at age fifty-six on January 27, 1922. Her death was reported with modest headlines and short obituaries. Though the *Journal* called her "the best reporter in America," the *World* hardly noted the passing of its most famous reporter. She was buried in Woodlawn Cemetery

in an unmarked grave. In 1978 the New York Press Club erected a head-
stone to "ease the loneliness from her last resting place."

Nellie wrote three books based on her newspaper pieces: *Ten Days in a
Madhouse* (1887; the book does not follow the same sequence as the newspaper articles. Paragraphing was changed, and Nellie added bits of description, particularly about herself), *Six Months in Mexico* (1888), and *Nellie
Bly's Book: Around the World in Seventy-Two Days* (1890). The following
article is the second installment of her story on her stay at Blackwell's Island.

INSIDE THE MADHOUSE.
Nellie Bly's Experience in the Blackwell's Island Asylum.
Continuation of the Story of Ten Days with Lunatics.
How the City's Unfortunate Wards Are Fed and Treated.
The Terrors of Cold Baths and Cruel, Unsympathetic Nurses.
Attendants Who Harass and Abuse Patients and Laugh at Their Miseries.

New York World, October 16, 1887

As the wagon was rapidly driven through the beautiful lawns up to the asylum my feelings of satisfaction at having attained the object of my work were greatly dampened by the look of distress on the faces of my companions. Poor women, they had no hopes of a speedy delivery. They were being driven to a prison, through no fault of their own, in all probability for life. In comparison, how much easier it would be to walk to the gallows than to this tomb of living horrors! On the wagon sped, and I, as well as my comrades, gave a despairing farewell glance at freedom as we came in sight of the long stone buildings. We passed one low building, and the stench was so horrible that I was compelled to hold my breath, and I mentally decided that it was the kitchen. I afterward found I was correct in my surmise, and smiled at the signboard at the end of the walk: "Visitors are not allowed on this road." I don't think the sign would be necessary if they once tried the road, especially on a warm day.

The wagon stopped, and the nurse and officer in charge told us to get out. The nurse added: "Thank God! they came quietly." We obeyed orders to go ahead up a flight of narrow, stone steps, which had evidently been built for the accommodation of people who climb stairs three at a time. I wondered if my companions knew where we were, so I said to Miss Tillie Mayard: "Where are we?" "At the Blackwell's Island Lunatic Asylum," she answered sadly. "Are you crazy?" I asked. "No," she replied; "but as we have been sent here we will have to be quiet until we find some means of escape. They will be few, though, if all the doctors, as Dr. Field, refuse to listen to me or give me a chance to prove my sanity." We were ushered into a narrow vestibule, and the door was locked behind us.

In spite of the knowledge of my sanity and the assurance that I would be released in a few days, my heart gave a sharp twinge. Pronounced insane by four expert doctors and shut up behind the unmerciful bolts and bars of a madhouse! Not to be confined alone, but to be a companion, day and night, of senseless, chattering lunatics; to sleep with them, to eat with them, to be considered one of them, was an uncomfortable position. Timidly we followed the nurse up the long uncarpeted hall to a room filled by so-called crazy women. We were told to sit down, and some of the patients kindly made room for us. They looked at us curiously, and one came up to me and asked: "Who sent you here?" "The doctors," I answered. "What for?" she persisted. "Well, they say I am insane," I admitted. "Insane!" she repeated, incredulously. "It cannot be seen in your face."

This woman was too clever, I concluded, and was glad to answer the roughly given orders to follow the nurse to see the doctor. This nurse, Miss Grupe, by the way, had a nice German face, and if I had not detected certain hard lines about the mouth I might have expected, as did my companions, to receive but kindness from her. She left us in a small waiting-room at the end of the hall, and left us alone while she went into a small office opening into the sitting or receiving-room. "I like to go down in the wagon," she said to the invisible party on the inside. "It helps to break up the day." He answered her that the open air improved her looks, and she again appeared before us all smiles and simpers.

"Come here, Tillie Mayard," she said. Miss Mayard obeyed, and though I could not see into the office, I could hear her gently but firmly pleading her case. All her remarks were as rational as any I ever heard, and I thought no good physician could help but be impressed with her story. She told of her recent illness, that she was suffering from nervous debility. She begged that they try all their tests for insanity, if they had any, and give her justice. Poor girl, how my heart ached for her! I determined then and there that I would try by every means to make my mission of benefit to my suffering sisters; that I would show how they are committed without ample trial. Without one word of sympathy or encouragement she was brought back to where we sat.

Mrs. Louise Schanz was taken into the presence of Dr. Kinier, the medical man. "Your name?" he asked, loudly. She answered in German, saying she did not speak English nor could she understand it. However, when he said Mrs. Louise Schanz, she said "Yah, yah." Then he tried other questions, and when he found she could not understand one word of English, he said to Miss Grupe: "You are German; speak to her for me." Miss Grupe proved to be one of those people who are ashamed of their nationality, and she refused, saying she could understand but few words of her mother tongue. "You know you speak German. Ask this woman what her husband does," and they both laughed as if they were enjoying a joke. "I can't speak but a few words," she protested, but at last she managed to ascertain the occupation of Mr. Schanz. "Now, what was the use of lying to me?" asked the doctor, with a laugh which dispelled the rudeness. "I can't speak any more," she said, and she did not.

Thus was Mrs. Louise Schanz consigned to the asylum without a chance of making herself understood. Can such carelessness be excused, I wonder, when it is so easy to get an interpreter? If the confinement was but for a few days one might question the necessity. But here was a woman taken without her own consent from a free world to an asylum and there given no chance to prove her sanity. Confined most probably for life behind asylum bars, without even being told in her language the why and wherefore. Compare this with a criminal, who is given every chance to prove his innocence. Who would not rather be a murderer and take the chance for life than be declared insane, without hope of escape? Mrs. Schanz begged in German to know where she was, and pleaded for liberty. Her voice broken by sobs, she was led unheard out to us.

Mrs. Fox was then put through this weak, trifling examination and brought from the office, convicted. Miss Annie Neville took her turn, and I was again left to the last. I had by this time determined to act as I do when free, except that I would refuse to tell who I was or where my home was.

THEY EXAMINE HER AGAIN

"NELLIE BROWN, the doctor wants you," said Miss Grupe. I went in and was told to sit down opposite Dr. Kinier at the desk. "What is your name?" he asked, without looking up. "Nellie Brown," I replied, easily. "Where is your home?" writing what I had said down in a large book. "In Cuba." "Oh!" he ejaculated, with sudden understanding—then, addressing the nurse: "Did you see anything in the papers about her?" "Yes," she replied, "I saw a long account of this girl in the *Sun* on Sunday." Then the doctor said: "Keep her here until I go to the office and see the notice again." He left us, and I was relieved of my hat and shawl. On his return, he said he had been unable to find the paper, but he related the story of my *debut*, as he had read it, to the nurse. "What's the color of her eyes?" Miss Grupe looked, and answered "gray," although everybody had always said my eyes were brown or hazel.

"What's your age?" he asked: and as I answered, "Nineteen last May," he turned to the nurse, and said, "When do you get your next pass?" This I ascertained was a leave of absence, or "a day off." "Next Saturday," she said, with a laugh. "You will go to town?" and they both laughed as she answered in the affirmative, and he said:

"Measure her." I was stood under a measure, and it was brought down tightly on my head. "What is it?" asked the doctor. "Now you know I can't tell," she said. "Yes, you can; go ahead. What height?" "I don't know; there are some figures there, but I can't tell." "Yes, you can. Now look and tell me." "I can't; do it yourself," and they laughed again as the doctor left his place at the desk and came forward to see for himself. "Five feet five inches; don't you see?" he said, taking her hand and touching the figures. By her voice I knew she did not understand yet, but that was no concern of mine, as the doctor seemed to find a pleasure in aiding her. Then I was put on the scales, and she worked around until she got them to balance. "How much?" asked the doctor, having resumed his position at the desk. "I don't know. You will have to see for yourself," she replied, calling him by his Christian name, which I have forgotten. He turned and also addressing her by her baptismal name, he said: "You are getting too fresh!" and they both laughed. I then told the weight—112 pounds—to the nurse, and she in turn told the doctor.

"What time are you going to supper?" he asked, and she told him. He gave the nurse more attention than he did me, and asked her six questions to every one of me. Then he wrote my fate in the book before him. I said, "I am not sick and I do not want to stay here. No one has a right to shut me up in this manner." He took no notice of my remarks, and having completed his writings, as well as his talk with the nurse for the moment, he said that would do, and with my companions, I went back to the sitting-room.

"You play the piano?" they asked. "Oh, yes; ever since I was a child," I replied. Then they insisted that I should play, and they seated me on a wooden chair before an old-fashioned square. I struck a few notes, and the untuned response sent a grinding chill through me. "How horrible," I exclaimed, turning to a nurse, Miss McCarten, who stood at my side. "I never touched a piano as much out of tune." "It's a pity of you," she said, spitefully; "we'll have to get one made to order for you." I began to play the variations of "Home Sweet Home." The talking ceased and every patient sat silent, while my cold fingers moved slowly and stiffly over the keyboard. I finished in an aimless fashion and refused all requests to play more. Not seeing an available place to sit, I still occupied the chair in the front of the piano while, I "sized up" my surroundings.

It was a long, bare room, with bare yellow benches encircling it. These benches, which were perfectly straight, and just as uncomfortable, would hold five people, although in almost every instance six were crowded on them. Barred windows, built about five feet from the floor, faced the two double doors which led into the hall. The bare white walls were somewhat relieved by three lithographs, one of Fritz Emmet and the others of negro minstrels. In the center of the room was a large table covered with a white bed-spread, and around it sat the nurses. Everything was spotlessly clean and I thought what good workers the nurses must be to keep such order. In a few days after how I laughed at my own stupidity to think the nurses would work. When they found I would not play any more, Miss McCarten came up to me saying, roughly: "Get away from here," and closed the piano with a bang. "Brown, come here," was the next order I got from a rough, red-faced woman at the table. "What have you on?" "My clothing," I replied. She lifted my dress and skirts and wrote down one pair shoes, one pair stockings, one cloth dress, one straw sailor hat, and so on.

AT SUPPER.

Rancid Butter, Weak Tea and Five Prunes
Her Uninviting Portions.

This examination over, we heard some one yell, "Go out into the hall." One of the patients kindly explained that this was an invitation to supper. We late comers tried to keep together, so we entered the hall and stood at the door where all the women had crowded. How we shivered as we stood there! The windows were open and the draught went whizzing through the hall. The patients looked blue with cold, and the minutes stretched into a quarter of an hour. At last one of the nurses went forward and unlocked a door, through which we all crowded to a landing of the stairway. Here again came a long halt directly before an open window. "How very impudent for the attendants to keep these thinly clad women standing here in the cold," said Miss Neville. I looked at the poor crazy captives shivering, and added, emphatically. "It's horribly brutal." While they stood there I thought I would not relish supper that night. They looked so lost and hopeless. Some were chattering nonsense to invisible persons, other were laughing or crying aimlessly, and one old, gray-haired woman was nudging me, and, with winks and sage noddings of the head and pitiful upliftings of the eyes and hands, was assuring me that I must not mind the poor creatures, as they were all mad. "Stop at the heater," was then ordered, "and get in line, two by two." "Mary, get a companion." "How many times must I tell you to keep in line?" "Stand still," and, as the orders were issued, a shove and a push were administered, and often a slap on the ears. After this third and final halt, we were marched into a long, narrow dining room, where a rush was made for the table.

The table reached the length of the room and was uncovered and uninviting. Long benches without backs were put for the patients to sit on, and over these they had to crawl in order to face the table. Placed close together all along the table were large dressing-bowls filled with a pinkish-looking stuff which the patients called tea. By each bowl was laid a piece of bread, cut thick and buttered. A small saucer containing five prunes accompanied the bread. One fat woman made a rush, and jerking up several saucers from those around her emptied their contents into her own saucer. Then while holding to her own bowl she lifted up another and drained its contents at one gulp. This she did to a second bowl in shorter time than it takes to tell it. Indeed, I was so amused at her successful grabbings that when I looked at my own share the woman opposite, without so much as by your leave, grabbed my bread and left me without any.

Another patient, seeing this, kindly offered me hers, but I declined with thanks and turned to the nurse and asked for more. As she flung a thick piece down on the table she made some remark about the fact that if I forgot where my home was I had not forgotten how to eat. I tried the bread, but the butter was so horrible that one could not eat it. A blue-eyed German girl on the opposite side of the table told me I could have unbuttered bread if I wished, and that very few were able to eat the butter. I turned my attention to the prunes and found that very few of them would be sufficient. A patient near asked me to give them to her. I did so. My bowl of tea was all that was left. I tasted, and one taste was enough. It had no sugar, and it tasted as if it had been made in copper. It was as weak as water. This was also transferred to a hungrier patient, in spite of the protest of Miss Neville. "You must force the food down," she said, "else you will be sick, and who knows but what, with these surroundings, you may go crazy. To have a good brain the stomach must be cared for." "It is impossible for me to eat that stuff," I replied, and, despite all her urging, I ate nothing that night.

It did not require much time for the patients to consume all that was eatable on the table, and then we got our orders to form in line in the hall. When this was done the doors before us were unlocked and we were ordered to proceed back to the sitting-room. Many of the patients crowded near us, and I was again urged to play, both by them and by the nurses. To please the patients I promised to play and Miss Tillie Mayard was to sing. The first thing she asked me to play was "Rock-a-by Baby," and I did so. She sang it beautifully.

IN THE BATH.

Scrubbed with Soft Soap and Put to Bed in a Wet Gown.

A few more songs and we were told to go with Miss Grupe. We were taken into a cold, wet bathroom, and I was ordered to undress. Did I protest? Well, I never grew so earnest in my life as when I tried to beg off. They said if I did not they would use force and that it would not be very gentle. At this I noticed one of the craziest women in the ward standing by the filled bathtub with a large, discolored rag in her hands. She was chattering away to herself and chuckling in a manner which seemed to me fiendish. I knew now what was to be done with me. I shivered. They began to undress me, and one by one they pulled off my clothes. At last everything was gone excepting one garment. "I will not remove it." I said vehemently, but they took it off. I gave one glance at the group of patients gathered at the door watching the scene, and I jumped into the bathtub with more energy than grace.

The water was ice-cold, and I again began to protest. How useless it all was! I begged, at least, that the patients be made to go away, but was ordered to shut up. The crazy woman began to scrub me. I can find no other word that will express it but scrubbing. From a small tin pan she took some soft soap and rubbed it all over me, even all over my face and my pretty hair. I was at last past seeing or speaking, although I had begged that my hair be left untouched. Rub, rub, rub, went the old woman, chattering to herself. My teeth chattered and my limbs were goose-fleshed and blue with cold. Suddenly I got, one after the other, three buckets of water over my head— ice cold water, too—into my eyes, my ears, my nose and my mouth. I think I experienced some of the sensations of a drowning person as they dragged me, agasping, shivering and quaking, from the tub. For once I did look insane. I caught a glance of the indescribable look on the faces of my companions, who had witnessed my fate and knew theirs was surely following. Unable to control myself at the absurd picture I presented, I burst into roars of laughter. They put me, dripping wet, into a short canton flannel slip, labeled across the extreme end in large black letters, "Lunatic Asylum, B.I., H.6." The letters mean Blackwell's Island, Hall 6.

By this time Miss Mayard had been undressed, and, much as I hated my recent bath, I would have taken another if by it I could have saved her the experience. Imagine plunging that sick girl into a cold bath when it made me, who have never been ill, shake as if with ague. I heard her explain to Miss Grupe that her head was still sore from her illness. Her hair was short and had mostly come out, and she asked that the crazy woman be made to rub more gently, but Miss Grupe said: "There isn't much fear of hurting you. Shut up, or you'll get it worse." Miss Mayard did shut up, and that was my last look at her for the night.

I was hurried into a room where there were six beds, and had been put into bed when some one came along and jerked me out again, saying: "Nellie Brown has to be put in a room alone to-night, for I suppose she's noisy." I was taken to room 28 and left to try and make an impression on the bed. It was an impossible task. The bed had been made high in the center and sloping on either side. At the first touch my head flooded the pillow with water, and my wet slip transferred some of its dampness to the sheet. When Miss Grupe came in I asked if I could not have a night-gown. "We have no such things in this institution," she said. "I do not like to sleep without," I replied. "Well, I don't care about that," she said. "You are in a public institution now, and you can't expect to get anything. This is charity, and you should be thankful for what you get." "But the city pays to keep these places up," I urged, "and pays people to be kind to the unfortunates brought here." "Well, you don't need to expect any kindness here, for you won't get it," she said, and she went out and closed the door.

A sheet and an oilcloth were under me, and a sheet and black wool blanket above. I never felt anything so annoying as that wool blanket as I tried to keep it around my shoulders to stop the chills from getting underneath. When I pulled it up I left my feet bare, and when I pulled it down my shoulders were exposed. There was absolutely nothing in the room but the bed and myself. As the door had been locked I imagined I should be left alone for the night, but I heard the sound of the heavy tread of two women down the hall. They stopped at every door, unlocked it, and in a few moments I could hear them relock it. This they did without the least attempt at quietness down the whole length of the opposite side of the hall and up to my room. Here they paused. The key was inserted in the lock and turned. I watched those about to enter. In they came, dressed in brown and white striped dresses, fastened by brass buttons, large, white aprons, a heavy green cord about the waist, from which dangled a bunch of large keys, and small, white caps on their heads. Being dressed as were the attendants of the day, I knew they were nurses. The first one carried a lantern, and she flashed its light into my face while she said to her assistant: "This is Nellie Brown." Looking at her, I asked: "Who are you?" The night nurse, my dear," she replied, and, wishing that I would sleep well, she went out and locked the door after her. Several times during the night they came into my room, and even had I been able to sleep, the unlocking of the heavy door, their loud talking, and heavy tread, would have awakened me.

THE HORROR OF FIRE.

Escape Practically Impossible in Case
the Building Should Burn.

I could not sleep, so I lay in bed picturing to myself the horrors in case a
fire should break out in the asylum. Every door is locked separately and the
windows are heavily barred, so that escape is impossible. In the one building
alone there are, I think Dr. Ingram told me, some three hundred women.
They are locked, one to ten to a room. It is impossible to get out unless
these doors are unlocked. A fire is not improbable, but one of the most likely
occurrences. Should the building burn, the jailers or nurses would never
think of releasing their crazy patients. This I can prove to you later when I
come to tell of the poor things instructed to their care. As I say, in case of
fire, not a dozen women could escape. All would be left to roast to death.
Even if the nurses were kind, which they are not, it would require more
presence of mind than women of their class possess to risk the flames and
their own lives while they unlocked the hundred doors for the insane prisoners. Unless there is a change there will some day be a tale of horror never
equaled.

In this connection is an amusing incident which happened just previous
to my release. I was talking with Dr. Ingram about many things, and at last
told him what I thought would be the result of a fire. "The nurses are expected to open the doors," he said. "But you know positively that they would
not wait to do that." I said, "and these women would burn to death." He
sat silent, unable to contradict my assertion. "Why don't you have it changed?"
I asked. "What can I do?" he replied. "I offer suggestions and my brain is
tired, but what good does it do?" he asked, turning to me, the proclaimed
insane girl. "Well, I should insist on them having locks put in, as I have
seen in some places that by turning a crank at the end of the hall you can
lock or unlock every door on the one side. Then there would be some chance
of escape. Now, every door being locked separately, there is absolutely none."
Dr. Ingram turned to me with an anxious look on his kind face as he asked,
slowly: "Nellie Brown, what institution have you been an inmate of before
you came here?" "None. I never was confined in any institution, except
boarding-school, in my life." "Where then did you see the locks you have
described?" I had seen them in the new Western Penitentiary at Pittsburg,
Pa., but I did not say so. I merely answered: "Oh, I have seen them in a
place I was in—I mean as a visitor." "There is only one place I know of
where they have those locks," he said, sadly, "and that is at Sing Sing." The
inference is conclusive. I laughed very heartily over the implied accusation,

and tried to assure him that I had never, up to date, been an inmate of Sing Sing or even ever visited it.

Just as the morning began to dawn I went to sleep. It did not seem many moments until I was rudely awakened and told to get up, the window being opened and the clothing pulled off me. My hair was still wet and I had pains all through me, as if I had the rheumatism. Some clothing was flung on the floor and I was told to take what I got and keep quiet by the apparently head nurse, Miss Grady. I looked at it. One underskirt made of coarse dark cotton goods and a cheap white calico dress with a black spot in it. I tied the strings of the skirt around me and put on the little dress. It was made, as are all those worn by the patients, into a straight, tight waist sewed on to a straight skirt. As I buttoned the waist I noticed the underskirt was about six inches longer than the upper and for a moment I sat down on the bed and laughed at my own appearance. No woman ever longed for a mirror more than I did at that moment.

I saw the other patients hurrying past in the hall, so I decided not to lose anything that might be going on. We numbered forty-five patients in Hall 6, and were sent to the bathroom, where there were two coarse towels. I watched crazy patients who had the most dangerous eruptions all over their faces dry on the towels and then saw women with clean skins turn to use them. I went to the bathtub and washed my face at the running faucet and my underskirt did duty for a towel.

THE FIRST MORNING.

Combed with a Public Comb, the Breakfast and the Uniform.

Before I had completed my ablutions a bench was brought into the bathroom. Miss Grupe and Miss McCarten came in with combs in their hands. We were told to sit down on the bench and the hair of forty-five women was combed with one patient, two nurses, and six combs. As I saw some of the sore heads combed I thought this was another dose I had not bargained for. Miss Tillie Mayard had her own comb, but it was taken from her by Miss Grady. Oh, that combing! I never realized before what the expression "I'll give you a combing" meant, but I knew then. My hair, all matted and wet from the night previous, was pulled and jerked, and, after expostulating to no avail, I set my teeth and endured the pain. They refused to give me my hairpins, and my hair was arranged in one plait and tied with a red cotton rag. My curly bangs refused to stay back.

After this we went to the sitting-room and I looked for my companions.

At first I looked vainly, unable to distinguish them from the other patients, but after a while I recognized Miss Mayard by her short hair. "How did you sleep after your cold bath?" "I almost froze, and then the noise kept me awake. It's dreadful! My nerves were so unstrung before I came here, and I fear I shall not be able to stand the strain." I did the best I could to cheer her. I asked that we be given additional clothing, at least as much as custom says women shall wear, but they told me to shut up; that we had as much as they intended to give us.

We were compelled to get up at 5:30 o'clock, and at 7:15 we were told to collect in the hall, where the experience of waiting, as on the evening previous, was repeated. When we got into the dining-room at last we found a bowl of cold tea, a slice of buttered bread and a saucer of oatmeal, with molasses on it, for each patient. I was hungry, but the food would not down. I asked for unbuttered bread and was given it. I cannot tell you of anything which is the same dirty, black color. It was hard, and in places nothing more than dried dough. I found a spider in my slice, so I did not eat it. I tried the oatmeal and molasses, but it was wretched, and so I endeavored, but without much show of success to choke down the tea.

After we were back to the sitting-room a number of women were ordered to make the beds, and some of the patients were put to scrubbing and others given different duties which covered all the work in the hall. It is not the attendants who keep the institution so nice for the poor patients, as I had always thought, but the patients, who do it all themselves—even to cleaning the nurses bedrooms and caring for their clothing.

About 9:30 the new patients, of which I was one, were told to go out to see the doctor. I was taken in and my lungs and my heart were examined by the flirty young doctor who was the first to see us the day we entered. The one who made out the report, if I mistake not, was the assistant superintendent, Ingram. A few questions and I was allowed to return to the sitting-room.

I came in and saw Miss Grady with my note-book and long lead pencil bought just for the occasion. "I want my book and pencil," I said, quite truthfully. "It helps me remember things." I was very anxious to get it to make notes in and was disappointed when she said: "You can't have it, so shut up." Some days after I asked Dr. Ingram if I could have it, and he promised to consider the matter. When I again referred to it, he said that Miss Grady said I only brought a book there; that I had no pencil. I was provoked, and insisted that I had, whereupon I was advised to fight against the imaginations of my brain.

After the housework was completed by the patients, and as the day was fine, but cold, we were told to go out in the hall and get on shawls and hats for a walk. Poor patients! How eager they were for a breath of air; how eager for a slight release from their prison. They went swiftly into the hall and there was a skirmish for hats. Such hats!

THE VIOLENT PATIENTS.

Unspeakable Scenes in the Yard— The Evil of Enforced Idleness.

We had not gone many paces when I saw, proceeding from every walk, long lines of women guarded by nurses. How many there were! Every way I looked I could see them in the queer dresses, comical straw hats and shawls, marching slowly around. I eagerly watched the passing lines and a thrill of horror crept over me at the sight. Vacant eyes and meaningless faces, and their tongues uttered meaningless nonsense. One crowd passed and I noted, by nose as well as eyes, that they were fearfully dirty. "Who are they?" I asked of a patient near me. "They are considered the most violent on the island," she replied. "They are from the Lodge, the first building with the high steps." Some were yelling, some were cursing, others were singing or praying or preaching, as the fancy struck them, and they made up the most miserable collection of humanity I had ever seen. As the din of their passing faded in the distance there came another sight I can never forget:

A long cable rope fastened to wide leather belts, and these belts locked around the waists of fifty-two women. At the end of the rope was a heavy iron cart, and in it two women—one nursing a sore foot, another screaming at some nurse, saying: "You beat me and I shall not forget it. You want to kill me," and then she would sob and cry. The women "on the rope," as the patients call it, were each busy on their individual freaks. Some were yelling all the while. One who had blue eyes saw me look at her, and she turned as far as she could, talking and smiling, with that terrible, horrifying look of absolute insanity stamped on her. The doctors might safely judge on her case. The horror of that sight to one who had never been near an insane person before, was something unspeakable. "God help them!" breathed Miss Neville. "It is so dreadful I cannot look." On they passed, but for their places to be filled by more. Can you imagine the sight? According to one of the physicians there are 1600 insane women on Blackwell's Island.

I was annoyed a great deal by nurses who had heard my romantic story calling to those in charge of us to ask which one I was. I was pointed out repeatedly.

It was not long until the dinner hour arrived, and I was so hungry that I felt I could eat anything. The same old story of standing for a half and three-quarters of an hour in the hall was repeated before we got down to our dinners. The bowls in which we had had our tea were now filled with soup, and on a plate was one cold boiled potato and a chunk of beef, which, on investigation, proved to be slightly spoiled. There were no knives or forks, and the patients looked fairly savage as they took the tough beef in their fingers and pulled in opposition to their teeth. Those toothless or with poor teeth could not eat it. One tablespoon was given for the soup, and a piece of bread was the final entree. Butter is never allowed at dinner nor coffee or tea. Miss Mayard could not eat, and I saw many of the sick ones turn away in disgust. I was getting very weak from the want of food and tried to eat a slice of bread. After the first few bites hunger asserted itself, and I was able to eat all but the crusts of the one slice.

Superintendent Dent went through the sitting-room, giving an occasional "How do you do?" "How are you to-day?" here and there among the patients. His voice was as cold as the hall, and the patients made no movement to tell him of their sufferings. I asked some of them to tell how they were suffering from the cold and insufficiency of clothing, but they replied that the nurse would beat them if they told.

I was never so tired as I grew sitting on those benches. Several of the patients would sit on one foot or sideways to make a change, but they were always reproved and told to sit up straight. If they talked they were scolded and told to shut up; if they wanted to walk around in order to take the stiffness out of them, they were told to sit down and be still. What, excepting torture, would produce insanity quicker than this treatment? Here is a class of women sent to be cured. I would like the expert physicians who are condemning me for my action, which has proven their ability, to take a perfectly sane and healthy woman, shut her up and make her sit from 6 a.m. until 8 p.m. on straight-back benches, do not allow her to talk or move during those hours, give her no reading and let her know nothing of the world or its doings, give her bad food and harsh treatment, and see how long it will take to make her insane. Two months would make her a mental and physical wreck.

BAD FOOD AND WORSE HELP.

When One Falls Ill the Natural Thing is to Simply Die.

I have described my first day in the asylum, and as my other nine were exactly the same in the general run of things it would be tiresome to tell about each. In giving this story I expect to be contradicted by many who are exposed. I merely tell in common words, without exaggeration, of my life in a mad-house for ten days. The eating was one of the most horrible things.

Excepting the first two days after I entered the asylum, there was no salt for the food. The hungry and even famishing women made an attempt to eat the horrible messes. Mustard and vinegar were put on meat and in soup to give it a taste, but it only helped to make it worse. Even that was all consumed after two days, and the patients had to try to choke down fresh fish, just boiled in water, without salt, pepper or butter; mutton, beef and potatoes without the faintest seasoning. The most insane refused to swallow the food and were threatened with punishment. In our short walks we passed the kitchen where food was prepared for the nurses and doctors. There we got glimpses of melons and grapes and all kinds of fruits, beautiful white bread and nice meats, and the hungry feeling would be increased tenfold. I spoke to some of the physicians, but it had no effect, and when I was taken away the food was yet unsalted.

My heart ached to see the sick patients grow sicker over the table. I saw Miss Tillie Mayard so suddenly overcome at a bite that she had to rush from the diningroom and then got a scolding for doing so. When the patients complained of the food they were told to shut up; that they would not have as good if they were at home, and that it was too good for charity patients.

A German Girl, Louise—I have forgotten her last name—did not eat for several days and at last one morning she was missing. From the conversation of the nurses I found she was suffering from a high fever. Poor thing! she told me she unceasingly prayed for death. I watched the nurses make a patient carry such food as the well ones were refusing up to Louise's room. Think of that stuff for a fever patient! Of course, she refused it. Then I saw a nurse, Miss McCarten, go to test her temperature, and she returned with the report of it being some 150 degrees. I smiled at the report, and Miss Grupe, seeing it, asked me how high my temperature had ever run. I refused to answer. Miss Grady then decided to try her ability. She returned with the report of 99 degrees.

Miss Tillie Mayard suffered more than any of us from the cold, and yet she tried to follow my advice to be cheerful and try to keep up for a short time. Superintendent Dent brought in a man to see me. He felt my pulse and my head and examined my tongue. I told them how cold it was, and assured them that I did not need medical aid, but that Miss Mayard did, and they should transfer their attentions to her. They did not answer me, and I was pleased to see Miss Mayard leave her place and come forward to them. She spoke to the doctors and told them she was ill, but they paid no attention to her. The nurses came and dragged her back to the bench, and after the doctors left they asked, "After awhile, when you see that the doctors will not notice you, you will quit running up to them." Before the doctors left me I heard one say—I cannot give it in his exact words—that my pulse and eyes were not that of an insane girl, but Superintendent Dent assured him that in cases such as mine such tests failed. After watching me for awhile he said my face was the brightest he had ever seen for a lunatic. The nurses had on heavy undergarments and coats, but they refused to give us shawls.

Nearly all night long I listened to a woman cry about the cold and beg for God to let her die. Another one yelled "Murder!" at frequent intervals and "Police!" at others until my flesh felt creepy.

The second morning, after we had begun our endless "set" for the day, two of the nurses, assisted by some patients, brought the woman in who had begged the night previous for God to take her home. I was not surprised at her prayer. She appeared easily seventy years old and she was blind. Although the halls were freezing-cold, that old woman had no more clothing on than the rest of us, which I have described. When she was brought into the sitting-room and placed on the hard bench, she cried: "Oh, what are you doing with me? I am cold, so cold. Why can't I stay in bed or have a shawl?" and then she would get up and endeavor to feel her way to leave the room. Sometimes the attendants would jerk her back to the bench, and again they would let her walk and heartlessly laugh when she bumped against the table or the edge of the benches. At one time she said the heavy shoes which charity provides hurt her feet, and she took them off. The nurses made two patients put them on her again, and when she did it several times, and fought against having them on, I counted seven people at her at once trying to put the shoes on her. The old woman then tried to lie down on the bench, but they pulled her up again. It sounded so pitiful to hear her cry: "Oh, give me a pillow and pull the covers over me, I am so cold."

At this I saw Miss Grupe sit down on her and run her cold hands over the woman's face and down inside the neck of her dress. At the old woman's cries she laughed savagely, as did the other nurses, and repeated her cruel action. That day the old woman was carried away to another ward.

MADE MAD BY THE SURROUNDINGS.

The Tragic Case of Miss Tillie Mayard—
Very Near to Detection.

Miss Tillie Mayard suffered greatly from cold. One morning she sat on the bench next to me and was livid with the cold. Her limbs shook and her teeth chattered. I spoke to the three attendants who sat with coats on at the table in the center of the floor. "It is cruel to lock people up and then freeze them," I said. They replied she had on as much as any of the rest, and she would get no more. Just then Miss Mayard took a fit and every patient looked frightened. Miss Neville caught her in her arms and held her, although the nurses roughly said: "Let her fall on the floor and it will teach her a lesson." Miss Neville told them what she thought of their actions, and then I got orders to make my appearance in the office.

Just as I reached there Superintendent Dent came to the door and I told him how we were suffering from the cold, and of Miss Mayard's condition. Doubtless, I spoke incoherently, for I told of the state of the food, the treatment of the nurses and their refusal to give more clothing, the condition of Miss Mayard, and the nurses telling us, because the asylum was a public institution, we could not expect even kindness. Assuring him that I needed no medical aid, I told him to go to Miss Mayard. He did so. From Miss Neville and other patients I learned what transpired. Miss Mayard was still in the fit and he caught her roughly between the eyebrows or thereabouts, and pinched until her face was crimson from the rush of blood to the head, and her senses returned. All day afterward she suffered from terrible headache, and from that on she grew worse.

Insane? Yes, insane; and as I watched the insanity slowly creep over the mind that had appeared to be all right I secretly cursed the doctors, the nurses and all public institutions. Some one may say that she was insane at some time previous to her consignment to the asylum. Then if she were, was this the proper place to send a woman just convalescing, to be given cold baths, deprived of sufficient clothing and fed with horrible food?

On this morning I had a long conversation with Dr. Ingram, the assistant superintendent of the asylum. I found that he was kind to the helpless beings in his charge. I began my old complaint of the cold, and he called Miss Grady to the office and ordered more clothing given the patients. Miss Grady said if I made a practice of telling it would be a serious thing for me, she warned me in time.

Many visitors looking for missing girls came to see me. Miss Grady yelled in the door from the hall one day: "Nellie Brown, you're wanted." I went to the sitting-room at the end of the hall, and there sat a gentleman who had known me intimately for years. I saw by the sudden blanching of his face and his inability to speak that the sight of me was wholly unexpected and had shocked him terribly. In an instant I determined, if he betrayed me as Nellie Bly, to say I had never seen him before. However, I had one card to play and I risked it. With Miss Grady within touching distance I whispered hurriedly to him, in language more expressive than elegant: "Don't give me away." I knew by the expression of his eye that he understood, so I said to Miss Grady: "I do not know this man." "Do you know her?" asked Miss Grady. "No; this is not the young lady I came in search of," he replied, in a strained voice. "If you do not know her you cannot stay here," she said, and she took him to the door. All at once a fear struck me that he would think I had been sent there through some mistake and would tell my friends and make an effort to have me released. So I waited until Miss Grady had the door unlocked. I knew that she would have to lock it before she could leave, and the time required to do so would give me opportunity to speak, so I called: "One moment, senor." He returned to me and I asked aloud: "Do you speak Spanish, senor?" and then whispered, "It's all right. I'm after an item. Keep still." "No," he said, with a peculiar emphasis, which I knew meant that he would keep my secret.

CHOKINGS AND BEATINGS.

The Nurses Amuse Themselves by Worrying their Helpless Charges.

People in the world can never imagine the length of days to those in asylums. They seemed never ending, and we welcomed any event that might give us something to think about as well as talk of. There is nothing to read, and the only bit of talk that never wears out is conjuring up delicate food that they will get as soon as they get out. Anxiously the hour was watched for when the boat arrived to see if there were any new unfortunates to be added to our ranks. When they came and were ushered into the sitting-room the patients would express sympathy to one another for them and were anxious to show them little marks of attention. Hall 6 was the receiving hall, so that was how we saw all newcomers.

Soon after my advent a girl called Urena Little-Page was brought in. She was, as she had been born, silly, and her tender spot was, as with many sensible women, her age. She claimed eighteen, and would grow very angry if told to the contrary. The nurses were not long in finding this out, and then they teased her. "Urena," said Miss Grady, "the doctors say that you are thirty-three instead of eighteen," and the other nurses laughed. They kept up this until the simple creature began to yell and cry, saying she wanted to go home and that everybody treated her badly. After they had gotten all the amusement out of her they wanted and she was crying, they began to scold and tell her to keep quiet. She grew more hysterical every moment until they pounced upon her and slapped her face and knocked her head in a lively fashion. This made the poor creature cry the more, and so they choked her. Yes, actually choked her. Then they dragged her out to the closet, and I heard her terrified cries hush into smothered ones. After several hours' absence she returned to the sitting-room, and I plainly saw the marks of their fingers on her throat for the entire day.

This punishment seemed to awaken their desire to administer more. They returned to the sitting-room and caught hold of an old gray-haired woman whom I have heard addressed both as Mrs. Grady and Mrs. O'Keefe. She was insane, and she talked almost continually to herself and to those near her. She never spoke very loud, and at the time I speak of was sitting harmlessly chattering to herself. They grabbed her, and my heart ached as she cried: "For God sake, ladies, don't let them beat me." "Shut up, you hussy!" said Miss Grady as she caught the woman by her gray hair and dragged her shrieking and pleading from the room. She was also taken to the closet, and her cries grew lower and lower, and then ceased.

The nurses returned to the room and Miss Grady remarked that she had "settled the old fool for awhile." I told some of the physicians of the occurrence, but they did not pay any attention to it.

One of the characters in Hall 6 was Matilda, a little old German woman, who, I believe, went insane over the loss of money. She was small, and had a pretty pink complexion. She was not much trouble, except at times. She would take spells, when she would talk into the steam-heaters or get up on a chair and talk out of the windows. In these conversations she railed at the lawyers who had taken her property. The nurses seemed to find a great deal of amusement in teasing the harmless old soul. One day I sat beside Miss Grady and Miss Grupe, and heard them tell her perfectly vile things to call Miss McCarten. After telling her to say these things they would send her to the other nurse, but Matilda proved that she, even in her state, had more sense than they. "I cannot tell you. It is private," was all she would say. I saw Miss Grady, on a pretense of whispering to her, spit in her ear. Matilda quietly wiped her ear and said nothing.

SOME UNFORTUNATE STORIES.

A Few of the Apparently Sane Women
Tell of Their Troubles.

By this time I had made the acquaintance of the greater number of the forty-five women in hall 6. Let me introduce a few. Louise, the pretty German girl whom I have spoken of formerly as being sick with fever, had the delusion that the spirits of her dead parents were with her. "I have gotten many beatings from Miss Grady and her assistants," she said, "and I am unable to eat the horrible food they give us. I ought not to be compelled to freeze for want of proper clothing. Oh! I pray nightly that I may be taken to my papa and mamma. One night, when I was confined at Bellevue, Dr. Field came; I was in bed, and weary of the examination. At last I said: 'I am tired of this. I will talk no more.' 'Won't you?' he said, angrily. 'I'll see if I can't make you.' With this he laid his crutch on the side of the bed, and, getting up on it, he pinched me very severely in the ribs. I jumped up straight in bed, and said: 'What do you mean by this?' 'I want to teach you to obey when I speak to you,' he replied. If I could only die and go to papa!" When I left she was confined to bed with a fever, and maybe by this time she has her wish.

There is a Frenchwoman confined in hall 6, or was during my stay, whom I firmly believe to be perfectly sane. I watched her and talked with her every day, excepting the last three, and I was unable to find any delusion or mania in her. Her name is Josephine Despreau, if that is spelled correctly, and her husband and all her friends are in France. Josephine feels her position keenly. Her lips tremble, and she breaks down crying when she talks of her helpless condition. "How did you get here?" I asked.

"One morning as I was trying to get breakfast I grew deathly sick, and two officers were called in by the woman of the house, and I was taken to the station-house. I was unable to understand their proceedings, and they paid little attention to my story. Doings in this country were new to me, and before I realized it I was lodged as an insane woman in this asylum. When I first came I cried that I was here without hope of release, and for crying Miss Grady and her assistants choked me until they hurt my throat, for it has been sore ever since."

A pretty young Hebrew woman spoke so little English I could not get her story except as told by the nurses. They said her name is Sarah Fishbaum, and that her husband put her in the asylum because she had a fondness for other men than himself. Granting that Sarah was insane, and about men, let me tell you how the nurses tried to cure her. They would call her up and say: "Sarah, wouldn't you like to have a nice young man?" "Oh, yes; a young man is all right," Sarah would reply in her few English words. "Well, Sarah, wouldn't you like us to speak a good word to some of the doctors for you? Wouldn't you like to have one of the doctors?" And then would ask her which doctor she preferred, and advise her to make advances to him when he visited the hall, and so on.

I had been watching and talking with a fair-complexioned woman for several days, and I was at a loss to see why she had been sent there, she was so sane. "Why did you come here?" I asked her one day, after we had indulged in a long conversation. "I was sick," she replied. "Are you sick mentally?" I urged. "Oh, no; what gave you such an idea? I had been overworking myself, and I broke down. Having some family trouble, and being penniless and nowhere to go, I applied to the commissioners to be sent to the poor-house until I would be able to go to work." "But they do not send poor people here unless they are insane," I said. "Don't you know there are only insane women, or those supposed to be so, sent here?" "I knew after I got here that the majority of these women were insane, but then I believed them when they told me this was the place they sent all the poor who applied for aid as I had done."

"How have you been treated?" I asked. "Well, so far I have escaped a beating, although I have been sickened at the sight of many and the recital of more. When I was brought here they went to give me a bath, and the very disease for which I needed doctoring and from which I was suffering made it necessary that I should not bathe. But they put me in; and my sufferings were increased greatly for weeks thereafter."

A Mrs. McCartney, whose husband is a tailor, seems perfectly rational and has not one fancy. Mary Hughes and Mrs. Louise Schanz showed no obvious traces of insanity.

NURSES WHO SWEAR.

Patients Hurried Into the Asylum
Without Sufficient Examination.

One day two new-comers were added to our list. The one was an idiot, Carrie Glass, and the other was a nice-looking German girl—quite young, she seemed, and when she came in all the patients spoke of her nice appearance and apparent sanity. Her name was Margaret. She told me she had been a cook, and was extremely neat. One day, after she had scrubbed the kitchen floor, the chambermaids came down and deliberately soiled it. Her temper was aroused and she began to quarrel with them; an officer was called and she was taken to an asylum. "How can they say I am insane, merely because I allowed my temper to run away with me?" she complained. "Other people are not shut up for crazy when they get angry. I suppose the only thing to do is to keep quiet and so avoid the beatings which I see others get. No one can say one word about me. I do everything I am told and all the work they give me. I am obedient in every respect, and I do everything to prove to them that I am sane."

One day an insane woman was brought in. She was noisy, and Miss Grady gave her a beating and blacked her eye. When the doctors noticed it and asked if it was done before she came there the nurses said it was.

While I was in hall 6 I never heard the nurses address the patients except to scold or yell at them, unless it was to tease them. They spent much of their time gossiping about the physicians and about the other nurses in a manner that was not elevating. Miss Grady nearly always interspersed her conversation with profane language, and generally began her sentences by calling on the name of the Lord. The names she called the patients were of the lowest and most profane type. One evening she quarreled with another nurse while we were at supper about the bread, and when the nurse had gone out she called her bad names and made ugly remarks about her.

In the evenings a woman, whom I suppose to be head cook for the doctors, used to come up and bring raisins, grapes, apples, and crackers to the nurses. Imagine the feelings of the hungry patients as they sat and watched the nurses eat what was to them a dream of luxury.

One afternoon, Dr. Dent was talking to a patient, Mrs. Turney, about some trouble she had had with a nurse or matron. A short time after we were taken down to supper and this woman who had beaten Mrs. Turney, and of whom Dr. Dent spoke, was sitting at the door of our dining-room. Suddenly Mrs. Turney picked up her bowl of tea, and, rushing out of the door flung it at the woman who had beat her. There was some loud screaming and Mrs. Turney was returned to her place. The next day she was transferred to the "rope gang," which is supposed to be composed of the most dangerous and most suicidal women on the island.

At first I could not sleep and did not want to so long as I could hear anything new. The night nurses may have complained of the fact. At any rate one night they came in and tried to make me take a dose of some mixture out of a glass "to make me sleep," they said. I told them I would do nothing of the sort and they left me, I hoped, for the night. My hopes were vain, for in a few minutes they returned with a doctor, the same that received us on our arrival. He insisted that I take it, but I was determined not to lose my wits even for a few hours. When he saw I was not to be coaxed he grew rather rough, and said he had wasted too much time with me already. That if I did not take it he would put it into my arm with a needle. It occurred to me that if he put it into my arm I could not get rid of it, but if I swallowed it there was one hope, so I said I would take it. I smelt it and it smelt like laudanum, and it was a horrible dose. No sooner had they left the room and locked me in that I tried to see how far down my throat my finger would go.

LAST DAYS.

One Good Nurse—Sitting Still for Five Days—Soap Only Once a Week.

I want to say that the night nurse, Burns, in hall 6 seemed very kind and patient to the poor, afflicted people. The other nurses made several attempts to talk to me about lovers, and asked me if I would not like to have one. They did not find me very communicative on the, to them, popular subject.

Once a week the patients are given a bath, and that is the only time they see soap. A patient handed me a piece of soap one day about the size of a thimble. I considered it a great compliment in her wanting to be kind, but

I thought she would appreciate the cheap soap more than I, so I thanked her but refused to take it. On bathing day the tub is filled with water, and the patients are washed, one after the other, without a change of water. This is done until the water is really thick, and then it is allowed to run out and the tub is refilled without being washed. The same towels are used on all the women, those with eruptions as well as those without. The healthy patients fight for a change of water, but they are compelled to submit to the dictates of the lazy, tyrannical nurses. The dresses are seldom changed oftener than once a month. If the patient has a visitor, I have seen the nurses hurry her out and change her dress before the visitor comes in. This keeps up the appearance of careful and good management.

The patients who are not able to take care of themselves get into beastly conditions, and the nurses never look after them, but order some of the patients to do so.

For five days we were compelled to sit in the room all day. I never put in such a long time. Every patient was stiff and sore and tired. We would get in little groups on benches and torture our stomachs by conjuring up thoughts of what we would eat first when we got out. If I had not known how hungry they were and the pitiful side of it, the conversation would have been very amusing. As it was it only made me sad. When the subject of eating, which seemed to be the favorite one, was worn out, they used to give their opinions of the institution and its management. The condemnation of the nurses and the eatables was unanimous.

As the days passed Miss Tillie Mayard's condition grew worse. She was continually cold and unable to eat of the food provided. Day after day she sang in order to try to maintain her memory, but at last the nurse made her stop it. I talked with her daily, and I grieved to find her grow worse so rapidly. At last she got a delusion. She thought that I was trying to pass myself off for her, and that all the people who called to see Nellie Brown were friends in search of her, but that I, by some means, was trying to deceive them into the belief that I was the girl. I tried to reason with her, but found it impossible, so I kept away from her as much as possible, lest my presence should make her worse and feed the fancy.

TRANSFERRED TO ANOTHER WARD.

She is Cursed Before She Leaves and Gets No Better Quarters.

When Pauline Moser was brought to the asylum we heard the most horrible screams and an Irish girl, only partly dressed, came staggering like a drunken person up the hall yelling, "Hurrah! I have killed the divil! Lucifer,

Lucifer, Lucifer," and so on, over and over again. Then she would pull a handful of hair out, while she exultingly cried, "How I deceived the divils. They always said God made Hell but he didn't." After she had been there an hour or so, Dr. Dent came in, and as he walked down the hall, Miss Grupe whispered to the demented girl, "Here is the devil coming go for him." Surprised that she would give a mad woman such instructions, I fully expected to see the frenzied creature rush at the door. Luckily she did not, but commenced to repeat her refrain of "Oh, Lucifer." After the doctor left, Miss Grupe again tried to excite the woman by saying that the pictured minstrel on the wall was the devil, and the poor creature began to scream, "You divil, I'll give it to you," so that two nurses had to sit on her to keep her down. The attendants seemed to find amusement and pleasure in exciting the violent patients to do their worse.

I always made a point of telling the doctors I was sane, and asking to be released, but the more I endeavored to assure them of my sanity, the more they doubted it. "What are you doctors here for?" I asked one, whose name I cannot recall. "To take care of the patients and test their sanity," he replied. "Very well," I said. "There are sixteen doctors on this island, and, excepting two, I have never seen them pay any attention to the patients. How can a doctor judge a woman's sanity by merely bidding her good morning and refusing to hear her pleas for release? Even the sick ones know it is useless to say anything, for the answer will be that it is their imagination." "Try every test on me," I have urged others. "and tell me am I sane or insane? Try my pulse, my heart, my eyes; ask me to stretch out my arm, to work my fingers, as Dr. Field did at Bellevue, and then tell me if I am sane." They would not heed me, for they thought I raved.

Again I said to one: "You have no right to keep sane people here. I am sane, have always been so, and I must insist on a thorough examination or be released. Several of the women here are also sane. Why can't they be free?" "They are all insane," was the reply, "and suffering from delusions."

After a long talk with Dr. Ingram, he said: "I will transfer you to a quieter ward." An hour later Miss Grady called me into the hall, and, after calling me all the vile and profane names a woman could ever remember, she told me it was a lucky thing for my "hide" that I was transferred, or else she would pay me for remembering so well to tell Dr. Ingram everything. "You d--n hussy, you forget all about yourself, but you never forget anything to tell the doctor." After calling Miss Neville, whom Dr. Ingram also kindly transferred, Miss Grady took us to the hall above, No. 7.

In hall 7 there are Mrs. Kroener, Miss Fitzpatrick, Miss Finney and Miss Hart. I did not see as cruel treatment as downstairs; but I heard them make ugly remarks and threats, twist the fingers and slap the faces of the unruly patients. The night nurse, Conway, I believe her name is, is very cross. In hall 7, if any of the patients possessed any modesty, they soon lost it. Everyone was compelled to undress in the hall before their own door, and to fold their clothes and leave them there until morning. I asked to undress in my room, but Miss Conway told me if she ever caught me at such a trick she would give me cause not to want to repeat it.

The first doctor I saw here—Dr. Caldwell—chucked me under the chin, and as I was tired refusing to tell where my home was I would only speak to him in Spanish.

THE "RETREAT" AND "ROPE GANG."

Some of the Cruel Atrocities Practised There—the Last Good-By.

A Mrs. Cotter told me that for speaking to a man she was sent to the Retreat. "The remembrance of that is enough to make me mad. For crying the nurses beat me with a broom-handle and jumped on me, injuring me internally, so that I shall never get over it. Then they tied my hands and feet, and, throwing a sheet over my head, twisted it tightly around my throat, so I could not scream, and thus put me in a bathtub filled with cold water. They held me under until I gave up every hope and became senseless. At other times they took hold of my ears and beat my head on the floor and against the wall. They pulled my hair out by the roots, so that it will never grow in again."

Mrs. Cotter here showed me proofs of her story, the dent in the back of her head and the bare spots where the hair had been taken out by the handful. I give her story as plainly as possible: "My treatment was not as bad as I have seen others get in there, but it has ruined my health, and even if I do get out of here I will be a wreck. When my husband heard of the treatment given me he threatened to expose the place if I was not removed, so I was brought here. I am well mentally now. All that old fear has left me, and the doctor has promised to allow my husband to take me home."

I made the acquaintance of Bridget McGuinness, who seems to be sane at the present time. She said she was sent to Retreat 4, and put on the "rope gang." "The beatings I got there were something dreadful. I was pulled around by the hair, held under the water until I strangled, and I was choked and kicked. The nurses would always keep a quiet patient stationed at the window to tell them when any of the doctors were approaching. It was hopeless to complain to the doctors, for they always said it was the imagination of our diseased brains, and besides we would get another beating for telling. They would hold patients under the water and threaten to leave them to die there if they did not promise not to tell the doctors. We would all promise, because we knew the doctors would not help us, and we would do anything to escape the punishment. After breaking a window I was transferred to the Lodge, the worse place on the island. It is dreadfully dirty in there, and the stench is awful. In the summer the flies swarm the place. The food is worse than we get in other wards and we are given only tin plates. Instead of the bars being on the outside, as in this ward, they are on the inside. There are many quiet patients there who have been there for years, but the nurses keep them to do the work. Among other beatings I got there, the nurses jumped on me once and broke two of my ribs.

"While I was there a pretty young girl was brought in. She had been sick, and she fought against being put in that dirty place. One night the nurses took her and after beating her, they held her naked in a cold bath, then they threw her on her bed. When morning came the girl was dead. The doctors said she died of convulsions, and that was all that was done about it.

"They inject so much morphine and chloral that the patients are made crazy. I have seen the patients wild for water from the effect of the drugs, and the nurses would refuse it to them. I have heard women beg for a whole night for one drop and it was not given them. I myself cried for water until my mouth was so parched and dry that I could not speak."

I saw the same thing myself in hall 7. The patients would beg for a drink before retiring, but the nurses—Miss Hart and the others—refused to unlock the bathroom that they might quench their thirst.

Hall 7 looks rather nice to a casual visitor. It is hung with cheap pictures and has a piano, which is presided over by Miss Mattie Morgan, who formerly was in a music store in this city. She has been in the asylum for three years. Miss Mattie has been training several of the patients to sing, with some show of success. The artiste of the hall is Under, pronounced Wanda, a Polish girl. She is a gifted pianist when she chooses to display her ability. The most difficult music she reads at a glance, and her touch and expression are perfect. On Sunday the quieter patients, whose names have been handed in by the attendants during the week, are allowed to go to church. A small Catholic chapel is on the island, and other services are also held.

A "commissioner" came one day, and made the rounds with Dr. Dent. In the basement they found half the nurses gone to dinner, leaving the other half in charge of us, as was always done. Immediately orders were given to bring the nurses back to their duties until after the patients had finished eating. Some of the patients wanted to speak about their having no salt, but were prevented.

The insane asylum on Blackwell's Island is a human rat-trap. It is easy to get in, but once there it is impossible to get out. I had intended to have myself committed to the violent wards, the Lodge and Retreat, but when I got the testimony of two sane women and could give it, I decided not to risk my health—and hair—so I did not get violent.

I had, toward the last, been shut off from all visitors, and so when the lawyer, Peter A. Hendricks, came and told me that friends of mine were willing to take charge of me if I would rather be with them than in the asylum, and I was only too glad to give my consent. I asked him to send me something to eat immediately on his arrival in the city, and then I waited anxiously for my release.

It came sooner than I had hoped. I was out "in line" taking a walk, and had just gotten interested in a poor woman who had fainted away while the nurses were trying to compel her to walk. "Good-bye; I am going home," I called to Pauline Moser, as she went past with a woman on either side of her. Sadly I said farewell to all I knew as I passed them on my way to freedom and life, while they were left behind to a fate worse than death. "Adios," I murmured to the Mexican woman. I kissed my fingers to her, and so I left my companions of hall 7.

I had looked forward so eagerly to leaving the horrible place, yet when my release came and I knew that God's sunlight was to be free for me again, there was a certain pain in leaving. For ten days I had been one of them. Foolishly enough it seemed intensely selfish to leave them to their sufferings. I felt a Quixotic desire to help them by sympathy and presence. But only for a moment. The bars were down and freedom was sweeter to me than ever.

Soon I was crossing the river and nearing New York. Once again I was a free girl after ten days in the madhouse on Blackwell's Island.

NELLIE BLY

9

Elizabeth Garver Jordan
(1865–1947)

WHEN ELIZABETH JORDAN was promoted to assistant Sunday editor of the *New York World* in 1897, it was rare for a woman to hold such a title. Her achievement proved that women could seek careers—not just jobs—in journalism, and as she moved on to even higher positions in magazine and book publishing, she demonstrated that journalism skills could be used in various fields. She left the *World* to be editor of *Harper's Bazar* (the spelling was changed to *Bazaar* in 1929), then went on to be literary adviser to Harper and Brothers, where she accepted Sinclair Lewis' first novel. At Goldwyn Pictures, she worked briefly and unsuccessfully, to her mind, as editorial director in charge of acquiring scripts. She had a Broadway play that flopped after thirteen performances, perhaps because the subject matter was ahead of its time. Called *The Lady from Oklahoma*, it ridiculed women's interest in permanent waves and cosmetic treatments, a theme that would later be picked up by Clare Boothe Luce in *The Women*. Wherever Jordan worked, she always found time to write, producing twenty-eight novels and short-story collections, collaborating with Dr. Anna Howard Shaw on the suffragist leader's autobiography, and devising the concept of a round-robin novel with *The Whole Family* (1908), which had chapters by Henry James, William Dean Howells, and others. Indeed, with such a résumé, she was a perfect role model for the new century's career woman.

What's more, Jordan was glamorous, admired by Mark Twain as well as composing-room typesetters for her wardrobe of well-tailored clothes. Even with a work schedule that often kept her at the office for eighteen hours a day she found time for music, golf, ice skating, letter writing, entertaining, and travel. Along with being ambitious, energetic, and well-organized, she had that uncommon talent of being a good listener, which earned her the loyalty of many friends, in particular, Frances Hodgson Burnett, the author of *Little Lord Fauntleroy*. She never married, but did live quite independently and elegantly in a Gramercy Square house with two professional women, her mother, a butler, and a secretary. A decent pianist, she enjoyed hosting dinner parties for witty, intelligent guests like bachelor Henry James, with whom she had a flirtation, and playing Chopin for them by candlelight.

Jordan was as relaxed and charming in the composing room as she was in the drawing room. At the *World* she was responsible for editing and laying out the Sunday edition of the paper. She spent long hours in the dirty, hot, and airless composing room bending over the stone, the newspaper form into which type was placed and locked up. A major technological change was sweeping newspapers at the end of the century: compositors who were used to handsetting type were being introduced to the linotype machine, a revolution akin to the more recent changeover from hot type produced on the linotype to computer typesetting. Compositors were disgruntled by the change, and one day a printer turned to Jordan and said, "Good heavens! What a job! Can you imagine anything worse?" To which Jordan replied: "Oh, yes! To lose it!"

Often asked for her advice on journalism as a career for a woman, she would say:

Self-confidence is the journalistic armor she will select first and wear on the outside. That she should have a good education and some worldly experience goes without saying. She will also need tact, a cool head, clear judgment, the ability to think and act quickly, a good understanding of human nature, and above all, an up-again-and-take-another spirit which no amount of discouragement can break. . . . Her sex will hinder her one hundred times to once that it will help her. Her best work will be taken as a matter of course, and anything less than her best as a deliberately planned and personal injury.

Jordan established her career with a daily fictionalized column, "True Stories of the News." At its inception the city editor told her to dig up all the facts behind news leads and write each story as fiction. She selected those bits of drama that are often covered with only a few lines in the paper—an unidentified body found in the river, the suicide of an unknown girl, an incident in a prison or courtroom or hospital. It was no simple task, as Jordan pointed out in her autobiography, *Three Rousing Cheers* (1938), to find enough dramatic ideas and all the facts surrounding them to be able to write two to three columns six days a week. People all over town gave her tips, and her day usually started with someone calling on the phone and saying: "I think I have a true story of the news here for you."

One true story turned out to be a source of many unpleasant dreams. Jordan interviewed a prominent woman who had escaped from an insane asylum and was suing her family for illegally reincarcerating her. As Jordan bent over the bed to say goodbye, the woman caught her by the throat and whispered, "Aren't you glad I'm sane now?" Tightening her hold, the woman wouldn't let go until a nurse pried Jordan loose.

"True Stories" ran without a byline, but the feature stood out in a generally gray paper: several headlines announced the themes, and line drawings broke up the eight-column, half-page layout. Jordan introduced to newspaper readers some magazine-style techniques that would later be used in the New Journalism of the 1960s. With a fictionalized narrative approach, she could describe, interpret, and write as though she were actually at a scene, watching over a sleeping child, observing a high-spending gambler lose his money. Still, every story had sources, dates, background, quotes. To produce a feature with such detail six days a week required not only prodigious reporting but remarkably fast writing.

"True Stories" was often the only human-interest story in the *World*. The human-interest angle had always been important to the undercover reporting done by Nellie Bly and Annie Laurie. When it was no longer fashionable for women to misrepresent themselves, however, the human side of the news became the province of the feature story, and undercover reporting techniques were confined to investigative pieces or in-depth series. Jordan once told an interviewer that she felt undercover assignments in the interest of reform rather than sensationalism made valuable contributions to newswriting. She added, though, that she was glad she posed as someone else only once, when she went without money to a girls' home and asked for shelter.

The "True Stories" style came naturally to her, so when she was waiting for copy to be set for the Sunday paper she started writing short stories based on her experiences at the *World*. She scribbled in pen and ink, the preferred tools of the time, and then had the manuscript copied on a typewriter. In 1898 Charles Scribner's Sons published *Tales of the City Room*, a book that influenced many women to work as journalists. In one story Jordan introduces Mrs. Ogilvie, an insecure reporter who laments that her lack of real-world experience prevents her from writing with flair. The story begins with this newsroom scene:

The trouble with my writing," said Mrs. Ogilvie, pensively, "is that it lacks local color." She was leaning on Miss Herrick's [Jordan's alter ego] desk in the city room, reading with much self-control a story of her own which had appeared in "the Searchlight" [the *World*] that morning. Not more than half of it had survived the ruthless blue pencil of Hunt, the copy-reader, whose muttered words as he had toiled over it the night before had not been prayers. In the interval between the rewriting of the last paragraph and the "building" of the "head" for the article, that gentleman had refreshed himself by confiding to a fellow-sufferer at the next desk a frank opinion of Mrs. Ogilvie's work which would have been of the greatest value to her if she had overheard it.

"All I have to do with it," he ended grimly as he lit a cigarette, "is cut out eighteen pages [pages were written in longhand] from the beginning, twenty-two pages from the end, and rewrite the middle. If only she'd begin and end her stories in the middle, it would be the salvation of us both!"

Even today these tales make interesting reading, with curious twists and O. Henry surprise endings. When Mrs. Ogilvie's husband dies after a freak accident (a safe lowered out a window falls and kills him), her ability to grieve and relate to suffering transforms her writing. It gains not just local color, but soul.

Good writing and stylistic expression, Jordan rightly believed, were necessary for any quality publication. And she put this philosophy to work during thirteen years as editor of *Harper's Bazar*, a women's magazine that did not address its subscribers as "Dear sisters in imbecility." Seeking intelligent articles for the cultivated and progressive woman, she called on many of her literary friends like James, Howells, and Charlotte Perkins Gilman for contributions.

Jordan was born to be right at home in New York's literary world. Although she would eventually have to support her parents after her father lost a fortune in the panic of 1893, she could look back on a secure childhood. The eldest of two daughters, she was born Mary Elizabeth Garver Jordan on May 9, 1865, in Milwaukee, Wisconsin, to William Francis Jordan, a prosperous meat-market owner and real-estate broker, and Margaretta (Garver) Jordan. Brought up in her father's Catholic faith and educated at St. Mary's High School in Milwaukee, as a child Jordan wanted to be a nun, while her mother envisioned a career for her as a concert pianist. Her father encouraged her to write and helped get her a job editing the women's pages of *Peck's Sun*, a paper run by his friend George W. Peck, the author of *Peck's Bad Boy*. Pictures from this time show a woman of erect posture, with a full face, gray eyes, dark hair, and an air of self-assurance.

She complained that the job was boring, so her father again used his influence to get her a position as secretary to the Milwaukee superintendent of

Elizabeth Garver Jordan

schools. During this time she had stories published in the *Chicago Tribune* and the *St. Paul* (Minnesota) *Globe*. In 1890, without any paternal connections, she went to New York and like Nellie Bly before her sought out the *World*'s managing editor, Colonel John A. Cockerill. She found him enjoying a cigar after lunch. "It is on such small details as this that vital turns in fortune often rest," she recalled in her autobiography. "The Colonel did not know my name or anything about me. He was idle for a moment or two, while he finished that cigar—and I had my chance!"

Cockerill thought Milwaukee a long way to come for a job and decided to interview her. "Did she know New York?" She didn't, but promised she would in a week. "Had she any reporting experience?" No. "Had she done interviewing?" No, but she hoped he would give her lots of it. Three years earlier Nellie Bly's energy and story ideas had charmed him; now Jordan's blend of self-confidence and modesty won him over. She was hired, but at a bad time, for Cockerill was engaged in a power struggle with Ballard Smith, an ambitious young man in charge of assignments, who would soon be the paper's editor. Smith sent her to Brooklyn to write feature stories, including a series on Long Island summer resorts that proved enjoyable: her mother came along and they went from one hotel to another on an extended holiday.

If this was the life of a reporter, Jordan had some doubts. She would later recall: "I put in from one to three hours on the actual writing. I felt guilty about it. Was I earning my salary? As a matter of record, I was very definitely doing so. I was writing on an average ten columns a week, which at the space rates then paid would have cost the *World* seventy-five dollars. I was getting thirty dollars a week and all my expenses."

Jordan would later tell women eager to follow in her footsteps that what she brought to New York was an excellent wardrobe and no experience. The wardrobe proved valuable when Smith sent her on a difficult assignment to Cape May, New Jersey, where President Benjamin Harrison, his wife, daughter, and 5-year-old grandchild were spending the summer in seclusion. Ishbel Ross in *Ladies of the Press* recorded: "Elizabeth Jordan so overawed Benjamin Harrison's butler with her elegant costume and ostrich feathers that she got an interview at Cape May when the door was closed to all other reporters." Evidently Jordan didn't see herself quite that way. She set the record straight in *Three Rousing Cheers*:

It was a very hot July morning when I rang the door-bell of that Cape May cottage, and what I wore was a fresh white linen tailor-made suit, white canvas shoes, a white sport hat, and white wash gloves. I suppose I looked clean and informal and very much alive when I asked the butler if Mrs. Harrison was at home, but I certainly did not impress him by my elegance. He said she was, and stepped aside to let me pass him. As I entered the hall Mrs. Harrison walked out of an inner room, wearing a beach hat, leading Baby McKee by the hand. Again I am impelled to remark that on such slight things as this do vital changes in fortune rest! If I had been formally announced, if Mrs. Harrison had been upstairs, it is almost certain that I would not have seen her. As it was, I went forward at once, told her exactly where I came from and what I wanted, and gave my attention to Baby McKee during the moment in which she took me in and decided that it was safe to accept me.

The fact that Jordan got this story without any fuss impressed Smith. He also noticed that she could write proper English, an ability he found lacking in many male reporters. Assigning her to a special staff with six other writers, he took it upon himself to teach her to write terse, clear, forceful prose, and to do it quickly. As she learned not to overwrite, she remembered—and was never to forget—the advice of her favorite girlhood teacher, Sister Ethelbert: "Let your readers shed their own tears."

Although the World had few bylines, credit was given to good stories. Every week a "model story" was displayed on the newsroom bulletin board, and shortly after the Harrison scoop, Jordan's "The Death of Number Nine" was posted. A nurse at Bellevue Hospital had called her about a destitute mother who had brought her dead baby in, asking for burial. Jordan wrote a story ending with a plea for contributions; by the next morning there was money not only for the burial but also for the mother's support.

For the World Jordan also covered the Lizzie Borden murder trial in New Bedford, Massachusetts (she always believed that Lizzie did not ax her parents to death). She spent a night in a haunted house in Sea Cliff, New Jersey; she went to the mountains of Virginia and Tennessee and wrote sympathetic stories about the mountain people. Although she became known as a feature writer, she could also work under deadline pressure. One night she had to digest hundreds of pages of legal documents, affidavits, and evidence about the death of Helen Pott. There was a suspicion that Carlyle Harris, a medical student, had poisoned his fiancée by giving her a prescription laced with opium. When the World learned that Harris was to be arrested, Ballard Smith asked Jordan at 6 p.m. to write a story with all the background leading up to the arrest. His instructions were to have a full page ready when he returned from dinner. For five hours she pored over the mounds of material, translating the legalese into a thrilling, sinister tale of love, murder, and deceit: it was done on time and to space specifications.

In 1893 to help support her parents she started selling short stories to the Ladies Home Journal. Four years later she was promoted to assistant Sunday editor at the World, working with the renowned Sunday editor, Arthur Brisbane, whom she ranked as one of the five best male conversationalists she knew. In 1900 she was asked to succeed Margaret Sangster as editor of Har-

per's Bazar, a challenge she couldn't turn down. The job also gave her more free time for writing popular novels, which were serialized in *Cosmopolitan*, the *Saturday Evening Post*, and *Harper's Magazine*.

After William Randolph Hearst bought *Bazar* in 1913, Jordan stayed with Harper & Brothers for another five years as literary adviser. She introduced the works of Zona Gale, Eleanor H. Porter, and Dorothy Canfield, but her major coup was detecting the talent of Sinclair Lewis when he brought her his first novel, *Our Mr. Wrenn*. She was personally impressed with the gangly red-haired Lewis, who would later marry the journalist Dorothy Thompson. Lewis would eat lunch with Jordan on the roof of her apartment, and they would go over revisions and editing for the novel. Lewis inscribed a copy, thanking her for making suggestions that were "inspiring and creative finishing touches," and for helping him "to make a book of this"—a dedication to an editor perhaps unmatched until Thomas Wolfe lyrically dedicated *Of Time and the River* to Maxwell Perkins of Scribner's. Jordan edited three more of Lewis' novels before she left and he changed publishers for his most famous novel, *Main Street*.

She gave her support to the women's suffrage cause, speaking on occasion and publishing the autobiography of Dr. Anna Howard Shaw, president of the National Women's Suffrage Association. Jordan had been interested in Shaw's story for a long time and seized the opportunity to collaborate when Shaw broke her ankle and was confined to bed for six weeks. *The Story of a Pioneer*, published in 1915, was dictated to Jordan, whose secretary took everything down in shorthand. The transcriptions totaled 200,000 words, which Jordan edited into the autobiography. She also edited *The Sturdy Oak* (1917), a novel based on the suffrage movement.

In 1918, an offer of $25,000 a year for a three-day-a-week consulting job with Goldwyn Pictures at its Fort Lee, New Jersey, studio was sufficient temptation for Jordan to leave Harper & Brothers. Before entering a new field, she took a three-month leave, and during this time the studio incurred major financial losses. The producers needed a hit and asked for "drama." Jordan offered lists of classic and modern books "whose titles were as familiar in my circle as our own names" but were unknown to her new associates. She kept the list and noted later that they were all eventually produced by various studios. At the time, however, they were as "alien to the picture world as I was myself." When Goldwyn moved its headquarters to California, the one unsuccessful stint in Jordan's career ended, and without remorse she returned to fiction writing.

She continued to turn out a novel nearly every year. Some of the titles were: *Tales of the Cloister, Lovers' Knots, Miss Blake's Husband, The Four-flusher, The Life of the Party*, and *Faraway Island*. In 1922 she began a column on the theater for the Catholic weekly *America*, which she wrote until her retirement in 1945. Failing eyesight prevented her from working for two years before she died on February 24, 1947, at the age of eighty-one.

Elizabeth Jordan's long career was in many ways a transition from the old-style journalism practiced by the sob sisters and the "intrepid" stunt reporters to a different kind of journalism in which a reporter functioned as critic and commentator. Her clear, concise writing style was imitated by novices; her elegant wardrobe was copied by the new generation of young writers; and her varied and successful career as reporter, editor, and novelist was pointed to as proof that women were indeed becoming professionals.

The following is one of the "True Stories of the News," which made Jordan's reputation on the *World*.

TRUE STORIES OF THE NEWS
A STRANGE LITTLE EAST SIDE GIRL
Why Did Maggie Gilbert Throw Herself Out of Her Bedroom Window at 369 First Avenue?
She Is a Dreamer, a Nomad, a Fragile, Delicate Bit of Humanity.
Whom Nobody In the Work-a-Day World of the East Side Pretends to Understand.

The New York World, February 12, 1891

Maggie Gilbert is a little dreamer, who lives away up in the top of a five-story tenement-house at No. 369 First avenue.

She is the same little girl who, on Tuesday evening, in a fit of despair or in a spirit of adventure—no one knows quite which—threw herself out of her bedroom window down on to the roof of the adjoining house.

She is an odd mite of humanity, this little nine-year-old Maggie Gilbert. Gossips in the tenement say that Maggie's stepmother punished her Tuesday evening, and that she jumped out of the window in desperation. But there is very slight foundation for such a story. Maggie Gilbert is a little child, who moves about always as if walking in a dream. And the matter-of-fact people in an east-side tenement, who battle day by day against heavy odds for their bread and beer, can't understand her, that is all.

She is a pretty thing, as fragile as a flower. Why she did not break her body into bits when she leaped from the window is a marvel. It is quite a fall to the roof of the next house. They picked her up almost unconscious. Very soon after she was found she became fully so. Then the doctor gave her medication and she fell into a quiet sleep. When she awoke yesterday morning she was a trifle weak but otherwise was as whole as if she had never taken the jump. At noon she was frolicking with other children in the household.

A VERY PECULIAR LITTLE GIRL

Maggie is one of eight children. Tommy and Mamie are older than she and Hannah came next after Maggie's birth. Then there are three chubby, flaxen little fellows, and last year the baby came. All but Maggie romp about and laugh and play and scream together just like other children in an east side tenement. But Maggie is different. She is an accident in their midst. They call her "queer."

No one has ever been quite able to interpret her strange ways. She loves to wander out when the rest of the family, after a long day's work or play, are fast asleep, and watch the life of the east side as it moves and hurries and eddies along in the three broad avenues nearest the river.

Sometimes she romps with the other children. But often she leaves them to their play and saunters away to stroll up and down the streets alone. When she is in those moods she never talks much. And when her mother and father ask her what she is thinking about when she walks up and down the pavements all alone she never says. There is a side to this little east-side dreamer which she never shows to her brothers and sisters and which her father and mother can no more comprehend than they can Greek.

Tuesday afternoon the child played truant. She goes to the public school on East Twenty-third street but for a long time it has been Maggie's habit to leave her lessons suddenly when the vagrant mood had hold of her and wander away at her own sweet will. Sometimes she does not go to the school at all.

A NOMAD OF THE EAST SIDE

At other times, when school is out, instead of returning home with her companions she disappears. Supper is spread, but Maggie's little chair is empty. Sometimes it is 8, sometimes 9, sometimes 10 o'clock before she returns. Sometimes, too, she doesn't return at all and her father and mother have had on several occasions to search the streets for her till midnight.

When they have found her she returns willingly enough, but they can never get her to explain her conduct. She closes her tiny mouth in a quietly determined manner and is deaf and dumb to all entreaty. When she has so been found she has invariably been alone. She was hopping up and down the pavements, bathing herself in the glare of the gas lights and electric lamps, gazing into the shop windows, watching the passers-by, drinking in, like another "Petit Daniel," the glamour and music of a great city till she was drunk with it all.

THE BOWERY A FAIRY LAND TO HER

You may smile at the magic and the glamour of Third avenue and the thoroughfares lying between it and the East River. It is all paltry enough, to be sure. But you must remember that this little Maggie Gilbert had hardly ever been out of the east side, during the day, in her life. And at night she slept in a stifling room with three or four sisters lying beside her in the same bed.

What wonder that the Bowery by night was a sort of fairyland to her and by day the far-off squares and parks into which she stumbled became as dreamlands.

Whether she strolled further away at times during her nocturnal rambles no one except Maggie herself knows. She never says. She loves books and flowers and pictures and music. She, of course, has had little enough of all these things in her life, with seven brothers and sisters to demand their share of the week's earnings.

Perhaps she got far away enough some afternoon or evening to learn that all these beautiful things existed, if she could manage to walk long enough to find them.

At any rate her disappearances from home and school became more and more frequent. Her parents scolded her and tried to reason with her. Once her father whipped her. But nothing availed with the child. Tuesday afternoon she played truant again. When Maggie's mother learned of it she scolded the girl and threatened to tell her father of her conduct. Maggie had eaten her supper, and at 9 o'clock, as was her custom, she left her mother, who was reading to the two older children, and went into the room where she slept.

The flat which the Gilberts occupy is on the top, on the south side of the tenement. It has the regular east-side tenement-house arrangement. There is a room facing the street and one facing the court. Between these there are two more rooms. In most houses these two middle rooms are window-less and dark. The room where Maggie slept, however, was a full story above the adjoining tenement and had a window in one corner looking toward the South.

It is such a little window. It is only about three feet high and a foot and a half wide. In fact, it isn't any bigger than the child who leaned out of it Tuesday evening. How she got out of it—for it only opened half way—sprung and made the leap down to the roof of No. 367, is as much a mystery as the little girl's whole life to her comrades. But do it, somehow, she did, and she cleared an alley way at least four feet in width which lay between the houses.

Two of Maggie's sisters were asleep in the big bed in the small room when she climbed up to the window-sill. They didn't hear her pull up the sash, nor did they wake when she lay moaning on the tiles outside. The doors were open through into the room where Mrs. Gilbert sat reading, but the sound of her voice must have drowned the creaking window. No one in the back room heard that. But they heard the child moaning, and Mrs. Gilbert ran in to see what the trouble was. Two children were sound asleep on the pillows. Maggie, however, was not there, nor was she in the front room.

THEY FOUND HER ON THE ROOF

Mrs. Gilbert noticed the half-open window, and she looked out. She saw something white down on the roof outside.

She cried out: "Is that you, Maggie?"

"Yes'm," came back in a faint reply.

Mrs. Gilbert ran down the four flights of stairs and up onto the next tenement. A tenant by the name of Armstrong had already heard the child groaning and had gone up to her assistance. He took up the fragile form in his arms and carried it downstairs. There Mrs. Gilbert met him.

The child was in her night-dress and her feet were bare. But she had put on her little cloak before she took the leap. When Armstrong found the child she was conscious, but she became insensible very soon after she was taken into the house.

An ambulance was sent for immediately, but Mrs. Gilbert would not allow the girl to be taken to the hospital. The patrolman on beat picked Maggie up and bore her to the Gilberts' flat. There they laid the child on the best bed and Dr. Holden was sent for.

He examined Maggie's body and found, as if by miracle, that no bone had been broken by the fall. A sedative was given the child and she soon was peacefully asleep.

SHE LIES ON THE BED LIKE A WAX DOLL

She was still asleep when a WORLD man called at the flat yesterday. She looked as delicate as a leaf, and her two tiny arms were folded above her head. That little head was one mass of golden hair, which was cut short, and her deep-blue eyes, which were repeated in every one of her brothers and sisters, were hidden. She looked like a wax doll, put there by one of the other children, and in no wise suggested as she slept there—hardly breathing it seemed—the upheaval that her strange short existence on earth must have undergone.

Mrs. Gilbert was sitting by the child as she was sleeping.

"I don't know why Maggie did it," she was saying to THE WORLD reporter. "She is such a queer little body. No, no; it couldn't have been because I scolded her. I didn't scold her. I only told her that I would tell her father that she had run away again."

"And that was an old story to Maggie. She has given us so much trouble by her strange ways. We can't make her out. Her father once was for putting her out to Father Drumgoole's. She couldn't run away there. But I said: "Oh, wait a little longer. The child is a bit queer now, but she will outgrow it." And I think she will."

"I never laid a hand on her, nor have I on any of my husband's children. He had six when I married him, the youngest a year old. Maggie has given us more trouble than them all. But she is quiet enough generally. If she would only stay at home like the rest!"

DIFFERENT FROM ALL HER PLAYMATES

"She is always wanting to do something different from her playmates," Mrs. Gilbert went on. "She wanted excitement and is always hankering after adventure. I think that is the reason she jumped out of the window. If she wanted to kill herself, why didn't she drop down in the alleyway instead of leaping over it? No, I think she meant to steal out again last night and roam the streets. Poor child, I don't know what she will do next."

The fact that Maggie had only a night-dress does in no way discountenance her mother's theory. For her father and mother have again and again hidden away her little shoes and stockings, but she would run out just the same in her bare feet. One of her vagrant moods was strong upon her Tuesday, and she began by playing truant in the afternoon. When she was sent to bed the mood still held her, and she intended to clear the alley, gain the next roof and steal down through the next house out into the avenue.

Two months ago Maggie's parents found that she had been going about among their friends and borrowing money. Once it was 25 cents she got in this way; once it was 50 cents. Another day she obtained $1. Then her father discovered what she had been doing and whipped her. The child took her strapping without a word—without a murmur. But no endeavor could wring from her the motive for her wrongdoing.

It was discovered afterwards that the child had spent some of the money in candies; some of it in fancy colored prints; some of it went no one knows where.

And now the little golden-haired creature lies in her bed, saying nothing about her action, sleeping at times, and at times again playing with the babies. Thomas Gilbert is an honest, hard-working engineer. His wife is a stout, hearty, good-natured woman, who spends her days mending, cooking, washing and tending eight children, six of which came to her as a wedding gift. The parents work hard by day and sleep sound by night. Seven of their children go to school, eat three meals a day till they have become as sturdy and fat a little race as it would be possible to find in the whole east side, and then at nights, like their father and mother, go to bed tired out, glad to get there.

AN ODD BIT OF HUMANITY

But this odd little bit of humanity, who lies in the big bed in the front room there, she is different. Her brothers and sisters go to school; she dislikes the restraint and sighs to get away. They don't care much to go to the Church of the Epiphany every Sunday. But the little Maggie loves that, for she hears music there. When the others are asleep she is wide awake. When the boys and girls whom she knows are tumbling in rough sports she goes away by herself and dreams. What does she dream about?

They call her up in the tenement "odd" and "queer." No one seems to understand her there. Poor little Maggie Gilbert! There is no place for dreamers in a work-a-day world like the east side.

10

Anne O'Hare McCormick
(1880–1954)

COMPASSIONATE, GENEROUS, often humorous, and always perceptive, Anne O'Hare McCormick was one of those rare journalists whose goodness overshadows their work. During thirty-two years on the *New York Times* that spanned the period between two World Wars and the Cold War, she interviewed Mussolini, Hitler, Chamberlain, Stalin, and Churchill, but it was her empathy for ordinary people trying to survive economic and political hardship that distinguished her analysis of foreign affairs. That she did not begin her career as a reporter until after she married at age thirty made her achievements even more remarkable.

Long before other journalists, she recognized the coming power of Mussolini and Hitler. In fact, at a press conference once, Britain's Foreign Secretary Anthony Eden remarked that reporters had understood the menace of these two leaders before Britain's ambassadors. To which McCormick retorted: "And why not? An ambassador is only a badly trained reporter."

On the basis of her articles from Italy the *Times* hired her as a roving correspondent in 1922, and she later became the paper's first foreign affairs columnist and the first woman appointed to its editorial board. In 1937 she was the first woman to win a Pulitzer Prize in journalism (in the category of correspondence), and she was the only winner in the history of the Pulitzers who was so honored on the basis of all her work rather than a particular entry.

She seldom took notes, saying, "It makes people too cautious." Her style was that of the beat reporter, talking to people on the street, those affected and vulnerable, and adding her interpretation. In a dispatch from France in 1945, just before the end of World War II, she surveyed the wreckage of Europe and wrote that she had found "the woman with a broom trying to clear away the debris that used to be her home." In this image she saw both "symbol and promise." When the Russians took over Budapest, she described the rows of empty food stores and the cattle being driven down the street, and in a few sentences captured the mood of an occupied city.

In 1947 Lester Markel, Sunday editor of the *Times*, credited her success to "an extraordinary ability to get along with people, to be on intimate terms with more important people than anyone else in the business." After hearing Mussolini's first speech, she thereafter interviewed him many times, writing that of the public figures she had met he was the only one who seemed "interested not only in what he says himself but in what you have to say; he appears to weigh your suggestions, solicits your opinions."

She was a conversationalist with a natural sense of humor, and President Franklin D. Roosevelt felt so relaxed in her company that he often broke his ban on giving individual interviews just to talk with Anne O'Hare Mc-Cormick. Their talks often would last three hours, but her stories never took the form of ". . . the President said." She had known FDR before his first nomination in Chicago in 1932, and he was known to favor those who were with him, as he termed it, B.C. (before Chicago). "When I first saw Franklin D. Roosevelt at the Cox notification ceremonies in 1920," she wrote, "he was a handsome and radiant figure, faring forth on a hopeless campaign with a smile of gay good humor. Twelve years later he swooped down from the skies to accept his own nomination from the Chicago Convention. In the interval he has suffered one political defeat, mostly vicarious, and a physical disaster so valorously surmounted and lightly borne that it has been almost an asset."

President Roosevelt called her a reporter who knew what she was writing about. "She thinks deeply," he noted. "And she is a wonderful human being." As McCormick gained prominence as a columnist, competing with Dorothy Thompson of the *Herald Tribune*, interviewers sought in vain to find flaws. She did not smoke, sipped an occasional Old Fashioned, was a devoted wife. The most serious criticism leveled against her in print was that she believed blindly that the League of Nations could secure peace. "Nothing better or more stable can be established by more war," she wrote in 1935, "but in the long view it is equally certain that there must be war—not all the sanctions in the world can stop it—until there is a league not only to enforce but to create peace."

She once described Pope Pius XI as a leader "who suggests force in repose." The phrase could have applied to McCormick as well. When she started at the *Times* at age forty-two she was middle-aged in appearance: five-foot-two, plump, with reddish hair, blue eyes, an expressive Irish face, and a conservative wardrobe. She was given to only one excess: ornate hats. At sixty-six, when she was in Berlin and Frankfurt reporting on the aftermath of World War II, colleagues noted the contrast between Mrs. McCormick of the *Times* and other pushy, domineering women journalists, notably Dorothy Thompson and Marguerite Higgins, both of the *Herald Tribune*.

Although McCormick was a fine reporter and writer who made deadlines and needed little editing, tributes from friends and colleagues after her death stressed her human qualities. Clare Boothe Luce called her "a rare combination of brilliance and goodness." James Reston described her as "that saintly woman." In the introduction to *The World at Home* (1956), a posthumous collection of her columns, Reston wrote, "She literally twinkled when she talked, and what talk! Everything and everybody interested her, and she illuminated every subject she touched. I remember her showing up at the 1952 Republican convention wearing a lovely white silk dress with tiny Democratic donkeys on it, and appearing the following week at the Democratic convention in another white silk dress with small blue Republican elephants . . . Anne McCormick was an extraordinary reporter primarily because she was an extraordinary human being . . . a poet with a sense of style about everything she did."

Repeatedly she refused to be interviewed about her personal life or to have articles written about her. She believed that journalists should not become media personalities because fame would interfere with what she termed "the kind of impersonal and uncolored reporting . . . on which the maintenance of a free press and therefore a free society depend." Although she never actively supported feminist causes, she encouraged women to seek careers. In an observation about herself and other newspaperwomen, she once noted: "We had tried hard not to act like ladies or to talk as ladies are supposed to talk—meaning too much—but just to sneak toward the city desk and the cable desk, and the editorial sanctum and even the publisher's office with masculine *sang-froid*."

After her death, in a lengthy tribute published in the *Times*, colleague Harold Callender wrote:

I have heard it said by colleagues that Anne had a masculine mind. This was meant as extreme praise, the inference being that the male intellect excels in logic, clarity and objectivity in dealing with the realities of politics and economics. Anne had these

Anne O'Hare McCormick

qualities to a superlative degree and she amazed the experts by the questions she put to them . . . I am not sure that the intellect is a peculiarly masculine faculty. To the contrary might be cited the intellects of Jane Austen, Charlotte Bronte, George Eliot and others, including Anne O'Hare McCormick. Nor am I sure how far intuition may be considered feminine. But I am sure that the intellect alone is a feeble instrument unless it be supplemented by the kind of perception, non-intellectual or super-intellectual, that comes of a broad human sympathy.

Luther Huston, who handled her copy as general manager of the *Times'* Washington bureau, once told an anecdote that showed McCormick's special personality. After the 1944 Republican convention in Chicago, a group of reporters in search of a good steak during meat rationing ended up at a North Side restaurant. They had a few drinks at the bar, and Huston lingered to pay the bill, joining the group to sit at the empty seat reserved for him at the head of the table. "I'll be father," he said jokingly, "but I will not say grace." There was laughter, followed by silence, and then Anne McCormick said, "I'll say grace."

"All of us bowed our heads," Huston said, "and there in that saloon amid the whisky fumes and the red-checked table cloths, Anne McCormick said the most moving grace I ever heard. It was like a benediction. It wasn't forced. It didn't dampen or frost up the party. With her saying it, it was a perfectly normal and natural thing to do."

McCormick came from a devout Catholic family. Born Anne Elizabeth O'Hare on May 16, 1880, in Wakefield, Yorkshire, England, she was the eldest of three daughters of American parents, Thomas J. O'Hare and Teresa Beatrice (Berry) O'Hare. Shortly after her birth the family moved to the United States and settled in Columbus, Ohio, where Anne attended the Academy and College of Saint Mary of the Springs. When she was in high school, her father, a regional manager for Home Life Company of New York, deserted the family. To earn money, Teresa O'Hare ran a dry goods store and sold door-to-door a book of her poetry, *Songs at Twilight* (1898).

After Anne's college graduation, the family moved to Cleveland, where she and her mother worked for the weekly *Catholic Universe Bulletin*. Her mother wrote a column and edited the women's section, and Anne became associate editor, working on the *Bulletin* until she married Francis J. McCormick, eight years her senior, on September 14, 1910. The couple moved to Dayton, and in the following decade she sold articles to *Catholic World Reader Magazine* and the *New York Times Magazine*, and poetry to *Smart Set* and *Bookman*. She also wrote a history of her former parish church entitled *St. Agnes Church, Cleveland, Ohio: An Interpretation* (1920).

Her husband, an importer and engineer, made frequent business trips to Europe after World War I, and Anne accompanied him, spending her time talking with taxi drivers, waiters, and shopkeepers, and discovering a talent for making astute connections. These trips stimulated her interest in foreign affairs. She started off keeping a journal of a Europe recovering from World War I, and in 1921 wrote to Carr V. Van Anda, managing editor of the *New York Times*, about sending dispatches to the paper. He wired back: "Try it." Hired as a regular correspondent in 1922, she wrote exclusively for the *Times* after 1925, with the exception of a series on Europe published in the *Ladies Home Journal* in 1933 and 1934. Although known for her thrice-weekly foreign affairs column, "In Europe" (from 1936 titled "Abroad"), which alternated in the *Times* with Arthur Krock's "In the Nation," she was equally at home covering political conventions or writing a series on the new South or the Florida boom.

The McCormicks led peripatetic lives, leaving New York in the fall and traveling through Europe till spring. They never established a home, preferring the amenities of the Carlyle or Gotham hotels while in New York, the Ritz or Crillon in Paris, and Claridges in London. They had no children, and eventually their roles reversed: her husband traveled with her, assisting with work, taking care of travel arrangements, making sure she left functions in time to make train connections. Even after her husband became infirm and deaf, they continued to travel together, caring for each other with touching tenderness, according to colleagues.

C. L. Sulzberger, who took over the "Abroad" column after her death, renaming it "Foreign Affairs," recalled in his memoirs, *A Long Row of Candles*, an incident that occurred in 1940:

> Already over sixty, she still retained boundless energy and feminine charm. With plain, merry face, square jaw and upturned nose, she radiated warmth and kindness; everyone loved her and, what was important for a journalist, also confided in her. As always, Anne was accompanied by her elderly husband who had suffered a stroke some years past and was but a shadow of his former courtly self; yet she adored him and never traveled without him, pretending to rely upon his counsel. She would not even dictate one of her perceptive articles without Frank standing beside her, often in a tiny telephone booth, gravely turning the pages. . . .
>
> When they arrived at Belgrade's suburban station after a train trip from Romania, Anne descended, embraced me and began to chatter like a machine gun shooting platinum bullets while poor Frank stood in puzzlement before a mound of luggage, objurgating equally puzzled Serbian porters. When we rescued him and led him to my car he turned with an air of grave knowledge and said: "Aha, Jugoslovakia. Tell me, Cy, who's president now?" Anne chided him affectionately: "Stop teasing the boy, Frank. You know Jugoslavia's a kingdom."

In her mid-sixties, *Time* magazine noted that she was "absorbent, imperturbable and apparently immune to minor excitements, as tireless as a self winding watch." At sixty-seven she was clambering up and down the mountains of Greece, covering the guerrilla war. Following an inspection of refugee and prison camps, she wrote:

It is easy enough to say that the Greek war is an affair of daily raids in which armed bands . . . swoop down from the cracks and crevices of a mountain . . . to sack or burn villages and carry off able-bodied men and girls to forced service in their armies. But the imagination cannot picture the desolation that this hit-and-run fighting leaves behind it . . . Everywhere the atmosphere was heavy with suspense. In such fearful quiet must the early settlers in the West have waited for the descent of the Indians.

When she was in Europe, no matter what time it was there, her column was cabled to the *Times* to arrive at 9:30 p.m. New York time. At home, in the office, she typed newspaper style, with the index fingers. Early in her career some *Times* copy editors labeled her "Verbose Annie," and cut her copy down to size, but she eventually learned to write seamlessly. Unlike her colleague Arthur Krock, she never complained about editing.

When Arthur Hays Sulzberger became publisher of the *Times* on May 7, 1935, one of his early announcements was her appointment as the first woman on the paper's editorial board. Sulzberger urged her to be the "freedom editor: to stand up and shout whenever freedom is interfered with in any part of the world." From 1936 to 1954, when she wasn't traveling, she wrote two unsigned editorials weekly, in addition to three weekly columns.

During World War II she was named to the Advisory Committee on Post-War Foreign Policy, a select government body that was secret at the time, and was often mentioned as a candidate for diplomatic positions. The National Federation of Business and Professional Women's Clubs named her Woman of the Year in 1939; she was elected to the National Institute of Arts and Letters and awarded sixteen honorary degrees from colleges and universities.

She wrote only one book on foreign affairs, *The Hammer and the Scythe: Communist Russia Enters the Second Decade* (1928). In addition to *The World at Home*, another posthumous collection of her writings, *Vatican Journal, 1921–1954*, was published in 1957, both edited by Marion Turner Sheehan.

When Anne O'Hare McCormick died on May 29, 1954, at the age of seventy-four, the *Times* blackened the border of the "Abroad" column and published a tribute, describing her as a "reporter in a rare sense. She understood politics and diplomacy but for her they were not the whole truth and no abstraction was ever the whole truth. The whole truth lay in people."

The following article of March 28, 1945, is one of Anne O'Hare McCormick's more memorable columns; it was the inspiration for Marion Turner Sheehan's 1955 book *The Spiritual Woman: Trustee of the Future*.

ABROAD
Bulldozer and the Woman With a Broom

By ANNE O'HARE McCORMICK

The New York Times, March 28, 1945

Every correspondent who has been near the front has seen the woman with the broom described by John MacCormac in a dispatch from the United States Ninth Army Headquarters east of the Rhine. In a devastated town two miles behind the fighting line he observed a woman emerge from a cellar and, though her house was a ruin, proceed to sweep away the dust and rubble that covered the doorstep.

This woman happened to be German but in every war-ravaged country the woman with a broom trying to clear away the debris that used to be her home is as familiar and monotonous a sight as ruin itself. In one flattened village in Holland after another dazed old men were standing in wavering clusters in the shell-pocked fields, but the women were working in the dooryards that a few hours before had led to houses. Several were trying to tie their chrysanthemum stalks to the poles that held them up. The chrysanthemums were still blooming, bright yellow beside piles of brick dust, and the housewives were mechanically starting to save the one whole thing that survived the wreck of the shattered cottages.

The Dutch, it should be remembered, have suffered terrible things in this war. The process of liberation has been harder, slower and therefore more ruinous than in France or Belgium, and the Germans in the occupied part of the country have treated the population and the countryside itself, reclaimed from the sea with infinite labor, with superlative cruelty—perhaps the Netherlanders say, because the Nazis expected more "cooperation" from them and were goaded to fury by the obstinate resistance they met in Holland.

For Americans, living in conditions unimaginably different from those prevailing in occupied and liberated countries, it is vital to understand the bitterness of overstrained and underfed people who have suffered too much and too long. It is one reason why refugee Governments are bound to be unstable and short-lived. It is why every provisional regime, including the French, by far the strongest of all, seems to move in a political vacuum. It explains the "ingratitude" that irks our soldiers in the land they are fighting to free. The temper of dispossessed and hungry people, and their sudden swings from violence to apathy, constitute one of the human and—or, for they are the same thing—the political problems which Mr. Hoover, in the series of articles appearing in this newspaper, rightly rates as taking priority over all other problems.

But the woman in Evreux, in battered Normandy, was not thinking so far ahead when she appeared with her broom that bleak Sunday morning and began raising the dust in the path of General de Gaulle and the distinguished visitors from Paris. With a dash and energy as impatient as General Patton's as he sweeps across the German plain, she was making a broomstick attack upon the crumbled stones that lay atop a tiny patch of garden. She paid no attention to the cortege skirting the shell holes in the road until a woman in the party stopped to ask her what she thought she was doing with a broom in the wake of 2,000 pound bombs. "Who's to save the cabbages and onions if I don't? They're all that's left of all the work of all my life," she said fiercely. "And somebody has to begin clearing away this mess."

Then there was the old woman sweeping out a cowshed in the Argo Romano, near Rome. The land had been flooded by the Germans and was once more a breeding place for malarial mosquitos, banished by the efforts of fifty years. The house was gone. In a fifty-mile radius not an animal was left. The farmer, who had lost a hand in a minefield, looked at us with hopeless eyes; but the woman kept on sweeping, clearing a little space in the wreckage to begin life anew.

The woman with a broom is both symbol and promise. It's pretty futile to start attacking the ruins of great cities with a kitchen broom. Yet everywhere, before the monster bulldozers arrive to clear paths for the armies through the debris left by the bombers, women instinctively seize their brooms in this futile, age-old gesture of cleaning up the mess the men have made.

There's no assurance that they can clear it up this time, but today there are more women than men in Europe, widows of soldiers, widows of hostages, widows of the last war, and they are bound to try. In Paris an association of widows of men executed by the Germans is headed by a lovely girl widow who said months ago exactly what Miss Horsbrugh, one of the two Englishwomen who will join Dean Virginia Gildersleeve as delegates to San Francisco, says of the responsibility of representatives who will assemble at the conference. "We are the trustees of the future," the French girl asserted. "We can't leave it to the next generation because they won't have seen what we have seen, and they won't understand."

It isn't chance that women are named for the first time to a conference called to set up the framework of international order. There should be more of them, for they are in the wars now, and millions of them have nothing much left but a broom. Whether they could do better than the men is a question, but they are somehow angrier over destruction, and at least there's not much danger of doing worse. Certainly it's a sound and self-protective instinct that impels the men to hand over to the women a little of the responsibility for the hardest job in history.

11

Emma Bugbee
(1888–1981)

IN THE SPRING OF 1966, the staff of the *New York Herald Tribune* knew that their newspaper, known as "the writers' paper," would be merged with the *World Telegram and The Sun* and the *Journal-American*, bringing together what once represented seven distinct journalistic voices into one paper, the *World Journal Tribune*. The dubious pleasure of working for this hybrid was based on seniority, and no one on the *Trib* had more of that than Emma Bugbee, who had been a reporter for fifty-six years. She had been on Park Row with the *Tribune* and then moved uptown after the merger of the *Herald* and the *Tribune* in 1924. She felt she had seen the best days of New York journalism, and on April 22, 1966, she announced that she would retire. She pinned a corsage on the shoulder of her blue suit, adjusted one of her perky flowered hats, and went downstairs to the *Trib's* pub, Artist and Writers, for some champagne. "She left and took part of the business with her," wrote *Trib* columnist Jimmy Breslin.

But she was not yet to receive her last newspaper "good night," the traditional nod that there is no more work. The next day she was back on the job for what would be the newspaper's final edition of April 24. Fittingly, for her last story she covered the dedication of a United Nations memorial to Eleanor Roosevelt, a close friend whose activities she had reported on from 1928 until Mrs. Roosevelt's death in 1962. Printed with the story was a wide-angle photograph of Emma Bugbee seated in the memorial, a semi-circular bench, engraved with Adlai Stevenson's famous tribute to Eleanor Roosevelt: "She would rather light a candle than curse the darkness, and her glow has warmed the world."

Emma Bugbee had many of Eleanor Roosevelt's characteristics. She was warm but shrewd. She was calm in a crisis, generous to a fault, and always supportive of her colleagues, especially women. Since 1924 Bugbee had always covered the woman's angle at the national political conventions, but in 1952, the paper decided it was time for a change and gave the assignment to Judith Crist, who recalled hiding for days, trying to avoid the sixty-four-year-old reporter. "I thought that if I were her I would feel terribly slighted," Crist said, "but then one day Emma came over and congratulated me, and started offering some tips on how to do the stories. She was such a lady and she taught me how to be one." Dick West, an editor who handled Bugbee's copy for more than thirty years, remembered her as "a lady who in a tumultuous, sophisticated world learned to adjust, but still preserved the virtues and manners of a simpler, homier time."

I also worked with Bugbee at the *Trib* and remember her as totally unflappable, even under deadline pressure. She would casually walk into the newsroom after an assignment, appearing as if she had just taken a stroll down Fifth Avenue. Everyone on the *Trib* had an "Emma" story. Once she was given a short to write about a ninety-four-year-old man who had become a father for the first time. She handed in the copy and shortly afterward the copy editor walked over to her desk, put the yellow paper on top of her typewriter and gently suggested: "Gee, Emma, he's ninety-four. Don't you think his age should be in the lead?" She nodded, gave one of her toothy grins, and rewrote the lead.

Bugbee reported mostly on women. If there was a woman's angle to a story, she was there to get it. Her articles, if put together, would make a progressive history of the women's movement. She was there for the suffrage marches and rallies: for the 1924 convention, the first where women were voting delegates; and for the introduction of the Equal Rights Amendment by the Women's Party in Washington in 1923. When she died at ninety-three, she was still optimistic about its passage.

It was her coverage of Eleanor Roosevelt, however, which brought her prominence as a reporter and writer. She was well into middle age when she became one of Mrs. Roosevelt's "girls," a group of women reporters who traveled with the President's wife. This association broadened her outlook, and one colleague felt that reporting on such a vivid personality brought a vigor and firmness to her writing that was previously lacking.

In 1933, for Franklin Delano Roosevelt's inauguration, the staunchly Republican *Trib* sent her to Washington to interview the First Lady. In the past, presidential wives had rarely talked to the press on their own. After a press conference, Bugbee, who had covered Mrs. Roosevelt's activities when her husband was governor of New York, hung around to say goodbye. Ishbel Ross, who also worked with Bugbee on the *Herald Tribune*, describes the scene in *Ladies of the Press*:

"I've always been crazy to know what things were like upstairs," said Miss Bugbee, without any special guile. A good New Englander, fond of the institutions of her country, she had great interest in the White House. She had picketed during suffrage days, attended diplomatic receptions, seen the Easter eggs rolled on the lawn.

"Oh, I'll show you upstairs any time," said Mrs. Roosevelt cordially. "Come and have lunch with me some day."

"That would be wonderful," said Miss Bugbee, "but my paper has called me in. I'm leaving to-morrow."

"Well, come to lunch to-morrow and bring all the New York newspaper girls with you."

That was the beginning of the new order. After they had lunched Mrs. Roosevelt took them on a tour of the White House. "Now this is Franklin's room," she said, "and here is where Anna sleeps."

They went from room to room. They inspected pictures, chintzes, hangings, favorite books, bibelots, antiques, rugs, photographs; they got an accurate picture of the home life of the President's family.

And they wrote about what they saw. Thereafter, Mrs. Roosevelt held regular Monday morning press conferences—for women only. Her decision to exclude men was not without reason. There was a Depression, and such conferences would make women more useful to their papers, ensuring their continued employment and forcing other organizations, notably the news services, to hire women for the first time. Mrs. Roosevelt also wanted control over the news coming from the White House; she wanted to make announcements, not have cooks or staff members leak details to reporters.

The first Monday conferences drew about thirty to thirty-five women, a number that exceeded the chairs, so latecomers sat on the floor. After a newspaper cartoonist drew a scene with women seated at the feet of the President's wife, more chairs were provided. Still, the conferences always had a feeling of informality, with the tone set by Mrs. Roosevelt who would freely discuss just about everything—education, pensions, minimum wages, housing, recreation, farms, factories, labor. It was understood, though, that she would not comment on her husband's politics, but her wide-ranging comments would often illuminate political problems. And sometimes there was spot news. Male colleagues may have referred to the conferences as "hen parties," but they didn't scoff when the women scooped them with the announcement in 1933 that beer would be served at the White House, and then again a year later when Mrs. Roosevelt announced that wines, preferably American, would be served at formal dinners.

Emma Bugbee

Any woman who covered Eleanor Roosevelt tended to refer to herself as one of the "girls." There was, however, a core group chosen to travel with the First Lady to such places as Appalachia to visit the coal mines or to Puerto Rico to investigate conditions in the garment factories. Besides Bugbee, the group included Lorena Hickok and Bess Furman of the Associated Press, Dorothy Ducas of International News Service, Ruby Black of United Press, and Kathleen McLaughlin of the *Chicago Tribune*.

These trips yielded many memories for the "girls," including home movies they took on a Puerto Rican beach of Mrs. Roosevelt skipping rope in a bathing suit. Bugbee once recalled a scene from the election night of 1944, when FDR ran in spite of poor health and political opposition. It was the last time she saw the Roosevelts together:

We were all at the President's home in Hyde Park. Every election night, the Hyde Park neighbors came out with torchlights and serenaded the family. I can still see that tableau. It was kind of a misty, cold night, and the Roosevelts stood out there on the veranda of the Hyde Park house. He always wore a long, navy-blue cape. He loved that cape. I can still see her [Mrs. Roosevelt] pulling that cape up around his shoulders and neck to keep him warm. That's a memory that I treasure very much.

During her husband's burial in the rose garden of their Hyde Park home on April 15, 1945, Mrs. Roosevelt maintained her composure. After the dignitaries and the worshipful crowd had left and only a few reporters remained, she paid a second visit to the grave with her daughter, Anna. As she returned to the house, she saw Emma Bugbee, and for the first time, started to cry. They threw their arms around each other and wept.

When Mrs. Roosevelt died in 1962, Bugbee wrote an award-winning tribute to the woman she admired so much. Concluding the story on the funeral, she noted: "Those of us who traveled with Mrs. Roosevelt on that spectacular tour [to a West Virginia coal mine] have often had occasion to reply to persons who thought it unnatural. To her it was just like visiting a depression village or an experimental farming plot or a new housing project. She was always interested in what was going on. Once someone complained that tramping through hospital wards killed her feet, and Mrs. Roosevelt laughed, replying, "I am always so interested I don't get tired."

As a Boswell to Mrs. Roosevelt and much earlier as a child, Emma Bugbee had strong role models. She was born in Shippensburg, Pennsylvania, on May 18, 1888, the first of three children of Edwin Howard Bugbee and Emma (Bugbee) Bugbee, who had met because friends thought two people with the same unusual last name should get together. Throughout their marriage, Emma's mother refused to wear a wedding ring, considering it symbolic of a kind of slavery. Her father, a French and Greek teacher, died when Emma was twelve, and her mother took over his job. Emma's niece,

Mrs. Norma Starr, described the mother as a determined and dedicated woman who worked most of her life to support her family and to put three children through college. Emma grew up in Methuen, Massachusetts, and after high school went to Barnard College in New York.

At Barnard she joined the press club, whose members wrote up college events for the various newspapers. Bugbee selected the *Tribune* as her paper and wrote to the editor, "I'd like to be your correspondent at Barnard College." She received a return letter asking, "Where were you yesterday? We wanted you to cover the basketball game." At graduation, rather than pursuing a newspaper career, she chose to teach Greek at her alma mater, Methuen High School. A year later the school dropped the course, but before she could find another teaching position, she heard from a Barnard classmate, Eva vom Baur, a reporter at the *Tribune*. Vom Baur wanted to visit relatives in Germany during the summer and asked Bugbee to work as a substitute.

Bugbee arrived at the *Tribune*'s Park Row offices on July 23, 1910, an eager twenty-two-year-old. She was asked to write women's news, which at that time consisted mainly of cute fillers or recipes such as "an eccentric Eastern salad consists of pineapple and celery, dressed with mayonnaise and served with lettuce." After vom Baur decided to stay abroad, Bugbee was hired permanently. Although assigned to the city desk, she was not allowed to have a desk in the all-male newsroom and instead worked in an alcove on another floor.

It was four years before she had her first byline—for a classic "undercover" story done earlier by Nellie Bly and Annie Laurie. Dressed in the blue serge uniform of a Salvation Army lass, she rang a bell at a collection pail on the corner of Fifth Avenue and 42nd Street. Dismayed by the apathy of shoppers who hurried by, hands in pockets, she started off her story: "Is it the hearts or the hands of New Yorkers that are so cold . . . ?" Earlier, of course, she had covered major stories but without a byline—for example, a three-week march of suffragists from New York to Albany to petition the governor for support. It took place during a cold, snowy December of 1911, and at first her editor didn't want to send her, thinking the march would be too arduous. She insisted on the assignment, however, and trudged up the Hudson River's east bank, leaving the marchers each day at 5 p.m. to hitchhike to the nearest telegraph station and file her story.

One day the city editor came over to her and said, "Go up and scream with the eagle," which meant to go to the Garden City airport and take a trial flight in a new fighter aircraft the government was testing. Using familiar imagery, she noted her reactions: "For thrills it cannot be compared to a Fifth Avenue elevator on the downward career. For fears and shrieks it is outclassed by any ordinary automobile on a chicken-strewn road. Actually, it was as steady as a cook stove."

Bugbee was a true generalist. She covered murders and local politics as well as some annual favorites: the cat and flower shows and the circus. For many years she wrote the main story for the *Herald Tribune*'s Forum, a feature which profiled national leaders in various fields. And, of course, she was the dutiful chronicler of the "firsts," from first woman judge to first woman governor. Yet, if the news was big enough, like a major suffrage parade, the policy was to give the front-page stories to the men.

On the eve of one big parade, a delegation of women from several departments decided it was time for a change. They sent a representative to talk to editor Ogden Reid, who said it was fine with him for women to do all the stories if the managing editor agreed, which he did. Four reporters from the women's department worked with Bugbee and they filled nine columns in the morning paper. Not a word of their copy was changed.

As the suffrage movement grew, with more marches to Washington, more speeches and incidents that demanded coverage, women reporters gained more status. In 1915, Bugbee got a desk in the newsroom and women's news became part of the daily assignments. Her colleagues respected her shrewd political views, but as a Republican she avoided heated discussions of the New Deal. A taciturn New Englander, she never boasted about her knowledge, particularly in a room filled with men who generally were not college educated. She had all the qualities of a wonderful wife and mother, but she never married, and no one recalled her having any strong attachments.

She accepted the fact that she covered the famous women and not the famous men. As was true of many of the early women journalists, she tended not to think in terms of discrimination, but in terms of what she did well. Certainly she worked as long and hard as her male colleagues. "We worked six days a week. And right up through Saturday night if necessary," she told writer Jean Collins. "If anything was happening, if women suffragists were having meetings somewhere, why we had to go, even on Saturday night. . . . And when the five-day week came in—it was part of Roosevelt's reforms—the old guard in the newspapers thought it was terrible. My city editor said, 'Why I love newspaper work.' And I said, 'Well I do too, but I can love it five days a week just as well as six.' "

In 1922, she helped to start the Newspaper Women's Club of New York, and served three terms as its president. In 1936, she published the first of the five "Peggy" books based on her experiences as a reporter. The series, which influenced many women to try journalism, is something of an old-fashioned classic and can still be found in public libraries. Helen Rogers Reid, wife of the *Herald Tribune*'s editor, and a strong advocate for women who was later responsible for helping Dorothy Thompson and Marguerite Higgins accelerate their careers, noted in the foreword of *Peggy Covers the News* (1936):

One of the difficult obstructions to clear thinking on the part of the male is that the success of a woman is always rated as individual, as an exception, whereas that of a man, in addition to honoring him, is credited also to general male prestige . . . The history of the race, however, is a fair illustration that any place, whether for work, play or residence, from the Garden of Eden down, has been more successful for having the supplementary points of view of the man and the woman and I am one who believes that newspapers are no exception. Some day the attitude toward applicants for work will function more normally and the obstacles to becoming a reporter will be sexless. The only measuring stick then will be ability to hold a job and to make it grow.

When she celebrated her first half-century as a reporter in 1960, a record unapproached by any other woman on a single New York paper, Bugbee noted that people always thought she was the city's "only" woman reporter. In fact, she said, with eleven newspapers in town, "there were lots of us. And we all covered the votes for women campaign." At her retirement, six years later, she counted up 18,911 days spent as a newspaper reporter.

For several years she traveled and spent her time painting landscapes in oil and water colors at her summer home in Bethel, Connecticut. Her last eleven years were spent in the Sunny View Nursing Home in Warwick, Rhode Island. She died there on October 6, 1981—two days before she was to be interviewed for this book. My memories of Emma will always be special. We met on the IRT subway line each morning on the way to work, and she helped me, a new young "Peggy" on the staff, in any way possible. She was a great lady. Her kind will not be seen again in the newsroom.

The following story, written on the day of Mrs. Roosevelt's death, won the Newspaper Reporters Association's feature award of 1963.

MRS. ROOSEVELT: PORTRAIT OF A BELOVED WOMAN

By EMMA BUGBEE

New York Herald Tribune, November 8, 1962

The wintry road was lonely in the twilight. Down it went running a tall woman with a long blue cape billowing out behind her. Hurrying toward her was a burly man with bandaged head. Both were smiling, their hands outstretched.

The woman was the wife of the President of the United States; the man was a motorcycle policeman who, earlier in the day, had been injured when his cycle got caught in a rut and threw him as he was guiding her car through traffic in Tarrytown, N.Y. Mrs. Franklin D. Roosevelt had gone to the hospital with him. There, she had been assured that his injuries were not serious.

Later, on her way back to New York, she saw him again on his motorcycle. At about the same time, he spotted her car, dismounted and started toward her to thank her for her solicitude.

"I will not have that poor man running to me," she exclaimed, darting down the road.

They met, chatted briefly, shook hands and parted.

Recollections of such incidents are in many hearts now, because they happened so often with countless persons here and in far corners of the world—soldiers and mothers of soldiers, the dispossessed, refugees, discouraged farmers, ailing and crippled people, ambitious college students, friends of high and low degree. Stories about Mrs. Roosevelt's kindness and generosity will go around the world for years.

A Do-It Yourself Original

She found it hard to think of herself as First Lady. In moments of state, of course, she acted with the requisite formality, but when the public curtains were drawn she was unpretentious, self-sacrificing, energetic, a do-it-yourself original.

I remember a scene at the Hyde Park swimming pool, where a considerable number of persons had borrowed bathing suits to join the President in the water. An hour later, everybody else was enjoying a picnic lunch. It was Rannie Hurst who looked up and said:

"Will you look at our First Lady now!"

She was hanging out a dozen bathing suits to dry.

She seldom rode in a parlor car on her trips to Hyde Park.

"All my life," she said, "I have been going up and down the Hudson River Valley in the day coach, and I'm not different now."

Eventually, the years in the White House taught her discretion. She found she must use a drawing room on long trips because strangers would interrupt her work, and she invariably had planned to devote those railroad hours to her correspondence or writing. The whole first version of her book, "This Is My Story," was dictated to her secretary, the late beloved Malvina Thompson Scheider, on a cross-country railroad trip in 1936.

"Tommy" was beloved not only because she was utterly faithful and endlessly competent, but because she had the gift of a salty tongue and could make her employer laugh when things became difficult.

"Much Better Than Her Pictures"

If Mrs. Roosevelt was ever hurt by the cartoons and the unflattering photographs that appeared in newspapers, she never showed it. Next day she would again oblige the photographer who confronted her at railroad stops. The late Heywood Broun once wrote that she had the best manners in the United States.

Sometimes the photographs did her justice. They showed a pleasant expression, a sweet smile or a moment of gaiety. These were the things that impressed persons who met her face-to-face, and noticed the kind blue eyes, the smooth skin, the fair hair. "Why, she's so much better looking than her pictures," was the universal comment.

Good pictures or bad, she went on about her business with no thought for such trifles. I believe she honestly accepted the fact that news photographs, like news stories, were inevitable. Like the rain, they were bound to happen to a person in public life, and nothing she could do would halt them. Therefore, no fretting. Get them over with as quickly as possible.

There was a little group of newspaper women who were often in her company on state occasions and sometimes behind the scenes.

It is difficult now to sort out the memories of those days and tell what seem most revealing of her character.

Perhaps one should describe the scene on Election Day in 1932 when Franklin D. Roosevelt was first elected. She was not yet ready to don the mask of First Lady.

As a newspaper woman I called at the house on East 65th St. to inquire where she would be later in the evening, after the returns were in, when she would be expected to make a statement for publication (assuming Mr. Roosevelt was elected).

She answered the door herself, because, she said, "the maids are busy."

"Come in," she said, "and I'll try to find out from Franklin where we'll be, probably at Democratic headquarters. Meantime, have you had dinner?"

"No, I really haven't," I said, "But——"

"Well, come on in and have some supper," she said. "It's just a buffet with scrambled eggs and salad, because we've all just returned from Hyde Park and there are lots of people here. But you have to eat somewhere."

So there I was eating and watching the President-to-be, who sat regally in a big armchair while all around him laughing and joking were the important Democratic men of his circle—James A. Farley, Louis McHenry Howe and others.

And there was Mrs. Roosevelt dishing up scrambled eggs that later were to be famous as the President's favorite supper dish. She stopped only when someone read aloud the first election bulletin. It was the return from a safe Democratic district downtown, but it was a good omen and everybody shouted for joy.

Mrs. Roosevelt's ease with newspaper women (and men) was among the White House innovations for which she was criticized, but I always believed it—and the others—stemmed from the same simplicity and distaste for pomp which marked her in other fields.

She disliked the idea of the White House as a palace. She said repeatedly that the White House belonged to the people of the United States and therefore they had a right to know what it looked like and even (within reason) to know what its occupants did.

The day after the first inauguration she showed some of us through the house, not only the state chambers but the upstairs private quarters—the bedrooms, the President's study, the cozy west room which was to become the family sitting room—all showing signs of a family not yet settled in.

Later, there were many occasions when Mrs. Roosevelt invited one or more newspaper women to spend the night. It happened to me first when I was flying with her to Washington where I was to attend some convention or other. She turned to me as the White House car met her at the airport, and she said:

"I hate to think of you alone in a hotel tonight. Why don't you stay with us overnight?"

Of course, there was no reason why not.

That night, or some time later, I was to sleep in the Lincoln bed.

"I always like to have everybody sleep at least once in the Lincoln room," she would say.

Lent Reporter Her Cottage

Another picture in my memory shows Mrs. Roosevelt in a blue bathing suit, standing on the edge of a swimming pool in Puerto Rico, after a breakfast with her newspaper entourage. One of the party was the late Ruby Black, a Washington reporter, who at the moment was racked with a severe cough which had bothered her despite the summer weather of the palmy island. Mrs. Roosevelt was on an NRA inspection trip—at the President's request— to see the slums and thatched cottages where toiled the makers of inexpensive embroidered garments.

Mrs. Roosevelt paused before diving into the water, and turned to me. "I'm so worried about Ruby," she said. "Do you think she would take our cottage at Campobello for August? We shall not be using it, and I always like to give it to somebody."

(Ruby and her family did take the cottage, to her great benefit.)

Mrs. Roosevelt's White House press conferences, at first planned only to cover her official engagements as a convenience to the reporters, soon became a channel for her crusades in the field of social welfare. More than any other First Lady and to an extent unique in American history, Mrs. Roosevelt conceived it to be her duty to help promote the national welfare— in the Depression, and then in the war—by pressing at every opportunity for the measures she considered important.

Once we asked if the President okayed these pronouncements.

"No, it's not necessary," she replied. "Franklin and I think alike on these matters, so there's no need to waste his time."

Aware And Not Afraid

Then she added with a chuckle:

"Once I did think it advisable to ask him, and he said, 'Lady, this is a free country. You may say anything you please!' And then he laughed. 'I have my own way of getting my views across to the American people. If you get me in hot water, I'll manage to save myself.'"

Those pronouncements often touched on inflammatory topics, not only about the then increasingly explosive Negro problem but Left-wing youth groups and communism. Once someone observed that she would "get into trouble" by a certain statement.

"I am aware of that and not afraid," she answered. "You may not realize that I often raise these points deliberately, believing it is important for people to talk about them. If I can start more discussion—on both sides—it is all to the good."

Those 12 years (plus a few weeks) of her White House pronouncements on public matters gave her the assurance that enabled her later to take her place effectively in the United Nations, and in Democratic party affairs.

In recent years she spent the greater part of her energies in an endless round of speaking engagements, always urging greater understanding for the United Nations, a self-imposed dedication to the organization her husband had founded. By this time her views were well known. The limelight of the White House no longer beat upon her, and her speeches had less newspaper value. But that never caused her to waver in her purpose.

Once she told us she was going that evening to a small meeting in the suburbs—a tiresome place to reach. Some one protested that she should spare her energies for important gatherings. Why did she have to waste herself on a small group?

"Because nobody else will," she replied.

12

Henrietta Goodnough Hull "Peggy Hull"
(1889–1967)

T HE CHINESE WERE in retreat as advancing Japanese troops and bombers shelled Shanghai in the brief war of 1932. Caught in the middle while on her way to interview Chinese General Tsai Ting-kai, Peggy Hull of the *New York Daily News* and her driver abandoned their car, raced across an open field, and took refuge in the first protection they saw—a mound-shaped Chinese tomb. Huddled silently in the small space at the end of the grave, they felt the earth shudder as shells hit the ground around them, listened as bullets whistled overhead, and through a crack in the door watched the dim silhouettes of Japanese soldiers coming toward them. Suddenly, in a panic, the driver Sasha, who only recently had escaped from Russia into China, crawled out of the tomb, bolted across the field into the path of the oncoming soldiers and was shot.

"I had been frightened many times, but I had never known the extreme of terror that was now forcing its way into my mind," Peggy Hull later recalled in *I Can Tell It Now*. "Hunching over my knees, I continued to stare out the partly ajar door. Seeing Sasha killed had unnerved me, I realized, and the prospect of dying in an already occupied grave filled me with a macabre horror. Yet I could not escape. . . . They were coming directly toward the grave and as they moved they stopped every few feet, aimed, and fired."

To run as Sasha had or to stay in the tomb meant certain death. Peggy dumped the contents of her pocketbook onto the ground, looking for a piece of unbleached muslin stamped with a design and message in Japanese, which had been given to her by a Japanese admiral during the early days of the war to be used for safe passage through Japanese lines. But she couldn't find it and in her panic couldn't remember for certain whether she had taken it with her from the hotel. She searched every crevice in her pocketbook, flipped through her address book, checkbook, reporter's notebook, and finally found the small square tucked into her passport. Reasoning that they would shoot at her heart, she pinned the message to her coat with hairpins, let down her hair so they could see she was a woman, and crawled out the entrance, emerging with her hands up. The column stopped and a young officer, revolver in hand, approached while Peggy pointed to the muslin on her coat. He looked at it, then looked at her with incredulity and bowed, inquiring in English: "You are lost?" Peggy explained that she had not known of the fighting, and the officer assured her safe transport to Japanese headquarters. She had met the Japanese general when she covered the American Occupation Forces in Siberia in World War I as the first woman to be accredited by the War Department as a foreign correspondent. When she entered his office thirteen years later, he remembered their previous meeting and said: "You know, if you do not give up your war corresponding, you are surely going to end your life on a battlefield."

Although Peggy Hull spent thirty-one years covering military actions on six fronts, the brief Sino-Japanese conflict, in which American troops were not involved, was the only opportunity she had to write firsthand accounts of battles and troop movements. On other assignments she had covered the "woman's angle," filing stories about the soldiers in training camps or on leave in cafés and clubs. The soldiers talked to her about the mess food, their girlfriends, and their fears. In many ways she was a female Ernie Pyle, writing, as she described them, "the little stories, the small unimportant stories which meant so much to the G.I., but for which no editor would use his wire service and which no 'spot news' correspondent had time to seek out and write." One article on "How to Beat the Censor When You Write to Lovers" suggested that soldiers cut out a love poem from a magazine and mail it home.

One of her specialties was to eat at the enlisted men's mess and interview the soldiers, filing a story about the food and using many names and hometowns. She visited the chapels and in her articles told the folks back home that the boys did indeed go to chapel and sing hymns. In one story from the

Pacific in 1944, she wrote that the chaplain told her the only sins the soldiers committed were "sins against purity and sins against charity."

Peggy Hull is remembered today, if at all, as the first woman accredited to be a foreign correspondent. She received no major journalism awards, had few front-page stories, and during her early career had no major newspaper to help her get overseas. Wanderlust characterized her career. She worked for some fifteen newspapers and news syndicates from Hawaii to New York, including papers in Kansas, Colorado, Minnesota, Ohio, Texas, and California. Her longest associations were with the *Cleveland Plain Dealer* as a freelancer covering the 1916 Mexican border incidents and as a World War II syndicated correspondent stationed in Honolulu covering the Pacific in 1944 and 1945, and with the now defunct North American Newspaper Alliance, which distributed her copy on and off for twenty years.

During World War I she started off her correspondent's career wearing a trim officer's tunic, calf-length skirt, polished boots, Sam Browne belt, and a campaign hat; she finished as the only woman accredited for both world wars covering the Pacific, wearing the uniform of a WAC officer with a green and white "C" (for correspondent) band on her left arm and three army campaign ribbons for the Mexican, French, and Russian fronts. At age fifty-three she told an *Editor & Publisher* reporter: "I'll never tire of doing this work, and as long as we have American boys in isolated parts of the world, I want to write their story for them."

Irene Corbally Kuhn, a long-time friend who first met Hull in Paris in the 1920s and sailed with her to Hong Kong, said she was a "small, slender, brown-eyed blonde who wore her short hair bleached long before it was fashionable. She was as feminine as a kitten, and she had a will of iron. She was also the kindest, most generous and compassionate human being I've ever known, a woman all men loved and no woman ever disliked." Hull was also a great cat lover and would keep several when she stayed in one place for any length of time, but curiously chose to have the cats put to sleep when she moved on rather than entrust their care to anyone else.

Peggy Hull traveled from a Kansas farm in Bennington, where she was born Henrietta Eleanor Goodnough on December 30, 1889, to become what she wanted most—a foreign correspondent. She was the eldest of two children of Edwy Goodnough and Minnie Eliza (Finn) Goodnough, who divorced before she was five. Her father, more a dreamer than a farmer, had overcome a boyhood speech impediment and liked to pass time telling stories; Peggy's paternal grandfather, the Rev. Edward Goodnough, had been bishop of Wisconsin for the Episcopal church. When her mother remarried the family moved around a lot, and her education stopped at sixteen when she began her newspaper career on the *Junction City* (Kansas) *Sentinel*, where she worked until around 1908.

In 1910, at twenty-one, Peggy married George C. Hull, a newspaperman she met in Denver while working on the *Republican*. The next year they went to Honolulu where he became city editor of the *Honolulu Evening Bulletin* and she worked as a reporter. Irene Kuhn recalled that George Hull was "a charming man, but like so many newspapermen of the time, a terrible drunk." Peggy endured his antics, Kuhn said, until the night he climbed naked to the top of a flag pole. In 1914 she returned to the continental United States, working on newspapers wherever she could and having her first experience as a correspondent when the United States militia was sent to the California-Mexico border in 1914. She stayed there four months, writing stories at space rates for a San Francisco weekly.

After this, according to David Len Jones' unpublished thesis on Hull, she worked for the *Minneapolis Tribune* as a general assignment reporter and replaced her cumbersome byline of Henrietta Goodnough Hull with the *nom de plume* "Peggy," but kept her married name Hull.

Her next job was at the *Cleveland Plain Dealer*, where she originated the idea of writing "buy lines" copy that advertised local businesses. A skillful promoter of her own ideas, Hull dreamed up publicity stunts and once had herself held up by a masked bandit to advertise a bank. When the Ohio National Guard was sent to the Mexican border in 1916 to help capture Pancho Villa, the Mexican revolutionary, she covered the story for the *Plain Dealer*. Although she was not at the front lines, she marched right along with the soldiers, slept on the ground rolled up in a poncho, and wrote stories reflecting these experiences. The journalist Floyd Gibbons once suggested she write a book and call it *I Slept with a Million Men*.

Whatever military front Hull happened to be covering, said Irene Kuhn, the other correspondents liked her because she was "fun and a good sport." It should be noted, though, that her stories in no way competed with those of male reporters and her abilities did not show up the male reporters' inadequacies. While at the Mexican border some correspondents dreamed up a stunt so that she could meet General John J. Pershing as he led his forces out of Mexico into El Paso. Photographers and newsreel cameramen were told to be in a specific place for the best shots, and when Pershing appeared on his horse, Hull emerged from the sidelines on a white horse, a huge bouquet in her arms, and trotted into position alongside him. Pictures appeared throughout the world carrying the headline: "American girl correspondent leads troops out of Mexico with General Pershing."

"Black Jack" Pershing, Kuhn said, never forgave Hull and stymied her

Peggy Hull

early efforts to get accreditation to go to France in 1917 with the American forces. Finally the *El Paso Morning-Times* agreed to give her press credentials. When General Pershing went to Europe, Hull was right behind, docking in Liverpool four days after him and arriving in Paris in time to see the first American troops parade on July 4. In Paris she started selling articles to the *Chicago Tribune*'s Paris edition and had her first foreign byline in August with a story of "How Peggy Got to Paris." She also wrote a weekly non-byline column called "The Letter From Home," from July 20 to September 30, 1917. The format featured two Chicago friends, Hank in the United States and Mike in the service somewhere in France. Hank would write about events at home and give advice to his friend. Other articles appeared in the Paris and Chicago editions of the *Tribune* bylined only "Peggy." One described a visit to an army training camp at Le Valdahon near Besançon. Other correspondents read the dispatches and wanted to know who this "Peggy" was, since no woman had been accredited to the American Expeditionary Forces. The stories were chatty and informal, mostly about the adventures and problems of a young woman in the midst of several thousand soldiers. Although nothing she wrote was competitive with the work of reporters based at Neufchâteau, the men nevertheless decided to make an issue out of her presence. Hull appealed to General Pershing to help her stay, offering a compromise that would have her accredited to the *Tribune*'s Paris edition and also to General Peyton March, whose troops she had reported on for two months. Eventually, after all the military memos had been routed and initialed, Hull lost out to the disgruntled male correspondents. Ordered back to Paris, she learned that her mother was ill and went home to Kansas.

When her family duties ended, she wanted to return to Paris. It was the summer of 1918 and President Woodrow Wilson had agreed to limited American participation in an allied invasion of Russia, landing troops at Vladivostok on August 16. Determined to go to this distant front, and this time properly accredited, she sent telegrams to fifty papers, offering her services. Meanwhile she sought out General March, who had returned from Paris and was chief of staff in Washington. According to a story by Jack O'Donnell in the April 1920 *Ladies Home Journal*, at their meeting General March told Hull:

Your stories are the sort that give the people at home a real idea of what the American soldier is like and what he likes and dislikes. I'd like to see you go with the Siberian expedition. These men are likely to be lost sight of in view of the big things that are happening in France. If you can get an editor to send you, I'll accredit you!

When all fifty papers turned down her request, she wrote to S. T. Hughes, editor of Newspaper Enterprise Association (NEA), who knew of her reporting from the Mexican border. At last, he gave her the assignment. Still, there was more red tape, for she needed to get a written order from General March to the Military Intelligence Branch which stated: "If your only reason for refusing Miss Peggy Hull credentials is because she is a woman, issue them at once and facilitate her procedure to Vladivostok." On September 24, 1918, she received the first war correspondent accreditation granted a woman and on November 15 started her 10,000-mile journey to Siberia, arriving after the armistice but in time to join an allied celebration of the end of World War I.

NEA promoted Hull with advertisements headlined:

Russia—Land of Blood and Bolshevism!
Siberia—Scene of Murder and Mystery!

Into these twin regions of dense ignorance and eternal terror, an American girl reporter, one of the ablest of American newspaper women is penetrating today to obtain exclusive news of happenings there.

Hull remained in Siberia for ten months, then traveled to China where she worked on the *Shanghai Gazette*, returned home for a while, and in the 1920s went back to Paris. She and Irene Kuhn lived in a cheap hotel on the Rue St. Antoine, became friends, and decided to go to Shanghai together— a journey that Kuhn records in her autobiography, *Assigned to Adventure* (1938). The high point of the seven-week sail from Marseilles to Hong Kong was Peggy Hull's meeting with Captain John Kinley in Singapore. Peggy told Irene after meeting him and being invited to breakfast: "I've fallen for him hard. It happened between the grapefruit and the eggs." They were married on February 22, 1922, in Hong Kong. As a Yangtze River pilot, Kinley could earn from $2,000 to $10,000 a month, depending on the tidal difficulties encountered on the river. His wife traveled with him, continuing to file stories for various papers, and using her former merchandising expertise to publish a shopping guide for passengers. Kinley, a seafaring man from the Isle of Man, was as hard drinking as her first husband had been. After two years they separated—though they did not divorce until 1933—and she returned to the *Shanghai Gazette* for a while.

During this second stay in China she started her own syndicate, selling freelance articles to United States papers about life in Asia. By 1927 she was living in New York, working as a freelancer and a publicity writer. While in New York she renewed a friendship with Harvey Vail Deuell, managing editor of the *New York Daily News*, whom she had met seventeen years earlier in Denver. Deuell was a forty-two-year-old bachelor who was very close to his mother. A journalist who had worked on papers in Denver and Chicago, he had joined the *Daily News* and become committed to the concept of an illustrated newspaper. He had studied photography at the Eastman Kodak Company's school in Rochester, New York, and was fascinated with the problems of taking photographs under adverse conditions. The idea of surreptitiously photographing murderess Ruth Snyder as she died in the electric chair at Sing Sing has been attributed to him. According to *Time* magazine, he was the highest paid managing editor in the country for 1938, with a salary of $140,000.

Hull returned to Shanghai in late 1931 for the *Daily News* and was there when the Japanese attacked the city in 1932. Returning to New York, she received her divorce from Captain Kinley, and the *News* announced the wedding plans of Deuell and Hull on June 17, 1933. Big, shaggy Harvey Deuell prized the wife that he had married late in life and bought her a lovely old mansion called Saxton Hall in Cornwall-on-Hudson overlooking the training fields of West Point. Despite the Depression, they traveled to South and Central America, lavishly entertained journalists and writers, many of whom Hull befriended and lent money to finish books. (*Chicken Every Sunday* by Rosemary Taylor and *Whistle Stop* by Marietta Wolff were just two of these.)

During her third marriage, judged by Irene Kuhn to be the happiest, she lived quietly, surrounded by cats in her columned mansion. One room alone was filled with her collection of needles and embroidery thread. She did work on her memoirs, but according to Kuhn, the perfectionist Deuell didn't think the early chapters were good enough, and she lost interest. After six years, Deuell died of a heart attack while driving to work on October 29, 1939. His will put everything in trust for his wife and mother, with Saxton Hall to be turned into a resort hotel and the income used for Hull's living expenses. Kuhn said he made such conditions to curb what he saw as his wife's spendthrift inclinations. Her close friends at this time were Hobert and Hubert Skidmore, twins and writers, who lived in a cottage on the grounds of Saxton Hall. She continued to live at the estate, preferring to use income from her husband's insurance rather than turn her home into a resort. But eventually boredom and the need for more funds compelled her to return to reporting again.

In late 1943, at the age of fifty-four, she approached Paul Bellamy, editor of the *Plain Dealer*, who had been city editor at the time Hull covered the Mexican border action. Sponsored by her old newspaper and the North American Newspaper Alliance, Hull set off to the Pacific to cover the final days of World War II. Her accreditation credentials had never been cancelled. Again she wrote motherly stories about the soldiers designed to reassure anxious relatives. In her first dispatch there was more poetry than fact.

Today I am writing my first story in the second World War. I am writing while planes drum and sputter across a blue sky filled with tiny white puffs of clouds; while a turtle dove croons persuasively in a palm tree outside my room and flocks of birds scramble and fight for the crumbs I have just thrown to them.

Recalling Hull at that time, retired Navy Rear Admiral Harold Blaine Miller told David Jones in 1979 that she was a motherly type who "always wore a funny knit hat. She was somewhat heavy set; in short, she was sort of a mother to many and even a grandmother to most of us. She never failed to have her sewing kit which she would break out to sew on a button or a torn sleeve. In her mild manner you might wonder how she could write, but she did."

After the war, she sold Saxton Hall and moved to Carmel Valley, California, with Hobert Skidmore as a companion and surrogate son. In the early 1960s she converted to Catholicism and would sit for hours on the veranda of a nearby convent talking with the nuns. She again attempted to write her memoirs, but never published them. Outside of newspapers, Peggy Hull's only published works were the lead articles for two Overseas Press Club books: in *The Inside Story* (1940) she detailed the Mexican raid on Columbus, Texas, in 1916, and in *I Can Tell It Now* (1964) she wrote about her experiences in Shanghai in 1932.

On June 19, 1967, she died of cancer at the age of seventy-seven in a Monterey, California, hospital. During her exciting career, Peggy Hull covered the news in her own insightful way, adding much warmth and folksy emotion to her stories from distant fronts. Her achievements demonstrated that women, indeed, could set out on their own and become foreign correspondents, though mostly on a freelance basis. She had talked her way into many assignments and frequently bucked the governmental bureaucracy by the time she concluded in an article of March 31, 1945, in the *Honolulu Star-Bulletin* that "to know the fullness of a well-rounded life it is necessary to have struggled; to have pitted one's initiative and courage and wits in a competitive field, to have ventured into the world with ideas and hopes and projects."

The following dispatches are examples of Peggy Hull's Siberian reporting: an opinion piece, and the soldier interview, a story style that she perfected.

PEASANTS ARE TORTURED
For Refusing to Aid New Russian Army

Cincinnati Post, June 6, 1919

When I think of the carnage and massacre of the past week I feel that Siberia, grand, magnificent and irresistible in its natural beauties, is still doomed to house the bitterness and tragedy of the days of czarism and exile.

A punitive expedition from Vladivostok visited a village near here. They came to draft the sons of the peasants into the new Russian army which the Omak government is organizing. All the young men ran away into the hills and when their fathers and grandfathers denied knowledge of their whereabouts 11 were taken from their homes, beaten with whips and rifle butts and then taken to an attic, where they were tortured. They first were hung to the beams by wires and ropes, and their hands tied.

Finally Shot to Death

Scalding water and hot irons blistered and scarred their bodies. They were flogged until the blood from their wounds spattered the walls and formed little pools on the floor—then, mercifully, they were propped against a wall, and shot!

The peasants were so aroused over this action they armed themselves and drove the punitive expedition out. They were immediately called Bolshevists and the allies were asked to send troops to fight them, but they didn't and I don't think they will—under the circumstances.

Refuse to Fight

Peasants refuse to fight for Kolchak and his government and at the same time they refuse to fight for the Bolsheviki. They maintain that Admiral Kolchak elected himself to his present place as dictator and that his methods are as high-handed as the czar's.

They clamor for the privilege of personal political expression, yet they refuse to see that there must be a unity of desire before that is possible. They cannot read and they cannot write. They are confused and bewildered over the thing they clamor for and if they were left to pursue their lives as farmers with military exemption I believe they would be contented with the Kolchak government. That is, if the agitators were bound and gagged.

Lie About Americans

They go among villagers and spread unhappiness and fear in the wake of their lives. They have lied about the Americans. They have lied about the ambitions of the allies. They keep the peasants in a continuous state of uncertainty, and consequently they are not willing to support anyone or any government.

Such tactless and undiplomatic moves as the punitive expedition add fuel to the agitator's fire or the Bolshevist's arguments. They cry for reprisals and invariably they get them. We hear that a Russian officer has been captured and his eyes gouged out.

Bodies Mutilated

In the translations from the Russion press under the headline "More Bolshevik Atrocities," I read that two officers of the Kolchak army had been found murdered in their room. Their bodies were mutilated and their hands nailed thru the palms to their shoulders. A message was pinned to one of them, "This is what will happen to all officers of the autocrats, Admiral Kolchak and General Horvat."   PEGGY HULL

RUSSIAN YOUTH WAR VETERAN
Tho Only 17, Boy Serves Three Years at Front.
By PEGGY HULL

Cincinnati Post, June 10, 1919

WITH THE AMERICAN ARMY IN SIBERIA: Nicholas Gukuvin is a strange product of a great war.

He is small, slender, smooth-cheeked and 17, altho he looks 10, in spite of his three years' service with the Russian army on the eastern front. He showed me a saber cut and several bullet wounds to prove it.

Nicholas is a peculiar combination of a boy and a man. He is intensely anti-Bolshevik, vehement and bitter because the allies are not putting forth greater and more active efforts to help Russia. I found him hanging around an American garrison in northern Siberia.

Longs to Fight Again

When a fatherly doughboy asked Nicholas if he would like to go to America and live in a land of peace he was almost insulted and answered sharply, "I don't want a peace job—I want to be a soldier in a fighting army."

"I was in an orphan asylum in Petrograd when the war came," he told me, with the aid of an interpreter. "My mother and father died when I was 3. Lots of the boys were running away to join the army so I went along. I belonged to a Baku regiment as a scout and had a horse.

Wounded in Battle

"One night after I had been with the regiment two years we ran into some Turks. They outnumbered us five to one. That's how I got this," and he pointed to the saber cut on his head. "The Turk thought he had killed me or I couldn't have escaped.

"It put me in the hospital for about a year—that was worse than fighting. We ran out of food and medicine and they shipped me from Moscow to Petrograd and from Petrograd to Chellabinsk. I got well, and when the Czechs came along and the Bolsheviks started trouble I joined the Seventh Regiment. I just transferred myself from the Russian army.

Fights Bolshevists

"We had a lot of fighting after that all along the line to Vladivostok and—" He opened both his hands with a quick significant gesture, smiling one of his boyish smiles—"I got more than that." He meant more than 10.

"Yes," he went on, "I got more Bolsheviks than I can count."

But the old wounds and the saber cut began to hurt and the Czechs shipped him to Vladivostok, where he was discharged as unfit for further service, but Nicholas is Russian and 17 and hope never dies in a heart so young.

PART II

BOLD BYLINES

BY THE FIRST DECADE of the twentieth century, women going into journalism no longer had to hide behind *noms de plume*. They had earned their bold bylines and used their maiden or married surnames, depending on when they started their careers. The bravura style of writing so much admired in every cityroom during the previous century gradually disappeared. New reporting and writing techniques were being developed to chronicle the vast political, social, and economic changes that were to follow as the country moved through World War I, the Depression, World War II, Korea, the Cold War, the civil rights movement, Vietnam, the women's movement, Watergate, and upheavals in Central America.

Trials still made compelling front-page stories and victims still unburdened themselves to women reporters, but new storylines were spawned with Prohibition and the exploits of underworld thugs such as John Dillinger and Lucky Luciano. The investigation of mental institutions, so sensationalized by Nellie Bly, would continue in the name of public service, but in a sober rather than a sob sister tone. Investigative reporters would specialize in uncovering scandals, pay-offs, and graft involving elected officials in all levels of government. By the early 1960s specialists in the business, science, environmental, and cultural fields would be added to the ranks of the general assignment reporter, and by the early 1970s the term "lifestyle" would be added to the newspaper lexicon.

Newspapers were also changing. By the end of the second decade of the new century readers could choose between the yellow press with its sensational news coverage and the conservative papers that covered the same news but "without a Rabelaisian wink," as one critic put it. Hearst's reckless journalism served as the prologue for a new era that began on June 29, 1919, with the publication of the country's first tabloid, the *New York Illustrated Daily News*, later called the *Daily News*. In England the tabloid had already become the most popular newspaper form. Alfred C. Harmsworth (Lord Northcliffe), one of Britain's famous press lords, had started the *Illustrated Daily News*' British prototype, the *Daily Mirror*, as a paper written for and by women. When the idea of a female journal did not attract readers, Harmsworth changed the newspaper into a half-penny illustrated, the English term for tabloid.

Whereas the yellow press editors had called for "gee whiz" stories, the tabloid editors sent their reporters out for "hot" news. Good copy was called a "sizzler," something that would "burn 'em up," suggesting an actual physical sensation. In his 1931 book *Hot News*, Emile Gauvreau of the *Evening Graphic*, New York's third tabloid, described the new phenomenon as "tabloid mania." He recalled how a rival editor, in a desperate effort to win back his paper's readers, instructed a handsome reporter to insinuate himself into the confidence of a murderer's sister: "If necessary," he said, "marry her to get the story. But get it." Hearst's *Journal* and *American*, although not tabloid size, reflected the same sensibility. Pulitzer's *World*, which had lived down its lurid past, joined other conservative papers such as the *Herald Tribune* and the *Times* in moral indignation against sensational writing.

Nonetheless, the tabloids were important for the careers of many women in American journalism. In her book *Ladies of the Press*, Ishbel Ross noted that the tabloids in the 1920s and 1930s provided jobs and opened the door to different types of women reporters. Tabloid editors, she wrote, "have fewer prejudices against the species. A girl has much more hope of walking in and landing a job than she has on a conservative paper. Stunt girls and beauties are welcome. It isn't essential for them to know how to write if they are exceptionally good at getting facts, or have the knack of finding their way in where other reporters are barred."

The tabloids also ushered in the era of the columnist, which created still more opportunities for women. There had, of course, been columns by women as early as 1893 when Nellie Bly was given a Sunday column in the *World* that announced: "This is all my own. Herein every Sunday I may say all I please and what I please." By the mid-1930s, Hearst's *Mirror* had a signed column on every page, with many written by women. Fay King wrote on personal matters, Frances Dutton on fashion, Gladys Glad on beauty, and Sally Martin on problems of the lovelorn. Nellie Bly's legacy now belongs to Ellen Goodman of the *Boston Globe,* whose syndicated column runs on editorial pages in nearly 400 papers.

Another domain for women was film criticism, often published on the women's pages because such reviews were not considered important enough to be in the theater section. Much of the early criticism was puffery to attract advertisers. By the 1960s, however, a newspaper critic like Judith Crist of the *New York Herald Tribune* was able to stand up to such commercialism. When she panned a movie and the distributor subsequently withdrew its advertising from the paper in retaliation, the *Herald Tribune* published an editorial supporting Crist's integrity as a reviewer.

Athough women continued to excel in feature coverage, there were news reporters like Ishbel Ross of the *Herald Tribune,* who covered the Lindbergh kidnapping, a front-page story for seventy-two days. The "front-page girls," as Ross described them in her book, competed with male reporters from other papers and according to custom did not receive bylines, which were handed out mostly to the feature writers. Mildred Gilman of the *New York Evening Journal,* International News Service, and the *Washington Herald* wrote some of the wonderful jazz-age stories of the 1920s, then covered the grim years of the Depression, the emergence of Hitler's Germany, and the New Deal.

When Franklin D. Roosevelt became President in 1933, the world of Washington politics was opened to women through Eleanor Roosevelt's press conferences held "for women only." Emma Bugbee of the *Herald Tribune,* Doris Fleeson of the *New York Daily News,* and other women reporters became known as Mrs. Roosevelt's "girls," traveling with the First Lady and reporting not only on her but on all aspects of life in the White House.

Today, of course, it is commonplace to see women reporters at presidential press conferences, in the halls of the Capitol, in palaces and parliaments around the world, and at the front lines of wars and revolutions. But such equality was not easily won. It was far more difficult for women to become Washington or foreign correspondents than it was for them to enter the newsroom as reporters. One exception, however, was Mary McGrory of the *Washington Post,* whose syndicated Washington columns give a liberal view of a conservative world and are read for her personal style as well as opinion. McGrory moved from book reviewing on the old *Washington Star* to covering the capital without having to pay her dues on the local or national desks.

From the time Margaret Fuller covered the ill-fated Italian revolution of 1849, there has been an intermingling of adventure, romance, and partisanship in women's desire to report or interpret wars and revolutions, domestic and foreign politics. For many women, the life of a foreign correspondent had to be shelved in favor of other reporting when obstacles to gaining an overseas posting became too frustrating. Prior to World War II newspaper editors gave foreign assignments to male reporters as rewards for work well done. During wartime the military didn't want the responsibility for women, explaining euphemistically that there were no "facilities" for them. To which Maggie Higgins once replied that she would use any available side of the road. The only option for a woman foreign correspondent was somehow to get abroad and then try to impress a newspaper or news agency with exclusive stories, a technique used earlier by Peggy Hull and Anne O'Hare McCormick and later by Sigrid Schultz, Dorothy Thompson, and Georgie Anne Geyer.

Schultz and Thompson became Berlin bureau chiefs for their papers in 1925, and Maggie Higgins headed a bureau there in 1947. In pre- and postwar Berlin these journalists excelled as hostesses at "purpose parties," gatherings to which important military and diplomatic sources were invited. Guests were carefully selected, meals were elegant, dress was formal, and the atmosphere was thick with foreign intrigue as image-makers plied reporters with flattery and propaganda. As hostesses, the women correspondents circulated freely, talking to sources, gathering bits of information, trying to sift out truths. When they attended as guests, however, the protocol was often different. Higgins once recalled attending a party where, in Victorian fashion, the men and women were separated after dinner, and while she spent time in idle chit-chat over coffee with the women, she worried that her competition was interviewing an important official over cigars and brandy.

No women covered World War I combat, but by the next war, with at least twenty-one women reporters present at various fronts, the military had grudgingly accepted their presence. Women correspondents asked for no special favors. If a Jeep wasn't available, they hiked and sloshed through the mud. They often slept hunched over their typewriters. When they were interviewed by other reporters about life at the front, the invariable question was what they packed. Hull carried a sewing kit along with her typewriter, for she loved mothering the soldiers and would darn their socks and mend their clothes. Higgins traveled with only a typewriter, toothbrush, towel, insect powder, and lipstick. Still, she was always recognized as a woman. "Of course, the GI's whistle and wolf-call as you Jeep down past a convoy on a road," Higgins wrote in *War in Korea.* "But when the shelling and the shooting starts, nobody pays any attention. No one has offered me his foxhole yet. And they didn't have to. I early developed a quick eye for protective terrain and can probably hit a ditch as fast as any man."

Foreign correspondents have always seen themselves as special, and when women joined the ranks they were no exception. "Although some newspaper editors maintain that regular street reporters are the same as—and can be exchangeable for—foreign correspondents, they are really two very different types of people," Geyer wrote in *Buying the Night Flight*. "To be a foreign correspondent means being of a particular, somewhat manic temperament, always seeking to conceptualize and bring things down to their roots . . . to love the entire process, in fact, to love the life."

Eventually women—Dorothy Thompson and Ellen Goodman, for example—moved from chronicling the news to interpreting it, making their reputations not as reporters but as columnists whose views were frequently printed on the editorial page. In all areas of the arts, not just film criticism, women's bylines could be noted throughout the country. As the first architecture critic for a daily newspaper, Ada Louise Huxtable was as boldly outspoken in her opinions on architects, city planners, and developers in the 1960s as Margaret Fuller, the first literary critic, had been in the 1840s in her appraisals of Edgar Allan Poe and Henry Wadsworth Longfellow. Huxtable's columns, which earned her a Pulitzer Prize, were influential in saving historic buildings and stopping developers' bulldozers, as well as in defining the role of architecture critic for daily newspapers.

Reporting on issues of concern to women started in 1873 when Jennie June began writing about the latest fashions and promoting stores and brand-name products. By the turn of the century many papers had pages devoted to society announcements, but they were mostly pallid compendiums of weddings, engagements, and pictures of women planning events over cups of tea. By the 1950s the "women's pages" had started to grow up and readers found stories for women—and men—about the facts of modern life. In sections later retitled "View," "Living," "Lifestyle," and "Outlook" there were stories on housewife alcoholics, lesbian mothers, child abuse, joint custody, abortion, the elderly, and the Equal Rights Amendment. By the mid-1970s these "pages" had become special sections in four-part papers, along with sections on home, design, food, sports, business, science, and the arts.

As a result, the concept of the feature changed—in all sections of the paper. The sob sisters and the tabloid writers had specialized in emotional accounts of people coping with death, loss and violence, but rarely did they go beyond reactions to a tragic situation to examine why something had happened and who—if anyone—was accountable. With the awareness that life was more than a soap opera, that social issues affected every aspect of living, reporters working on human interest stories began to probe the ethics and responsibility of government, business, and religion, often instigating change in the process. This new feature style called for longer in-depth stories, multi-part stories, or cover stories in a newspaper's Sunday magazine. Madeleine Blais of the *Miami Herald* has specialized in this magazine-style account. Indeed, the newspaper of the 1980s, with its bold graphics, picture stories, and special sections, often looks and reads more like a magazine than a "news" paper.

The dozen newspaperwomen presented in this section were—and are— venturesome and dedicated, but they came into journalism better prepared to deal with the modern complexities of the profession than their predecessors. With the exception of Ishbel Ross, who received the traditional public girls' school education in Scotland, all earned college degrees, and three have graduate degrees in journalism. Among them they have been awarded two Fulbright Fellowships, one Guggenheim, one Neiman, one Maria Moors Cabot award, four Pulitzer Prizes, and numerous other honors given to journalists of distinction. These women and the younger generation of newspaperwomen who now have the opportunity to report from anywhere in the world—as well as the public which benefits from their contributions—owe a debt of gratitude to the courageous women with the bygone bylines who came before them: Margaret Fuller, Jane G. Swisshelm, Nellie Bly, Jennie June, Annie Laurie, Polly Pry, Ida Wells-Barnett, and Elizabeth Jordan.

13

Sigrid Schultz
(1893–1980)

T O BE A FOREIGN CORRESPONDENT in Berlin in 1935 was to be in constant combat with the Nazi propaganda machine. Largely unimpressed with the new government's touted superiority and efficiency, journalists filed stories on arrests, persecutions, and rigged trials. For the Nazis to expel a correspondent who reported the truth only attracted attention; a better strategy was to tame the press corps. To this end, Herman N. Göring, Hitler's second in command, devised a clumsy spy plot: a reporter would be tricked into sending a dispatch containing secret military information, arrested for espionage, and publicly tried. Other correspondents, Göring reasoned, would be intimidated and come around to writing what Germany wanted the world to know. The plan was executed with an obvious cloak-and-dagger scenario: shabby-looking characters started dropping in on correspondents to offer secret plans for weapons and plants. Soon the word went around to be careful.

At that time, no American correspondent knew more about behind-the-scenes Germany than Sigrid Schultz, the *Chicago Tribune*'s bureau chief, who had lived in Berlin since World War I. She was immediately suspicious when a man came to her office offering details on a weapon only a spy would want. She ordered him out, but a few days later an envelope was delivered to her home, with the message that the information could wait until Schultz returned. Her mother, with whom she was living, immediately called her about the visit, and Schultz grabbed her coat and rushed home. She burned the unopened envelope in the fireplace, sifting through the embers to make sure no scrap remained that could be identified. When she left to return to work, she noticed the man who had been in her office; with him were two secret-police officers. "Don't bother to go in," she shouted at them as she got into a taxi. "I just destroyed the information."

The Nazis referred to Schultz as "that dragon from Chicago." Her colleagues had other descriptions: "a female bloodhound," "a small Sherman tank in motion," and "well-informed, buoyant and cheerful." Always more outspoken than diplomatic, she decided that the entrapment incident should be thrown back in the face of its creator. She knew Göring. In fact, she had invited him to her dinner parties because, she said, he had "good table manners." Shortly after the envelope burning, she was to be co-hostess at a luncheon honoring Göring and his new actress bride. Schultz arranged to be seated on his right.

The Nazi arrived at his party in bad temper. He was particularly enraged about what he termed "sentimental" coverage of the concentration camps and complained loudly to Schultz and any other correspondents who would listen. Choosing the right moment, Sigrid Schultz leaned toward Göring and, in a conspiratorial whisper, told him how she had foiled his little spy plan, adding that the American Embassy had been informed. Göring's feigned disbelief quickly turned to new anger, and he snarled, "Schultz, I've always suspected it. You'll never learn to show the proper respect for state authorities. I suppose that is one of the characteristics of people from that crime-ridden city of Chicago." After the confrontation, Schultz later wrote that she "felt as proud as if I had scored a coup and netted gratifying headlines."

One of the first correspondents to warn readers of the Nazi menace, she noted in the introduction of her book, *Germany Will Try It Again* (1944):

In 1930 I realized that the Nazis would play a decisive role in European history and I began studying them most closely. Until then they could have been defeated by a militant democracy. In the first interview I had with Hitler he staggered me by asserting, at the top of his voice: "My will shall be done," and by showing very clearly that he felt he had the right to speak in religious terms. At a dinner at my house . . . Goring gave me an insight into Nazi mentality by describing in detail the joy he had felt in 1914 when his sword had cracked through the bones of his first French adversary.

Fluent in French, Polish, and Dutch, and with a colloquial command of German, she used her language ability and a talent for entertaining to bring together journalists and other guests, including Hohenzollerns, Nazis, and Communists. She had a natural grace as a hostess, for she had been around notable people since childhood, traveling throughout Europe while her father painted portraits of the "wealthy, the important or the beautiful." Her journalistic rival Dorothy Thompson was certainly more glamorous and impressive, but Schultz, far from being "that dull woman" (as Thompson's novelist husband, Sinclair Lewis, called her), was an astute observer and listener—and most importantly, an interpreter. When Schultz interviewed Hitler in 1931, she immediately sensed his power; Thompson, by contrast, interviewed him the same year and pronounced him "a man of startling insignificance"—a misjudgment that haunted her till her death.

Frequent parties, with abundant food and speculative conversation, played an important newsgathering role in the postwar period in Berlin, an era of decadent living captured in one mood by Christopher Isherwood through his character Sally Bowles of I Am a Camera. "A good kitchen and cellar are the best requisites for getting news," Schultz once said. At these parties Göring, for one, was never at a loss for words, remarking once between mouthfuls of his hostess' excellent cooking, "You people gorge yourselves while the masses are starving," and another time, "The only way to treat a woman is to beat her."

Even though she freely entertained Nazi leaders, she was always one step ahead of being expelled for her outspoken views and articles.[1] The Propaganda Ministry wanted to get rid of her, wrote fellow correspondent William L. Shirer in Berlin Diary, "because of her independence and knowledge of things behind the scenes." Indeed, the Chicago Tribune waited until the end of the war to reveal that a series of highly critical articles, "The Truth About Nazi Germany," published in its Graphic magazine in 1938 and 1939, had been written by Schultz, under the byline John Dickson. Her daily dispatches never failed to warn about the dangers of war, and even though the Tribune was an isolationist paper, it backed up her stories with editorials condemning Hitler and Mussolini. Her warnings never stopped. "To be fooled once is tragic," she concluded in Germany Will Try It Again. "To be fooled twice is unforgivable."

In an effort to avoid constant censorship, she would cross the border into Denmark or Norway and send dispatches under her nom de plume. Her articles exposed the concentration camps, the persecution of Jews, the secret

[1] In the 1930s many rumors circulated about Sigrid Schultz. Because of her surname, some thought her to be German; because of her strong anti-Nazi feeling, others thought her to be Jewish. The most slanderous untruth, however, is attributed to the novelist Katherine Anne Porter and is quoted by Joan Givner in Katherine Anne Porter: A Life (1982). "Porter, calling her 'Sigrid Somethingorother,' said that she was raised in the United States of German parents and described her as 'indeed a beautiful woman—treacherous, devious, fiendishly clever and always scheming—but a real beauty nonetheless. Hitler and his sordid clique could not have hoped for a more attractive ally.' "

Sigrid Schultz

arrests, the attacks on churches. As "Dickson," she accurately predicted the Munich agreement between Hitler and Chamberlain and revealed that Hitler was fully prepared for war.

As early as 1931 Hitler told her that she would never understand the Nazi movement, because she "thought with her head and not with her heart." He was wrong, of course, on both counts, for Schultz had been analyzing Germany and the German character, both intellectually and emotionally, since the end of World War I. In fact, she pinpointed the date for the beginning of the Nazi push as shortly before the guns ceased firing on November 11, 1918. After twenty-five years in Germany, and alarmed by Americans' romantic notion of that nation, she decided to return home and write her only book. As stated in the title, her thesis was that Germany started preparing for a second war as soon as it was clear that the first one was lost. And when the Germans lost the Battle of Britain in 1940, they began preparing to win the peace even if the war was lost, thus setting the stage for World War III. New York Times reviewer Orville Prescott praised the book's effective propaganda, noting: "Until the peace has been won and Germany disarmed, in fact as well as in theory, it would be well if we had books like this once a month."

Years later, in 1977, she was convinced that such a situation could still happen. At this time, the eighty-four-year-old Schultz was quoted as saying: "Germany has tremendous influence behind the scenes in world politics. It has not given up its hope for reunion of the two Germanys. The inevitable moment will come when they will be reunited and ultimately join in the formation of the United States of Europe. Whether or not it will be a German-dominated united Europe, I cannot say, but the old pan-Germanic, nationalist element in Germany is still strong." Fearing that history would repeat itself, she stressed that the military mind had to be controlled. "When the military men have too much power and the political leaders have too little vision, that's when you get into trouble."

If Sigrid Schultz had not lived and studied in France and Germany, her journalistic career would have been far different. Her Norwegian parents, Herman Schultz and Hedwig (Jaskewitz) Schultz, came to Chicago for the 1893 World's Fair, and their only child, Sigrid Lillian, was born there on January 5, 1893. The family lived in Chicago for seven years and then went to Europe, where her father, a well-known artist, did portraits of royalty. His connections with the German court would eventually be useful to his daughter as a journalist. The family traveled frequently from their home base, Paris, and Sigrid attended the Lycée Racine and the Sorbonne, graduating in 1914.

That same year the family was in Germany and witnessed the Kaiser's declaration of World War I, a scene Schultz would later compare to Hitler's announcement of September 1, 1939, that Nazi troops had marched into Poland. As American citizens, the Schultzes were considered neutral but endured the same food shortages as others during the war; a dish of cooked crow on the table was considered a delicacy. Although times were difficult, she decided to do graduate study in history and international law at Berlin University, choosing a difficult and competitive program for a woman at that time.

When America entered the war, the Schultzes were declared enemy aliens and had to report daily to the police. They chose to remain in Germany, however, because of her mother's poor health. To earn some money, Sigrid attended law classes and translated lectures into French for a fellow student, the mayor of Baghdad, who didn't speak German. (He became smitten with her and wanted to put her in his harem.) In 1919, after completing her studies, she worked for Richard Henry Little, the *Chicago Tribune*'s Berlin correspondent, a veteran reporter who had covered the Spanish-American War, the Russo-Japanese War, and World War I. Her school of journalism was typing Little's letters and deciphering cryptic cables from the *Tribune*'s home office. Multilingual, well-educated, and well-connected, Sigrid Schultz was a remarkably versatile young woman. On her own she became an authority on military strategy and armaments. Even so, she had to start out as a freelancer for the *Tribune* (her first story was on former Kaiser Wilhelm's wedding) before the paper took her seriously. *Tribune* editors started to notice her, though, when she dodged bullets in the Tiergarten and stepped over corpses in frequent street battles and riots during Germany's postwar reconstruction. "I practically got myself killed before the *Tribune* saw my value," she once said.

One of her early scoops was an exclusive interview with Friedrich Ebert, first president of the Weimar Republic, who was dying in a hospital. All press representatives had been barred from his room, but Schultz, who had a bronchial infection, had herself admitted to the hospital and from there smuggled out reports of his last days, writing that she had shared some lemonade with him only minutes before his death.

In 1924, she became the first woman to be elected to the board of directors of the Foreign Press Club in Berlin, a position that gave her access to valuable sources, and the following year she was named Berlin bureau chief. Anticipating war and gas rationing, she bought a Fiat Topolino, which she called "just about the smallest car in creation." She was often afraid to drive her car in Berlin because of a Gestapo tactic to keep unfriendly reporters in line. The Gestapo cars were equipped with a specially built front which was used as a ramming device to push a car over a bridge or into a river. "Even walking," she once said, "I was careful in getting to my office since my stories had to be filed at one in the morning." Visitors to her tiny office in the Esplanade Hotel would often find the five-foot blond working in blue gingham overalls, smoking a pipe, and drinking Sanka coffee.

William L. Shirer, in his memoir 20th Century Journey (1984), wrote of her in this period, "Though attractive Sigrid never married. After I came to know her well I had the feeling that she would have liked to but that the luck of life was against her on that. She was a good correspondent, well informed, hardworking, energetic. But, unfortunately, she was not a good writer. She had a passion for politics, but no feeling for the American language."

When she was made bureau chief, she observed that "nobody in the new Germany seemed surprised to find a woman in charge. The only one to worry occasionally about my status was the Chief of Protocol," who worried about the dress code for the launching of a battleship where men were to be in military or formal dress. "Years later he told me of the negotiations between his office and the Navy about the clothes the lone woman correspondent was to wear. By that time, infinitely more serious problems confronted us."

In addition to running the bureau, she was a weekly radio broadcaster for WOR-Mutual from September 1938 to the end of 1940. All her scripts had to be submitted to the censor to make sure no information unfavorable to Germany was transmitted. Two days before the German invasion of Norway she warned listeners that "all eyes are on Scandinavia" and was immediately cut off the air. After the invasion she persisted in references to "little Norway" and "strong Germany." When the censor objected to her choice of adjectives, she turned her intelligent blue eyes on him and inquired, "Well, aren't you strong?"

Never a correspondent to settle for just chronicling the news, Schultz preferred to anticipate the next Nazi move by piecing together bits of conversations, evaluating German news reports, and making prescient connections. In July 1939, again as "Dickson," she predicted the Nazi-Soviet pact, which stunned the world less than two months later and paved the way for World War II. "The newest toast in high Hitler guard circles is: 'To our secret ally, Russia,'" she wrote. Over Mutual Broadcasting she announced the outbreak of World War II seconds before Shirer's voice was heard on CBS.

On August 26, 1940, she and Shirer were trying to get to the broadcast studio through the British air attacks on Berlin. Shirer made it first, and the engineer insisted he speak close to the microphone, so that the bombing would not be transmitted to the United States. A few minutes later he picked up his broadcast via shortwave and heard Elmer Davis comment on the realistic sound of guns and bombs in the background. The German officials listened and scowled. On her way to the studio Schultz stumbled and got a mass of shrapnel lodged in her leg. Hobbling in, she went on the air, but the same transmitter that had earlier functioned perfectly for CBS and NBC suddenly broke down and the broadcast did not get through.

In *Berlin Diary,* Shirer described the scene:

Until almost dawn we watched the spectacle from a balcony. There was a low ceiling of clouds, and the German searchlight batteries tried vainly to pick up the British bombers. The beams of light would flash on for a few seconds, search the skies wildly, and then go off. The British were cruising as they swished over the heart of the city and flying quite low, judging by the sound of their motors. The German *flak* was firing wildly, completely by sound. It was easy, from the firing, to follow a plane across the sky as one battery after another picked up the sound of the motors and fired blindly into the sky.

After Schultz contracted typhus in 1941, she returned to America, stayed to write her book and returned to Europe two years later as a war correspondent with the First and Third Armies and the Air Power Press Camp for the *Chicago Tribune.* She also filed stories for *McCall's* and after the war reported from Europe for Mutual and for *Collier's* magazine.

A founder of the Overseas Press Club, an organization for foreign correspondents, she collaborated on three club-sponsored books. She edited the *Overseas Press Club Cookbook* (1962), which offered recipes for the Aga Khan's favorite chocolate dessert and the oyster stew *à la Orata* served to Göring. For *How I Got That Story* (1967), she told of the spy caper and how she stood up to Göring, and in *I Can Tell It Now* (1964), a collection of behind-the-news stories, Schultz wrote about the final hours of Adolf Hitler, pieced together through interviews she had with Nazis who had been in the bunker. One source was a friend of Kaete Haeusermann who was the assistant to Hitler's dentist, Dr. Hugo Blaschke, a long-time Nazi and a graduate of the University of Pennsylvania. On the day that Hitler and Eva Braun committed suicide, Hitler had given Haeusermann a poison capsule in case she wanted to end her life. Instead she left the bunker and returned home. Shortly afterward she was picked up by Russian intelligence officers and taken to a hospital outside Berlin to identify any of the smashed and half-burned jaws displayed on a table. According to Schultz's source, she identified two bridges and a distinctive old-fashioned "window crown" as belonging to Hitler. On July 6, 1945, Schultz filed a story on the identification, noting that Haeusermann had been summoned a second time in May by the Russians and had not returned home. Since the Russians had denied that there was any proof of Hitler's death, this was a major story.

In her last years Sigrid Schultz lived in Westport, Connecticut, where her home, interestingly, was in the middle of a parking lot. (Friends had convinced developers, who wanted to demolish her house, to pave around it.)

Interviewed at this time by the oral history library of the American Jewish Committee, she revealed that she had helped numerous Jews escape the Nazis.

She died at her home on May 14, 1980, at the age of eighty-seven. One of her most enduring comments advised Americans "to take into consideration not only the nature and ambitions of our enemies, but also to remember our own psychological make-up. We are very kindhearted, and that may prove dangerous to us."

When Hitler led his mechanized forces into Austria on March 11, 1938, Sigrid Schultz telephoned her report from Vienna, the first full-length dispatch received by the *Chicago Tribune* via trans-Atlantic telephone. The report, which appeared the following day, has the urgency of a radio broadcast.

BERLIN JUBILANT AS VIENNA FALLS TO HITLER'S AIDS
Troops Rushed to Border All Day Long.
By SIGRID SCHULTZ

Chicago Tribune, March 12, 1938

BERLIN, March 11—German troops were converging toward the Austrian border all day and crossed into Austria tonight a few minutes after Reichsfuehrer Adolf Hitler received a telegram from Austria's new provisional chancellor, Dr. Arthur Seyss-Inquart, asking the Austrian born dictator of Germany "to send troops to Austria to help restore order and prevent bloodshed."

The telegram was read with jubilance over the radio at 10:30 o'clock tonight, ending a day of uncertainty in which soldiers and officers of Germany's new powerful army kept thundering toward the Austro-German border while officials steadily asserted there was "no abnormal movement of troops in Germany."

7th Corps First to Cross

The seventh army corps, which is stationed in Bavaria under its commander, Knight von Schobert, was the first to cross the age old border line.

The joy felt in Nazi circles was expressed in the hopeful assurance that the "day has come when German Nazis together will pull out all border posts which divided the Austrian and German nations and divided them both."

Until they received the Seyss-Inquart plea for military help, officials barely dared to hope that he would be able to fulfill the tremendous promises he gave the Hitler envoys, Wilhelm Kepler and Joseph Buerckel, that he would be strong enough to enforce "absolute reconciliation between the brother nations."

Deny Seizure Ultimatum

German Nazis continue to deny with vehemence that today's victory was enforced by Germany's ultimatum, asserting that the "army and police refused to obey Chancellor Kurt Schuschnigg and made it impossible for him to enforce the plebiscite he had ordered and remain at the helm of the government."

[Chancellor Schuschnigg resigned today in accordance with an ultimatum from Germany.]

Until late today rooms had been reserved in a Berlin hotel for Dr. Seyss-Inquart who had planned to come to Berlin for further advice if he and Hitler's envoys failed to break Schuschnigg.

In the course of the day, German representatives in Paris and London called on the foreign offices and informed them of the action Hitler planned in Austria.

15,000 Return to Austria

Fifteen thousand men of the Austrian legion of refugees who fled to Germany when in danger of arrest for Nazi activities in Austria now are crossing the border into their homeland. They are to serve as reinforcements for local police of districts from which they came.

All day long, German papers continued their vicious attacks on the ousted Austrian chancellor, branding him as "a traitor to the German cause," and comparing his policy to that of Prince Clemens Metternich of Austria, and former Empress Zita of Austria, who during the world war "opened negotiations with enemies behind the back of German allies." The privy council on foreign affairs met late today and was meeting again tonight to discuss developments.

Women Rule Brown House

The most amusing sight in Munich today was presented at the Brown house where sturdy Storm Troopers and Schutz Staffel men usually are on duty. It was an all female organization today, with offices occupied by women holding down the fort while the men of the Brown house were doing emergency duty as police to replace mobilized policemen.

Nazi propaganda offices carefully disseminated news asserting that Czechs had invaded Austria "to help the reds in Vienna," and that French reds were rushing to Vienna to fight the Austrian Nazis. The purpose of these rumors was to increase the people's willingness to see their sons and brothers march toward border countries which still are foreign territory.

Ordered to Police Duty

The Deathshead battalion of Schutz Staffel men was ordered to report to Munich to do police duty while 3,000 men of Hitler's Berlin bodyguard rushed to the Austrian border during the course of the night.

In Berlin early this morning truckload after truckload of policemen and troops of all descriptions poured out of the capital toward Germany's famous automobile road, which for the first time served the purpose for which it was built—military mobilization.

An eyewitness who was on the motor road at Hermsdorf, between Berlin and Nuremberg, saw the exodus toward the border. For hours, he said, cars loaded with officers, state police, secret police, army cars of all descriptions from lorries to tiny two man vehicles; eight wheeled military trucks and tanks that can be equipped with caterpillar tread, and big private limousines rushed by. Searchlight cars towing mounted machine guns on trailers and field kitchens followed.

A vast number of motorcyclists in gray uniforms had rifles slung across their shoulders. Only small groups of men in the black uniforms of the Schutz Staffel were in the cars of the state police.

A striking feature of the military procession out of the Berlin regions toward the Austrian and Czechoslovakian borders were hundreds of big yellow town buses full of blue uniformed police.

Police Have Military Training

Military experts explained that mobilization of the police was comprehensible since the greater part of the police force has received full military training. It also must be remembered that shortly before Germany occupied the Rhineland she sent squads of police to prepare the ground for the arrival of the military forces.

Airplanes flying in military formation passed over Potsdam and Wittenberg heading south.

At headquarters of the motorized forces in Berlin a vast number of motorized units coming from Wuerzburg and Leipzig pulled in this morning. Equipment was carried into the cars and officers and soldiers rushed into them. Motorized field kitchens struck the fancy of Berliners, who stared at them with fascination.

The police force of Berlin has been warned it cannot expect a day off for some time to come. In Berlin a number of men who were released from military service last October, after serving two years, received orders this morning to report to military offices for "field exercises."

Cross Into Austria

The first units to cross into Austria were motorized detachments which entered Salzburg half an hour before the general order to advance was issued at 10 o'clock. They were followed quickly by 10,000 men, artillery, and motorized units which pushed forward over bridges at Kufstein, Salzburg, and

Mittenwald, under orders of Gen. Hoffman, second in command of the Munich division.

The Augsburg division was the next to move into Austria. Troops stationed at Rosenheim, Reichenhall, and Traunstein are being rushed forward.

Reenforcements were coming from Baden and Wurtemberg through Munich tonight, headed for Austria.

With news of the marching German troops in Austria still ringing in their ears, the Nazis already have turned eyes toward Czechoslovakia, which remains as the unfulfilled point in the program to unite all Germans. The official organ for labor service, Der Arbeitsmann, points to Czechoslovakia which "not only has the same mountain valleys but the same people as Germany."

Chancellor Hitler has cancelled his trip to Hamburg for the launching of the ship built with funds obtained through the "strength through joy" movement.

14

Dorothy Thompson
(1893–1961)

IN 1936 JAMES THURBER drew a *New Yorker* cartoon showing an angry husband attacking a typewriter while his wife explained to a guest: "He's giving Dorothy Thompson a piece of his mind." The scene captured the mood of the time and the reaction that many had to the outspoken, often belligerent *New York Herald Tribune* columnist, who had more than seven million readers in 1939. During the twenty-one years her "On The Record" column ran on editorial pages across the country, she probably won as many enemies as friends.

Dorothy Thompson subscribed to Aristotle's definition of politics as "the art of discerning what is good for mankind." Whenever she did not agree with the way of the world, she self-confidently announced: "I'll fix it; I'll write a column about it." And she did, vehemently arguing for unpopular positions that ranged from her pro-interventionist attacks on the United States' isolationism before World War II to her anti-Zionist advocacy of Arab rights in the Middle East after World War II.

Indignation was her reaction to most things, even clipping her nails. John Gunther, author of the "Inside" books and a close friend, entitled an essay on Thompson, "A Blue-Eyed Tornado," writing that "two things happened to central Europe during the decade of the '20s—the world economic crisis and Dorothy Thompson."

Heywood Broun added his assessment that "Dorothy Thompson is greater than Eliza [a reference to the character from *Uncle Tom's Cabin*] because not only does she cross the ice but breaks it as she goes. Moreover, she is her own bloodhound." Although not an early Roosevelt supporter, she did speak out for FDR as a leader who could deal with the wartime crisis in 1941. The President, like Thurber's agitated character, was put off by her strident and shrill stance. He reportedly wrote in a letter: "Dorothy Thompson is the only woman who ever had a menopause in public and got paid for it."

Her public persona was further enhanced by her marriage to Sinclair "Red" Lewis, the first American awarded the Nobel Prize in literature (1930). Gossip circulated concerning her intense relationships with women friends, particularly a frequent traveling companion during the 1930s, Baroness Hatvany of Budapest, who under the name of Christa Winsloe had written the lesbian novel *Mädchen in Uniform.*

Two years after starting her column in the *Herald Tribune,* Thompson was featured on *Time* magazine's cover of June 12, 1939. The story coupled her with Eleanor Roosevelt as the two most influential women in America. At that time her column was carried by 196 papers, with a readership estimated at 7,545,000. She was, *Time* wrote, "the embodiment of an ideal, the typical modern American woman that they [other women] think they would like to be: emancipated, articulate, and successful, living in the thick of one of the most exciting periods of history and interpreting it to millions."

Like many complex, irritating personalities, Dorothy Thompson had a childhood tainted with difficult adjustments that altered her sense of self. Born on July 9, 1893, in Lancaster, New York, she was the eldest of three children of Peter Thompson, a British-born Methodist clergyman, and Margaret (Grierson) Thompson. According to Thompson's biographer Marion K. Sanders, when Dorothy was eight, her mother died from blood poisoning after a bungled abortion performed by Dorothy's maternal grandmother. Her father, whom she idolized, was a poor, small-town minister and a committed preacher who moved his family around upstate New York towns, earning from $700 to $1,200 a year. "His life did not represent in my youthful eyes anything that could be called success or anything that was greatly to be desired," she would later say.

A precocious problem child, Dorothy rebelled against many of her father's restrictions, and when he remarried two years after her mother's death, she set out to displease her stepmother, Elizabeth Abbott, the church organist, with willful acts at home and in school. So successful was her rebellion that at age fourteen she was sent from Gowanda, New York, to live with an aunt in Chicago, where she went to high school, and later to Lewis Institute. She was an indifferent scholar, but popular with other students and captain of the basketball team.

By the time she entered Syracuse University, aided by the scholarship available to children of Methodist ministers, she had developed a talent for public speaking and a penchant for embracing causes. At Syracuse she became a vigorous campaigner for votes for women, and a heroine of sorts to many women students. During the summers she earned money for college by selling ice-cream cones on the boardwalk at Ocean Grove, New Jersey, rolling taffy in a candy factory, waitressing, and selling encyclopedias door to door. This experience made her a tough taskmaster in later life, who frequently told aspiring journalists that they had to pay their dues by performing menial tasks like filing and typing.

After graduating from Syracuse in 1914, she came to New York to take the teacher's examination, but failed the English grammar section and decided to find a job. She first worked in Buffalo, New York, addressing envelopes in the local women's suffrage headquarters and making speeches at county fairs and town squares through the state. During this time she was blonde, skinny, and angular (a short-lived state, for she later became statuesque and buxom, fighting a lifelong weight problem). She learned to handle hecklers and to project her beliefs with force and sincerity. In one town she was talking from the back of a truck, dressed in a shiny blue serge suit, the model of a feminist, when a band started playing nearby, drowning out her words and attracting her audience. She went into a store, bought a child's blackboard and some chalk, hopped back on the truck and wrote out sentences on the slate. The crowd applauded her ingenuity, and the band stopped playing.

Unable to qualify for overseas work during World War I, she spent the war years in New York, in small upstate towns, and in Ohio, doing copywriting for an advertising agency, and social work in Cincinnati for the Social Unit, a New York-based reform group working in the slums. Bored with social causes and seeking adventure, she committed herself to becoming a freelance writer and sailed for Europe in 1920 with a college chum and her entire savings of $150. On board she met a group of Zionists en route to London for a conference, and after the twelve-day sail she felt knowledgeable enough to convince International News Service (INS) to let her cover the conference. Later she traveled throughout Europe selling articles at space rates to INS, the Associated Press, the *London Star*, the *Westminster Gazette*, and the *Manchester Guardian*.

Of these halycon days in Europe between the wars, Thompson said: "It's a wonderful thing to be a freelance and to be poor, provided you are young and not condemned for life. You really get to know people. When I was first in Europe, I seldom had much money. I had to travel third class. So I met the average people. I slept in hundreds of little hotels where there were bedbugs and dirt and had to shop around for places where I could afford to eat. It was hard, but it was an awfully good way for a journalist to study countries."

During this period, Thompson skillfully picked the brains of Fleet Street reporters, who advised her to go to Ireland. There she had the last interview with Mayor Terence MacSwiney of Cork, the Irish independence leader, before he died in jail after a seventy-four day hunger strike. A union organizer she knew from New York, Joe Schlossberg, directed her to Milan, and she arrived in time to cover the street riots of the striking Fiat metalworkers.

Other correspondents were soon talking about Dorothy Thompson and her luck at being on the scene for major events. She was developing sources, but feeling lonely. She wrote to a friend: "To be twenty-seven and loverless in Italy is a crime against God and man."

Returning to Paris, she learned of her father's death and reflected on how different her worldly adult life was from her early years in the parsonage. To earn more money, she took a publicity job with the American Red Cross, writing releases for one cent a line and making her margins wide enough to get thirty lines to a typewritten page. She also began an eight-year association with Cyrus H. K. Curtis' *Philadelphia Public Ledger*, becoming its Vienna correspondent at space rates.

The postwar news focus had shifted to Austria, Germany, and the Balkans, and Thompson arrived in Vienna on the day of the first Karlist Putsch, the attempt of Emperor Karl to regain the Hapsburg throne for himself and Empress Zita. She also met the Hungarian-born correspondent for the *Manchester Guardian*, Marcel Fodor, a thirty-year-old bachelor who fell in love with her. He had to settle for a platonic relationship, though, helping Thompson get stories past the censors and advising her on foreign affairs. It was Fodor who alerted her to a special flight to Budapest just as the emperor was defeated in a second attempt to regain his throne. Using her Red Cross connections, Thompson gained admittance to Esterhazy Castle, interviewing the royal couple and scoring a major exclusive for the *Ledger*. She was immediately placed on staff and in 1925, at age thirty-one, was sent to Berlin as Central European bureau chief for the *Ledger* and the *New York Evening Post*, another Curtis paper. She arrived shortly after Sigrid Schultz was appointed *Chicago Tribune* bureau chief, also at the age of thirty-one, the two thus basically tying for the honor of being the first woman to head a major European bureau.

Within six years, Thompson married, divorced, and remarried, meeting both husbands at parties, where she always made sure she was the center of attention. At a Budapest reception in 1922, Marcel Fodor introduced her to Josef Bard, a romantic-looking Hungarian Jew, who was a moody and mel-

Dorothy Thompson

ancholy writer of philosophy, without family money or income. Thompson married him soon after, but his womanizing led to a divorce in 1927. At her thirty-fourth birthday party, which also celebrated her divorce decree, she met Sinclair Lewis, eight years her senior, who was in the midst of a divorce from his first wife. He immediately asked Thompson to marry him, and when she refused, he ardently pursued her across Europe. They wed in London in 1928 and spent their honeymoon touring the English country-side in a gypsy caravan. Returning to the United States, they settled on a 300-acre estate called "Twin Farm" near Barnard, Vermont. Their only child, Michael, was born in 1930, and for the next five years Thompson and Lewis traveled and worked in Europe.

Before her marriage to Lewis she had toured the Soviet Union, writing a series of articles for the *Ledger* and publishing her first book, *The New Russia*, in 1928. That same year Theodore Dreiser published *Dreiser Looks at Russia*, and Thompson publicly charged him with plagiarism, saying he had used 3,000 words from her newspaper series. Sinclair Lewis, who was totally captivated with his new wife, calling her the "greatest woman on earth," came close to a fist fight with Dreiser at the Metropolitan Club over his wife's claims. For all of Lewis' fame, though, he was, according to biographer Mark Schorer, jealous of his wife's talent as a writer and her emergence as a public figure. Moreover, he did not share her fascination with international politics, which he referred to as "it," and would sneak solitary drinks in the kitchen when Dorothy held court analyzing the news from Germany.

A good part of her eight years in Europe had been spent trying to interview Hitler, and finally in 1931 he agreed to see her at his headquarters in Berlin but kept her waiting eight hours, a fact that may have contributed to Thompson's monumental underestimation of him. In her article for *Cosmopolitan* magazine, she portrayed the Nazi leader as "inconsequent and voluble, ill-poised, insecure . . . [a man] of startling insignificance . . . I was convinced that I was meeting the future dictator of Germany," she wrote. "In something less than fifty seconds I was quite sure that I was not." She turned her impressions into a book, *I Saw Hitler* (1932), and spent many years living down her misjudgment. In 1934 she was expelled from Germany, by decree of the secret police, and thereafter proudly kept the framed document on her desk, next to the framed Thurber cartoon. And according to a two-part *New Yorker* profile in April 1940, out of some 238,000 words she wrote in the *Herald Tribune* during 1938 and 1939, nearly 147,000 words—or more than three-fifths of the total—were devoted to attacking Hitler's regime.

Dorothy Thompson dated her real journalistic career from 1935, when she became an interpreter rather than a chronicler of events. "I don't like doing a lot of legwork," she explained. "In fact, I don't like reporting. Ideas are what I'm after. I like to write more in the essay form." Her ideas attracted the attention of Helen Rogers Reid, wife of the *Herald Tribune*'s publisher Ogden Reid, and Thompson was asked to write 1,000 words three times a week. "On The Record," alternating with Walter Lippmann's "Today and Tomorrow," made its debut on the editorial page of March 17, 1936, with this disarming opener: "I, like 120,000,000 other Americans, will probably never grasp the truth about the money system. Professor Einstein also admits that he doesn't understand it."

Mostly she continued her one-note theme, warning of Hitler's power not only in her columns but in articles for magazines like *Cosmopolitan* and the *Saturday Evening Post*. An article in *Foreign Affairs* on the refugee problem was credited with aiding in the formation of the Intergovernmental Committee on the Refugees by President Roosevelt.

As her reputation grew, that of her husband waned. Their marriage was further agitated by Lewis' increased drinking, and in 1937 the pair separated. But that did not stop her fame from spreading. To the contrary, during 1938 and 1939, in addition to her writing, she did commentaries on NBC radio stations heard by five million listeners. In 1938 alone her earnings were reported to be somewhere over $103,000. She was the first woman invited to speak to the all-male bastions at the Union League Club, the Harvard Club of New York, and the National Association of Manufacturers. One year she received 7,000 requests to lecture, most of which she refused, particularly those from women's clubs which she found dull. For all her early feminist oratory, Thompson preferred the company of men whom she considered her intellectual equals.

She had her share of detractors, though, who found her views strident and emotional. And she was labeled a war monger by many as a result of her campaign for intervention and against the isolationism favored by Americans before World War II. A St. Louis radio station cut her off the air, explaining that she was "against everybody." When a collection of her columns was published in 1939 as *Let The Record Speak*, one reviewer suggested that it be retitled *Let The Record Shout*. Even so, millions of readers enjoyed her columns for their clarity of thought and uncomplicated writing style.

Helen Rogers Reid had suggested Thompson's column as a way for wives to understand events without having to ask their husbands, and her readership tended toward women at the start, but eventually she attracted a substantial male readership intrigued by her definitive—and changing—views about everything. An early fan of Charles Lindbergh, lauding his "humanitarian instincts," she turned on him when he favored neutrality in World War II and publicly labeled him a Nazi, although this charge was never printed in a column. Sometimes her columns were humorous, particularly when she brought Lewis into them as "The Grouse," and in many she successfully used modern idioms and metaphors to promote causes.

When the staunchly Republican *Herald Tribune* dropped her column in 1941 following her support of President Roosevelt's re-election against Wendell Willkie, she went to the Bell Syndicate, with her New York outlet the liberal but less prestigious *Post*. During her six years with the *Post* she embraced another cause—Arab rights in the Middle East—declaring that the partition of Palestine for the establishment of Israel was an invasion of the Arab world. She offended Jewish readers with such views, and in 1947 the paper dropped her column, although she continued her sympathy for the uprooted Arabs.

Despite career setbacks, Dorothy Thomspon at fifty found some personal happiness. In 1943, a year after she and Lewis were divorced, she embarked on her third marriage. Her new husband, Maxim Kopf, an Austrian-born Czech painter, could fling the heavy-set Dorothy up in the air and expressed a raw sexuality she secretly yearned for. When Kopf died in 1958, she decided to end her syndicated column and wrote in a farewell:

When events have proved me right, I've been most unpopular. And when they have proved me wrong, I have been most popular. I remember losing a great many outlets [for "On The Record"] when I wrote against the division of Germany. Lately I have been severely criticized for my views on the Middle East situation. I have been predicting for eight years that the West would lose the Middle East if it supported Israel wholeheartedly. If I had it all to do over, of course, I'd do a lot of things differently. It seems that one knows increasingly less in this world. So much truth is clouded over by propaganda and misinformation. It's hard to get at the truth nowadays. I don't believe in regrets. I have written objectively and honestly.

At her retirement she had plans to read and to work on her autobiography in the Dartmouth College library. With work barely underway, she traveled to Lisbon to visit her daughter-in-law (recently divorced from Thompson's son) and two grandsons. There on January 30, 1961, she died at age sixty-six following a heart attack while reading in bed. The *New York Times*, in an editorial on February 1, observed:

Dynamism alone does not hold so many readers. Dorothy Thompson had two qualities often obscured by the flamboyance that is sometimes the hallmark of excellence. First, she was a good reporter; she dug deeply for her facts. Secondly, she spoke out unremittingly for what she felt was right, in large things and small. Readers, agreeing or not, sensed that here was a go-getter who was go-getting for all.

The following is Dorothy Thompson's famous column comparing the compromising actions of British Prime Minister Neville Chamberlain to those of *Alice in Wonderland*.

LET THE RECORD SPEAK
Chamberlain and Alice

By DOROTHY THOMPSON

New York Herald Tribune, April 5, 1939

There is a reason why "Alice in Wonderland" is pre-eminently *the* English classic. It is a tender and humorous glorification of the age of innocence.

Alice is the very well-brought-up, polite and extremely reasonable English child who finds herself in a world full of unreasonable foreigners—a world where the bottles labeled "Drink Me" are not marked "poison," the way all bottles in the nursery medicine closet ought to be, and which, nevertheless, when you drink their contents, "shut you up like a telescope."

If the bottle had only been decently marked, as a proper English bottle would have been, Alice would not have drunk it, "for she had read several nice little stories about children who had got burnt and eaten up by wild beasts and other unpleasant things, all because they *would* not remember the simple rules their friends had taught them; such as that a red-hot poker would burn you if you hold it too long, and that if you cut your finger *very* deeply with a knife it generally bleeds, and she had never forgotten that if you drink much from a bottle marked 'poison' it is almost certain to disagree with you sooner or later."

However, as you remember, this bottle was not marked 'poison,' so Alice ventured to taste it, and "finding it very nice (it had, in fact, a sort of mixed flavour of cherry tart, custard, pineapple, roast turkey, toffee, and hot buttered toast), she very soon finished it all."

Now, what happened to Alice after that was that she became only a fraction of her former size, and since this sudden diminution made it impossible for her to do some of the things she very much wanted to do, she sat down and cried. But being a well-brought-up little English child, she took herself severely to task, saying, "There is no use crying like that!"

And we learn that Alice was in the habit of scolding herself and even sometimes of boxing her own ears "for having cheated herself in a game of croquet she was playing against herself, for this curious child was very fond of pretending to be two people. 'But it's no use now,' thought poor Alice, 'to pretend to be two people! Why, there's hardly enough of me left to make one respectable person!'"

And you remember that, pulling herself together and seeing a box marked "Eat Me," Alice figured that she might as well eat it, "for if it makes me grow larger I can reach the key, and if it makes me grow smaller I can creep under the door. So either way I can get into the garden."

For those who find it difficult to understand Mr. Chamberlain I recommend a re-reading of the English classic.

Mr. Chamberlain followed the "Drink Me" policy at Munich, and the "Eat Me" policy in the House of Commons last week and this. It is called the muddling-through policy when translated into political terms, and is totally ununderstandable to anything except an English mind. It is a combination of responsibility without reasoning.

It has its uses in English statesmen. I use the word "English" advisedly. It is certainly not Scottish. And it is, above all, not Welsh or Irish. One can perfectly imagine Mr. Chamberlain at six as the masculine of Alice. One cannot imagine Mr. Lloyd George as anything but a very distant relative. Its usefulness is that the qualities of Alice—her niceness, her reasonability and her incredible foolishness—attract the English people.

If Alice makes a mistake it is because of her innocence, because she is really much too nice to live in a world full of falsely labeled bottles and boxes, perverted nursery rhymes, vicious old Father Williamses and ugly Duchesses. She is confused and misled, but in the end it all turns out to be a nightmare.

And she wakes up in her secure nursery, comforted by her tea, recalling the shriek of the gryphon, the choking of the suppressed guinea pigs and the distant sob of the miserable mock turtle as a fantastic experience.

Yes, Alice is beloved by England because of her unconquerable simplicity.

And so, strange as it may seem to any type of mind except the English, it is extremely probable that Mr. Chamberlain is stronger in his leadership because he turned out to be wrong than he would have been had he been always right.

At any rate, as the result of making incredible blunders, one has Monday's spectacle in the House of Commons, where an entire nation, from the Labor Opposition to the most Bourbon Tories, is united behind the counterpart of Alice.

Perhaps this uncoerced unity, which has been convinced not by using its reason but purely empirically, will turn out to be of more importance to history than all the lost strategical bases. Perhaps, to paraphrase another English poet, there is some method in this madness. For mad it certainly appears to be.

The nation which was not prepared to defend Czechoslovakia, a country which had meticulously kept all of its international engagements, is now prepared to defend Poland, a country which has pursued a most dubious diplomatic course and which is at least as difficult to defend.

Some will look for every explanation except the simple one. But I am inclined to believe that the simple explanation is the true one.

It is very difficult to believe that when Chamberlain went to Munich he did not know that he was giving Hitler a free hand in the east and that he did not know exactly what giving that free hand would mean. But since Mr. Chamberlain is English it is possible that he really thought that Hitler would behave like an Englishman and take what he wanted in such a way as not to shock and horrify the world and stop at the right moment.

I doubt whether Mr. Chamberlain has ever in his life met anybody who was not either just a gentleman or a "gentleman in trade." But Hitler is neither a gentleman nor a trader.

I am inclined to believe that when Mr. Chamberlain said, on the eve of Munich, "If I were convinced that any nation had made up its mind to dominate the world by fear of its force, I should feel that it must be resisted," he meant it—but didn't believe. Since then he has come to believe.

What has made him believe has been the *method* of Hitler. What has made him believe is the speed of Hitler.

If Chamberlain had ever read "Mein Kampf"—which I am reasonably sure he has not done—he might have been aware a long time ago. But, being English, even that is doubtful. For the English mind believes only what it sees. It believes in the event, not in the plan.

And the German mind has its equal weakness. It believes in the plan and fails to observe the event.

That is perhaps one reason why Germany won all the first battles but lost the last war. It is not written in history that this will always be so, but it is curious that Hitler, who prides himself on having invented something absolutely new in diplomacy and who attacked Wilhelm's Germany for its idiocy in making an enemy of England and Russia at the same time, has managed to repeat Wilhelm's mistakes.

15

Ishbel Ross
(1895–1975)

AFTER ISHBEL ROSS left daily journalism in the 1930s, she wrote *Ladies of the Press* which researchers still turn to for source material on America's early women journalists. Published in 1936 and reprinted in 1974, it is, in many cases, the only reference with original anecdotes and background on those reporters who never wrote their autobiographies. Omitted from the index, perhaps out of modesty, was the author's name. It is time, though, for the record to be amended. For Ishbel Ross was not only a chronicler but a pathmaker, a notable newspaperwoman. To Stanley Walker, her city editor, woman journalists were often "slovenly, incompetent vixens, adept at office politics, show-offs of the worst sort," but Ross, he noted, had "unflustered competence" and came as near as any woman did to being able to cover any assignment. She was often referred to as the perfect newspaperman.

From 1919 to 1934 she wrote front-page leads for the *New York Tribune* and the merged *Herald Tribune*, assignments that on rival papers were routinely given to men. She covered the crimes of the twenties and thirties: the 1926 Hall-Mills murder trail and the 1932 kidnap-murder of Charles A. Lindbergh's infant son. She interviewed the future King Edward of England on his visit to the United States, covered the return of Lindbergh from his triumphant Paris flight, and reported the inaugurations of Presidents Harding, Coolidge, and Hoover. Aviation was one of her specialties, and she spent many long nights at airports waiting for the arrival of those first trans-Atlantic airplanes. She covered the city's fires, its subway explosions, even its prize fights. She wrote a major series on the lives of European immigrants. She interviewed the jazz-age college youth about drinking, dancing, and dating.

Some of her stories carried her byline, others didn't. Her monumental second-day story of the Lindbergh kidnapping, for instance, carried no credit. However, she did get bylines for her stories on the Hall-Mills trial and the death of Pulitzer's *World*. In a letter to Joy Stilley of the Associated Press, Ross explained the *Trib*'s byline policy: "I never kept a clipping, even of my major stories. I rarely got bylines since I was not a feature writer and it was not the custom at that time. Few signed clippings of my work are in existence. When doing my biography of Mrs. Coolidge [*Grace Coolidge and Her Era: The Story of a President's Wife*, 1962], I wanted to use a lot of period atmosphere, and I just had to plough through the old newspaper files day by day, trying to identify my stories."

Her career, for at least one reason, was more interesting than those of most other women reporters, for she often competed with her husband, Bruce Rae, described by a colleague as the "most brilliant writer" on the *New York Times* after the renowned feature writer, Meyer Berger. Ross and Rae met when they both covered the James A. Stillman divorce case and married in 1922. The next major story they worked on as rivals was the Hall-Mills trial, described earlier in the chapter on Dorothy Dix. The highlight of that trial was the testimony from a hospital bed of the "pig woman," who claimed she saw the double murder of the minister and his mistress. As a study in the different styles and approaches of both the morning papers and their reporters, here are the two leads for that day, November 19, 1926. Ross's version is studded with visual images:

Jane Gibson, the Amazon "pig woman," who rode Jenny the Mule in her sturdier days and guarded her farm with a shotgun, was borne into court on a stretcher today—a helpless, mummified figure, wrapped in blankets and close to death.

For four blistering hours she dominated the Hall-Mills trial from the pillows of a hospital cot—an eerie figure waving waxen fingers at the four persons she now links with the murder scene on the Phillips farm in September, 1922. . . . Her wild eyes blazed from their sunken sockets at Mrs. Hall. Her skinny arm was leveled at the still form in black. A faint smile of pitying scorn touched the lips of the rector's widow. Her calm was untouched in the midst of a hysteria that she visibly despised.

Ross received a byline for this story, but the same coverage in the *Times* had no credit. By all accounts, though, Bruce Rae wrote the lead story. The *Times* played down, in its headlines and lead, the reference to Mrs. Gibson as the "pig woman," dropping the first reference to the second paragraph.

Propped in bed in the hushed court-room, her face as waxen white as the coverlets, Mrs. Jane Gibson told her story yesterday in the Hall-Mills murder trial at Somerville, N.J. The recital took her only twenty minutes, and a white-clad nurse stood at one side of the bed and a physician at the other as the painfully slow sentences of accusation were uttered.

It was a story of shots in the darkness and of faces dimly seen in the flare of a flashlight, a narrative of mumbled voices, curses and a struggle, and the dull sound of the falling of the Rev. Edward W. Hall and Mrs. Eleanor R. Mills before four bullets. A story that was simple, yet one that clutched the auditors in a spell of silence broken only by the words issuing from the parched lips. Down through the night of the murder the "pig woman" rode again on her mule. Along the winding way of De Russey's Lane to a crabapple tree, leaves a rustle in the whisper of a breeze to the scene of the crime.

Same story, but different styles indeed. Rae approached the story—the facts of which were well known to every reader—with a new sense of mystery and foreboding, while Ross highlighted the dramatic action in the courtroom, noting gestures, reactions, feelings.

Also different were their attitudes toward journalism. Rae, variously described as a "quixotic man with great mood swings," and a "martinet with a caustic wit and a sharp tongue," had started at the *Times* as an office boy in the business department, working his way up to reporter, night city editor, and assistant managing editor. He was a perfectionist in all things and, like many newspapermen, wouldn't leave for home until the first edition came out early in the morning. "My idea of a journalism school," one of his former reporters once said, "is that dour little Scotsman slumped in his chair, glaring over his ulcers at a reporter and daring him not to write the best damn story of which he was capable."

By contrast, his wife was a quiet, solitary person, with many acquaintances but few friends. One colleague recalled, "She was on the reporting staff—but not of it. She did her work and went home." Home was a small apartment on Manhattan's East 76th Street, crammed with glass water tanks filled with tropical fish, a passion of Rae's. In such close quarters, a friend remembered, their forceful personalities often clashed, although both maintained, particularly with the Hall-Mills trial, that at home they never discussed that case or others they covered together.

On the evening of March 1, 1932, after receiving her "good night" from the desk, Ross was at her apartment when the news flash came over the wires that Lindbergh's son had been kidnapped. Dick West was on rewrite that night and recalled how the editors met at 2 a.m. to plan the next day's coverage. "It was a measure of Ishbel's stature," he said, "that no one thought of anyone else to do the lead." Reporters were to be driven within the hour by hired limo to Hopewell, New Jersey. L. L. Engelking, night city editor, started making calls to get the staff out of bed. A six-foot-four-inch hulking man of gentle manners, Engelking hesitated about waking up Ross. When she answered the phone, his first words were apologetic, but thirty minutes

Ishbel Ross

after the call Ross walked into the city room with "every curl in place," according to West. Engelking offered another apology, to which Ross briskly replied, "Oh! That's all right. I hadn't been to bed yet."

Fourteen hours later the limos returned and Ishbel Ross sat down to a desk covered with wire copy, phone messages, memos, and a stack of afternoon papers. She conferred with Engelking and described the chaotic scene at the Lindbergh home. Then from 8 p.m. to 2 a.m. she typed out eight columns, while keeping track of new developments, inserting updates from wire copy, changing leads. In all she wrote some 10,000 words and this lead:

> The attention of millions all over the world was centered last night on the fate of the infant Charles A. Lindbergh Jr., who was kidnapped from his crib on Tuesday night as he lay sound asleep in the nursery of his home on his father's estate near Hopewell, N.J.
>
> After a day's pursuit of seemingly fruitless clues, a state trooper said soon after 8 o'clock last night that Colonel Lindbergh expected his son to be returned to him within thirteen hours. No information was given on the source of this new expectation. At 2 o'clock this morning the Associated Press said that Colonel Lindbergh had just told a party of state troopers that he was "very confident that the baby will be returned by noon."

"She was fast and accurate," recalled *Trib* editor Everett Walker, "and it was interesting how she and Bruce Rae tried to outdo each other on the Lindbergh story." Stanley Walker, who praised Ross in his book *City Editor*, wrote the foreword to *Ladies of the Press*, stating that "Miss Ross, with her lack of giddiness, her clear and forthright mind, her amazing and unfailing stamina on the toughest assignments and her calm judgment, seemed to come closer to the man's idea of what a newspaperwoman should be. . . . I could detect only two mild flaws in her during my entire association with her: (1) she was inclined to regard life as a fairly serious business and never laughed enough, and (2) she was lacking in venom."

It appears that her male colleagues were often intimidated by such poise and bearing. "Her intense blue eyes made you feel that she was sizing you up, coolly and completely," said Dick West. "She spoke very little and in a very soft voice with a slight Scottish lilt. She had a dignity, a self-possession that inspired respect. To everyone, she was always 'Miss Ross.'" West also admired her intuition and her use of rhythm and pacing in her writing. "All her stories had a depth and a texture that no one could match," he said. "Her insights brought people and events to life in print."

This sense of dignity, said West, was evident one long night in 1929 at Lakehurst, New Jersey, where the press waited in the attic of an immense hangar for the arrival of the dirigible, the Graf Zeppelin, which was on the last leg of its round-the-world trip of 21 days, 7 hours, and 34 minutes. As the hours dragged on, the whiskey bottles were emptied and the atmosphere grew rowdy. In the midst of the disorder and confusion, West remembered Ishbel Ross sitting on a table, dressed with impeccable taste as always, "swinging her legs, smiling and chatting with anyone who walked by completely oblivious of her surroundings."

Talking about her childhood in Sutherlandshire, Scotland, where she was born Ishbella Margaret on December 15, 1895, the second of two children of Grace (McCrone) Ross and David Ross, she was once quoted: "Even as a little girl I was determined to be a writer. I can remember seeing Rudyard Kipling walking his children in the Far Highlands and thinking, Oh, to write like him someday. I used to haunt the libraries and read anything I could get my hands on."

She was educated at the Tain Royal Academy in Ross-Shire and at age twenty went to Canada where she worked first as a publicist for the Canadian Food Board, and then in the library at the old *Toronto Daily News*, where she waited to get her first assignment. Her break came, she told Marion Marzolf for her book *Up From the Footnote*, when she convinced the suffragist Emmeline Pankhurst to give her an interview. "I owe my career to Mrs. Pankhurst," said Ross, "although I was never a great suffrage sympathizer."

In 1919 she left Canada for New York and the *Tribune*. "I had no trouble at all getting my job because so many of the men reporters were still in the Army," she wrote years later to journalist Pegge Parker. Emma Bugbee had been the only woman on cityside for nine years and now she was joined by Ross, who had an adjoining desk. Ross was a facile writer and a fast touch typist, skills that later helped her turn out five novels and twenty biographies and historical works. She was still a reporter in 1931 when she wrote her first book, *Through the Lich-Gate: A Biography of the Little Church Around the Corner*.

After the Hall-Mills case ended in 1928, the Raes, who were paid at space rates, had accumulated so much money that they each took a six-month leave of absence and made a round-the-world cruise. Out of that experience, Ross wrote her first novel, *Promenade Deck* (1933), a best-seller that was later made into a movie. In 1934 she left the paper to write at home and bring up her daughter, Catriona (Gaelic for Catherine), who was born in 1935.

In the period from 1934 to 1937 she wrote four more novels but found that form difficult. One critic noted that she was "acting as a reporter not as a novelist." In *Fifty Years A Woman*, published in 1938, she examined five birthdays in a woman's life, each separated by a decade, and used them as connections to bring a character from 1880 to 1930. "I do best with facts

rather than with creating," she once said. She also liked the research necessary for her biographies and, with the success of *Ladies of the Press* in 1936,
she turned her attention exclusively to nonfiction. Her books received favorable, but not rave reviews; at their core was a journalist at work, not a historian. She was, however, introducing notable and unknown women to the
reading public and was in demand to lecture and appear on radio talk shows.

Along with many other newspaper reporters, she worked with the Office
of War Information during the early 1940s, writing magazine articles for
overseas publications. In the next decade her reputation as a writer grew, but
Bruce Rae was having problems at the *Times*. Never able to play office politics the diplomatic way, he was taken out of the newsroom in 1955 to head
the paper's news service, a syndicate operation sending *Times* articles to other
newspapers.

After her husband's death in 1962, she devoted herself with a disciplined
passion to turning out books as fast as possible. In a thirteen-year period she
published ten books, including one of her most ambitious works, a history
of the Taft family from 1658 to 1964. Her last book was a biography entitled
Power with Grace: The Life of Mrs. Woodrow Wilson. Friends from this time
speculated that she needed money to pay for her daughter's frequent medical
treatments for mental illness. Ross wrote letters as an outlet for her concern
about Catriona, lamenting in one: "All parents today seem to have dreadful
problems." Concerning her work, she observed, "The prospects grow dim
when one is seventy-four; yet for me to write is to live. I have been doing it
since I was sixteen."

During this time she enjoyed helping other writers, and once started, a
relationship continued, with frequent letters and notes. She was particularly
helpful to Doris Faber, who had once worked for Bruce Rae at the *Times*.
Faber had written numerous biographies for teen-agers, and in the mid-1960s,
when she signed a contract for a book on all the Presidents' mothers, she
sought out Ross's advice on such a research project. "I think she enjoyed
being consulted as an outstanding example of how a reporter could become
a historical biographer without benefit of academic training," Faber said.

Faber adopted Ross's folder method of research, which involved taking notes
on yellow legal pads, cutting the notes into sections and filing them according to chronology and subject. Faber found Ross "delightfully quaint," describing her as a "plump, short, pouterpigeon of a woman who wore '20s
finery like a coat with bands of fur around the hem and wrists." Through
the years the two kept in touch, Ross writing on her favorite blue stationery
about her work and always inquiring about Faber's family. On August 17,
1975, Ross wrote: "I am relieved to have the Wilson book out of the way—
it was one of the most troublesome jobs I ever worked on. I am busy now

straightening out papers, answering letters that always follow the publication of a book, and keeping up with the daily activities of my household. I'm as healthy as a horse, and it will be eighty years I reach next December."

The following month, on September 21, early in the morning, Ross died in a fall from a fourth-story window of her East 76th Street apartment. Police ruled her death a possible suicide, and if that was the case, friends still remain baffled as to the motivation.

Ishbel Ross's feature story on the "Boy Trotzky of Harlem," carried no by-line, but she was given full credit when it was selected as one of the best news stories of 1923 for a collection edited by Joseph Anthony.

Boy Trotzky of Harlem, 11, Arrested by Bomb Squad

His Pockets Stuffed With Red Literature and Dis-Patches From Russia, He "Waited for Mother"

Taught Doctrines To Workers, 7 to 14

Stands High in School, His Communistic Field, Though Often Is Tardy

New York Tribune, November 28, 1923

Leo Granoff, the Boy Trotzky, whose dark doings in Harlem have suddenly been uncovered by the police, is not so much of a terror to meet. To begin with, he's only eleven years old, a little shaver with snapping brown eyes and unkempt black hair that blows in a communistic wave over his head.

It wouldn't be true to form if it blew any other way, for Leo's a Communist from the crown of his head to the soles of his feet—and not in theory alone. Didn't he organize the Harlem branch of the Young Workers' League? And didn't the cops pick him up at the corner of 107th and Lexington Avenue after midnight yesterday and find a sheaf of pamphlets in his pocket with the Internationale, the Red Flag and other songs of "anarchistic tendencies?"

"Only Waiting for Mother"

"Gee! I was only waiting for my mother to come back from the Moscow Art Theater. I was afraid to be home alone and the wind was blowing and I stood in the druggist's door to get shelter and the cops got me and searched me," said Leo, in explaining how he happened to fall into the hands of the law.

Told like this it sounds simple, but he knows very well that the bomb squad is after him. In fact, Lieutenant J. Gegan and Detective Louis Herman, both of the aforementioned squad, are making a serious investigation of the activities of Leo, who is declared to be rapidly converting the youth of Harlem into red-hot communists. It is further reported that many mothers handed out spankings in the same part of town after Detective Herman had called around to say that young Sadie, Emmanuel et al. were on the accredited list of members of the league.

Youngest, Seven. Oldest, Fourteen

The youngest was seven and the oldest fourteen, but eleven-year-old Leo unquestionably is the youngest person who has ever engaged the attention of the bomb squad in this city. When he came before Judge Hoyt in the Children's Court and was charged with juvenile delinquency he was put on probation until December 15. In the meantime his Red activities will be investigated.

Leo is rated A No. 1 in his school. Public School 171, 19 East 106th Street. Both Myron T. Wilson, principal, and Miss Nancy Kirkman, his assistant, say his conduct is impeccable. As for Leo, he thinks the way they teach grammar, spelling and arithmetic is all right, but history—! Gee! it's nothing but patriotism. And when Leo thinks of patriotism he tugs at his green sweater and grows inarticulate. But Leo has naive ideas on many subjects. He is a vegetarian, scorns candy, gave up Nick Carter years ago and reads only Russian Communistic literature, prances around the halls of his tenement without the gross encumbrance of his clothing and is only staying in this country because he thinks they need him a little more here than they do in Russia.

Gets "Red" Dispatches Direct

Mention Russia and Leo's eyes blaze with enthusiasm. He is frank to admit that all his knowledge of that country comes from letters received by a friend of his from "a fellow out there." But Russia certainly is the place to be if one were not so badly needed here! He is of Russian parentage. His father died about two years ago. Leo was born in this country and grudgingly admits to being an American. There are two other children in the family and they are in a home. Mrs. Granoff is a shirt maker. Leo runs his life according to his own ideas.

He took to his roller skates and fled when reporters and photographers called yesterday at his home, 114 East 108th Street. Finally, induced into his own kitchen, it was necessary to remind him that many of his worthy prototypes in the communistic world had submitted to being photographed before he would pull a cloth away from his face and look at the camera.

He explained at length that he had organized the Junior Harlem branch of the Young Workers' League, which had headquarters at 1008 North Street,

Chicago. As far as Leo knows, there are three of these branches in greater New York, and they meet for athletic purposes.

One is in Williamsburg, one in "Chinatown" and the third is his own. The pamphlets he had in his pocket came from headquarters, he said. He alone took responsibility, however, for roping in the young Harlemites. Indeed, the youngest member, who came recently from southern Virginia, was given the "Internationale" set to music to take home and play on her violin. Her mother was shocked and tore it up. There was a spanking in this house.

The membership cards are a violent red, symbolical of the purpose of the club. The children pay 10 cents a month, one nickel going to the league, the other for the social purposes of the club. Harry Fox is the director and the last meeting was held at 143 East 103rd Street last Saturday.

Soothes Hearts of Lovelorn

No one knows how the police came to learn that Leo was a Red. It may have been the accident of finding the pamphlets in his pocket. Every one in his block knew all about him, however. In fact, he was counsellor and friend to the fat, the lovelorn and the sick. He knows all about protein and calories and has frequently advised the fat ladies of his block to eschew—here is his own list—milk, cheese, potatoes, cream, candy and most kinds of bread.

"This is no political club," he explained. "We're an athletic club, but I'll tell you one thing—we don't allow no bourgeoisie into it. We won't have any paraseets (parasites) like the Rockefellers in it—no, or less richer men than him. We wouldn't have the rich man's children."

Leo was sure he would rather see a Soviet in this country than the present form of government, but it took him several minutes' meditation to tell why. He rubbed his hair, crinkled his brows in deep thought and finally gave a series of disjointed reasons.

Free Speech Only for "Bourgeoisie"

"You know this country is supposed to be a free country for free speech and free assemblage," he said. "But there's only free speech and free assemblage for such things as I call the bourgeoisie. My mother works in a shop. Other men, women, and children work in shops. They don't get enough pay. The workers don't get any chance at free assemblage."

It was to help the cause he could only vaguely define that Leo organized the league, he said. It seems to him that patriotism must be done away with. He will never sing "America" in school and it is told of him that one day when the preamble to the Constitution was being recited he put up his hand and asked his teacher why they should talk about justice when children were employed in the Pennsylvania mines. It appears that Leo once visited some of the mines and has made the employment of the young in mines one of the many planks in his elastic platform.

Has Al Fresco Views on Life

Having airily dismissed America's national figures Leo went on to give his views on al fresco living, little clothing, less food and free love. People don't live naturally, he thinks.

Although he is all for free love he doesn't believe it is practical with the way the world is now.

Asked if he'd like to go to the Russia he admires so much, Leo became a little firebrand. With arms outspread and blazing eyes he said: "In Russia they don't need me so much. They need me more here than in Russia, for conditions are worse here than in Russia."

And Leo was so serious that no one laughed.

Next minute he owned up to the commonplace ambition of wanting to be a civil engineer.

"But what about helping the cause of communism?" he was reminded.

"Oh," rather vaguely, "I'll do that too."

Chills Even Bomb Squad "Cop"

The truth was Leo was getting tired of answering questions, although he has the reputation of being able to talk sustainedly for hours on his favorite subject. He repeats like a parrot all the favorite communistic theories. He burns with fervor as he goes along. Even Herman, of the bomb squad, was impressed. He is the man specially delegated to look into activities of the league. They have been meeting in a hall owned by the Workingmen's Circle.

Leo's mother lets him talk. She is away all day and, according to Miss Kirkman, has been responsible for Leo being late many mornings. She came to the school to announce that she would not get up at any set time in order to have Leo there promptly. There was no other complaint against him in school. He is the brightest boy in 6–B. Patrolman Thomas J. Donegan arrested him when he found him in the street after midnight.

16

Mildred Gilman
(1896–   )

You see, Jane, you're trying to turn yourself into sort of a human catalogue, an engine that takes human beings and mangles them into copy. I'm afraid of you. You can turn a little crank and cry real tears. I've seen you do it. You've lost your respect for everything simple and beautiful and really kind. . . . The sympathy you feel for human beings is paid sympathy. It looks real to them. They don't know it's all part of earning your salary.

IN THIS PASSAGE from Mildred Gilman's 1931 novel, *Sob Sister*, a thinly disguised account of her Hearst newspaper days, Jane Ray's boyfriend, in effect, has told her that she is turning into a monster. As Gilman's alter ego, Ray has doubts about the way she is forced to report and write stories. After her city editor offers her to the police as a decoy to lure a murderer, she quits her job, marries her boyfriend, and lives happily ever after without deadline pressure. In real life, Gilman did much the same thing.

Now in her eighties, fit and slim (she bicycles three miles a day), Gilman admits that being a Hearst reporter as the Roaring Twenties moved into the Jazz Age was exhausting and often unethical work. "Sure we slanted stories and made characters more interesting," she said. "Embroidered facts were sometimes necessary to titillate the readers. Nowadays, of course, everything is different in journalism, but back then it was all in good fun—it was a crazy era, people were sitting on flagpoles and walking backwards across the country."

During that era of wonderful nonsense, there were few discussions about journalistic ethics. Back then, a Janet Cooke affair wouldn't have "caused such a fuss," Gilman said, referring to the *Washington Post* reporter who wrote a story on an eight-year-old heroin addict and won a 1980 Pulitzer Prize, but was later stripped of the honor when she admitted that she had fabricated the character of "Jimmy." Cooke later said she made up the story because she wanted "to be first, to be flashiest, to be sensational," a style of tabloid thinking that Mildred Gilman knew well.

During three years as a *New York Journal* reporter, Gilman never strayed as far into fiction as Janet Cooke, but then, as she pointed out, a reporter didn't have to because bizarre stories abounded. There was, for instance, the saga of Edward West "Daddy" Browning, a wealthy New York realtor with a passion for young girls. He adopted fifteen-year-old Frances "Peaches" Heenan, sent her to boarding school and married her when she reached legal age. Browning was a publicity hound who papered his Broadway office with clippings from the tabloid press, which loved him. To keep his picture in the news, he would go about town handing out five-dollar bills to bums at the Tub, a free-coffee hangout.

"I had to ride to the Tub with 'Daddy,'" Gilman recalled, "in a Robin's-egg-blue Rolls Royce and try to keep out of his iron embrace. The destitute men at the Tub went berserk. Daddy tried to mollify them with one-dollar bills. But we refused to photograph that. One photographer posed as a derelict and collected several bills. I had to write a humorous story, not the indictment of the times—The Depression, the press, and depraved 'Daddy'—as it should have been. Later I wrote his obituary, which was a masterpiece. It was thrown out. Even his obit had to be treated as a joke."

Recalling how she stretched ethical standards on some assignments, she said she has never felt guilty since she never hurt anyone. Part of being a sob sister, as her book tells, was getting people to trust her immediately, so she could get the story first. When she was covering the Colin Close torch murder (torchings to destroy the body were popular in the 1920s) in New Jersey, she convinced Mrs. Close to let her inside the family home, promising to protect the distressed woman from the mob of reporters outside. "I helped her put her three little girls to bed, tried to ease her shock at finding out a few hours earlier that her husband had killed a mail-order bride he had married for her money." Gilman stayed in the house for forty-eight hours, using the phone to dictate stories to the *Journal*. Finally, the irate reporters sent for the police, who found Gilman posing as a nurse, with the woman's consent. The deception was harmless, she said, and she used it only to fake out her competition.

When pressed, though, she does admit to two "reprehensible" things. One involved a fairly complicated abduction, murder, and suicide. As a sixteen-year-old girl stood waiting for a school bus, she was abducted by her girl-friend's father, who whisked her onto the running board of his car. The man had been smitten with the girl for some time, and this infatuation was well known in the community. When she refused to run away with him, he took a revolver that had been secreted in a hollowed-out copy of the *History of Scotland*, shot her, then swallowed poison and shot himself.

Found by police in his pocket was a "love diary," which all the papers wanted to get their hands on. When Gilman was dictating her story to the *Journal*, the city editor, Amster Spiro, told her to get it even if she had to give the state trooper $100. Gilman told the trooper about the offered bribe, saying she didn't want to have to do that. The trooper replied he wouldn't have taken the money anyway.

Then Spiro called back with the news that Hearst's competing *Mirror* had published parts of the diary. "When he read them to me over the phone," she recalled, "I knew they were fake. I asked him if he wanted the same kind of diary and to call me back in fifteen minutes. I dictated some copy and Leo Carroll [the state trooper who had the diary] said my fake diary was bet-ter than the original."

The other bit of fakery involved a poor American Indian woman who had been convinced to pose nude by a sculptor who promised to marry her. When the reluctant model found out he already had a wife, she arranged for a friend to shoot him. Gilman, with her instinct for tabloid journalism, persuaded the model to write a letter to the wounded sculptor, which the *Journal* re-produced in her original handwriting on the front page.

Years later, in a 1933 article for the *American Mercury*, Gilman looked back on the practice of slanting stories:

Sometimes a criminal finds it pretty hard going when he falls into the wrong news-paper category. There is no way of getting out of it. Once a Torch Fiend, always a Torch Fiend. The first reporters at the scene of the crime set the tone of it . . . There is an unwritten law among the thrill papers for the protection of their readers: never admit that a killer is insane until you have to, and fight even then for his sanity. Insanity ruins a story. It detracts from the menace and brilliant wickedness of the killer, it cheapens the crime, it ruins the lugubrious threat of the last walk to the electric chair.

Gilman has always felt that Ruth Snyder, the first woman to be electro-cuted and the subject of a much-criticized picture taken surreptitiously for the *Daily News* when she died in the electric chair, would have escaped with a life sentence had she played a different role with the press. She slipped into the "iron woman" category instead of the "sympathetic, misunderstood wife," Gilman said.

When the facts were bent, it was usually to make personalities more

Mildred Gilman

glamorous. "A playboy always had to be rich, a matron always from society, and if a murderer took a girl out for a ham sandwich then the description became 'wild parties with a sweetie,' " Gilman said. If stories couldn't be boring, then they couldn't be shocking either. Gilman once covered the funeral of a gangland czar, arriving at the tenement where the wake was being held with the private knowledge that the gangster had left all his insurance to his mistress. When she asked the widow what she thought about that fact, the woman attacked her, and relatives shouted curses at the body laid out in the living room. Rather than write a story of an angry widow attacking her dead husband, Gilman started off this way: "There is one little woman who has clung to the murdered beer baron, Johnnie the Sheik, in spite of his cruel neglect of her—his wife."

Gilman was usually assigned to murder cases because she could bring a novelist's touch to the stories. (Before she started at the *Journal* in 1928, she had written three novels: *Fig Leaves, Count Ten,* and *Headlines.*) Still, life was not one murder after another, for her career spanned Prohibition, the stock market crash of 1929, and the Great Depression. She covered the imaginative stunts of the era (a talk marathon was called a "larynx handicap"), and participated in some herself. The stunts at the *Journal* were thought up by Henry Paynter, the assignment editor. After reading about the death of Peter Trans, a Canadian bridge worker who had his lines tangled in a cofferdam and suffocated, Paynter got the idea to send Gilman down in a diving suit to write about what Trans might have felt when he was trapped. "I couldn't refuse the assignment," said Gilman, "since I was being paid more than male staffers." On February 2, 1930, she put on an old-style 200-pound diving suit with a fish-bowl headpiece and descended into the Hackensack River to inspect the new Turnpike Bridge. Hers was the only diving suit available, so no one was standing by to dive after her in an emergency. Her impressions were written with a characteristic light touch:

From the minute your eighteen pound lead shoes leave the last rung of the ladder and your heavy canvas rubber mittens let loose their friendly clasp—you're in a remote terrible different world. This scenery is supposed to resemble what Peter Trans saw . . . No sight but the dark water, the darker movement of little fishes—no sound but the rushing air. I'm millions of miles from civilization—there isn't any bottom to the river. Yes—my shoes touch something, bounce a little. I'm too light to walk in this two hundred pound suit . . . There's no cofferdam [a watertight enclosure] in this river, they've mislaid it—I can't see with my hands . . . Maybe they've lost the rope, I've slipped away—floated down to the ocean or something.

On another assignment, she tested out the range of airplane-relay telephone calls. The headline noted: "Earth and Sky are Linked by Human Voice." From 3,000 feet, she placed her first call to the paper only to have the city editor bawl her out for not being in the office. He had forgotten about the assignment. When the rewrite man got on the phone, Gilman told him she was calling him from an airplane. He replied, "Yeah, well, what's the story?" She called her mother in Grand Rapids, Michigan, and she called her local delicatessen and ordered dinner. Then she called Robert Wohlforth, her future husband, at his parents' home in Spring Lake, New Jersey. When he picked up the telephone, Gilman said, "Hello," and he answered, "Hello, Josephine, I have my bathing suit on. I'll be down on the beach in a few minutes." A reporter on the ground who had heard the conversation called Walter Winchell, who put an item in his column noting that Gilman not only had made the first and highest telephone call, but also had been stood up the highest of anyone on record. Pictures in the paper for the story show a smiling Gilman with her blond hair cut in the 1920s flapper style. Along with ice-blue eyes and a lithe, tall figure, she was indeed striking. As an octogenarian, she is still stunning and still a vigorous talker with a slight touch of the Midwest in her voice.

She was born Mildred Evans on October 1, 1896, in Chicago. Her father, George Dickinson Evans, was a furniture manufacturer who was forced to go on the road as a salesman when his factory burned. The family moved around—to St. Louis, Grand Rapids, and to Espanola, New Mexico, for summers with relatives. Both her mother, Eva Elizabeth (Campbell) Evans, a typist, and her godmother, Mary Agnes Chase, who worked at the Smithsonian Institution cataloging the grasses of the world, were very supportive of Gilman's desire for an education. "They counteracted the influence of my New England father who didn't want to spend the money to send me to college," she recalled. An older sister had died before she was born, and Mildred grew up feeling that her younger brother was her father's favorite. "I had to prove constantly that females were equal or superior to males. I did daring things, set records, followed rigid health regimes my mother set for me and wrote constantly at her insistence." When she was six, her mother told her she would be a writer and made her keep a diary, which "bored" her but "proved effective." Chase took her on suffrage marches, and Gilman remembered being at a Washington protest during Woodrow Wilson's inauguration.

She went to the University of Wisconsin where she was the first woman editor of the *Wisconsin Literary Magazine*. While at college she was selling magazine articles and finishing her first novel, *Fig Leaves*, a thinly disguised autobiography describing her teen-age rite of passage in Grand Rapids, trying to avoid "the furniture people and become a literate person." Right out of college she married James Ward Gilman, a writer and teacher. They had a son and for a time ran a bookshop in Springfield, Massachusetts. After her marriage broke up, she moved to New York where her cousin was working as Heywood Broun's secretary. Coincidentally, Broun had read *Fig Leaves*, and when they met told her it was unusual to read a book written from an adolescent's point of view. Shortly thereafter she took over as his secretary. Such an association was invaluable for a young writer. Broun, a founder of the American Newspaper Guild, was for thirty-one years a liberal journalist who distinguished himself not only as a columnist and drama critic, but also as a sports writer and foreign correspondent. She became friendly with Broun's wife, Ruth Hale, a newspaper reporter who was active in the Lucy Stone League, a feminist group named after an early suffragist who advocated use of a woman's maiden name in marriage. Through Broun, Gilman met the legendary personalities of the Algonquin Round Table, that gathering of wits which included H. L. Mencken, George S. Kaufman, Alexander Wooll-cott, Dorothy Parker, and others. "I was a kibitzer," she said, "but as the last surviving member of the table group, many interested in that period are calling me for background information."

During her college years, Gilman had begun to correspond with Mencken and Sherwood Anderson simply by sending them fan letters. "In my day," she recalled, "you could write a famous author, tell them how much you admired them—and receive an answer. Not any more. I had a wonderful correspondence with Sherwood Anderson about writing techniques. It was like having him as a teacher."

Working for Broun, whom Gilman described as a "big loveable bear," and whom others have called "an unmade bed," was never routine. His column "It Seems to Me" bounced from the *New York Tribune* to the *World* to the Scripps-Howard chain and was destined for the *New York Post* when he died in 1939. He was an unpredictable, opinionated, combative liberal. As his personal secretary, Gilman worked out of his apartment, where part of the job was getting him out of bed, finding his clothes, and getting him on his way. Then she took care of correspondence and forged his signature to letters. One day, at lunch with her successor, the author John O'Hara, the two decided to compare each other's forgeries. "You couldn't tell them apart," she said.

There was a bit of fakery, too, when Mildred Gilman got her first newspaper job. As she tells the story, a newspaper friend wrote a job-application letter praising her work, using a deceased editor for a recommendation so it couldn't be checked. On the way to deliver the letter to the editor of Hearst's *American*, Gilman got off the elevator on the wrong floor and handed it instead to the *Journal*'s city editor, Amster Spiro, who said he had read her book *Headlines* (a novel with fictionalized stories built around real newspaper headlines). He thus assumed she had some newspaper experience and asked her how much she would work for.

Although fifty-six years have passed since this encounter, Mildred Gilman clearly delights in the retelling of the story. When she told it to me, she was sitting in a suite at the Princeton Club, where she stays when in New York. She was dressed in grey tweeds set off by silver jewelry. Her ice-blue eyes twinkled as she recalled, naughtily: "I looked him right in the eye and said, 'I have never worked for a newspaper for less than $100 a week.' " The scale at that time for men was $60. Spiro hired her. Looking back, did such deception bother her? "I didn't mind a bit," she said. "I saw the whole thing as a great joke."

When she started reporting in 1928, life was fun and Gilman, tutored by the Round Table sages, was better equipped than most to bluff her way through. With the general feature story, where she could use her talents for scene setting and characterization, she had no problems; she couldn't, however, handle the inverted pyramid for news stories. Soon the copy editor discovered she didn't have a clue about how to write hard news. Graciously, he would take her out in the hall, tell her what the lead should be, and Gilman would blithely return to her typewriter to write it as dictated. Along the way, she learned how to do it on her own. Since many of her big stories were out of town, she dictated them to rewrite men, and in the translation, there were, of course, changes. But the fact that a really gutsy newspaperwoman was the one calling in the story was by far the most significant change.

Occasionally she claimed to be from the *New York Times* in order to gain entry to a respectable place that would have barred a tabloid reporter. As she emphasized, it was all in good fun. Outside of work, New York's reporters enjoyed the illicit life of Prohibition and at a party she met Robert Wohlforth, a reporter on Hearst's *American* who would become her second husband. Wohlforth fell asleep on her shoulder at the party, after drinking too much bootleg liquor. "I fell in love with him that night," she said. He worked nights and she worked mornings, so they didn't have much time together. But there was the telephone.

One telephone call led to Gilman nearly being arrested for murder. She was in New Jersey, covering the arrest of Gladys Mae Parkes, who was accused of killing her two wards. The woman was definitely insane, said Gilman, but the press had to work to make her appear sane. They labeled her the "Iron Mae" and the "Sphinx Woman" because she refused to confess. After a long day waiting for a confession, Gilman returned to her hotel in Camden and called her husband. She recalled that the conversation went something like this: "Haven't they found out anything yet?" he asked. "Not a thing they didn't know—only that they're dead and their bodies were in a suitcase," she replied. "Ah, come on home," he said. "You can't stand the strain."

An hour later there was a loud banging on the hotel-room door. When Gilman opened it, two detectives barged in and started interrogating her as she sat huddled in her fur coat in the middle of the bed. The detectives demanded that she repeat what she had told her husband. Finally they said they knew all about how she had killed a man and buried his body in a suitcase. It seems that the New York long-distance operator had listened in, embellished the facts, and called the New York police, who in turn called the Camden police, who then sent detectives over to the hotel. Gilman produced her press card, and a call to the *Journal* verified the identification. That night she ended up getting no sleep, but she wasn't in jail.

Mildred Gilman might have continued her newspaper career if she had been assigned to run-of-the-mill stories. Instead, her editors continued to assign her dangerous ones. It was the 3X murderer and Robert Wohlforth's own trickery that convinced her to retire. The 3X case started in 1930 when the *Journal* received notes announcing that murders were going to take place in Queens. The paper dismissed the messages as the rantings of a crank— until the first body was found. The 3X killer, a name he chose for himself, had approached a couple in a parked car, murdered the man, and then escorted the woman home, giving her a lecture on morality.

The next time he declared his intentions, Gilman and a photographer were sent out as decoys. Nothing happened. Later the killer wrote the *Journal* that he had observed the decoys "making fools of themselves." He also said that he would spare "7Y—the tall, blonde Miss Gilman," indicating that he knew who she was. The last letter he sent said he was flying to Germany in his biplane and would circle the *Journal* building. He killed twice and was never apprehended.

At this point, Wohlforth, who had had enough of daily journalism himself, took Gilman to a medical student friend, but told her he was a doctor. After an examination, the student announced that Gilman had low blood pressure and if she continued working there could be serious consequences. So both Gilman and Wohlforth left their newspapers. Gilman wrote *Sob Sister* and sold it to the movies for $10,000. Anyone with cash during the Depression could buy anything, and it had always been Gilman's wish to return to the area around Ridgefield, Connecticut, the scene of the "love diary" case. They found a 1730 farmhouse, which had once been a cobbler's shop, and purchased it from Cass Gilbert, architect of the Woolworth building in New York and the Supreme Court building in Washington. They had two sons, and they've lived there ever since. After his newspaper career,

Wohlforth was an executive with the publishing firm of Farrar, Straus and Giroux for twenty-five years.

Gilman followed *Sob Sister* with two more novels, *Divide by Two* and *Love for Two*. She contributed to many magazines, and her portrait of Paul Robeson, the black singer, actor, and political activist, was an early *New Yorker* profile, published in 1928. She returned to reporting twice. When Hitler came to power, she went to Germany for International News Service (INS) and was able to interview Herman Göring because she had a personal letter to him from a friend of his late wife. Göring met her dressed in blue velvet robes, accompanied by a lioness. "He was trying to emulate the ancient conqueror Julius Caesar," she said.

While in Germany she covered the Reichstag arson trial and each morning had to be searched before entering the courtroom. After interviewing someone who had been released from Dachau, she started asking too many questions about the concentration camp and thereafter was followed everywhere by Gestapo agents. One night they came to where she was staying and took all her notes and correspondence. Of particular interest to them was a letter from her INS editor in Berlin, who had written down the latest joke from America: "Why are they sawing all the toilet seats on Wall Street in two?" "Because there are so many half-assed bankers." The Gestapo thought this was a special code. Ordered to return home on the next boat, she was followed to the train station at dawn. She got the agent following her to help with her heavy suitcases.

In 1934, when her husband had a government post in Washington, she worked for the *Herald* covering Eleanor Roosevelt and reporting on the projects that were coming out of the New Deal—the National Recovery Act (NRA), the Tennessee Valley Authority (TVA), and the Works Progress Administration (WPA).

Since her time in Germany and Washington, life has never been dull. She has lectured about her newspaper days, worked for Planned Parenthood for twenty years, started a society magazine in Miami Beach, and in 1983 began working on her autobiography. Her husband still commutes to New York, where he is finance-committee chairman of his former publishing company. Together they dance, swim, exercise, and, most recently, sailed to Nova Scotia with their sons and grandchildren. Above all, Robert Wohlforth has been the focus of her life. He is seven years younger, and she recommends that "every girl marry someone younger, particularly if he is witty and has the proper feeling about women. We have had a good fifty-three years together, and I am not a widow as most women are at eighty-six years of age. When I married him, I outweighed him and made more money.

Now, he weighs more than I do and he has all the money. Everyone should choose a mate with a sense of humor," she said, all in fun, of course.

Mildred Gilman tended to become emotionally involved with many of the victims she wrote about. One was Harry Hoffman, who created his own circumstantial evidence that led to his being charged with the murder of Maude Bauer. A neighborhood girl had recognized his car near the scene of the crime. Learning of this, Hoffman panicked, painted his car, and mailed his gun to his brother. At his fourth trial, with previously suppressed evidence, it was proved that his gun could not have fired the fatal shot. Gilman interviewed Hoffman before his last trial, was convinced of his innocence, wrote touching stories, and sent presents in his name to his child in the orphanage. This story celebrates his acquittal.

Hoffman's Ex-Wife
Would Rewed Him

By MILDRED GILMAN

New York Evening Journal, May 23, 1929

Freedom—after "five years of hell—"

"It's like waking up suddenly from a bad dream. I don't know how I feel. My emotions are too mixed up."

Harry Hoffman spoke hesitantly, dazed from the sudden shock of finding himself free of prison bars and the menace of the electric chair.

And now the former wife, Mrs. Agnes Keating Hoffman-Rankin, a frail, nervous little woman, wants to go back to the husband she discarded, the man who has faced four trials for his life in the slaying of Maude C. Bauer on March 25, 1924, in a lonely Staten Island road.

Always "Loved Harry"

Mrs. Rankin remained inconspicuously in the background while her former husband was on trial for his life, but when he won acquittal she ran to him in the hall of the Brooklyn Supreme Court and threw her arms about him, breaking into tears.

Then, while Hoffman went to the reporters' room to pose for cameramen Mrs. Rankin hovered shyly in the background. To the *Evening Journal* reporter she said:

"I have always loved Harry. I was frightened and hysterical after he was put in jail.

Listened to "Stupid Advice"

"But I always knew that he was innocent. I listened to stupid advice of people trying to turn me against him. He was a wonderful husband and father. He came home every night directly from his work. This talk of his meeting other women is ridiculous.

"In the first place he always was a home man; in the second place there wouldn't have been any time for such things. I want to return to him, to get

Dorothy, our baby who is six years old, out of the Israel Orphanage and begin where we left off on that day five years ago."

"When are you going back to Mr. Hoffman?" she was asked.

To Seek Divorce

She replied with a sheepish smile.

"I've got to get a divorce first. But I don't suppose that will be so hard. I haven't seen my husband for three and a half years and never got any sort of support from him. And now that the children's name is cleared, I want to go back to Harry to start over again.

"I haven't any idea what Harry will do, but I guess he can get a job somehow. If he can't he can come and live with me."

And Harry Hoffman is anxiously looking forward to his meeting today with his "baby Dorothy." He hasn't seen her since the day five years ago when he was first arrested. The girl now is six.

"Come Home Now!"

Little Mildred Hoffman, "Beany," his ten-year-old daughter, threw herself into his arms.

"Can you come home with us now, Daddy?" she asked. "We've waited such a long time."

She has been living with her mother in Jersey City.

Hoffman, through Samuel Liebowitz, his counsel, had refused to plead guilty to a manslaughter charge, which would have meant death in the electric chair in the belief he would be acquitted.

The accused man was with his wife and daughter in his cell beneath the courtroom during the five hours the jury was out. He was very confident, and although his face was pale as he was led into court by two deputy sherifs when the jury returned, he wore a faint smile. The jurors were grave, and experienced courtroom spectators "feared the worst."

No Demonstration.

Justice Humphrey solemnly said the bare half hundred persons in the room might remain provided they made no demonstration when the verdict was announced.

Reginald C. Thomas, tall, dignified foreman of the jury, hesitated a moment before saying:

"We find the defendant not guilty."

There was a prolonged silence. Hoffman turned to Liebowitz, and they hugged each other. Tears dimmed Hoffman's eyes as he put out his hand

and groped for that of Liebowitz. They did not "shake" hands, merely rocking backward and forward, both powerfully moved by the emotion of the moment.

Hoffman, with his wife and daughter and his lawyer, went to Liebowitz's office at No. 66 Court street. When they came out an enthusiastic woman kissed Liebowitz. The party went by subway to The Bronx, where Hoffman spent the night with his brother, Albert.

Four times the quiet, well-mannered little man has stood trial, accused of the brutal attack and murder on March 25, 1924, of the pretty Staten Island wife and mother, Maude C. Bauer. A blue ribbon jury after three hours deliberation said at last the words Hoffman has prayed for so long— "not guilty."

He strained tensely forward, seemed on the verge of collapse when the welcome words were pronounced. Then a smile appeared on his tired face.

Fach Takes It Gracefully

District Attorney Albert Fach, who has prosecuted Hoffman in all four trials, conceded his final defeat gracefully. He made a motion before Supreme Court Justice Burt J. Humphrey that the assault charge pending against Hoffman, on Staten Island, be dismissed.

Crowds of people surrounded the man who has put up the stiffest legal struggle ever staged in the State of New York to prove his innocence. He accepted their congratulations in a daze, tears of happiness in his eyes.

Harry, trembling with emotion, on the verge of a breakdown, followed his lawyer, Samuel S. Liebowitz, through cheering Brooklyn crowds collected in front of the court house, past flashlight flares, around the corner to the lawyer's office.

What It Is Like

There, after a few minutes of rest, he tried to put into words the emotions of a man who steps out into the free air at last after losing home, family, position and wasting five years of his life in prison—for a crime of which he was declared innocent.

"I can't tell you what it is like to sit day after day, year after year in prison, knowing of your own innocence, waiting for the law to take its slow, laborious course.

"The jury gave me what I most wanted—complete vindication. I would not accept a compromise and would have fought to the end of my days for freedom—or death.

"What am I going to do now? First I am going to the Israel Orphanage to see my baby Dorothy." As he talked he clung to little Mildred. "These two children are all that has kept me alive and fighting, all that has prevented my going insane in that prison hell."

Hoffman spent his first night of freedom at the home of his lawyer in Brooklyn.

Job Awaiting Him

"Then I will try to start life over again," he said, "try to forget the bitterness and shake off the prison feeling."

The motion picture machine operator's union has a job waiting for Hoffman, according to Mr. Liebowitz, in one of the larger New York City theatres. They are going to send him first to recuperate in the Adirondacks to aid in the rehabilitation of the former motion picture projectionist, whose health has been seriously impaired by his imprisonment.

Hoffman was asked by a reporter if he would change his name.

"Why should I change it?" he countered. "The name of Hoffman is vindicated; it belongs to a free man. 'Hoffman' means in German the 'man who hopes.'"

Hoffman has not seen his baby girl, Dorothy, for five years, during which the father's secret has been kept by attendants at the Israel Orphanage. Dorothy, who is six, does not know of the taint of murder that had been placed on her father.

Today she was to greet him and was to be taken to a home of her own.

The tiny girl has won for herself a place in the hearts of the Orphanage officials, attendants and inmates. She has endeared herself to Judge Gustave Hartman, head of the home, and his wife, honorary superintendent.

"We are both happy and sorry Dorothy is to leave us," Mrs. Hartman told the *Evening Journal* today. "Of course, we are delighted to hear that Mr. Hoffman has won his freedom, but at the same time we are sorry to learn that Dorothy will leave us. I'm so glad of the acquittal of Mr. Hoffman for Dorothy's sake."

The tiny girl, by her ever smiling, always correct behavior, has become a pet at the home and with her companions.

17

Doris Fleeson
(1901–1970)

O N A SUNDAY EVENING in May 1960 Edward R. Murrow's guests on his television show *Small World* had it out on the quality of newspapers. Marya Mannes, the critic, called the nation's press "parochial, trivial and inadequate," with the one exception of the *New York Times*. Doris Fleeson, labeled a "stormy petrel" by some of her journalistic colleagues, replied, "I consider it extremely parochial to insist that there's only one great newspaper in the United States. And that paper, against which I have competed for 30 years . . . is very often, and often largely, overwritten." As a Washington political columnist for thirty-four years, Doris Fleeson said a lot in 600 words, and was called "the columnists' columnist." Proud of her tabloid experience, where you had to beat the competition and grab the reader in the lead, she once said, "We belonged to the who-the-hell-reads-the-second-paragraph school."

In a biographical sketch of Fleeson for *Notable American Women*, Mary McGrory, now a columnist for the *Washington Post* and a close friend, wrote, "Doris Fleeson was not just the first syndicated woman political columnist; she was the only one of either sex to approach national affairs like a police reporter." Indeed, Fleeson was the perfect 1930s tabloid reporter. She loved the police beat, saying it was the best way to learn how politics works, and in a 1959 speech at the University of Minnesota she boldly suggested that Washington correspondents be returned to their home papers and assigned to the police and the department of sanitation to "restore those with comfortable connections to reality and restore their perspective."

A feisty five-foot-two, with flashing green eyes that were quick to register trust or disdain, she was a Washington spitfire. For nine years she and her first husband, John O'Donnell, wrote their trenchant views on politics and politicians in "Capitol Stuff," one of the *New York Daily News*' most popular features. The paper's style book, which specified type size for double bylines, specifically excluded their column, which ran in larger type. After their marriage broke up, Fleeson started her own column, which was syndicated in ninety papers. It was, she said, a forum to practice what she preached and to earn a "few figs—with thistles."

Doris Fleeson covered the terms of five Presidents, working in nearly the same way as a columnist that she had as a general assignment reporter. She made sure she had the best contacts, was a permanent member of President Roosevelt's press touring group, and was one of Mrs. Roosevelt's "girls." Moreover, she had an instinctive understanding of how government works and the ability to interpret political complexities in simple terms. In 1952, *Time* magazine noted: "Her pipelines into the administration are so well placed that her columns on what the Fair Dealers are thinking often reveal what the Democrats will do long before they are ready to announce it or are quite sure themselves."

Any press roundup on Washington views always included excerpts from her furiously opinionated columns. She was a staunch New Deal Democrat even after O'Donnell and the *Daily News* became critical of the Roosevelt administration in the late 1930s. Never hesitant about telling any President how to run the country, she wrote once: "The trouble with Eisenhower is that he seems to think 'politics' is a dirty word." Her barbs were fairly distributed, however, as *Newsweek* magazine observed: "There is almost no Washington figure, Republican or Democrat, who has not felt the sharp edge of her typewriter."

She uncovered a feud between the Supreme Court Justices Robert H. Jackson and Hugo Black, and created a stir when she printed a quote from President Truman about U.S. military deserters during the Korean War. Truman claimed that the 46,000 deserters were "principally from areas reached by the influence" of the *Chicago Tribune* and the Hearst and Scripps-Howard newspapers, which supported General Douglas MacArthur, who the President said was "insubordinate." MacArthur replied that Truman's "lack of faith" and policies of appeasement in Korea could have caused the desertions and could also cause another war.

Fleeson supported Adlai Stevenson, continuing to write hopefully of his 1956 presidential campaign long after other journalists had counted him out.

A week before the election, she wrote that Stevenson's challenge rested on two things: "a demonstrated and admitted strength of the Democratic Party and the possibility that there is a silent vote in the country." A few months after John F. Kennedy took office, she noted that the "golden boy" was dealing with hard tasks with "something less than the grace expected of him."

Universally respected by her colleagues, Fleeson was described by James Reston of the *New York Times* as an "alert reporter with a facility for making difficult questions sound innocent." Eric Sevareid, the television commentator, once told an audience: "Look carefully at the column written by Doris Fleeson. If you are a reader intimate with the whole cargo of background she is writing against on any given day you cannot fail to be impressed by the Swiss-watch economy of her construction. There is scarcely a wasted or replaceable word. She is probably the finest woman reporter of the time and in the field of purely party politics has no superior."

A woman of great style, she favored tailored clothes us' ally with a designer label, Sally Victor hats, and expensive French perfumes. She helped younger journalists like Mary McGrory get started in Washington and worked tirelessly for liberal causes, fighting for the installation of women's restrooms in congressional galleries, and in 1953 sponsoring the first black applicant for membership in the Women's National Press Club. Twenty years earlier she had joined Heywood Broun and other reporters to help found the Guild of New York Newspaper Men and Women, a forerunner of the American Newspaper Guild, and to fight for a minimum wage of $35 a week for reporters.

"To be a woman reporter in the man's world of Washington in the 1940s and 1950s was to be patronized or excluded," McGrory wrote, adding that Fleeson "submitted to these indignities with tearful rage. She knew that few of the men were her peers and none her superior, and she was, well in advance of the women's liberation movement, a militant feminist." Retired columnist Joseph Alsop, looking back at this time in Washington and the women reporters who worked there, recalled: "We never thought of Doris Fleeson or May Craig [correspondent for numerous Maine newspapers] as women. They were reporters. They were uncommonly gifted and idiosyncratic. None of them would have liked to have been called Ms."

As the youngest of six children and the second daughter, Doris Fleeson learned early to be a fighter and an individualist. She grew up in rural Sterling, Kansas (population 2,239), where she was born on May 20, 1901. Her father, William Fleeson, ran a clothing store and "ran the town from the back room," she often said. Her mother, Helen (Tebbe) Fleeson, raised the large family, and young Doris often helped out in the rooming house operated by her grandmother.

She attended local schools and went to the University of Kansas to study journalism. During her junior year she took her first job on the *Pittsburg* (Kansas) *Sun*, covering school board meetings and labor disputes. After graduation in 1923 she went to New Haven, where her sister, Elizabeth, was studying for a doctorate at Yale. Doris tried unsuccessfully to find a newspaper job, and supported herself by making up production schedules in a wire factory.

Moving to Chicago, she tried again to become a reporter and took another clerical position until 1926 when she was hired as society editor by the *Evanston News Index*, a suburban paper. Restless after a year, she returned East and found a job at the *Great Neck News* in Long Island, reporting, writing, editing, making up pages, proofreading—in short, putting out the paper.

Her eye, though, was always on the *Daily News*. She proudly told a reporter how she got that job. "One dark November night in 1927, I walked into the *New York Daily News* and demanded that I see the editor. In fifteen minutes I got him and in the next fifteen minutes I did myself no injustice whatever. He had a vacancy, wonderful to relate, and I was a fullfledged New York reporter at last."

Writing in the flamboyant style of the time, she reported on crimes, trials, and scandals. Later assigned to local politics, she covered Fiorello H. La Guardia's first campaign for mayor when he was defeated by dapper Jimmy (Gentleman) Walker, and the Seabury investigation into official corruption in New York City. She asked Judge Samuel Seabury to delay Mayor Walker's testimony, the highlight of the inquiry, while she had her first and only child. Two days after the birth of her daughter, Doris, Fleeson was back in chambers to hear Mayor Walker testify.

Her excellent city reporting earned her a coveted assignment to the Albany bureau, and when President Roosevelt was inaugurated in 1933 she went to Washington as a correspondent in the *News'* newly opened bureau, joining her husband of three years, a dashing, tall, dark Irishman described by colleagues as "brilliant and unpredictable." "Capitol Stuff" was hard-nosed, sprightly, and provocative, capturing the flavor of the New Deal era. On January 20, 1937, the couple's column described President Roosevelt's second inaugural:

Head bared to an angry sky, his face lashed by the chill fury of a wind-whipped rain, Franklin Delano Roosevelt took the oath of office for his second term as President and pledged his administration to continue the fight against need and poverty, which still are the lot of millions. Standing on the spot where four years ago he rallied a stricken country to battle against the forces of Depression, the President reconsecrated himself to the goals of that earlier day.

Doris Fleeson

Around Washington, the O'Donnells were a striking couple, but there were problems both personally and politically. Her husband and the *Daily News* became disenchanted with the New Deal, and Fleeson's and O'Donnell's views became increasingly disparate as the nation moved toward World War II. On July 26, 1939, the family sailed for a working vacation in Europe, putting their daughter in a Swiss boarding school and continuing on to Berlin where they filed a story predicting that war was imminent. O'Donnell left for London, and Fleeson, after collecting young Doris, caught the last boat out of France before war broke out.

In 1942 the reporter team divorced; O'Donnell was kept as a Washington correspondent, with Fleeson recalled to New York to write radio news, a sad commentary on the rights of women at that time. For several months, she did "rip and read" announcements for the hourly news programs, waiting for something good to happen to her career. Ed Quinn and Frank Holeman, former *News* copy boys who brought her wire copy, remembered how this "star" reporter was "so gracious in a grinding low estate." When she left the paper in 1943, she immediately signed on as a roving war correspondent for *Woman's Home Companion*, covering the battlefronts from Salerno to Omaha Beach. In 1945 she became a columnist, writing twice-weekly for *United Features Syndicate*. According to Mary McGrory, "She roamed the Capitol, a tiger in white gloves and a Sally Victor hat, stalking explanations for the stupidity, cruelty, fraud, or cant that was her chosen prey." Her scrappy columns frequently skewered politicians, leading President John F. Kennedy to quip that he "would rather be Krocked than Fleesonized," referring to the gentler *New York Times* columnist Arthur Krock.

Fleeson lived in a century-old Georgetown house, which she said was furnished "mostly in books," and she prided herself as a meticulous housekeeper. The columnist Inez Robb was a close friend, and the two carried on a competition to see who was neater. Robb once said that they both had simple tastes: "All we want is the best." Fleeson's daughter, Doris, went to Vassar and made her debut in Washington. When not at a press conference, traveling, or on a convention floor, Fleeson was dining or lunching with someone important, from her idol, Eleanor Roosevelt, to Dan Kimball, Navy Secretary under President Truman, whom she married in 1958.

McGrory wrote that the Kimballs were "aggressively happy in their house on S Street. She was fiercely domestic . . . and Sunday afternoon often found the scourge of statesmen sewing fresh white collar and cuffs on her dark-blue dress, looking for all the world like Kitty Foyle."

Fleeson's last campaign was in 1964 with Lyndon Johnson. She collapsed while traveling with the press corps, suffering from circulatory problems, and in 1967 semi-retired. On July 30, 1970, Dan Kimball died: thirty-six hours later on August 1, the couple's twelfth wedding anniversary, Doris Fleeson died of a stroke at the age of sixty-nine. Joint funeral services were held for the couple, and they were buried at Arlington Cemetery.

Fleeson was fond of quoting a Senator who addressed the Senate with, "I am not, sirs, a statesman. I am, sirs, a politician, and I hope a good one." She would say, "I am not a pundit. I am a reporter, and I hope a good one." A long list of awards and honorary degrees attest to that. More importantly, though, Doris Fleeson represented one of the last of the "hit-'em-in-the-eye" political commentators to come out of Washington.

In 1937 the New York Newspaper Women's Club gave Doris Fleeson its first annual award for outstanding reporting for her coverage of the 1936 Republican convention. She was honored again in 1943 for the following article on Wendell L. Willkie.

Willkie Fighting for '44—Party or No Party

By DORIS FLEESON

New York Daily News, December 29, 1942.

Wendell Willkie today is a man without a party, but not a man without a country.

He is probably second only to President Roosevelt in his ability to command a nationwide—and an international—audience. He speaks, writes, debates, discusses, is interviewed, dines out incessantly. All channels to the public opinion on which he now relies for his political "it" are open to him. A flood tide of mail and telephone calls washes daily into the sedate downtown law office which is his only base of operations.

His energy is prodigious and his industry titanic.

Some years ago, when the late banker-philanthropist, Otto Kahn, was at his zenith, a wit remarked that whenever you found as many as three people dining in public, one of them was bound to be Otto Kahn. The modern version would substitute the name of Wendell Willkie. Alice Roosevelt Longworth, who is bitterly hostile to Willkie's internationalist views, put it another way. She said it was no longer necessary to invite Willkie to a party— you just put a lighted candle in the window and he would drop in.

A cursory glance at his speeches for the last year shows that no public forum of any consequence omits him. To a mass meeting in the Hollywood Bowl he expounds ideas which he will later air at the Lincoln's Birthday dinner of the Middlesex Club in Boston, Mass. A churchmen's dinner, a campaign to modernize St. Vincent's Hospital, the awards dinner of the Academy of Motion Picture Arts and Sciences—come one, come all, and hear Willkie.

His Audience, Now Worldwide

Since his far-flung travels to the world battlefronts, his audience has been the world. The London Times interviews Willkie. The London Evening Standard asks for—and gets—a message to the British people on Pearl Harbor day. The Australian, Russian, Chinese and South African press are similarly favored.

All this Willkie writes himself or pours forth extemporaneously from the durable larynx which has never failed since the one time it blacked him out for two days on his first campaign swing westward in '40.

The Republican Party watches this scintillating performance with mixed emotions. The rank-and-file appear to approve. They like the Willkie gustiness, the curiosity and hardihood that put him aboard planes soaring over the China deserts. The Willkie outspokenness, his tangling with President Roosevelt, reassure them that it is still a free country.

On the other hand, the animosity which any gathering of Republican organization politicians displays toward Willkie is a major phenomenon. One reporter at the National Committee meeting in St. Louis last Dec. 7, described it ecstatically as "a lovely hate—full-blown, lush, expressive, one of the best political hates I've ever seen."

He had just been getting an earful from various committee members— including one notable so eager to participate in the hate-Willkie discussions that he cut short an interview on party affairs with the plaintive complaint: "But you haven't asked me what I think of Willkie."

Won His Battle On G.O.P. Chairman

Another '40 Willkie supporter suggested the best job for his ex-hero was India manager for Henry Wallace's international milk route.

With it all, they were compelled to bow to Willkie's edict that the able Werner Schroeder could not be National Chairman because he was supported by the isolationist Chicago Tribune.

Willkie is a candidate for the Republican nomination for President in 1944. Because of his popularity and unique access to public opinion, he is still formidable, despite his organization weakness. And he does not entirely lack organization support—from Oregon to Massachusetts, many of the ablest party leaders are in his camp. With the help of peacemakers within the party, the Willkie group was able to pile up 43 votes—close to one-half—for their stalking-horse in the Schroeder fight, an unknown from the West Coast. Perhaps two-thirds of this represented Willkie strength.

But it is not now upon organization support that Willkie relies. He believes that if his ideas—progressive domestic policies, international cooperation to keep peace—prevail, he will prevail.

If his ideas do not prevail, he will not and could not be nominated.

Lost Most Support Of Big Business

Willkie has always considered himself a progressive. But at Philadelphia in '40 the "We Want Willkie" stampede was engineered by a brilliant big business-political combination, which believed that the $75,000-a-year president of the great electric power holding company of Commonwealth and

Southern was an ideal ally. This support has largely fallen away from him. Now it will go to a "safe" candidate, such as they thought the business-nurtured Hoosier was.

Willkie is still popular with many middle-class groups, with the small country club sets, as well as with the general public. But like Roosevelt, he must look in the main to the ordinary man to give him political stature.

It is 18 months until the Republican convention, but it seems probable now that it will be a case of the field against Willkie. Probably Gov. John Bricker of Ohio, against Willkie. Bricker, the solid man with the clean record who has avoided all controversy, is easier to understand. It is easier to predict what he will do.

A Bricker-Willkie deadlock might eventuate, in which case Thomas E. Dewey of New York, who has removed himself from the picture, or another favorite son would profit.

Lacks Some Notable Bryan Advantages

Willkie in his present position is frequently compared to William Jennings Bryan of the silver tongued and popular following. Bryan's then unorthodox economic views drove everybody with a checkbook out of the Democratic Party, but he was able to secure his party's Presidential nomination three times against violent opposition.

It has been argued that Bryan always had a home state, Nebraska, for a base of operations, always a sure seat in the convention, always controlled a delegation. This Willkie lacks. A legal resident of New York, he has no chance of seizing party control from Gov.-elect Dewey, who will certainly maintain a firm grip on the New York sector of the G.O.P.

But Willkie has friends to help him in New York besides powerful newspaper support. And it was a Bricker supporter who declared in Ohio: "Never count out Willkie. If they try to read him out of the party, he'll read the party out of them."

It would take a lot of cold nerve to deny the 1940 standard-bearer, titular leader of the party, his chance in the national convention. Politicians, who have watched the cat jump some odd ways, are short of that kind of cold nerve.

During the Willkie-Roosevelt honeymoon after Willkie announced support of lend-lease, some Republicans wistfully thought the Democrats might welcome home their wandering boy and solve the G.O.P. problem. One Republican who was asked his opinion on whom the Democrats would nominate said: "Hadn't you heard? We're giving you back Willkie." Democrats, however, looked the gift horse in the mouth and declined.

Outspoken Attacks Annoy Washington

Besides, the great honeymoon is over. Willkie's attacks upon the deal with Darlan, his insistence that Great Britain be made now to discuss the postwar world, his demands for a unified command, his criticism of the flow of aid to China, his second front speeches while abroad—these are rifts in the Roosevelt lute.

Willkie has complaints, too. He was enraged while in the Middle East to learn of the Roosevelt attack on "people who didn't know what they were talking about" when they demanded a second front. By this time the North African offensive was under way, and Roosevelt had disclosed that it was projected in the Summer between himself and Churchill. Clearly Willkie had been left out, and his friend, Stalin, had not enlightened him. The effect was to ridicule Willkie.

Of his association with Roosevelt, Willkie states categorically:

"I have never had any political understanding with President Roosevelt. I say what I think. If it agrees with his views, okay. If not, okay. He and I have never had any political discussions."

Talked Plainly to F.D.R. at White House

In their famous hour-and-a-half meeting after Willkie returned to Washington, the President did the listening and Willkie did the talking. Roosevelt was effervescent and effusive when his caller entered the oval study. Willkie responded to the greetings, but then announced he had a lot to get off his chest. He said that it was Roosevelt's office and that Roosevelt could get rid of him at any moment, but declared that while there he proposed to tell his observations and opinions, gleaned from his journey.

When Willkie concluded, the President obliquely apologized for what F.D.R. termed a misunderstanding regarding the Roosevelt remarks on those who demanded a second front. Roosevelt blamed this misunderstanding on the "isolationist press." Willkie did not argue, but commented politely that the President's failure to correct the misunderstanding at once had made his task more difficult.

Willkie has been incensed by censorship of his speeches. Secretary of War Stimson insisted that he cut out of one address a caustic reference to the Darlan deal. Twenty-four hours later the President issued an explanatory statement condemning Darlan and justifying the deal on the ground of military expediency.

Willkie has also prodded the conscience of Britain and insisted that Churchill must discuss postwar aims now—a problem the Prime Minister has been notably reluctant to deal with, even under Roosevelt's urgings. But

Churchill in his most recent speech acknowledged that there was such a problem and that it was important.

Believes Darlan Deal Key to Postwar World

The Darlan deal, Willkie believes, stands at the heart of the postwar problem. He believes that the United Nations must never yield their moral leadership of the world.

"I believe the moral losses of expediency always far outweigh the temporary gains," he told a Canadian audience. "I believe that every drop of blood saved through expediency will be paid for by 20 drawn with a sword."

In his Darlan discussions, Willkie frequently cites the Emancipation Proclamation. When Abraham Lincoln lifted the freeing of the slaves from the realm of theory to that of fact by the famous proclamation, Willkie asserts that the people of England for the first time swung to the side of the North. "We've got to keep our colors bright and clean," he asserts vehemently. "Only then will the people flock to our standard and believe we mean what we say."

Always he contends that we "cannot rebuild the world on a strictly Anglo-American basis." He demands agreement now on the basic structure of peace between us and all our allies. Economic internationalism, he warns, must accompany political internationalism.

Sees No Security With U.S. Isolationist

And he harps upon the theme that if the United States again withdraws into itself after this war, there can be no peace or economic security in the world, at least under a democratic form of government.

Historically, the party in power in the United States during a war is not the party in power after the war is over. It is Willkie's hope to lead the resurgent Republican party down the path of international cooperation. He is in the fight to the finish to prevent a return to isolation.

The Willkies live quietly in a Fifth Ave. apartment. He still has his Indiana farms and a home in Rushville, Ind. Among his legal clients are great motion picture firms—and he has argued a civil liberties case for a Communist in the United States Supreme Court.

As with many other American families, the hearts of the Willkies are on the high seas. Their only son, Philip, a Navy ensign, is on patrol duty in the Caribbean.

18

Mary McGrory
(1918–   )

MARY MCGRORY is said to be the most-loved and respected journalist in Washington. Her grace and generosity are unbounded; her gutsy views make her one of the capital's most readable and controversial columnists; and her love for words makes her thrice-weekly syndicated column a literate joy. By virtually all accounts, she is an uncommon reporter, writer, and person. "Some reporters write with their hearts, some with their minds; Mary writes with both," said former *Washington Star-News* colleague Phil Gailey, now of the *New York Times*.

Whether she likes it or not, this petite woman from Boston who quotes Yeats and sings Irish ballads has become a legend among the press corps for her unselfishness and caring, though she would be the first to shrug off such accolades in a modest but beguiling way. In a city where many reporters revel in being media personalities and partygoers, McGrory just wants to be read. She saves her meanness for her prose and can be withering to those who don't meet her political or moral standards.

Many journalists who worked at the *Washington Star-News* where McGrory started her writing career, looked to her for advice and support. Mary Anne Dolan, editor of the *Los Angeles Examiner* and the first woman to run a major newspaper without owning it, recalled how McGrory read all her copy. "It made a difference to her that I did well," she said. "You can't imagine how it feels to have someone religiously read every word you write and discuss what is of value and what isn't." At one point, Dolan was conflicted about taking an editor's position at the *Star*. "Mary cautioned me, 'Remember, if you are going to be an editor your job is to bring your writers hot chocolate.' Mary knew that you have to serve writers, to reach out and be there for them."

Phil Gailey, who came to the *Star* in 1977 when the staff was filled with anxiety about its future, remembered how supportive McGrory was when the paper finally folded in 1981. "Mary was our rock," he said. "She spent so much time consoling and encouraging staffers who were distraught over their lack of job offers, so much time making phone calls to editor friends around the country to open up some jobs, so much time grieving with us over what was our shared loss, that she often had to stay around late into the night to write her column."

Her good friend Robert Kennedy once said, "Mary is so gentle—until she gets behind a typewriter." She lashed out at Kennedy in 1968 when he decided to challenge Eugene McCarthy for the Democratic nomination. "Kennedy thinks that American youth belongs to him, as the bequest of his brother," she wrote. "Seeing the romance flower between them [the college students who canvassed door to door in the New Hampshire primary] and McCarthy, he moved with the ruthlessness of a Victorian father whose daughter has fallen in love with a dustman."

References to Victorian life often nudge into her copy. Jane Austen, whom she rereads frequently, is one of her favorite authors. In 1982 when two congressmen were named as having engaged in sexual relations with teen-age pages, she wrote not about sex and drugs on Capitol Hill but about the characters of *Mansfield Park*, Fanny Price and Mary Crawford, and Austen's "celebration of virtue and right-mindedness." She concluded the July 11 column with: "I realize that she [Jane Austen] would censure me for devouring "Mansfield Park" in one gulp. She deplored unrestrained indulgence. But you can see that this week I am not in a position to judge undetailed excesses on Capitol Hill. How can I, at this time, pass judgment on addicts of any kind?" One fan letter noted: "I don't *always* agree with your opinions expressed in your column, but I surely agree with your words of praise for Jane Austen."

Passing judgment on political bullies is more Mary McGrory's style. In fact, she made the White House enemies list with two asterisks and a check mark during the Nixon administration and won a 1975 Pulitzer Prize for her etched-in-acid commentary on Watergate. Of the Watergate trial, she wrote: "The defendants came on like Chinese wrestlers bellowing and making hideous faces as if to frighten the prosecutors to death."

Of her work, McGrory said: "I have very few opinions, but powerful impressions. If you observe closely enough, you will write in truths, but not necessarily uncover truths." Any discussion of her columns elicits praise for her writing, her "poet's gift of analogy," as James Reston once said. Tom Winship, editor of the *Boston Globe*, added that she is "the undisputed best handler of the English language in the daily news business." All the fuss about her style sometimes amuses her, for she spent four years studying Latin and diagramming sentences at Boston's Girls Latin High School and after that, she said, "you learn how to put together a good sentence."

Mary McGrory is also one of those rare journalists who not only write but talk well. It was how cleverly she talked about things that impressed New-bold Noyes, the *Star's* national editor in the 1950s, who rescued her from the obscurity of book reviewing in 1954 to cover the Army-McCarthy hearings. Within days, everyone in Washington was talking about her impressions of the personalities and the proceedings. "No one paid any attention when I was writing book reviews," she said jokingly, "but after my coverage of the hearings people were calling and asking, 'Who is she? I'd like to adopt her.' And then others were complaining that I was a Communist."

She produced thirty-two stories on the hearings, with Noyes guiding and helping her. She recalled how, on the second day, she was stuck for a theme and sat down to talk through the day's events with him. He asked about Joe Welch, the elderly Boston attorney who was the Army's counsel. "I remembered then how I was impressed with how Joe Welch had this Dickensian silhouette," she said. "He was one of those people who carried his power with him." Noyes told her to write it that way. And she did:

In the floodlighted jungle of the hearing room Mr. Welch, who might have stepped out of the "Pickwick Papers," does not appear entirely in his element. His habitual expression is dubious. . . . A tall man, he has a long face and owlish eyes. He beams rather than smiles, and sometimes when he is listening to a witness he puts the tips of his fingers together and looks rapt, as one might who was listening to the fine strains from the Boston Symphony Orchestra. Mr. Welch proceeds at the measured pace of the minuet, with frequent, courtly bows. Senator McCarthy favors the tarantella, moving almost faster than the human eye can follow.

She saw McCarthy as an Irish bully, the kind she had "seen walk into rooms all my life. I didn't take him [McCarthy] seriously," she recalled. "It was the one thing nobody had done up until that time—laugh at him." Her trademark soon became the incisive thumbnail description: Roy Cohn looked like a "boy who has had a letter sent home from school about him, and has come back with his elders to get the thing straightened out"; Nelson Rockefeller campaigning "plunges into a crowd as into a warm bath"; Richard Nixon during his 1962 press conference after his defeat in the California gubernatorial election was "a kamikaze pilot who keeps apologizing for the attack."

After the McCarthy hearings McGrory moved to the national desk, an unheard-of jump without first going through the city desk. "Every reporter should have an editor like Newbold," she said. "He didn't wait for me just to write the lead, he waited until I had done the second paragraph, because he knew that was just as important." Noyes, now retired in Maine, is modest about his mentor role in molding McGrory: "Mary had the talent. I just gave her the opportunity." He remembers her as a "bleeder," a reporter who agonized over every word, sitting at her desk "chewing her pencil," moaning and groaning, and after a while producing a "marvelous piece of copy." She admits that even today she doesn't discard ideas quickly enough, but the 850 words go faster working on a video display terminal.

One of her habits is to try out ideas on colleagues. Noyes recalled that during lunch he would be "dazzled by the wittiness of her conversation," only to see what she had said almost verbatim in her next column. "Mary likes to quote herself," Noyes joked. Another co-worker said that after talking with her, his ideas turned up in the column. "It was flattering," he noted, "but only Mary could get away with that."

McGrory maintains that she has no special sources, that few high officials return her telephone calls, and that no one uses her column to leak news. "But they can't bar me from public events," she said, "and they are the most fun." Sometimes her Sunday columns will be essays on topics that interest her—gardening, mockingbirds, Jane Austen—but mostly she concentrates on domestic politics. A typical day will include a hearing, reading endless government handouts, documents, and all the papers, for she is a reporter who reads everything—even every word in her own paper. Unlike some columnists, who favor the armchair-sage approach, McGrory does her footwork to get what she wants.

It was Mary McGrory who mined the best human interest story out of the Three Mile Island nuclear reactor accident in 1979. Phil Gailey, who was also covering the story, remembers that she came to breakfast one morning with a crumpled newspaper picture showing the towers of the nuclear plant looming behind a house and a terrified mother fleeing, trying to protect her baby from radiation with a blanket. She showed the picture to her colleagues around the coffee-shop table. "This is the story I want to do," she said. "I have to find that mother." One reporter suggested she find another story since the mother had probably left town. McGrory, somewhat annoyed, replied, "This is the story!"

Gailey agreed to help her in the search, and together they showed the picture to merchants, residents, gas-station attendants, but with no luck. They drove around the roads within sight of Three Mile Island trying to find the house, and after hours of searching "the tableau finally popped into view," said Gailey. "Mary walked around the house, making notes on the flower

Mary McGrory

boxes in the windows, the children's toys in the yard, and anything else that was a reminder of the normal family life that had been disrupted. A neighbor said that the woman might have gone to an evacuation center, so we searched every one, looking for the face, showing the picture to civil defense workers. Then as a last effort, we called every person with the same last name in the telephone book, about a dozen names, and on the third call Mary found the woman staying with a relative seventy-five miles away, and got her interview over the phone."

Syndicated through Universal Press Syndicate, her thrice-weekly column in 1985 had 160 subscribers, with such major papers as the *Chicago Tribune*, *Boston Globe*, *San Francisco Examiner*, and *Los Angeles Examiner*. The number of subscribing papers has grown steadily over the years, but as she points out, "It's hard to be a liberal columnist in a conservative world."

Other journalists, often referred to as "McGrory's Bearers," are always on hand to help carry her typewriter and gear, including the likes of Harrison Salisbury of the *New York Times* and writer Murray Kempton. For those who betray or tarnish the integrity of her beloved profession, she has only harsh words. Of Janet Cooke, who lost a Pulitzer for faking a story, she said, raising her voice, a glint in her dark blue eyes, "I could slap her, and I'm not a violent person. What she and Daly [Michael Daly of the *New York Daily News* who faked a story from Belfast] did to journalism is unforgivable."

Her respect for honor and rectitude is most apparent when she speaks of her father, Edward Patrick McGrory, the eldest of eight children, who had to turn down a Dartmouth scholarship to help support his family as a postal clerk. "He was never bitter about this missed opportunity," she said proudly, and would spend his lunch hours reading at the South Boston library and browsing around second-hand bookstores. Her father died when she was twenty-one, and he more than her mother, Mary (Jacobs) McGrory, was her literary mentor. "He would quote Shakespeare, but would not be tiresome about it," McGrory said. "He was a gentle, delightful, humorous person, and was not as entertained as I was by the rogueries of Boston politicians."

McGrory was born in Boston on April 22, 1918. An older brother, John, now dead, was an English teacher, with "the gift of explanation, spontaneous, clear and logical," she said, a description that fits her as well. She has always been proud of her Irish roots, saying she inherited her love for flowers from her paternal grandfather, who was a gardener in Donnegal.

She went to the strict Girls Latin High School and then to Emmanuel, a Catholic girls' college in Boston, graduating in 1939 with a B.A. in English. Her first job was for the publisher Houghton Mifflin, cropping pictures for $16.50 a week. After three years she moved to the *Boston Herald*, working as a secretary and reviewing books in her spare time for that paper and the *New York Times*. John K. Hutchens, the book editor of the *Times*, took an interest in her, letting her know about a reviewer's job at the *Star*, which she applied for and got.

McGrory was twenty-nine when she arrived in Washington. For seven years she reviewed books, prompting Doris Fleeson, the *Daily News* columnist, to say once that McGrory was "curled up on a bookshelf" all those years just gathering strength to be a columnist. When McGrory started her column in 1960, Fleeson and Walter Lippmann reached out to help her, just as she later did for those coming after her. "The classier they are, the nicer they are to competition," McGrory noted. Fleeson saw to it that she was introduced to good sources, and Lippmann, she said, told her before she was syndicated, "Ignore it. Write what you want, and don't fret if a paper doesn't run it."

It was after she had moved to the national desk that she developed her "Mother McGrory" reputation. "Many of the younger reporters would take their cue from Mary, and if she disagreed about some management decision," said Noyes, "it could be a problem. She was in a position of leadership and was not always the easiest person to work with." During the mid-1970s, a time of office intrigue, with austerity measures and layoffs, "there wasn't a leaf that fell that I wasn't informed about or consulted on," McGrory said.

During the Vietnam War, in particular, there was tension between her and Noyes. The *Star* had a hawkish policy, and McGrory's one-note theme was that America should not be in Southeast Asia. "Mary was very upset that the paper wouldn't support her views," he said. "Sometimes she wouldn't even talk to me." The placement of her column also became an issue, for she saw herself as a news writer and "didn't want to be in the company of David Lawrence and Joe Alsop and all those she thought were stupid," said Noyes. "The amusing thing about her attitude was that even if all she did was comment, she still didn't want to be regarded as a commentator or columnist," he said, adding that, "sometimes we were uncomfortable with what she wrote, and it wouldn't have mattered if she had been on the editorial page."

At the *Washington Post*, where she went after the *Star* folded, she has her news position on page two twice a week and on page one of the Outlook section on Sundays. There is little office politics for her now, and she cherishes this serene life. "I just write my column, go home, cook a late dinner, read, and watch TV." She enjoys this solitude; in fact, she demands it. She still savors the classics and describes herself as "an illiterate" who never reads modern writers. Still, she's a *M*A*S*H* addict, refusing any phone calls while

it's on the tube, and a fan of silver screen gems such as Alfred Hitchcock's
Notorious. If she ever writes her book, she said, it will be about the demise
of the *Star*.

Surprisingly, it is her nonpolitical columns that often draw heavy mail.
The Jane Austen columns are always a hit, and an essay on a mockingbird
that landed on her kitchen windowsill brought out all the bird-lovers' stories.
It amuses her that such simple tales frequently excite more interest than her
insights into public policy. "You write about a mockingbird," she joked, "and
you knock 'em dead!"

After the Israeli invasion of Lebanon in 1982, she published an open letter to Prime Minister Menachem Begin telling him not to come to Washington, writing, "We are told you insist on coming because if you canceled,
people would think you had something to be ashamed of. In our opinion,
you do." The mail commentary on this stand ranged from, "Are you the
only courageous person who has access to the media?" to "From your last
name, it seems you may be Irish—I'm sure you are 100 per cent with them
in their struggle."

McGrory is indeed Irish. With a small but true mezzo voice, she sings
Irish songs for her friends and for the orphans at St. Ann's, her favorite charity. Singing and serving up food with gusto have made her a different kind
of hostess for her group, "The Lower McComb Street Choral Society," which
in addition to the regulars—a Salvation Army colonel, a retired federal worker,
other journalists, and good friends—often includes a politican or a judge.
All the guests must sing for their supper.

On these occasions, the hostess, with graying hair but a face that perjures
time, wears a long flowing dress and works between two kitchens (she has
incorporated two apartments into one) to fix and serve homemade lasagne
(she speaks Italian and makes frequent trips to Italy). Depending on the guests,
the songs will vary, but regulars remember Eugene McCarthy singing Irish
songs, Newbold Noyes singing again and again his fourth-grade school song,
longtime friend and aide Liz Acosta belting out "Lucky Charlie Lindbergh,"
and the hostess, among many favorites, doing "All I Want Is a Room Somewhere" from *My Fair Lady*.

Through the years, McGrory has forged a wide network of journalistic
friends who have moved on to other papers, and for thirty-five years she has
given her time to St. Ann's orphanage. Those who number themselves among
her friends have been expected to help with a car pool or a Santa role for
St. Ann's events. With such an extended family, she says she is never lonely,
but interviewers persist in asking why she never married, to which she often
quips, "I guess men think the best thing about me is my writing."

Close friends, however, speculate that her great admiration for and friendship with Adlai Stevenson and John Kennedy made it hard for any other man to measure up. The column she wrote following Kennedy's assassination is often cited for its moving prose. Noyes particularly remembered her "grace under fire" that November 23, 1963: "She had already written a personal tribute for the extra and wanted to do a piece for the next day's editorial page. I was waiting to take the copy out of the typewriter, and she was typing away, tears streaming down her face. For me, that situation always epitomized her skill as a reporter." In part, she wrote:

He brought gaiety, glamor, and grace to the American political scene in a measure never known before. That lightsome tread, that debonair touch, that shock of chestnut hair, that beguiling grin, that shattering understatement—these are what we shall remember. He walked like a prince and he talked like a scholar. . . . His public statements were always temperate, always measured. He derided his enemies—he teased his friends. He could be grave, but not for long. When the ugliness of yesterday has been forgotten, we shall remember him smiling.

And if she has her way, Mary McGrory will never stop writing the words she loves. Retire? Never, she says: "I am going to die in the newsroom—it's like oxygen to me."

Mary McGrory's perceptive eye and ear captured the mood of Watergate in a series of columns in 1974 that earned her a Pulitzer. One is reprinted here from *The Washington Star,* along with her spot-news coverage of Three Mile Island in 1979.

ENGLISH MAY SURVIVE

By MARY McGRORY

Washington Star-News, August 18, 1974

The English language, which underwent severe trials in the last five years, is recovering, revived, like much else, by the strong remedy of impeachment.

Thanks to the House Judiciary Committee, we have learned that words can say something, that they can lead instead of mislead, that they can reveal, not just conceal.

The Constitution, we find, not only prescribes government. It affords a kind of pageantry. Many Americans long for ceremony of the Old World, the changing of the guard, the trooping of the colors, the flash of the sabres of the Italian policemen, the swish of the cape of the gendarme. Well, we know now we don't need that. We have the Constitution instead, and because of six days when it paraded across the nation's television screens, it has become a living, breathing document again, cited by cabdrivers as they give their opinion of the great federal drama recently unfolded.

Enough has been said about the White House transcripts as the Thermopylae of language. That was a war in which words were almost wiped out. Through systematic abuse, they lost their meaning. "Protective reaction raid," one of the baser coinages, meant creating an alibi to bomb the enemy. When our former first citizen said, "I am not a crook," what he meant was "You can't prove it." When he said, "One year of Watergate is enough," he meant the fire was getting hot. When he said he was "Trying to get to the bottom of it," he meant he was trying to get out of it.

It may be a while before the country stops reading "down" for "up" and "white" for "black."

But a noble beginning was made in the House Judiciary Committee. Impeachment, like execution, wonderfully focuses the mind, and the men and women of that group tried with a care almost unknown hereabouts to match their feelings to the Constitution, and to say what they really thought and felt.

The language gradually came to life again during those six incredible days, when people sought to express anguish, dismay, resolution and anger.

The results were historic both for the country and declamation. The use of the simple declarative sentence was rediscovered.

Said James Mann of South Carolina: "The next time, there may be no watchman in the night."

Said Walter Flowers of Alabama: "To my friends I say I have pain enough for them and me."

Said Caldwell Butler of Virginia, in the single most fiery and liberating sentence spoken: "Watergate is our shame." He was the first Republican to slash the comforting myth that somebody else, of unknown party origin, was to blame.

The country has not heard language used like that in five and a half years.

And overlaying all was the language of the impeachment counts, sentences that marched like armies and tolled like bells.

"In his conduct of the office of President of the United States," each began portentously, "in violation of his constitutional oath faithfully to execute the office of President of the United States, and to the best of his ability to preserve, protect and defend the Constitution to take care that the laws be faithfully executed. . . ."

And each ended heavily, majestically: "Wherefore, Richard M. Nixon, by such conduct, warrants impeachment and trial and removal from office."

It was powerful stuff. And the country watched transfixed, as those phrases sounded through the ritual civilities: the Chairman addressing Barbara Jordan as "the gentle lady from Texas"; each speaker, no matter how wroth, on receiving recognition, saying politely, "Thank you, Mr. Chairman." The country has been famished for civility, it seems, along with truth.

Thanks partly to those men and women and their words, we now have a new President. On being sworn in, he promised "just a little straight talk among friends."

It is long overdue. The country will survive. So may the English language.

They Fled: 'She was Holding Baby, and Shaking All Over'

By MARY MCGRORY

Washington Star-News April 3, 1979

MIDDLETOWN, Pa.—Last Thursday morning, Catherine Mayberry stepped out of her small house on the Susquehanna River, under the shadows of the troubled towers of the Three Mile Island nuclear plant. She was carrying her year-old daughter, Kimberly. She had put a blanket over the baby's head—someone had told her "it might help."

An alert UPI photographer, one of the thousands of press people who have flocked here to record Pennsylvania's "silent spring," spied her, made a U-turn on Highway 441, and took her picture. For the thousands who saw Catherine Mayberry's strained face over her blanketed baby, the picture told it all—all that could be said about dread and futility when technology goes bad.

Catherine Mayberry is no longer in her house. She's not sure she will ever set foot in it again. Friday morning, after the second radiated belch from the monster—the one plant owners said was "controlled" and the Nuclear Regulatory Commission said was not—Catherine Mayberry packed up Kimberly and fled north to relatives in Sunbury, 70 miles away.

Her husband, Rick, a Buick salesman, has been staying at different family homes ever since, and went back to the house on Highway 441 only once, to get some papers for an insurance claim to the NRC for the expense and disruption of Cathy's flight.

"SHE'S SCARED to death," he said of his 22-year-old wife. "She woke me up at 4 on Friday morning because she heard a noise from the plant. I told her they were just working on the reactor, but she was holding the baby and shaking all over. I liked nuclear power before, because it was clean, but I'm afraid of it now."

Catherine Mayberry said on the telephone from Sunbury that she doesn't see how she could ever sleep in her own house again, "not knowing if we would wake up in the morning."

Kimberly is her main concern—"I wish people could see her face, she's beautiful. I want her to grow up healthy and I want to be around with her.

People say that only two-tenths of the population would be affected, but I don't want it to be her. If something happens to her 10 years from now, I would never be sure if this was to blame. Some of the people around got pamphlets telling them what to do if there was radiation, and what to take, but we didn't get any. We were totally unprepared for this."

In the door of Catherine Mayberry's house, there is a yellow evacuation notice. The primroses are blooming in the garden, watched over by an orange plastic owl. The doormat has two more owls and says, "Welcome to our nest."

TWO OF HER neighbors were still around on a rainy Monday, down the street from the fog-shrouded towers. David Barbaretta, a small, wiry furniture builder, had spent Sunday driving his wife and 7-year-old son to the safety of the mountains in Perry County. He had come home to find his house robbed of several guns and his television set. The NRC had turned down his insurance claim because, he was told, only preschool children had been required to evacuate, and his son was over-age.

Barbaretta has been thinking of selling his house, which is awash in daffodils, but has had no offers.

"Real estate has gone down," he said. "They can't guarantee it would never happen again. They don't know what they are doing up there. I hear they had robots in to close the vent. I just want to get out of here."

While he was talking, another neighbor who lives across the street came to collect her mail.

Louise Hardison was wearing a kerchief and a worn black coat, and she was mad. She raises goats, and "another had to be hauled away an hour ago." And since the worst nuclear accident in history had occurred, three newborn baby lambs who seemed perfectly healthy, "just curled up and died.

"I CAN'T BE evacuated. I can't leave those animals. I've got 17 pregnant goats. They'll have to lasso me."

Hardison has owned her property since 1957, and is a member of the small local nuclear protest group, "The Three Mile Alert."

"What can we do? Now the bubble is going down, people will say it's all over, and they'll forget it ever happened."

Catherine Mayberry is returning to her parents' home in Harrisburg tomorrow. It's 10 miles away from the plant and she thinks it will be safe. But she can't imagine living so close to the reactor again. She would like to see the plant shut down, but she doesn't think that will ever happen.

"If someone came to me with a petition, I'd gladly sign it," she said. "But what can one person or any group of persons do to stop anything that big. I thought about it, I could see the towers from my window, and I wondered what would happen if a plane from the airport—it's very near—crashed into one of them.

"I'm totally against nuclear power," she said. "I'm for coal or solar now. I would gladly turn out the lights. I'd go back to candles rather than go through another week like this. I just couldn't do it."

19

Marguerite Higgins
(1920–1966)

IN TIME, the life of Maggie Higgins, the glamorous and fearless war correspondent of the *New York Herald Tribune*, will be turned into a television movie, with the script writers further exaggerating the myth of the intrepid woman journalist, as they did for Nellie Bly in a 1982 production. A pert actress with golden curls tucked into a fatigue cap, sapphire-blue eyes, a wide, shining smile and a little girl voice will be cast to fit Higgins' physical characteristics. There will be scenes of Maggie and Keyes Beech of the *Chicago Daily News* bouncing over Korean backroads in their Jeep, bullets skimming over their heads; there will be innuendos about Maggie's romantic liaisons and how she charmed the generals and the G.I.'s and a dramatic depiction of Maggie landing with the fifth wave of Marines at Inchon. In two hours the reporter who inspired the women journalists of the 1950s to go to war will grow up beautiful and brave, a heroine in the newsroom and on the battlefield.

Higgins' career as a reporter began in earnest when she talked her way into Columbia's Graduate School of Journalism five days before classes began and ended with her death at forty-five from a tropical disease contracted during a tour to Vietnam, India, and Pakistan. Her ambition to be the best has been portrayed as ruthless; her femininity as coy and flirtatious, giving her an advantage over male colleagues; her sexual appetites as greedy and indiscreet.

The truth about Maggie Higgins, however, is that today she would not be an oddity, for in the climate of the 1980s her driven personality would be admired, her success would be considered both hard-earned and deserved, her life as a journalist, wife, and mother envied and emulated. She wanted *everything* and set out to get it. The Higgins who told a friend that she didn't plan to marry "until she found a man who's as exciting as war" was hardly the "war lover" that she would later be called, but a romantic with perhaps a naive sense of what constituted the adventurous life. When Lieutenant General Walton H. Walker ordered all women out of Korea's war zone except nurses, announcing "This is just not the type of war where women ought to be running around the front lines," she went to General Douglas MacArthur and said: "I am in Korea as a reporter, not as a woman." Higgins may have whined on occasion to get her way, but her commitment to being a journalist was never articulated so powerfully as in her confrontation with MacArthur, who overturned the order.

It was her insistence on taking as many or more risks covering Korea than the bravest of the 130 male reporters that brought her the most criticism. The men were forced to do more dangerous frontline stories just to show that they could keep up with her. Just as she beat the men of her class at the journalism school to get the campus correspondent's job at the *Herald Tribune*, she continued to beat them for front-page play in the final days of World War II and in Korea.

Russell Hill, her boss when she was first assigned overseas to the *Trib*'s Paris bureau, said in *Witness to War* (1983) that Higgins was the victim of a double standard. "Maggie was controversial," he said, "largely because her newspaper rivals felt she used unfair methods to achieve her ends. Maggie's own view was that since war correspondents were already discriminated against, she was merely righting the balance . . . her success was due largely to her courage. She would take great personal risks in order to get a story. . . . She had a talent for getting difficult stories and getting them right."

She once boasted to her Columbia classmates that she was going to be better known than Dorothy Thompson, who in 1941 was at the height of her fame. In many ways, she succeeded. At twenty-five, younger by six years than Dorothy Thompson and Sigrid Schultz, both of whom headed Berlin bureaus, she was named Berlin bureau chief for the *Trib*. By the age of thirty-six she had received more than fifty journalism awards, including the 1951 Pulitzer Prize for foreign correspondence (shared with five of her colleagues), the first woman so honored.

She was "a hell of a reporter, but a lousy writer," said Keyes Beech, with whom she shared a jeep when they covered the Korean conflict. This oft-repeated criticism was, as the record shows, something that Higgins always accepted. After her coup of getting into Columbia when all the places for women students were filled, she was asked to write a few paragraphs on her professional preferences. She wrote:

> People stopped to stare that day in Times Square when I accosted the man carrying the "Tony's Restaurant" sandwich sign. They stared even more while we stood there in the middle of the noon-time crowds as I interviewed him. But I didn't mind. It was fun. I was finding out something. It certainly was a test of my capacity to get facts from a total stranger. It was getting the news.
> And there you have it. That's my preference. It always has been. . . . I don't think I'm being romantic about it. I honestly think I do better in getting the information than in writing it.

Her most dramatic wartime writing never attempted stylistic turns, but took the "I was there" approach, which readers loved and editors noted with appropriate headlines. As one dispatch went:

> A reinforced American patrol, accompanied by this correspondent, this afternoon barrelled eight miles deep through enemy territory. . . . Snipers picked at the road, but the jeep flew faster than the bullets which nicked just in back of our right rear tire.

Beech noted in his memoirs that although not in direct competition, he and Higgins often fought. "Usually, these disagreements developed over what time we should return to the rear to file our dispatches. Higgins, who worked for a morning paper, usually wanted to stay until the last Communist was killed. I worked for an afternoon paper and had an earlier deadline."

Homer Bigart, sent by the *Herald Tribune* to help her cover Korea, tried to get her sent back to Tokyo or, it has been said, fired. The Korean front was too small an area for two reporters and Bigart, as the senior person, wanted it all to himself. Bigart could file a story relating that "this correspondent was one of three reporters who saw the action, and the only newsman to get out alive." But about Higgins' personal journalism he grumbled, "With her it was always me and the Marines did this today. She was out for herself."

The point, of course, was that if she wasn't with the Marines, she would have been out of harm's way in Tokyo, covering MacArthur's headquarters and rewriting releases. That was never her style. "First-rate war coverage," she wrote in her autobiography, *News Is A Singular Thing* (1955), "requires only two qualities that are not normally demanded of any first-rate reporter on a big story. They are a capacity for unusual physical endurance and the willingness to take unusual personal risk."

Maggie Higgins felt that as a reporter she was only as good as her last story; her life was a challenge to prove to herself and to others that she was the best. Her father, an Irish-American World War I flier who had captivated her childhood imagination with war stories, told a reporter in the 1950s:

"There was only one place for Marguerite and that was the top, regardless of what she was doing—learning to swim, to play the violin or whatever she went into."

She was the only child of Lawrence Daniel Higgins (O'Higgins was the ancestral name; the "O" was dropped when his parents emigrated to California) and Marguerite (de Godard) Higgins, a half-noble, half-peasant Frenchwoman from Lyon, who met in a Paris bomb shelter during World War I when Larry Higgins was serving with the Lafayette Escadrille. After the armistice the married couple went to Hong Kong, where Marguerite was born on September 3, 1920. Her father became an agent for the Pacific Mail Steamship company, and the family lived for some years in Mâcon in the south of France, moving to Oakland, California, in 1927. Larry Higgins took a job as a stockbroker, and Maggie was sent to the Anna Head School, an exclusive private girls' school in Berkeley. She was indulged to the limit of the family's often precarious finances and encouraged to achieve, to think of herself as special. A scholarship student, she maintained an "A" average, practiced piano and violin five hours daily, won the athlete's cup, and was yearbook editor. She went on to the University of California at Berkeley on scholarship, working summers, vacations, and part-time while in school to pay expenses.

Her freshman year she signed up as a reporter for the *Daily Californian*, receiving her first byline for an interview with Somerset Maugham. She met Lincoln Steffens, the muckraking journalist, advocated "free love" to her sorority sisters, and charmed Stanley Moore, a leftist philosophy graduate student, whom she later married in 1942, shortly after she completed graduate school. She expanded her journalism experience with a job on the *Tahoe* (California) *Tatler* the summer of her junior year, and the following summer went to the *Vallejo* (California) *Times Herald* where she took classified ads over the phone and hung around the newsroom at night hoping for an assignment. "She was as eager as a sophomore halfback," managing editor Will Stevens said years later.

She saved enough money for an airline ticket to New York, but failing to get a newspaper job, decided at the eleventh hour to go to Columbia. She convinced the deans to accept her, had references and transcripts telegraphed to the school, and joined the class of 1942, which included Flora Lewis, foreign affairs columnist for the *New York Times*, and Elie Abel, formerly NBC bureau chief in London and Dean of Columbia's Journalism School and now Chandler professor of communications at Stanford University. Although L. L. Engelking, the *Trib*'s city editor, had refused to hire her when she had applied for a job earlier, he now consented to give her the open position of campus correspondent.

Marguerite Higgins

Determined to have a full-time job after graduation, she impressed editors by seeing Madame Chiang Kai-shek, a patient at Columbia's Presbyterian Medical Center, who had refused to talk to the press. Higgins went to the hospital, waited outside Madame Chiang's hospital room, and, when a nurse entered, picked up a medicine tray and followed her in. After graduating fourth in her class, just behind Elie Abel, she went to work at the *Trib's* 41st Street newsroom. Challenged by the city editor to interview James Caesar Petrillo, head of the musicians' union, she knocked on his hotel door and was admitted because, he said, "she looked like my daughter."

During the 1940s Higgins lived in a cramped apartment on Horatio Street in Greenwich Village. For the first time she had some extra money saved from her $25-a-week salary and decided to take Spanish and Russian lessons, adding more languages to her already fluent French and basic Chinese. Her new husband, Stanley Moore, was in the service, but Higgins was not lonely, attracting, with her often untidy but innocent ingenue appearance, many admirers from the cityroom.

She had good assignments as a cub reporter—fires, a Connecticut circus disaster, celebrity interviews—but she wanted to get to Europe before the war ended. After only two years' experience on the paper, it was a bold move to ask Helen Rogers Reid, the editor's mother, for an overseas posting. Impressed with Higgins' determination as she had been earlier with Dorothy Thompson's, Mrs. Reid approved, and in August 1944 Higgins sailed on the Queen Mary. She worked first in the paper's London bureau and then, after the liberation, in Paris, where she lived at the Hotel Scribe, meeting other correspondents, including Ernest Hemingway. She filed up to 3,000 words daily on the political situation, food shortages, and health problems, in addition to writing stories on the fashion industry for *Mademoiselle*.

By this time she and Stanley Moore had decided to end their brief marriage, and she met George Reid Millar, a British journalist for the *London Daily Express* whom she singled out in her autobiography as the major love of her life. In many ways, Millar resembled Moore: He was from a wealthy family, well-educated, with a charismatic personality, but he had a sense of adventure which had been missing in the inner-directed, scholarly Moore. "With George I had discovered love," she wrote, "and the kind of need for another of which I had not imagined I was capable." They traveled together, to interview composer Franz Lehar, enjoying a romantic idyl, with picnics in forests and nude swims in lakes. Soon, however, Millar wanted to return to England and tend to his broken marriage, and when Higgins eventually followed him to London he had remarried, leaving her depressed and determined to concentrate on work.

She received her first prize from the New York Newspaper Women's Club for her story on—and participation in—the May 1945 liberation of Dachau. She and Peter Furst of *Stars and Stripes* beat the Allied forces to Augsburg, collecting surrendered German weapons in their jeep as they rode to the concentration camp. Higgins spoke to the guards in German, and twenty-two of them surrendered; she then announced to the 30,000 prisoners in French, German, and English that they were free.

At that time she was working out of the Berlin bureau, assisting Russell Hill. Following his transfer, she took his place, winning out again over male competition. Working with only a secretary, she was frantic about keeping up with Drew Middleton of the *New York Times*, who had a staff of nine. If she saw a *Times* man leave the Press Club, she was right behind him to check if he had a better story to file. During her assignment in Germany she covered the Nuremberg war trials and the Berlin blockade, traveled to Czechoslovakia to interview foreign minister Jan Masaryk, and drove alone into Poland to write about police terrorism during the first postwar elections. In the process she formed strong anti-Communist opinions, which she injected in her articles throughout her career. When the Chinese intervened in Korea she hawkishly advocated use of the atom bomb if they didn't pull back.

In 1948 the Berlin airlift and the staggering logistics involved in getting food and medical supplies to more than two million people were under the direction of Major General William Hall, director of Army intelligence. For the eleven months of the blockade, Hall was a major source for all journalists. As it happened, Hall, who had a wife and four children in the United States, and Maggie fell in love, but it would be four years before they married, following his divorce in Reno.

After the blockade ended, the news focus in Germany changed to West German Chancellor Konrad Adenauer's plans to rebuild the country. The *Trib* assigned Don Cook to cover Bonn and Frankfurt, with Higgins remaining in Berlin. That decision was not to her liking and subsequently, in 1950, she was assigned to head the Tokyo bureau—initially an even greater disappointment. She arrived in Asia, however, a few days before North Korean troops crossed into South Korea to begin their drive to Seoul on June 25, 1950. Teaming up with Keyes Beech, she flew to Seoul from Tokyo under fighter escort to cover the fall of the city and the evacuation of American personnel. The following is part of the story she filed:

Sixty United States Army officers and four newspaper correspondents [the others were Burton Crane of the *New York Times* and Frank Gibney of *Time*] escaped this morning by makeshift ferry across the Han River southward from Seoul after the South Korean Defense Ministry suddenly blew up all bridges, trapping the Americans for hours in the isolated capital . . . The dynamiting of one bridge took place while South Korean troops were crowded on the span, as were personnel of the American military mission . . . An entire truckload was blown straight into the air. A bright red sheet of flame was seen by this correspondent as I was about to cross the bridge. The structure was ripped by the explosion and two other correspondents [Crane and Gibney] were injured.

A month after this story, when General Walker ordered her out of Korea, the *Trib* supported her editorially with a statement from editor Whitelaw Reid that went far in advancing the rights of women foreign correspondents. The editorial concluded: "Newspaper women today are willing to assume the risk and in our opinion should not be discriminated against. We hope she [Higgins] will be allowed to continue her work." General MacArthur's telegram to the *Trib* read: "Ban on women correspondents in Korea has been lifted. Marguerite Higgins is held in highest professional esteem by everyone."

After covering the Panmunjom truce talks and publishing *War in Korea* (1951), Higgins was assigned to do a series of interviews with world leaders including Tito of Yugoslavia, Franco of Spain, Nehru of India, the Shah of Iran, and the King of Siam, all of whom were curious to meet the renowned Maggie Higgins. In 1953 during her first pregnancy (her daughter, born two months premature, died after five days) she continued to travel, going to Vietnam to interview President Ngo Dinh Diem, whom she supported. She made a 13,500-mile trip to the Soviet Union, the first American correspondent allowed into the country after Stalin's death, and wrote about her experiences in her third book, *Red Plush and Black Bread*, (1955).

With the publication of that book, she settled in Washington with her new husband, Bill Hall. She covered the State Department as a weekly columnist and diplomatic correspondent and subsequently had, within a year of each other, a son and a daughter. She continued to deliver exclusives, and in 1959 when eight months pregnant with her third child, accompanied Vice President Richard M. Nixon to the Soviet Union to record his historic confrontation with Premier Nikita Khrushchev.

In 1963 she made her seventh trip to Vietnam, convinced more than ever of America's error of involvement. At the same time she was in conflict with *Trib* editors over her Washington column. Their disagreements ultimately led to her resignation after twenty-two years with the paper. She became a twice-weekly political columnist in Washington for *Newsday*, the Long Island daily, which was just beginning a syndication service and wanted a big name. After three years, she was carried in fifty papers. Asked to do a book on Vietnam, she took the opportunity to promote her beliefs. In *Our Vietnam Nightmare* (1965), she blamed the United States "for the arrogance of seeking to impose our own values on a country that resents our demands because it does not understand them," writing that President Diem's overthrow and murder resulted from American policy interests.

On her tenth visit to Vietnam, a month-long tour in late 1965 that also took her to India and Pakistan, she contracted leishmaniasis, a rare tropical disease transmitted by the bite of a sandfly. Hospitalized in Washington on November 3, 1965, she continued to write her column until her death there at age forty-five on January 3, 1966.

Obituaries at the time noted her achievements, her feuds, her attractiveness. And twelve years after her death, Jim O'Donnell dedicated his book *The Bunker*, a chronicle of the last days of Hitler, to Marguerite Higgins.[1] "For all her shenanigans she was a good and loyal friend, the sort of person who went through life doing good deeds concealed," he said in *Witness To War*. "Maggie combined the realism of a French peasant with the idealism of an Irish drunk. There was a whimsical irony about her that I think many people missed." Others missed an even more important truth: She was a great reporter, way ahead of her time.

Marguerite Higgins' report on the landing at Inchon can be found in *A Treasury of Great Reporting*. The following story on the liberation at Dachau was the one that first brought her recognition.

[1] Two *romans à clef* loosely based on Marguerite Higgins' career were published. Toni Howard, wife of Jim O'Donnell, wrote *Shriek With Pleasure* (1950) and Edwin Lanham, a *Trib* rewrite man, wrote *The Iron Maiden* (1954).

33,000 DACHAU CAPTIVES
FREED BY 7TH ARMY
110,000 Are Liberated at Moosburg;
Nazi Doctor Admits Killing 21,000

By MARGUERITE HIGGINS

New York Herald Tribune, May 1, 1945

DACHAU, Germany, April 29 (delayed)—Troops of the United States 7th Army liberated 33,000 prisoners this afternoon at this first and largest of the Nazi concentration camps. Some of the prisoners had endured for eleven years the horrors of notorious Dachau.

The liberation was a frenzied scene. Inmates of the camp hugged and embraced the American troops, kissed the ground before them and carried them shoulder high around the place.

[At Moosburg, north of Munich, the United States 14th Armored Division liberated 110,000 Allied prisoners of war, including 11,000 Americans, from Stalag 7A.

[From United States 12th Army Group headquarters came the story of a captured Nazi doctor, Gustav Wilhelm Schuebbe, who said that the Nazi annihilation institute at Kiev, Russia, killed from 110,000 to 140,000 persons "unworthy to live" during the nine months he worked there. He himself, he said, murdered about 21,000 persons.]

The Dachau camp, in which at least a thousand prisoners were killed last night before the S.S. (Elite Guard) men in charge fled, is a grimmer and larger edition of the similarly notorious Buchenwald camp near Weimar.

This correspondent and Peter Furst, of the army newspaper "Stars and Stripes," were the first two Americans to enter the inclosure at Dachau, where persons possessing some of the best brains in Europe were held during what might have been the most fruitful years of their lives.

While a United States 45th Infantry Division patrol was still fighting a way down through S.S. barracks to the north, our jeep and two others from the 42d Infantry drove into the camp inclosure through the southern entrance. As men of the patrol with us busied themselves accepting an S.S. man's surrender, we impressed a soldier into service and drove with him to the prisoners' barracks. There he opened the gate after pushing the body of a prisoner shot last night while attempting to get out to meet the Americans.

There was not a soul in the yard when the gate was opened. As we learned later, the prisoners themselves had taken over control of their inclosure the night before, refusing to obey any further orders from the German guards, who had retreated to the outside. The prisoners maintained strict discipline among themselves, remaining close to their barracks so as not to give the S.S. men an excuse for mass murder.

But the minute the two of us entered a jangled barrage of "Are you Americans?" in about sixteen languages came from the barracks 200 yards from the gate. An affirmative nod caused pandemonium.

Tattered, emaciated men, weeping, yelling and shouting "Long live America!" swept toward the gate in a mob. Those who could not walk limped or crawled. In the confusion, they were so hysterically happy that they took the S.S. man for an American. During a wild five minutes he was patted on the back, paraded on shoulders and embraced enthusiastically by prisoners. The arrival of the American soldier soon straightened out the situation.

Prisoners Charge Tower

I happened to be the first through the gate, and the first person to rush up to me turned out to be a Polish Catholic priest, a deputy of August Cardinal Hlond, Primate of Poland, who was not a little startled to discover that the helmeted, uniformed, begoggled individual he had so heartily embraced was not a man.

In the excitement, which was not the least dampened by the German artillery and the sounds of battle in the northern part of the camp, some of the prisoners died trying to pass through electrically charged barbed wire. Some who got out after the wires were decharged joined in the battle, when some ill-advised S.S. men holding out in a tower fired upon them.

The prisoners charged the tower and threw all six S.S. men out the window.

After an hour and a half of cheering, the crowd, which would virtually mob each soldier that dared to venture into the excited, milling group, was calmed down enough to make possible a tour of the camp. The only American prisoner, a flyer, with the rank of major, took some of the soldiers through.

Stalin's Son Taken Away

According to the prisoners, the most famous individuals who had been at the camp had been removed by S.S. men to Innsbrueck. Among them were

Leon Blum, former French Premier, and his wife; the Rev. Martin Nie-moeller, German church leader; Kurt Schuschnigg, Chancellor of Austria at the time of the anschluss (he was said to have been alive a few days ago); Gabriel Piquet, Bishop of St. Etienne; Prince Leopold of Prussia; Baron Fritz Cirini, aide of Prince Leopold; Richard Schmitz, former Mayor of Vienna, and Marshal Stalin's son, Jacob.

The barracks at Dachau, like those at Buchenwald, had the stench of death and sickness. But at Dachau there were six barracks like the infamous No. 61 at Buchenwald, where the starving and dying lay virtually on top of each other in quarters where 1,200 men occupied a space intended for 200. The dead—300 died of sickness yesterday—lay on concrete walks outside the quarters and others were being carried out as the reporters went through.

The mark of starvation was on all the emaciated corpses. Many of the living were so frail it seemed impossible they could still be holding on to life.

1,200 Bodies Piled Up

The crematorium and torture chambers lay outside the prisoner inclo-sures. Situated in a wood close by, a new building had been built by pris-oners under Nazi guards. Inside, in the two rooms used as torture chambers, an estimated 1,200 bodies were piled.

In the crematorium itself were hooks on which the S.S. men hung their victims when they wished to flog them or to use any of the other torture instruments. Symbolic of the S.S. was a mural the S.S. men themselves had painted on the wall. It showed a headless man in uniform with the S.S. insigne on the collar. The man was astride a huge inflated pig, into which he was digging his spurs.

The prisoners also showed reporters the ground where men knelt and were shot in the back of the neck. On this very spot a week ago a French general, a resistance leader under General Charles de Gaulle, had been killed.

Just beyond the crematorium was a ditch containing some 2,000 more bodies, which had been hastily tossed there in the last few days by the S.S. men who were so busy preparing their escape they did not have time to burn the bodies.

Below the camp were cattle cars in which prisoners from Buchenwald had been transported to Dachau. Hundreds of dead were still in the cars due to the fact that prisoners in the camp had rejected S.S. orders to remove them. It was mainly the men from these cattle cars that the S.S. leaders had shot before making their escape. Among those who had been left for dead in the cattle cars was one man still alive who managed to lift himself from the heap of corpses on which he lay.

20

Ada Louise Huxtable
(1921–   )

As a young girl growing up in New York City on Central Park West and 89th Street, Ada Louise Landman would rollerskate across the park to the Metropolitan Museum of Art at 81st Street where she spent many solitary hours. The museum was her mentor. "If I had not had free access as a child to this museum [which now solicits a fee]," she said, "I would not have developed my interests in art and architecture." At the museum and later through studies her interest in architecture, which Frank Lloyd Wright called "the mother of the arts," grew into love. And by the time she went to the *New York Times* in 1963 as its first full-time architecture critic and the first on any daily newspaper, she had developed a personal vision of what she has termed "the inescapable art." The merits of a building's interior and exterior were important to appraise, but Huxtable also cared deeply about how a certain building affected the people who used it or lived near it, a perception that made her, for a decade, the most powerful of the *Times'* roster of critics.

She changed the way readers felt about cities and influenced a generation of city planners and architects. She continues to do so today even though she left the *Times* in 1981 to pursue her own research and writing. Her cogent—and often controversial—views performed a public service by making readers aware of the forces—private and governmental—that can affect them where they live and work. Often her views were at odds with the *Times'* vested interests, as she attacked unfair zoning regulations and called for historical preservation.

For eighteen years as a critic and an editorial writer she also influenced other papers to pay more attention to architecture. She made the job respectable by putting a journalistic imprimatur on the position of critic in a field that had hitherto been regarded as too esoteric for newspapers.[1] For her readers, many of whom became fans and followers, she took academic language and made it accessible, translating forms and feelings into a witty prose style peppered with idioms, metaphors, and not a few clichés.

Once read, her pithy descriptions stick in the memory. The Hirshhorn Museum in Washington will always be the "biggest marble doughnut in the world." Her stylistic devices enticed casual readers and teased them into a critical experience. Consider the opening of a March 13, 1966, column on New York's CBS building:

> The first observation that one must make about the new CBS headquarters that rises somberly from its sunken plaza at Sixth Avenue and 52nd Street is that it is a building. It is not, like so much of today's large-scale construction, a handy commercial package, a shiny wraparound envelope, a packing case, a box of cards, a trick with mirrors.
> It does not look like a cigar lighter, a vending machine, a nutmeg grater. It is a building in the true, classic sense: a complete design in which technology, function and esthetics are conceived and executed integrally for its purpose. As its architect, Eero Saarinen, wanted, this is a building to be looked at above the bottom fifty feet, to be comprehended as a whole.

Urban design, as she wrote in a July 6, 1969, column, is "the not so simple process of considering the city's patterns of growth, building and development on its people, neighborhoods, circulation, and living and working conditions, and, if you will pardon the expression, beauty and pleasures." To better her beloved New York she attacked the venality of developers, aided in the establishment of New York City's Landmarks Preservation Commission in 1965, and helped to save any number of threatened buildings, including the New York Customs House and the St. Louis Post Office.

Ada Louise Huxtable is universally described as a feminine, gracious lady, a critic of integrity with strong opinions and values, a writer and thinker who is respected for not being seduced by the architectural fancies of the time. This petite (five foot two) woman with soft brown eyes and a cultured voice

[1]Giorgio Vasari, a sixteenth-century Italian architect, is considered to have been the first architecture critic. The best known of the early American critics was Montgomery Schuyler, a New York newspaperman who free-lanced for *Architectural Record* between the end of the Civil War and 1914. The *Record* was written primarily for the general reader interested in learning about architecture. After Schuyler's death the magazine targeted its material at professional architects, a policy that has continued.

can be surprisingly feisty as well as determined and precise. Though passionate and sometimes even obsessive about her field, she is always humane. She has stood steadfastly against "blind mutilation" in the name of urban renewal, saying, "Our heritage is too precious to see it go down the drain without a struggle."

"I am terribly disturbed when I see places being ravaged and turned into non-people places," she once told an interviewer, "when I see the profit motive that overbuilds a city like New York. I'm just being polite—*greed* is the word I really use. I think we are entitled to wonderful cities and wonderful places to live and work."

Defining the role of responsible criticism in architecture, the least ephemeral of the arts, has strained her relationships with some architects, particularly Philip Johnson, for whom she once worked at the Museum of Modern Art. He was so "hurt" by her objections to his design of the AT&T building that he refused to comment on Huxtable's journalistic legacy. To the same question, a leading New York architect, Robert Stern, replied, "While I believe the critics should have their say about architects, I am not so sure about things the other way around."

Other architecture critics, who may not always agree with her appraisals, are, however, united in crediting her with creating the post of architecture critic in daily journalism. Her work was recognized in 1970 when she was awarded the first Pulitzer Prize for distinguished criticism, and over the years she has received numerous other prizes and more than twenty-five honorary degrees. Jane Holtz Kay of the *Christian Science Monitor* said, "She is still the major person in architecture criticism; there is no number two. She also made it possible for women to enter the field." Carter Wiseman of *New York* magazine praised her "vigorous pursuit of excellence which has always been a mark against which to judge yourself." Paul Gapp of the *Chicago Tribune* stated that she "has had a profound effect in paving the way for criticism that treats architecture not only as an art but as a business." And Bob Campbell of the *Boston Globe* added that her criticism proved that writing about architecture could change events and the world. "The preservation movement owes a great deal to her," he said.

When the *Times* cajoled a somewhat reluctant forty-two-year-old Ada Louise Huxtable into working at 43rd Street, the paper's editors realized they were selecting an expert. Professor Adolf K. Placzek, Avery librarian at Columbia University's School of Architecture, who knew her as a researcher in the 1950s, observed, "Ada Louise did not spring on the journalism scene unprepared, for she had remarkable insight and knowledge as an art and architecture historian," a fact confirmed by her Fulbright Fellowship to study

Italian architecture and design in 1950 and her Guggenheim Fellowship to study American architecture in 1958.

She had spent four years (1946 to 1950) as assistant curator for architecture and design at the Museum of Modern Art, had been a contributing editor for *Progressive Architecture* and *Art in America,* and had started another book, *Classic New York* (1964). In the early 1960s her occasional by-line had started appearing in the *Times'* Sunday magazine, after articles in professional journals attracted attention, "more for the writing than the content," she frankly admitted.

During this time Aline Bernstein, a friend and assistant *Times* art critic who did occasional pieces on architecture, married the architect, Eero Saarinen, and left the paper. She recommended Huxtable to E. Clifton Daniel, then assistant managing editor. When Daniel offered Huxtable the position, she turned it down. Recalling why, she said, "Most people are bright enough to calculate the angles, about where such a job would lead them, but I was just interested in my own work, and was afraid how the job would change my life." Daniel told her that the paper's editors were convinced that they needed a full-time critic and if she wouldn't take the post they would find someone else. She changed her mind.

At the *Times,* the label "an appraisal" was first devised to run with her columns when the paper wanted to make clear that she was not writing a critical column, but an evaluation presenting both sides. "A critical column was my own voice and it was not the same thing as an editorial, which is the newspaper's voice—and I have done them all," she said, referring to her time on the editorial board from 1973 to 1981 when she wrote only a Sunday article on architecture.

Since she left the *Times* in 1981 after receiving a MacArthur Foundation "genius grant," a tax-free stipend of $300,000 over five years, she has, in her own words, "her life back, the time to be inner-directed, to be able to think again." She has written long articles for *New Criterion* and the *New York Review of Books,* a book *The Tall Building Artistically Reconsidered: The Search for a Skyscraper Style* (1985), and a third anthology of *Times* columns, *Architecture Anyone?* (1985), which follows two earlier collections, *Will They Ever Finish Bruckner Boulevard?* (1970) and *Kicked a Building Lately?* (1976).

When I interviewed her in 1983, new architecture books were separated into piles behind a sofa in the five-room penthouse apartment on Park Avenue where she lives with her husband of forty-three years, L. Garth Huxtable, a retired industrial designer. She pointed to them and with a semi-sigh of relief said, "It's so wonderful that I now have time to read. What has

Ada Louise Huxtable

interested me is learning. I never particularly wanted to be a journalist. I was interested in researching what was of interest to me. There's nothing less valid than recycling in terms of a living art. I felt that I was doing a lot of recycling [at the *Times*] because I had a tremendous amount of knowledge and I could reach in and pull out what I needed—it was inevitable."

For lay readers, Ada Louise Huxtable has kept watch on what she calls "the four urban horsemen: expediency, obstructionism, stupidity and greed." The desire to teach is prominent in her writings, although space limitations sometimes have prevented full explanations of every proper name, date, or architectural term. In the introduction to *Bruckner Boulevard*, she noted: "The function of this broad kind of architectural criticism is educational; it must in many ways fill the gap that our schools have left so conspicuously vacant—the yawning chasm between the educated man's perception and understanding of the man-made world around him."

Five years later, she concluded in the introduction to *Kicked a Building Lately?*: "I measure success by the street-corner. My obsessions are now shared and my co-conspirators are everywhere. Assuming survival, the battle for the future is well-joined. I'll still be kicking buildings for a while."

Some of her more memorable prose kicks have been for the Pan Am building, a monumental addition to the New York skyline that she termed "a colossal collection of minimums . . . gigantically second rate" and for the John F. Kennedy Center for the Performing Arts in Washington, D.C., a white marble building with red carpets and crystal chandeliers that she described as a "superbunker" of which Nazi architect Albert Speer would have approved. One of her favorite buildings is the Seagram building in New York. Although she found Lincoln Center "dull and hardly dramatic," she praised the complex's sense of community, with outdoor space for restaurants, and a fountain-dominated plaza.

Often it has been the debate over Modernism and what has come after, the so-called Post-Modernist style, that has fueled Huxtable's skirmishes with the architectural elite. After putting down the Kennedy Center as a "banal box," she wrote to its architect, her friend Edward Durell Stone, saying that her critical remarks "hurt me more than you." It also hurt her to pan the much-debated AT&T building, notable for its Chippendale top and Renaissance-inspired base, which was designed by her former colleague Philip Johnson and John Burgee.

Those who have felt the sting of Huxtable's prose don't always sulk in silence. Vincent Scully, an art history professor at Yale, was so enraged by her review of his 1972 book, *American Architecture and Urbanism*, that he wrote a letter to the *Times*, stating: "It has never been possible to value Mrs. Huxtable's critical acumen or command of history. Its most positive quality has seemed to be a kind of hectic candor, but that, too, must be called into question now."

To be sure, Huxtable does tend to prefer the Modernist school, as represented by Louis Sullivan, Le Corbusier, Walter Gropius, and Mies van der Rohe, whose dictum "less is more" is embodied in the Seagram building he designed with Philip Johnson. Modernist architects strive for a purity of line, a sleekness, often through the use of glass and metal, that is both economical and functional. Some of the leading Modernists, however, have now begun to come up with designs that use fanciful blends of derivative classical ornamentation. Johnson, whose AT&T building is a prime example of this Post-Modernism, has been quoted as saying, "Architecture is no longer a matter of rules. We are as individualistic as painters. Post-Modernism isn't a style but a freedom."

Huxtable maintains that Modernism is "not dead, nor is it to be debunked. We are in a transitional period. There has been an unshackling of the profession, and new things are being tried. But some of it is very trivial." Post-Modernists, she has said, "have thrown away the rationale and the morality of Modernism. They've thrown out the good with the bad."

The Post-Modernists have designed a new generation of skyscrapers which, to their advocates, have a liveliness and flamboyance absent in the previous tall buildings. "I think we're so close to the new skyscraper now that we can't appreciate it," Huxtable said. "But if we were to stand away and look at the twentieth century and its skyscrapers, we would say, 'My God.' They will be viewed much as we now view the cathedrals of Europe."

It remains to be seen whether Ada Louise Huxtable's values will endure the test of history. Professor Placzek pointed out that she has "never deflected and has a remarkable fortitude and consistency in not being influenced by the prevailing success of current fashion." As Huxtable herself put it, "Good is good and bad is bad. It's rather a timeless thing." This sense of visual confidence was implanted by her parents, Leah (Rosenthal) Landman, a Bostonian whom she described as an "intensely visual woman with an impeccable eye and an abhorrence of anything fake," and Michael Louis Landman, a physician with a passion for art and writing plays. His first play, *Pride of Race*, which dealt with interracial marriage, was considered quite shocking when first produced in the 1920s.

Born in the city on March 14, 1921, Ada was an only child who led a solitary life exploring New York and its museums. Her father taught her iambic pentameter when she was seven, and she spent many hours writing poetry in "those lovely old marbleized notebooks." Her father's death when she was eleven changed the intensity of her education. "If he had lived, I perhaps would have been pushed too much intellectually." She was in the first graduating class at the High School of Music and Art, where she edited the school newspaper. At Hunter College a professor told her to give up writing because she wouldn't follow strict models for short-story structure.

After graduating *magna cum laude*, she had to help support her mother. First she worked at Bloomingdales, and then taught at the Institute of Fine Arts of New York University, where she took courses toward a master's degree. She left without graduating when her thesis proposal on nineteenth- and twentieth-century Italian architecture was turned down. She later explored the subject on a Fulbright, and out of that research came her first book, *Pier Luigi Nervi* (1960), on the Italian architect-engineer.

The Metropolitan had been an early mentor, but her career role model was Lewis Mumford, the *New Yorker* critic, to whom she is often compared. When she first started as a critic, he wrote to her praising certain columns, and once told an interviewer, "It wasn't until the *Times* got Huxtable that people really began to pay attention to architecture criticism."

Another mentor and colleague has been her husband, L. Garth Huxtable, whom she married at twenty, right out of college. He often takes photographs for her articles, and she shows him a copy of everything she writes. She in turn has collaborated with him on his projects, which have included designing tableware for the Four Seasons restaurant in New York. The Huxtables have no children and divide their time between the city and a summer home in Marblehead, Massachusetts. They frequently are in Paris, which she says is the "most beautiful city in the world," and in 1983 she was a jury member for a major project in Paris, a new building at La Défense.

Although her future criticism will be directed more to the nation's intelligentsia than to the lay newspaper reader, her achievement of teaching all readers—both professional and nonprofessional—to look at architecture multidimensionally will be her legacy. Buildings, like people, are very complex, she noted. "They are supposed to fulfill programs of such complexity, that it is easy to say a building succeeds on this level, fails on that level. I don't think there is a building that is a total success on every level. A perfect building doesn't exist. It is a matter of balance." A perfect architecture critic doesn't exist either, but on balance Ada Louise Huxtable may be as close as we can hope for.

The Huxtable touch, a fine blending of anger and satire, is evident in a column on the Architectural Follies. The tribute to architect Mies van der Rohe that follows reveals a different mood.

New York's Architectural Follies

By ADA LOUISE HUXTABLE

The New York Times, February 14, 1965

New York's longest-run show, the Architectural Follies, goes on. Performances as usual.

First, the comedy act. The New York Bank for Savings announced that it will build a 27-story apartment house next to its main office on Third Avenue at 72nd Street, utilizing the same "Colonial design" as the earlier building. Horace Ginsbern will be the architect.

Since the earlier building is a Williamsburg-type governor's palace, and a 27-story apartment building is a high-rise tower that was not only structurally and stylistically impossible but also as remote as a spaceship in Colonial times, this will be an amusing design trick. The "Colonial" label seems to be no more than a wistful thought, however, because the rendering shows a typical New York 27-story apartment house with familiar curtain wall and projecting balconies that might have made George Washington giddy. Funny? Boffo.

But this kind of joke is something that New York should have outgrown long ago. It is a hangover from the days before modern cities recognized their own magnificence. It doesn't work, as architecture or nostalgia.

Witness the original Bank for Savings building that is to inspire this addition. We banked there, until we were shifted to a newer neighborhood branch that was all "modern," with a wall-length pseudo-Mondrian subsequently painted out so that everything was reduced to safe, washable, plastic-coated middlin' gray and green, including the plants. Call it the Plastic Esthetic.

Saving money—considered a dubious virtue today, anyway—becomes a singularly depressing experience. Dreams die easily at the Bank for Savings. In the main office they die in an inflated, dehydrated, imitation Colonial shell, built with all of the handcrafted Colonial sincerity of big city commercial constructions, housing the unparalleled mechanical impersonality of the modern banking operation. Were banks first to reduce people to numbers? This one has the intimate eighteenth-century charm of its IBM computers. There is nothing sadder or funnier than this kind of misuse, or abuse of meaningful architectural style.

It's sad and funny to see it done again by the Franklin National Bank at Madison Avenue and 48th Street. Watching this building being transformed from twentieth century to eighteenth century was one of the top midtown acts of last season's Follies. First, there was the steel frame, strong, severe, handsomely rectilinear (the bones are best in most buildings), suggesting the logical shape and design that its covering surface might take, subject only to the architect's talent, imagination and respect for inspiration of the structure. Painstakingly, brick by brick, the lie was laid up for anyone to observe.

Eighteenth-century arches were hung on the facade like theatrical scrim. Originally, of course, arches like these were carefully built up to wedge-shaped, locking keystones to make openings in a brick wall without having the wall fall down. They were as natural and beautiful for masonry construction as the thin curtain wall is for the metal-framed building today.

Presto change. The hand is quicker than the eye. The arches aren't arches because the masonry is non-supporting. It's all backed by steel. Fooled you. What we have here is a kind of large architectural practical joke. It is tiresome, like most practical jokes. But the undertaking was carried out in consistent comic spirit to the end. The opening luncheon, which featured authentic Colonial cooking, was served by waiters in knee breeches. (Authentic Madison Avenue.)

So much for comedy. The tragedy was the razing of the Brokaw mansion. The hoarding went up at the end of the week and major demolition began on Saturday. Saturday, obviously, is not a normal building trades working day and the wrecking crew got double time for its efforts. The Campagna Construction Corporation, the owners and builders of a new apartment house on the site, were taking no chances. It was a dandy way to do enough massive damage at a time when no normal channels are functioning, to assure the building's doom.

No Marquesa de Cuevas had a chance to step forward with $2 million to save it, as with the Pyne house group on Park Avenue. By Monday it was too late. Perhaps the American Institute of Architects, which produced a nice scroll for the Marquesa, could arrange for a suitable trinket for the Campagna Corporation. Something like profit rampant on the seal of the city, upside down.

There is no denying that this is the most dramatic act in the Architectural Follies in a long time. There's nothing quite like a good house-wrecking. Come one, come all. You are cordially invited to a demolition-watching. It's a great performance of a kind being given with increasing frequency in Manhattan, one that could replace the "happening" as the most chic of avant-garde anti-cultural events.

Watch an architectural landmark demolished piece by piece. Be present while a splendid building is reduced to rubble. See the wrecking bars gouge out the fine chateau-style stonework. Hear the gas-powered saws bite into the great beams and rafters. Thrill to destruction. Take home samples. Hurry to the show.

On second thought, don't hurry. There will be many more performances. Good demolitions could outrun *Abie's Irish Rose*. Free demolition-watchings will be offered in all of New York's best styles and periods: High Victorian, Early Skyscraper, Cast-Iron Commercial in the path of the Lower Manhattan expressway, Greek Revival on the waterfront. If this isn't going to be faced as a public responsibility, it might as well be taken as a public spectacle. Anyone coming from City Hall?

MIES: LESSONS FROM THE MASTER

By ADA LOUISE HUXTABLE

The New York Times, February 6, 1966

A small, impeccable show of drawings of delicate precision and quiet power by Mies van der Rohe opened at the Museum of Modern Art this week to honor the architect's 80th birthday. It will run through March 20. The exhibition says a great deal about the artist's remarkable half-century of consistency as one of the supreme innovators of our time, but it leaves a great many things unsaid that could be discussed profitably at this moment.

The first are truisms that bear repeating, such as that Mies is one of the greatest architects of the 20th century, and, without really stretching the point, of all time. To the historian with a critical sense, he has obviously taken his place among the men of genius whose talents and contributions are such that the world is never quite the same again. Flesh and blood genius is seldom acknowledged by its own generation: we wait for the authentication of Charlton Heston playing Michelangelo as superman in supercolor.

Popinjays

But we have had our supermen: Frank Lloyd Wright playing himself, and Le Corbusier playing Scrooge while producing timeless spatial and sculptural delights. Both are gone. Only Mies remains, the last of the triumvirate that so decisively affected the course of architecture in the revolutionary years of the 20th century, evolving the look, structure and function of a new kind of man-made world in natural and inevitable synthesis with society's other radical changes. And he remains, at 80, at the peak of his creative powers, although crippled with arthritis, collecting the prime commissions that never came in his youth, now that his years to execute them are limited.

He is a massive, craggy man, given to few public pronouncements, whose person and work share a tacit monumentality. Measured against his stature, most of today's architects look like popinjays and pygmies. Measured against his work, most of today's architecture has a spurious creativity: an overanxious originality for its own or publicity's sake, that only incidentally may solve problems.

The world has mislearned the lesson of Miesian architecture, and then lost the ground he had gained for modern architecture, in the span of his own lifetime, and it is sadly instructive to see how and why.

The Miesian esthetic—strict, strong and subtle—is a correct, ordered and logical architectural solution for our day. That it is not the only solution goes without saying: but each artist must have his personal vision which he carries as close as possible to its ultimate perfection. Mies's vision rests on the acceptance of modern technology as it appeared, stunningly, in his youth.

Purity and Power

Trained as a stonemason, bricklayer and delineator of plaster ornament, he saw steel and glass as the fabric of a new world of shimmering skyscrapers and floating pavilions of stringently rational and elegant simplicity. He has produced work of a purity and power as great as anything the art of building has ever known.

But technology is not art, and form only follows function as a starting point, or life and art would be much simpler than they are. The key to the art of architecture is the conviction and sensitivity with which technology and function are interpreted esthetically, in solutions of practical social purpose.

Mies's structure, often the hard, straight-lined strength of the steel frame, is reflected in exterior metal detailing of painstaking refinement, that speaks directly and logically of the way he builds. His use of these details is as expressive as Sullivan's foliate ornament was of its underlying structure, is the quality and effectiveness of this expressive balance that marks the good, or great building.

The proportions of a Mies design are so sensitively adjusted, his understanding of the richness of marble, the brilliance of glass and the substantiality of bronze so sensuously sure, his feelings for the materials of our time so overwhelmingly rich and yet so far from vulgar, that no one has matched the precise and timeless beauty of his buildings. The Seagram building, for example, is dignified, sumptuous, severe, sophisticated, cool, consummately elegant architecture; architecture for the 20th century and for the ages.

The Miesian example is a lesson of principle. But in too many cases the Miesian principle has been ignored and the Miesian example simply "knocked off" in the cheapest Seventh Avenue terms.

Without fine materials and meticulous details, Mies's diamond-sharp doctrine of "less is more" becomes a most ordinary formula. Raised above the shoddy and speculative, however, it is a competent and appropriate formula, and it is here that Mies's signal importance, as the source of a genuine popular style, has been much misunderstood.

A Genuine Vernacular

The "glass box" is the most maligned building idea of our time. It is also one of the best. Whatever its deficiencies, and there are many, due to the complex factors of architects who are less than perfectionists and business-men who are less than philanthropists or sociologists, it is the genuine ver-nacular of the mid-20th century. It derives, legitimately, from Mies's mas-terful and meaningful innovations, and it serves, legitimately, the needs of a commercial society that builds on an industrial scale. It does this with sheer and brilliant modern magic, and with as much validity and suitability as the last great vernacular style, the Georgian.

The two are not dissimilar, except in their obvious disparity of scale. The Georgian expanse of plan brick, window-pierced wall with standard mold-ings and cornices made the kind of uniform, understated 18th-century back-ground that set off a good Wren church: the glass-walled streets today are a contemporary version of the same thing, background building for a Seagram tower or a handsome Beaux Arts survival.

The Miesian lesson has been equally misunderstood in the higher spheres of creativity. Today's architect is rushing lickety-split backwards into the kind of willful, whatnot Victoriana that Miles conclusively shattered. The triumph of modern architecture is becoming a strangely pyrrhic victory. The current pursuit of arbitrary dramatic effects resembles nothing so strongly as the Vic-torian pursuit of the picturesque, or 19th-century art for art's sake. It clings tenuously to the dubious rationale of the exploration of new structural tech-niques, reasoning that must be stretched like India-rubber to explain some of the anarchic, acrobatic results.

Mies stands for discipline, and this is becoming a lost architectural virtue. He stands for style, in its highest and most valid meaning of the expression of standards and techniques of a particular historical time.

"Architecture is the will of an epoch translated into space," he said in his most articulate period, the 1920's, which yields a handful of short state-ments. "My attack is against form as an end in itself. We create form out of the nature of our tasks, with the methods of our time." And finally, from St. Augustine, "Beauty is the splendor of truth." He has contributed both to an ancient art.

21

Judith Crist
(1922–   )

G OOD JOURNALISM is not ambiguous, according to Judith Crist, who lets
moviegoers know whether a movie is great or a clinker, and leaves no
question in a student's mind about what is good writing style. She has always been strongly opinionated, a quality which has made her not a few
enemies. "Inviting her to review your movies is like inviting the Boston
strangler to massage your neck," director Billy Wilder once quipped. "You
either love her or hate her," commented a student at Columbia's Graduate
School of Journalism, where as a member of the faculty she has weeded out
mixed metaphors and deplored muddy thinking for more than a quarter of
a century.

You can't call the most talked about picture of 1963, the $40 million epic
Cleopatra, a "monumental mouse" and "at best a major disappointment, at
worst an extravagant exercise in tedium," without bringing down the wrath
of the movie moguls. To be sure, Judith Crist plays the *grande dame* role
with style, shrugging off the nasty comments. She has even picked her favorite epithet, what she calls the "triple S sting," uttered in 1965 by a Twentieth Century-Fox publicist who called her "a snide, supercilious, sour bitch."

More to the point, perhaps, was Alfred Hitchcock's retort when asked
whether he thought the *New York Herald Tribune*'s film critic was blunt:
"Not blunt, sir, but very sharp." Crist has become controversial not only
because of what she writes about a movie, but also because of how she writes

it. She has been called "middlebrow" and "schmaltzy." Marsha McCreadie in *Women on Film, the Critical Eye* (1983) wrote that one reason Crist's laudatory blurbs and quotes can so often be seen on marquees and in newspaper advertisements is that she has the "ability to slangily toss together some phrases that when closely examined may make no logical sense but that on a fast read seem insightful."

Almost overnight Judith Crist became famous, publicly acclaimed and derided, just because she was, in her words, "honest and courageous." It all started in 1963 when she panned *Spencer's Mountain*, starring Henry Fonda and Maureen O'Hara. She called it "a film that for sheer prurience and perverted morality disguised as piety makes the nudie shows at the Rialto look like Walt Disney productions." In addition to trashing the movie, she questioned the standards of Radio City Music Hall where it was booked, writing that the theater management was exposing young people to the movie's "vulgar . . . mealymouthed piety."

Producers of the film, Warner Bros., retaliated and dropped all advertising in the *Trib*, with Radio City following along and reducing its lineage. The paper supported Crist, however, publishing an editorial on June 5 that stated, "A newspaper whose comments and critiques can be controlled by advertisers cheats its readers and ceases to be an honest newspaper. . . . We feel sorry for film producers who consider themselves above criticism. . . . They injure their own reputations, and hurt the critic not at all. Mrs. Crist is one of journalism's most competent critics. The Herald Tribune is proud of her talent and her integrity. We are also proud of journalistic standards which leave no room for such inane pressure tactics."

"The editorial was brilliant," said Crist. "It had never happened before in the history of newspaper criticism, and it changed the way editors throughout the country viewed their movie critics." Crist has always been on the side of the moviegoer who plunks down from $4 to $6 and wants to know what has to be endured or enjoyed for several hours. Her reviews are not for the cineastes, those interested in the artistic and technical aspects of film production, and she scoffs at critics who go from the college screening room to the professional screening room without experiencing anything in between.

Her eighteen years as a *Trib* general assignment reporter, covering politics, education, finance, crime, even sports, were a great asset for writing criticism, she said: "Reporting teaches you that you are the filter, and that you're dealing with the inevitable truth, whether it's the way you saw an event or the way you saw a film. I've always felt you have to be an egomaniac to be a critic, because at least while you're writing, you believe you're dispensing the truth."

She told the truth about *Cleopatra*, and she claims other critics felt the same way but didn't dare knock such an expensive movie, whose filming had involved an off-screen romance between Elizabeth Taylor and Richard Burton, broken marriages, dismissed directors, and so much pre-release hoopla. "But all that has nothing to do with the person who pays to see the movie," said Crist. There was even more of an uproar when she was unenthusiastic about the decent, home-loving, big-gross musical, *The Sound of Music*, with Julie Andrews, filmed in the Austrian Alps. She wrote:

But one star and much scenery do not a two-hour-and-fifty-five-minutes plus intermission entertainment make, and the issue must be faced. Squarely. That is the way to face "The Sound of Music." This last, most remunerative and least inspired, let alone sophisticated, of the Rodgers and Hammerstein collaborations is square and solid sugar. Calorie-counters, diabetics and grown-ups from eight to eighty had best beware. . . . For let me tell you that there is nothing like a super-sized screen to convert seven darling kids in no time at all into all that W. C. Fields indicated darling little kids are—which is pure loathsome.

This iconoclastic view of motherless children infuriated Crist's critics. She joked, "If I had beaten my mother to a pulp, strangled my small children and slit the throat of my little puppy dog, I wouldn't have seemed so odious."

In the 1970s, when she was reviewing in *TV Guide*, *New York* magazine, and on NBC's *Today* show, with a combined audience of 30 million, the Louis Harris poll showed that she was the most influential film critic in the United States. Her audience has dwindled since. In 1977, lured by a high salary, she took a job with the *New York Post*. She left after only nine months, and when a reporter asked why she quipped, "It was recently made clear to me that the *Post* felt I was overqualified and overcritical."

But she continues to write reviews for *TV Guide* and is seen on New York's WOR-TV. In California, she contributes criticism to *Beverly Hills* (213). Her books include *Take 22: Movie Makers on Movie Making* (1984) and two review anthologies: *The Private Eye, the Cowboy, and the Very Naked Girl* (1968) and *TV Guide to the Movies* (1974).

In *The Private Eye*, she set forth her critical philosophy:

I have subscribed to the James Agee premise that film criticism is a conversation between moviegoers; I relish agreement but I think quite frankly that my immediate goal is to keep the conversation going, to stimulate my listener into a response, whether it involves a reappraisal of his own opinions or an affirmation of his disagreement. Ours is the age of the expert, where we sit and wait to get the word from on high, to operate on a consensus of what the ephemeral "they" think. If I can prod a person or two into just thinking for himself, let alone organizing his thought into opinion form, let alone even articulating that opinion—critical mission practically accomplished.

David Ansen, *Newsweek*'s film critic, admires Crist's ability to maintain her enthusiasm over the years. He sees her as a very solid critic, but not one like Pauline Kael of the *New Yorker*, who has influenced younger critics. Kael has called Crist "the only film critic with balls." McCreadie, in her analysis, praised Crist's "lack of pretense and ability to cut through hokum," describing her, socially and politically, as often very middle-American, and "much to her credit and in the national vein, completely unsnobbish."

After reviewing for more than two decades, Crist concedes that she has mellowed a bit. The fast, punchy, grab'em-by-the-coat-lapels style of writing is still her hallmark. There is usually a catchy phrase, a rolling alliteration, but she is limited to 200 words for *TV Guide* and her reviews have to let the insomniacs know if it's worthwhile to turn the dial for the late late show or if a TV movie makes the grade. She does manage, in many of these brief reviews, to weave in historical context and draw on her vast knowledge of film history; the bitter edge that characterized her 1960s reviews, however, is infrequently found in her 1980s criticism.

"I realize now that values matter a lot to me," said Crist during an interview, punctuating her opinions with exclamation points. Sex-and-violence films such as *Dressed to Kill* and *Taxi Driver*, which received favorable reviews, don't interest her. She likes movies that "promote decency," and mentioned *Chariots of Fire* and *ET* as favorites. "I was an elitist in my youth," she joked, "so I could be a populist in my old age."

She has also added theater and opera to her reviewing repertoire. "I was totally involved with movies for so long that I now find other events of equal importance. I suppose that's mellowing." There aren't as many opportunities today, however, for the classic Crist acerbic review as there were twenty-two years ago when Hollywood churned out 450 movies a year. "Today, it's either trash or class!" she noted, her large hazel eyes widening, serving as subtitles to her emotions. "Nobody can afford to make those mediocre movies that you loved to get mad about. A *Cleopatra* would not be made today. Warren Beatty can spend the same money to make *Reds* and it's a class act!"

Born in New York City on May 22, 1922, Judith Crist was the second of two children of Solomon and Helen (Schoenberg) Klein, who were of Polish-Russian-Jewish background. Her father, an entrepreneur, had many business interests from furs to jewelry and invented a dry-cleaning machine. Her mother, a New York librarian and a translator, had been a revolutionary in the unsuccessful 1905 rebellion in Russia.

Judy saw her first movie at age five—*Seventh Heaven* with Janet Gaynor. But she spent part of her childhood in Montreal, where her father's business ventures had taken the family, and there you had to be sixteen to go to the movies. However, this only made the forbidden treat more alluring.

Judith Crist

Crist was bright and precocious, with a tested IQ at age 12 of 142. Skipping grades, she graduated from New York's Morris High School at fifteen. During her high school years she indulged her passion for movies, often taking 10 cents from her mother's change purse to attend the inexpensive afternoon double features at Loews or RKO. She went on to Hunter College, where she wrote for all the literary publications. "I always knew I was going to be a writer," she recalled. "You know that when you fall in love with words at an early age. I dreamed of being a movie critic, but knew that the odds were against it."

She did graduate study in eighteenth-century English literature at Columbia in 1941 and was a teaching fellow at the State College of Washington the next year. It was then that she decided she wanted to do graduate work in journalism, but she spent a year working as a civilian instructor of English with the Air Force before she entered the class of 1945 at Columbia. In her application she wrote, "My hope for success is supported by two great interests: people, and truth. A concern with them, coupled with a facility for fact and language, will, I believe, make me a journalist."

The making of this journalist began immediately after graduation from Columbia with a job as assistant to Dorothy Dunbar Bromley, women's editor of the *New York Herald Tribune*, who became both a mentor and role model for Crist. "She was a pioneering, self-made woman," said Crist, "second only in her time to Dorothy Thompson, and way ahead of her time when she wrote the book *Sex Habits of Vassar Girls*." Bromley is credited with changing the women's pages from a dreary listing of club activities to a lively montage of articles of social significance.

After four years in the women's department, Crist moved to the city desk and general assignment. Her city editor, Dick West, recalled that he would "save Judy for a story that was bound to break and be worth her mettle. She wasn't the kind of reporter you would waste on trivia." Co-workers acknowledged that she was a natural telephone interviewer; in fact, her first byline, on March 10, 1949, stemmed from getting the right person on the phone to give the perfect quote for her lead. She was doing a reaction story on an article published by *Pravda*, the Soviet Communist newspaper, which stated that American women were oppressed. To this actress Tallulah Bankhead replied, "*Pravda* is full of prune juice."

Crist's *Trib* colleagues, she said, taught her things they don't teach in the classroom. In her interview with me she fondly cited reporter Emma Bugbee: "She taught me how to be a lady." Labor reporter A. J. Raskin, Crist said, "took the dew off my eyes. I was terribly idealistic and still am." And rewrite man Bob Peck "taught me a better lesson in journalism than I had received in a whole year at Columbia."

To tell the Bob Peck story, Crist lit yet another cigarette and her eyes took on a twinkle. She was given a wire story from Rochester, New York, she said, about a girl who found a plaster statue of the Virgin Mary in a garbage can. The child took it home, put it on the mantle in her tenement apartment, and tears started flowing from the statue's eyes. "I started making calls," Crist recalled. "I called a priest for a quote, but all the clergy were being very reticent about the incident. I called the Associated Press in Rochester because I needed an eye witness. I talked to the reporter who had been in the apartment, and he told me, 'Look, I'm Jewish and I don't believe this, but there is water coming out of the statue's eyes.' I called the University of Rochester, and a scientist told me that the plaster might have absorbed moisture from the garbage since it had been raining heavily."

Skeptical about the facts, and with only second- and third-hand information, she sweated out the story and handed it in. Then she went downstairs to the *Trib*'s pub, Artist and Writers, to meet her husband, William B. Crist, a public relations executive specializing in education. They waited for the first edition to be brought down by the copy boy, and she saw that her story, in the right-hand corner of page one, had been rewritten by Peck into a "wonderful, visual account," right down to the detail of how the old tenement stairs creaked and swayed under the weight of the people rushing to see the statue. "It was just the way a reporter on the spot would have written it," she said, "and I never forgot that lesson."

Bill Crist has always been around in such situations, and his wife never fails to rave about the supportive man she married, who adjusted to her erratic schedule, which was often 1 to 9 p.m. Their son, Steven, is the *New York Times*' racing writer, and his mother once benefited from listening to his rock music. "When I reviewed *Hair* or *Jesus Christ Superstar*," she said, "I could write with some knowledge about the music."

During her years as a cityside reporter, she interviewed Queen Elizabeth II, Queen Juliana of the The Netherlands, as well as such diverse personalities as Maria Callas and Mrs. Nikita Khrushchev. A three-part investigative series on the Yonkers school system won her four prizes and led to a state inquiry on the lack of proper funds for education. Seeking a change of pace, she asked one day to review some Off Broadway plays and was assigned Maxwell Anderson's *The Golden Six*. She panned the effort of a famous playwright, learning at the same time that she could make a reputation for herself by being vicious and funny.

In 1958 she was named drama critic of the *Herald Tribune*, the first woman to hold such a title on a major metropolitan daily; two years later, she became editor for the arts, in charge of developing the *Trib*'s first culture section, a packaging concept copied later by papers across the country. Her childhood dream was fulfilled in 1963, when she became movie critic and associate drama critic. Before she could get started, though, a nine-month newspaper strike closed all the city's papers.

During this strike many print journalists were introduced to television, and Crist did regular theater and film reviews on ABC's morning and evening news programs. Viewers used to hearing propaganda criticism were startled by her "tell it as it is" approach, and Crist claims credit for launching an era of honest criticism in television journalism. She continued to do reviews for ten years on the *Today* show.

Being overcritical as a professor of writing at her alma mater, Columbia, has earned her a reputation as a "tough" teacher who bullies both novices and advanced writers into thinking about the words they so carelessly throw on paper. "She prunes all the bullshit, and what you're left with is style," said one former student. Her comments on papers are often "harsh and acerbic," but many Crist graduates agree with one student's appraisal: "one of the most memorable experiences of my educational life."

Judith Crist is still a deadline writer, although she works out of her home now, writing finished copy on an electric typewriter. She has a secretary to organize a full schedule that takes her from screening room to theater preview. She receives a "varied mail bag" of about fifty letters a month from *TV Guide* readers, which she describes as "intensely personal since TV movies come into the home." And for fourteen years she has coordinated weekend discussions with Hollywood personalities at Tarrytown, New York.

Occasionally she thinks about writing a thriller, which she would call *The Film Festival Murders*, but for now reviewing takes most of her time. "Movies are where things are happening," she said, and it is always with the expectation of something wonderful in store that she settles down in the plush seat of the screening room, lights up a cigarette, and waits for the house lights to dim.

Judith Crist's *New York Herald Tribune* reviews of the 1960s made her reputation. Reprinted here is the infamous pan of *Cleopatra*.

CLEOPATRA: A MONUMENTAL MOUSE

By JUDITH CRIST

New York Herald Tribune, June 13, 1963

Long months—if not years—ago, I suspect, the majority of moviegoers made up their minds either to see "Cleopatra" no matter what or to avoid being caught dead in its vicinity. It's for the undecided minority, therefore, that I must report that this film is at best a major disappointment, at worst an extravagant exercise in tedium.

It depends, of course, on what you have been waiting for. Certainly if you want to devote the best part of four hours to looking at Elizabeth Taylor in all her draped and undraped physical splendor, surrounded by elaborate and exotic costumes and sets, all in the loveliest of colors, this is your movie. And if you are able to adjust your focus from time to time, you will get two fine performances by Rex Harrison and Roddy McDowall, the lilting speech of Richard Burton and a couple of parades and divertisements that Flo Ziegfeld or Busby Berkeley might well have masterminded.

THE COSTS

But I think a bit more has been expected of this 1958–63 "Cleopatra" under the aegis of Walter Wanger, with script and direction by Joseph L. Mankiewicz. We were led to anticipate a fresh and sophisticated character-oriented approach to the story of Caesar, Cleopatra and Mark Antony, courtesy of Mr. Mankiewicz's past performances; a spectacular epic to take the breath away with panoramic scope and eye-filling extravaganza, courtesy of the $34,000,000 production cost; a vital history of turbulent times, alive with the excitement and fever of the politics and passions that framed them, courtesy of Mr. Mankiewicz's co-authors' researches and the scope Todd-AO can give to near-global events. But "Cleopatra" is none of these.

And I might note at the outset that an even greater disappointment awaits those whose interest has been titillated almost exclusively by the Taylor-Burton real-life parallel to their Cleopatra-Antony romance. They should be warned that Mr. Burton does not appear for the first hour and 20 minutes; that another hour and 15 minutes elapse before their first embrace and that, beyond much love talk and soulful ogling, their physical encounters are scarcely five degrees warmer than the Caesar-Cleopatra liaison—and that's a cool one. Perhaps the sexy bits ended up on the cutting-room floor.

I should prefer, in fact, to blame much of the film's inadequacies on the fact that it was cut from six to four hours. This might well account for the choppy incoherence of the action (we search for columns and hieroglyphics and uniforms to discover whether we're in Rome or Alexandria at times), for the sketchy portrayal of the pre-Cleopatra Antony (we know him only as a besotted, vain weakling—scarcely a man whose dying "should be shouted from the corners of the earth"), for the strangely abbreviated spectacle of the battles on land and sea and even of the "orgy" aboard Cleopatra's barge.

THE CUTS

But cutting would not account for the level of the film's dialogue, provided principally by Mr. Mankiewicz, hitherto one of our most adult and literate screenwriters. Certainly he faced stiff comparison with, let alone competition from Shaw and Shakespeare—but the resultant melange of cliches and pompous banalities is unworthy of him. "Nothing like this has come into Rome since Romulus and Remus," Antony remarks of Cleopatra's spectacular arrival; "A woman that cannot bear children is like a river that has run dry," Cleopatra notes, adding, "I will bear many sons—my breasts are filled with love and life."

Time and tides, the characters keep telling each other, are either running out or waiting for no one; "One world, one people, one nation" is Cleo's political plea, apparently making her a world Federalist at heart; "The way to prevent war is to be ready for it," she assures her generals. "Antony— what has happened?" "To me? You have happened to me." And so it goes.

THE CHARMS

And you want to weep for Rex Harrison—or, at least, to get some of Shaw's "Caesar and Cleopatra" lines into his mouth. He is so good an actor, however, that in spite of the script he manages to make Caesar the larger-than-life creature he must be to be believed. Slightly amused, always superior, steadily approaching the ultimate ambitions that would destroy him, he conveys both the intelligence and the stature of an emperor, particularly in the subtle suggestion that, though he might succumb to her charms and ambitious chatter, he still regards Cleopatra as not too much more than a serviceable doll.

And Miss Taylor makes little more of her than that, her accents and acting style jarring first with those of Harrison and later with those of Burton. She is an entirely physical creature, no depth of emotion apparent in her kohl-laden eyes, no modulation in her voice that too often rises to fishwife levels. Out of royal regalia, *en negligee* and *au naturel*, she gives the impression that she is really carrying on in one of Miami Beach's more exotic resorts rather than inhabiting a palace in ancient Alexandria or even a villa in Rome. And strangely, in the course of this 18-year history, she seems to reverse the aging process, looking a well-groomed 30-plus when she rolls out of the rug at Caesar's feet and a love-lorn 20 in her death throes.

THE COSTUMES

Miss Taylor's costumes are nothing short of sensational and her doing without any at all in a couple of scenes is equally impressive. But the fallacy is, alas, that neither her costumes nor her performance leaves anything to the imagination. We have on hand a rather unsubtle siren, a blatantly ambitious beauty in search of a man to conquer the world for her, with not even the illusion or suggestion of that eternally mysterious woman whose fascination would outlast the centuries.

With the mystique of Cleopatra missing, Antony loses heroic stature and winds up as a pathetic Caesar-ridden sot, given to occasional pangs of conscience, but a ninny. There's nothing grand about his passion for Cleopatra and no grandeur in his destruction. There is grandeur in Richard Burton's way with a line and a fit of remorse, but the monotony and inconsequence of his role limit this very able actor.

As Octavian, however, Roddy McDowall does bring to Caesar's heir an underlying shrewdness and strength under an impassive exterior that is fascinating. Kenneth Haigh is briefly interesting as Brutus, but of the other "names" scattered in the cast Hume Cronyn seems oddly uncomfortable as Cleopatra's adviser and Pamela Brown is strictly from Fu Manchu as her high priestess. There's the usual hodgepodge of accents, as in all made-abroad spectaculars, with the ludicrous achieved by the small boy, depicting Caesar's and Cleopatra's son at the age of four, who bursts out with a ripe Italian dialect.

There are of course the thousands of extras, the hundreds of Nubians, the dancing girls, the barges, the palaces, the statues, the sphinxes. But it is clear that Mr. Mankiewicz is not a spectacular man *au fond*. Aiming above, as he put it, "the Taras Bulba crowd," he has attempted to emphasize the main characters rather than the panorama. But so grand and grandiose are the sets that the characters are dwarfed, and so wide is his screen that this concentration on character results in a strangely static epic in which the overblown close-ups are interrupted at best by a pageant or dance, more often by unexciting bits and pieces of exits, entrances, marches or battles.

Mr. Mankiewicz's heart is all too obviously not in the large-scale action that a film of this subject and physical scope demands. He frustrates the requirements of the wide screen by reducing the naval engagement of Actium, after a few disjointed clips of the actual fighting, interrupted by static close-ups of his various characters, to a moving around of models on a map by Cleopatra's admiral aboard her barge. Given, at the outset, magnificent views of the battlefields at Pharsalia and Caesar's camp—after the battle—we hunger for more than the brief clash, clatter and fireworks at Moongate, the mere marching of legions, even Antony's abortive one-man attempt against Octavian's legions.

THE CAPERS

We are cheated of a sense of size and power in the Roman Senate; Caesar's assassination is downgraded by having it splotchily seen through the augury fires set for Cleopatra by her priestess—and not even his funeral pyre on the Forum steps—with Romans throwing what look like old pieces of furniture on it—achieves significance.

The orgies? A bit of wild dancing aboard the barge, with a suddenly drunken Antony joining in, is strangely skimpy—and not helped one bit by having one of the dancing girls decked out as a double for Cleopatra. We should not be reminded that other girls can look just like Elizabeth Taylor, particularly when she is trying to portray the Queen of Queens.

THE CLIMAX

Certainly Cleopatra's multimillion-dollar parade into Rome does beat the advent of Romulus and Remus; it's a mishmash of cavalry, burlesque-show girls and Ballets Africans—"Hot Mikado" performers, topped by Cleo and son, in cloth of gold, riding an arch-high sphinx on wheels. Unfortunately, the climax is dimmed for us by the unnerving but not illogical expectation that somewhere a tenor should burst out with "A pretty girl is like a melody."

The Queen's barge is impressive on the outside, what with pretty girls playing boatswain and lookout and all—and it's deceiving, because inside it's like the whole hotel Manhattan laid out on one floor. And the banquet! Flaming Shishkebab the Ambassador East never dreamed of, whole stuffed and fully feathered peacocks—"Fabulous feast," says Antony. "One is so limited when one travels by ship," replies Cleo.

A painstaking attention to tiny details makes it all too obvious that nothing has been spared on the set and costumes. There are indeed some beautiful and impressive photographic effects with transitions made by having faded frescoes slowly brighten into a live scene or a scene freeze and dim into a fresco. But the sets themselves never create an illusion of permanence within their time. The cardboard and paint are there. Even in their most dramatic moment, when Cleopatra and Antony are slapping each other around in her tomb, one's most immediate image is of Miss Taylor and Mr. Burton having it out in the Egyptian Wing of the Metropolitan Museum.

All is monumental—but the people are not. The mountain of notoriety has produced a mouse.

22

Georgie Anne Geyer

(1935–   )

GEORGIE ANNE GEYER, affectionately known as "Gee Gee," loves strange cities, hotels, room service, and "looking around and waiting"—her description of a foreign correspondent's life. An expert on Latin America, she was one of the first to report on this generation of Central America's guerrillas when in 1966 she and a photographer went into the Sierra de las Miñas mountains of Guatemala to interview leaders of that country's rebel armed forces. She waited around for five weeks before she made the right connections to get the story. Before she left the country, her life was threatened by a right-wing organization, the Mano Blanco (White Hand), and she was accused of being the mistress of a right-wing dictator, which she found even more alarming, because she said the dictator was "the single most unattractive man" she had ever met. In her autobiography, *Buying the Night Flight* (1983), one of the Radcliffe series on famous women, she wrote: "It doubtless was more dramatic to die in Spain during the Spanish Civil War, but in the sixties, in Latin America, to die in Guatemala was a respected business."

Her journey into the Guatemala mountains was dangerous and arduous; she sloshed through mud, lived off tortillas and black bean paste and was constantly uncertain about whether to trust her guides. The quest, however, paid off with an exclusive story of a week spent with the nascent guerrilla movement. She was the first outsider to appraise the situation, and this story gave her, at age thirty-one, a sense of personal accomplishment that has kept her roaming the globe ever since. "The sacrifices one makes to be a foreign correspondent," she wrote, "husband, children, the house with the view of the lake, the comforts of normalcy, and the reassurances of conformity, seem [at such times] quite simply, irrelevant."

Georgie Anne Geyer made her reputation on the old *Chicago Daily News*, where she worked for eleven years before becoming a thrice-weekly syndicated columnist for Universal Press Syndicate, writing on foreign, domestic, and women's issues. In 1985 her column appeared in eighty-five newspapers from California to Florida. As a roving columnist, she is free to pick her own destinations. In 1983, for example, she went to China for the first time, and she returns frequently to Latin America, where she says she feels most at home.

As a woman and a journalist, she is comfortable with her independent life. Although she could have married more than once, she consciously has rejected family life. "In this kind of work," she said when I interviewed her in 1983, "relationships tend to be fleeting. You aren't in one place long enough to maintain them." When she isn't traveling, home base is a three-and-a-half-room apartment across from the Watergate in Washington, cluttered with pottery, pillows, and inlaid furniture collected over twenty-two years of working abroad. Her household companion is Pasha, an imposing black-and-white cat, who Geyer is convinced is descended from the Egyptian god cats.

She is usually on one of her four phones, filling an appointment book with dates for conferences, lunches, dinners, and plane flights. There is a pleasure-loving energy in everything she does, and clearly she is not the "girl next door" or the "elementary school teacher"—labels thrust on her in interviews published in the 1960s. An attractive woman with a sensuality that recalls Marilyn Monroe's, she has never thought about camouflaging her femininity. "I prefer to dress as a woman, not a soldier," she said, indicating a favorite outfit she had on of a flowered skirt, pink gauze tie-blouse, and sandals. "You don't wear fatigues in Latin countries if you want to survive."

In Geyer's view there are advantages and disadvantages to being a woman foreign correspondent. Latins can be quite gracious and protective of women, she said, and through the years she has learned that men tend to open up and reveal themselves "with the proper psychological presence, particularly a female one." Male colleagues often thought that Geyer had all the advantages because she was young, blond, and female. "Frankly, I never quite understood the principle at work here," she noted in her book. "I just couldn't picture waking up at three in the morning with some stranger lying next to me and saying, 'Er, Che, *mi amor*, tell me where your missiles are?' Men apparently think this is the way it's done."

During a crisis or major news event, men in power will seek out the important correspondents, Geyer said, and they are usually men; but when powerful men have lots of time, they would rather be with a woman correspondent. People in "out" positions also prefer women, at least American women. "I am convinced that I had success in reaching the guerrillas because they, being anti-American and generally pro-Marxist, hated American men. It was American men who were representatives of the metropole, not American women."

A natural curiosity about people and customs makes Geyer a skilled conversationalist; she listens and makes others feel at ease. She has never joined the brittle, hard-edged, "one of the boys" school of women correspondents. One such person she does admire, though, is Oriana Fallaci, the Italian journalist known for her withering interviews of such leaders as the Ayatollah Ruhallah Khomeini and Henry Kissinger. In her book, she fantasized:

> I would like to spin on them [world leaders], crashing the door behind me, and say, "All right, Anwar, why don't you wipe out Kaddafi?" But I would not be capable of acting that way even if I were high on hashish. I work, rather, in what I call the absorptive style. I go into "His" office and sit there. I am sympathetic. I may well look a little pathetic. I present "Him" with a vacuum and he virtually always fills it. I do present questions—and I can present them very directively indeed if need be— but 95 percent of the time I have found that that is not necessary.

Generally she doesn't like leader interviews and does them only because they offer good background, people want to read them and they increase her own prestige. "They are so hard to arrange," she said, "that the chase itself is stimulating." Geyer was the first foreigner to interview Mrs. Anwar Sadat when she was Egypt's first lady and the only American to talk with Argentina's Juan Peron shortly before his death in 1974. He was "the single most charismatic man I have ever met," she recalled. "The pull was electric."

Certainly a part of the Geyer charm is her disarming candor. She readily admitted to me that she often initially judges famous people in terms of physical attraction. "It's never evident to them," she noted. "Everything is always very businesslike." Chile's Marxist president, Salvador Allende, reminded her of a "penguin"; Muammar Kaddafi of Libya had "the eyes of a Baptist preacher . . . tight, fanatic eyes"; Yassir Arafat, head of the Palestine Liberation Organization, was "a cross between GI Joe and Buddha"; and Lech Walesa, leader of Poland's Solidarity movement, was "a hyperactive bantam rooster." Khomeini of Iran she likened to a "huge black moth of a man who floated to the ground like a specter" when he sat down. Her favorite leader was Saddam Hussein of Iraq, whom she described as "charming, gracious, intelligent, rational." When she first met Fidel Castro of Cuba, she had no feelings whatsoever, finding him somewhat effeminate during an

Georgie Anne Geyer

eight-hour interview that ended at 1:30 a.m. when he suggested they get some ice cream at a modern, block-long ice cream parlor across from the hotel. She recounted the incident in her book:

Fidel looked at me and said with deadly seriousness, "We now have twenty-eight flavors."

I was astonished, confused. What was I supposed to say—"Do you have chocolate ripple?"

Then he said, again with total seriousness, "That's more than Howard Johnson's has."

Now I was absolutely nonplussed. Howard Johnson's? Was I in Communist Cuba or was I Alice in Wonderland?

Then he answered the riddle—and gave me some good insight into the Fidelian mind. "Before the revolution," he said, now with just a touch of humor in his eyes, "the Cuban people loved Howard Johnson's ice cream. This is the way of showing we can do everything better than the Americans."

Recalling her years as a foreign correspondent, Geyer stressed the need to be patient; in fact, "waiting around" is one of the most frequently used phrases in her autobiography. She listens, takes in the other person, relaxes into an easy give and take of ideas, as she did during an interview in her Washington apartment. The conversation often returned to her early love for Latin America. The empathy she feels in these countries, she said, stems from the basic question they face: independence or dependence, which she sees as analogous to a woman's life. "In truth, I was one of them."

Georgie Anne Geyer grew up on the uneasy South Side of Chicago where "there was a very real bully on every block," but this outside environment was tempered with a secure extended family, which added to her self-confidence. She was born on April 2, 1935, ten years after a brother, Glen, with whom she is very close. Her father, Robert George Geyer, owned a dairy which flourished under his strict Germanic management, but his remote personality was in counterpoint to that of her caring mother, Georgie Hazel (Gervens) Geyer, a warm, affectionate person whom she described as a "woman who created neighborhoods" wherever she went.

Her father's detachment made her over-achieve to "earn love," while her mother gave approval, eventually supporting her choice of a career over marriage and children. "All my life I suffered from the feeling that I wasn't doing the right thing because I didn't do what I was raised to do—get married and have babies," she said.

She entered Northwestern University's Medill School of Journalism at sixteen, spending a junior-year semester at Mexico City College. She was "seduced by the Latin culture," but it would be some time before she returned. She won a Fulbright to Vienna where she studied German and Spanish. There, in the aftermath of the failed Hungarian revolt of 1956, she fell in love with a Hungarian and worked with him to help refugees cross the border into Austria.

Her return home the following year was marred by a severe case of hepatitis. She was in bed for a year, an ordeal that taught her "respect for patience and waiting," for she could elevate her hands only inch by inch each month. After recovering, she spent four months on the *Southtown Economist,* a Chicago neighborhood paper. In 1959 she was hired by the *Chicago Daily News* as a society reporter.

Even in the late 1950s there were still vestiges of the rough-and-tumble days of old-style Chicago journalism immortalized in the play *Front Page.* Its co-author, Ben Hecht, as well as Carl Sandburg, John Gunther, and Ernest Hemingway, had all worked at one time for the *Daily News.* Reporters aggressively competed against the three rival papers but never against each other, and the word "scoop" had a ringing sound. "We were reporters," Geyer recalled, "not even journalists and certainly not media celebrities."

The undercover "sob sister" approach still intrigued the city editors, though, and when Geyer moved to the city desk after a year, she was assigned to pose as a waitress at a Mafia wedding. "It was a fun kind of story," she said. "It wasn't the kind of undercover story that rankles any ethical standards." The story won an award from the Chicago Newspaper Guild in 1962 for the best human-interest article.

After four years she felt restless as she watched the fifty- and sixty-year-old male foreign correspondents drift through the newsroom on their home leaves, and listened to them swapping war stories. Geyer wanted to be doing the same work, and she might have continued to just daydream had she not found a back door to Latin America. She applied for a Seymour Berkson (named after a publisher of the *New York Journal-American*) foreign assignment grant and at twenty-nine found herself in Peru for six months, filing stories to the *Daily News.* She began her education as a foreign correspondent with such useful rules as, "You don't call people at home. Interviews have to be arranged through intermediaries. Local journalists who know a country are the best sources."

In the mid-1960s there was little newspaper coverage of Latin America except for breaking stories. To give readers the needed background on their next-door neighbors, Geyer started covering trends, writing about real people and linking them to their history, tales, and legends. She established a reputation at her paper for fair, accurate reporting and in 1964 was appointed roving correspondent. Based mostly in Latin America, she also made special trips to the Middle East, Russia, Angola (where she was imprisoned for writing about the revolutionary government), and Vietnam (she never fully understood the war there, she said).

In 1972, three years before the *Chicago Daily News* folded, she left the paper to write a column for the Los Angeles Times Syndicate, switching in 1980 to Universal Press Syndicate. Her various assignments produced three books: *The New Latins* (1970), *The New 100 Years' War* (1972), and *The Young Russians* (1975). In 1970, she received the prestigious Maria Moors Cabot award for inter-American journalism.

In her *Who's Who in America* listing, Geyer included a personal credo, which stated in part: "the old injunction to 'Know Thyself' reaches women more than men. It has been a constant personal struggle, often with little personal approval or backing, which I feel also adds to a woman's inner strength." Somehow Geyer went through her early career without a professional mentor, although she was always looking for someone who would take her aside and tell her she had talent or encourage her to learn languages (she speaks Spanish, German, Russian, and Portuguese). "Once I had these things," she said, "then I received the encouragement."

In the 1960s she was often the only woman covering a revolution, and her position forced her to examine the problems women face in choosing a career over a family. She has no simplistic answers except, "You have to do what you love." One man she was romantically involved with but didn't marry was Keyes Beech, long-time foreign correspondent for the *Chicago Daily News*. He covered Korea with Marguerite Higgins of the *Herald Tribune* and Vietnam with Geyer. "They were both driven women," he recalled, "but different in their own ways. Gee Gee is an excellent political analyst, a conservative actually, who thought Maggie was an arch reactionary. Both of them had this murderous ambition to succeed—and who wants to be married to a driven woman?"

Jim Wallace, who covered Latin America for *U.S. News & World Report* in the mid-1960s and knew Geyer there, described her as a "realist" who at that time kept after stories that were difficult because she felt it was important that she be in the paper constantly. "It's the same today," he said, pointing to her column in the *Washington Times*, owned by the Rev. Sun Myung Moon's Unification Church. "She makes the best of this situation because she realizes the advantages of being read in the capital." Wallace rates her as a "better reporter than a manipulator of ideas." The more individual a column is, he said, the better it is. She wrote such a column on July 2, 1983. It carried the headline "Journalist's Death a Senseless Tragedy," and discussed the death of the *Los Angeles Times'* correspondent Dial Torgerson, who had been killed by a grenade while on assignment in Honduras near the Nicaraguan border. She concluded the column:

Unlike the television-news readers, who generally cover nothing, the Dial Torgersons "out there" remain relatively unsung. Unlike many of the fashionable new "investigative reporters" who are in journalism to make a name fast, the Dial Torgersons do not get the public recognition they should.

Yet virtually everything we know about other countries, about the world and our place in it, comes from conscientious men like him, who are "out there." Or were.

Geyer's outlets as a columnist are mostly in the second papers in major cities, and she, too, doesn't get the recognition she once had when she was often the only woman correspondent in Latin America. Still, her mother taught her that life was meant to be a "dedication, not simply a pastime." After twenty-two years of covering revolutions and wars, she is still full of enthusiasm, often tinged with a romantic's love of the unexpected. She sees her work as a "loving involvement with history" and made the following analogy in *Buying the Night Flight*:

To insert yourself lovingly into another culture means a very special kind of love affair. The director Robert Bolt has said, "The comparison between a love affair and the making of a film is not so exaggerated as it sounds. There is the same day and night preoccupation, the same switchback of elation and gloom, the same absurd intensity. A film-maker gives to his film the sort of anxious attention which is only properly bestowed upon a woman." It is the same being a foreign correspondent. Sitting alone sometimes in a cafe, I would be overcome by the mystery, by the joy, by the sense of watching or of being watched. I got a sensuous thrill out of the travel, the excitement, the observing and exploring. I have always felt sorry for people who couldn't love other peoples and other countries; I *adored* each new place. And the mysteries became ever more mysterious.

Georgie Anne Geyer has interviewed Fidel Castro several times. The following is a 1966 interview, characterized by her personal insights into the Cuban leader.

Our Girl's Talk with Dictator
'MENTIRA' ('LIE'), I SHOUTED at CASTRO

By GEORGIE ANNE GEYER

Chicago Daily News, September 6, 1966

When Fidel Castro eats grapes, the people around him say "delicious." When he shoots a bird with a submachinegun, they applaud.

But Castro is more than a fawned-upon leader. He's a man of ideas, and one who is compulsively anti-American.

Georgie Anne Geyer, The Daily News' Latin American correspondent, recently spent six weeks in Cuba during which she had four long talks with Castro.

In the following story—the first of a series—she gives an intimate picture of the man and his ideas.

BANAO, Cuba—The mysterious, contradictory man who is Fidel Castro strode restlessly back and forth in the old shed, eating grapes from deep-red bunches just plucked off the vine.

It was blazing-hot at midday in this valley in the rich agricultural center of Cuba. It had rained the previous night and around the shed were deep ruts of mud and water.

Occasionally Fidel, dressed in his usual immaculate fatigues, would say something about the grapes, like "delicious." Everybody would nod eagerly and agree: "Delicious."

It was here that I first sensed Castro's loneness and the isolation of so much power. He was the only one who talked, the only one who moved. Everyone else spoke or moved in response to him.

He finally roved outside, restlessly, picked up a Russian submachinegun and fired several bursts across the quiet valley. As the sound reverberated off the mountain, everyone applauded. Then he shot at some birds and one fell. Everyone applauded.

WHEN WE FINALLY sat down to eat—30 of us, most of them aides of Castro, who had just come down from visiting a teacher training school in the mountains—I was sitting directly across from him. We began to talk.

He took a bite of chicken and leaned across the table. "Would you be capable of joining a revolution?" he asked.

"Yes," I said, "but it would depend upon what kind of revolution and whether it were my country." I tried not to become involved in a personal conversation, but he persisted, just as all the Cubans I met in my six weeks there insisted on knowing my personal feelings.

"And don't you think that humanity comes before one's own country?" Castro went on. "If you had to choose between your family and humanity, which would you choose?"

It sounded like those unanswerable questions we used to ask each other in college and I brushed it aside.

"BUT YOU HAVE to belong to the good, don't you?" he continued. I nodded. "Do you believe in people dying of hunger, in children sick because there are no doctors?" I shook my head impatiently because, as he put it, not to agree with the Cuban revolution meant to agree with people dying of hunger.

I made some intemperate remark about the low caliber of Cuban journalism, which is pure propaganda, and Fidel agreed: "It is terrible, but it is because we do not have the people."

"You will never have the people," I said, "because if they're good you can't control them."

"There isn't one journalist in Cuba who could do what I'm doing. I come here and I can look objectively at what is happening. Could anyone from here go to the United States and write anything good about it?"

"Of course," he said with a tight sound in his voice and gesturing with his cigar, "We are not going to say anything favorable about the United States."

"And you would die for capitalism?" he was asking a few minutes later.

"I WOULD DIE," I answered, "for the liberties, for the freedom to speak, to question, to search, to publish, to demonstrate."

"You Americans are so rigid," he said. "There is always only one way, one truth."

This struck me forcibly, because it was what I had been thinking about the Cuban Communists. But then Fidel was saying, "What is your country? The United Fruit Co. Where is your democracy? A country ruled by millionaires!"

Here he mentioned the word "parliaments," and all the scorn and disgust that Fidel Castro can show so graphically came forth. "Parliaments!" he said, as though it were a filthy word.

I was angry, but I hit upon a new device. In his speeches about the United States, Castro often waves an arm and shouts. "Mentira, mentira," which means "Lie, lie."

So I leaned across the table, waved my right arm and shouted, "Mentira, mentira."

Luckily, Castro is a man with a good sense of humor and, I suspect, a desire for a little more spirit than he finds in his speechless, idolizing followers. He liked this. He laughed and chuckled, and now I took the offensive.

ONE THING is certainly typical of Castro—he brings every subject back to the compulsive Cuban anti-Americanism.

For three hours, our conversation wandered over many topics, as the others listened silently. Just before the end, we talked about "intervention," as what Latin American conversation would be complete without a few words on intervention?

Castro spoke of the Dominican Republic intervention and I spoke of his tricontinental conference on intervention. Castro's conference vows to support guerrillas in Latin America.

"Well, we have always said we would support wars of national liberation," he said finally. "And that is that."

"Why," I asked him, tongue-in-cheek, "don't you put me through your guerrilla school? I would like very much to learn to be a guerrilla."

"We aren't training any guerrillas," he said seriously. "Those are all lies."

"Come now," I said, "I've talked to students in Latin America who were trained here. (I had.) They told me all about it."

Castro grinned. "Of course, we have students here in the university studying all kinds of things, and if they learn shooting for the Olympics while they are here, what can we do about it?"

THE AFTERNOON was half gone by the time we left, the sun was sinking, the earth cooling. The jeeps jammed through the mud. Before he left, Castro came over to the car. "I don't want you to think that in any way we meant to be discourteous," he said. I said of course not, that I was delighted, and I was.

This was the fourth time I had a chance to talk at some length with Castro. Previously we had met at his beach house at Santa Maria del Mar, at the Havana Libre Hotel and at a mountain training school for teachers.

But even after our last meeting, the mystery of what kind of man Castro really is continued to disturb me. He comes across far different from his international image. Physically, of course, he is a big man, with powerful shoulders and a sportsman's delight in doing things, such as being able to stay underwater more than two minutes. (He can.)

IT IS PROBABLY his beard that gives foreigners the idea that he is sloppy, because he is actually extremely clean. His uniform always is pressed, and he apparently bathes several times a day since several times he left groups that I was in to shower.

In public speeches, he often uses gutter language, applied to the Americans and Chinese alike, or anyone who offends him at the moment.

But with me, he was gentlemanly, almost formal in an old-fashioned way. He said once, "Just because we talk of women's rights doesn't mean we give up the old courtesies."

IN OUR FIRST interview, he told me that Cuba was developing ice cream because the Cubans had always liked Howard Johnson's ice cream and they wanted to outdo them. When I wrote this for The Daily News and Howard Johnson's answered, saying they still had more flavors than Castro, Fidel literally shook with laughter.

"I am going to send them a bill for the publicity," he told me.

In his personal relationship with the Cuban people, with which his popularity is still extensive, Fidel's manner is like that of a father or an uncle.

I watched him one Sunday afternoon talking for three hours on the beach to a group of admirers about everything from sharks to ideology. He uses these informal meetings to get information from the people.

He did not promise them anything. Instead he said things like, "You have to realize there are priorities, that a child having a school or a person having enough to eat—that is not the same as having a bottle of cognac."

AT THE TEACHER training school at Topes de Collantes, his style was almost humble in speaking to the students.

"The thing I like least," he said, "is making speeches. I like to work in the greatest silence possible and with the least agitation. Above all, I like to visit the countryside and above all I like the mountains."

A great, soft "aaah" went up from the hypnotized students.

A few minutes later he mispronounced the word for "orphanage," then joked, "I hope they won't suspend me for that, or that my errors will serve as an excuse for yours."

Without understanding this personal side of Fidel Castro and the relationship he has with great numbers of the Cuban people, it is impossible to understand the Cuban reality. But there is the other Castro, the man of unlimited power, or—as one Western diplomat put it—"the one-man show."

THIS MAN who constantly roams about Cuba, never announcing where he is going, and well-protected when he does announce it, has more than absolute political power. He is using this power to change everything in Cuban life, from diet to social habits.

He is extremely interested in health. His only alcoholic drink is cognac. One evening at dinner I saw him putting bicarbonate of soda in his milk and asked him why.

"They say that milk gives people gas and that is why the Cubans don't drink it," he explained. "But if you put bicarbonate of soda in it, it is all right."

He reads constantly. In his car he always has at least 30 books on the back seat and more in the trunk. He concerns himself with every detail of everything in the country.

"If we tell him we have a medical problem, he starts reading medical books," Armando Acosta, Communist Party chief in Oriente Province, told me. "One factory prepared 50 questions and answers when Fidel was going to visit. He asked 160 questions, but none of the 50."

NOW, HOWEVER, the Communist Party apparatus is nearly formed, and the gigantic bureaucracy is beginning to grind away at every facet of Cuban life, leaving little breathing space. Some believe this will necessarily limit Castro's power. He himself is concerned about the dulling effects of the bureaucracy, and talks about it constantly.

As of now, the revolution is Fidel and Fidel is the revolution. As secretary-general of the party as well as prime minister, he holds absolute power.

When I asked Carlos Rafael Rodriguez, one of the old Communists considered the party theorist, whether Fidel has ever been overruled in high decision-making councils, he said:

"As far as I know—no. But there can be differences in opinions.

"In 90 per cent of the cases, Fidel's decisions are accepted and enriched and applied. Perhaps 10 per cent of the decisions are not accepted for reasons of applicability. But he always accepts the changes. This is not frequent."

BUT WHO is Fidel Castro?

He is, at times, an almost playful man who can lead a group of medical students up to Pico Turquino, the highest peak in Cuba, and then fly up hairdressers to do the girls' hair. On the same trip, foreign diplomats were flown by helicopters with packs on their backs. One Communist ambassador thought the pack was a parachute and that he would have to parachute out.

But he also is the man who controls a country where possibly as many as 80,000 persons are held as political prisoners, where justice is at the whim of those in control, where there are no controls except a final appeal to Fidel's wisdom.

He rules a country where abuse, venom and political and psychological destruction are heaped upon those who oppose or even doubt.

CASTRO IS A complex man. No one really "knows" him. But there are certain guidelines.

Castro is an absolutist. He is the Cuban Latin leader par excellence—physically powerful, brilliant with words, the "holder of absolute wisdom," the man who offers testimony rather than proof. Whereas the Anglo-Saxon accepts the limitations of man and therefore, imposes limitations on his power, Castro springs from the Iberian heritage that demands absolute truth committing everything in its name. (Castro's family has its origins in Galicia in Spain.)

Even scientifically trained Cubans accept the idea, common to many emotion-based mass movements, that "the leader and the people are one."

"In the square, there is a kind of dialog between him and the people," Dr. Claudio Palacios, an American-trained Cuban psychiatrist told me. "Oh, the people do not speak, but from time to time they applaud. And they find that the things he is saying are exactly what they are feeling."

But I could not get over the idea that Castro is often isolated and knows it.

AS TO LATIN AMERICA, he says he is the revolutionary leader. But I suspect he has doubts. The first time I met him, the first thing he said was, "They tell me you travel a great deal in Latin America and know a great deal about it." We talked about Chile, his ideological enemy that night, and privately he was far more moderate than he had been at lunch. Of the president of Colombia, whom he publicly reviles, he said, "Yes, he is a serious man."

When I told him I love the Andes of Peru and Bolivia, a far-away look came into his eyes. "How I would love to go there," he said. "But I would like to go as you go—anonymously."

But when he was giving a speech, it was different. Then the leaders of Chile were "prostitutes," the Colombian president was a reactionary. Then the Cuban revolution was the only revolution.

I suspect Castro knows what he could never admit and what, on the contrary, he must continue to deny—that the Cuban revolution has not become the model for Latin America. But he is now imprisoned in the gigantic myth he created.

And so, eight years after the Cuban revolution, Fidel Castro climbs in his jeep and everyone moves.

When Fidel smiles, everybody smiles. For only Fidel has the original motive power. Cars back up, people jump in, the motorcade falls into line.

And one wonders what the man in the first jeep really thinks.

23

Ellen Goodman
(1941–   )

E LLEN GOODMAN has been called many things: "the midwife of feelings," "the lay analyst of the mood of America," "one of the few journalistic chroniclers of the women's movement," and "the thinking woman's Erma Bombeck." Such appraisals stem from her twice-weekly columns, syndicated in 388 papers through the Washington Post Writers Group. "She writes about what is on people's minds," said *Boston Globe* editor Tom Winship, who started her as a columnist in 1971. Her saline aphorisms (e.g., "Losing privacy is a little like losing one's virginity. You can only do it once, and you can't get it back.") are passed along the party circuit, and she is frequently quoted as an authority on what is happening with women. On the relationship between business executives William Agee and Mary Cunningham when they worked together at the Bendix Corporation, she asked: "If women can sleep their way to the top, why aren't they there?"

Goodman can write about sterile zucchini one day and nuclear war the next. In her columns there is an abundance of wit, which is often missing in today's journalism. She resists being labeled, as she should, for she is neither a pundit nor a pontificator. She has created a special niche for herself in being able to write about everything, but always in terms of how it affects the private lives of her readers. Not surprisingly, the changing lifestyles of both men and women concern her most.

Many editorial-page editors who use her column say that Ellen Goodman draws a high reader response because of her talent for getting into issues without being overly sentimental. The young, the frustrated, the middle-aged, and the elderly all find comfort in her words. Women clip columns and mail them to friends in cities where the column doesn't appear. Even though her appeal is mostly to women, her position on the editorial or Op-Ed pages gives the column a significance it would not have on the lifestyle or women's pages where it started out.

Numerous local columnists mimic her approach, but no one yet has come close to matching her unique combination of non-strident commentary, humor, and moral values. "I want to make things important that the newspapers don't think that important," she said in defining her purpose. "These important subjects are the crises all women face, whether it's about food or home maintenance. The difference now is that such discussion has been elevated to the editorial pages."

In the introduction to *At Large* (1981), the second collection of her columns, she declared: "I worry about my weight and the bomb." That she so blithely embraces a range of topics is both a strength and a weakness of her writing. When she zeros in with wit, she can be very good indeed, but when she takes on too much in a limited 750 words, she can sometimes leave readers behind. Tamar Jacoby, reviewing *At Large* in the *New York Times*, noted: "She makes little effort to inform her readers. Indeed, she seems to make a virtue of being cranky and opinionated and rarely takes the trouble to test or probe or develop the often slight observations at the center of her columns." Molly Ivins, who reviewed her first collection, *Close to Home* (1979), pointed out: "Much of the difference [in the columns] is bound to be a matter of skill, but it is also possible that virtue is intrinsically less interesting than vice. Ellen Goodman on the joys of being a cheerful riser is not half as funny as Fran Lebowitz *[Metropolitan Life]* on the joys of sleeping late."

"It's more difficult writing this kind of column than a political column," Goodman admitted, "because you're always starting from ground zero and you're not 'covering' anything. The material comes from inside." Pontificating, she feels, is the worst thing a columnist can do. In a column on voter apathy, she chose not to preach on the responsibility to get out and vote, but instead focused on how it feels to get up an hour earlier and go out in the rain to cast a ballot.

A frequent response to her columns from other writers like James Reston of the *New York Times* is: "I wish I had written that." Still, there are many that she says are best forgotten. A hard grader, she admires Russell Baker of the *Times* for his consistent "B" columns. Goodman is seldom repetitive, however, and hasn't yet shown those early-warning signs of intellectual fallowness: columns built on trivia about what she saw on television or what her husband said at the breakfast table.

Each column is a fresh idea. "There are no evergreens in the filing cabinet," she said. Often, there are columns that come naturally from her experiences as a mother, as a divorcee, as a remarried woman, and her observations on working, partying, entertaining, gardening, and relaxing. Although she mines her personal experience, she seldom writes a "confessional" column such as the *New York Times'* lifestyle column "Hers." "There's a limit to what you share about your personal life," she said, adding, however, that she does try to create a persona in print, which she feels is necessary for rapport and credibility with readers. "As a writer, I've wanted to be seen as a person. Why should people believe what I have to say if they know nothing about me? I don't want to present myself as a disembodied voice of authority but as a woman, mother, vegetable gardener, failed jogger and expert on only one subject: the ambivalence of life."

Goodman was in her twenties during the height of the women's movement in the 1960s and feels that it had a profound effect on her personality, self-confidence, energy, and instincts. "The women's movement taught a lot of us that the personal is political and the political is personal," she said. "You can't deal with those things separately and make a whole lot of sense out of a life—and I think that is crucial to some of what I try to do. To draw the sense out of things."

Writing so that people hear themselves thinking, so that there is a coast-to-coast chorus of readers crying out, "This is what is happening to all of us," sounds deceptively easy when Goodman discussed her approaches and techniques. She has managed since the mid-1970s to tone down her anger and now can write for and about women without having to announce herself as a feminist. Molly Ivins wrote that if she could choose a voice for the women's movement she would "select Miss Goodman instantly over *Ms.* magazine and Germaine Greer."

Above all, Ellen Goodman has been the observer of change. She sees herself still changing, moving on, growing within and without the social trends and movements of the country. The difference between the shooting of President Ronald Reagan and the assassination of President John F. Kennedy in 1963, she wrote, was not that one died and the other survived, but that in 1963 the nation was stunned that such a thing could happen. "Back then, I did not believe what I read. But this time, when the news came into the city-room, I accepted it instantly. Indeed, the numbness of gruesome familiarity spread across the day." Her generation's youthful sense of possibilities coincided with Kennedy's call to get the country moving again, she noted. In 1979, however, at age thirty-eight, she wrote that her "choices no longer

Ellen Goodman

range from A to Z, but perhaps from A to E. This is not a complaint, just an observation. In mid-life most of us feel these limits. We don't squander our energy; we allot it with care. We call this maturing. The young call it aging."

There are few Goodman critics among the editorial-page editors who take her columns, but among woman journalists of her generation opinions can be tinged with envy. One generally admiring writer commented, "Ellen is much better now than when she started her column. But often she doth protest too much. Maybe readers outside of big cities don't have a credibility problem with some of her columns, but her personal struggles as a journalist, wife, mother or single parent have never been the struggles of the average person. Her life has been privileged, and it always will be."

It is true that Ellen Goodman, the muser on change, came to maturity with impressive credentials. By her fortieth birthday, she had earned a *cum laude* Radcliffe degree in 1963, a Nieman Fellowship (1974), and a Pulitzer Prize (1980). A tall (five foot eight) willowy honey blonde with blue-gray eyes, she is attractive not in the parts, but in the sum. There is a preciseness to her speech and a command of vocabulary appropriate to the topic. She can get a brittle edge to her voice, though, if she thinks she is being typecast as "pro" or "anti" anything. She is a third-generation Bostonian, and although change may have influenced other aspects of her life, she has maintained strong family ties. As she wrote in the introduction to her book *Turning Points* (1979), "I wanted to live in the same home, to go to the same school, keep the same friends . . . forever."

And to a great degree she has managed to do just that. She was born on April 11, 1941, in Newton, Massachusetts, and now lives just one-and-a-half miles away in Brookline, in a renovated nineteenth-century house with her daughter, Katie, and her second husband, Bob Levey, the *Globe*'s national editor. An aunt and uncle live next door, her older sister, Jane Holtz Kay, architecture critic for the *Christian Science Monitor,* also lives in the neighborhood, and her mother, Edith (Weinstein) Holtz, has her home in nearby Cambridge. The fact that she can live and work out of her hometown, rather than New York or Washington, has certainly influenced her perceptions. "I think it's good for papers to have columnists who live in their hometowns—it gives them an important web of associations that makes their writing specific rather than general," she said.

Goodman's mother was a traditional housewife, but was always supportive of her daughters' career goals. Her father, Jackson Jacob Holtz, who died in 1966, Goodman described as a "provocative, humorous man" who taught her how to debate and win an argument. Discussing politics and public issues was an important part of growing up in Brookline, where her father, a lawyer, was twice defeated in a Democratic bid for Congress.

Her high school years were spent at the Buckingham School in Cambridge, and then she followed her sister to Radcliffe, where she majored in history (a topic she still reads for relaxation). She had no real interest in journalism at college, and did not try out for a staff position on the *Crimson*, the school newspaper. She preferred to spend her free time performing in theater productions like *Damn Yankees, On the Town,* and *Guys and Dolls.* When her sister went to work for the *Quincy* (Mass.) *Patriot Ledger,* it was the first time Goodman thought seriously about journalism as a career choice.

After graduation, she married Anthony Goodman, who was completing his studies at Cornell Medical School in New York. Goodman got a $58.50-a-week job as a researcher in the television department of *Newsweek.* There is still bitterness in her voice when she speaks of how women were treated there. "Prejudice was so overt," she recalled. "Girls were researchers; men were reporters." Women have since broken that barrier at the newsweeklies, but back then, Goodman said, "it took a lot of maturity to be aware of the outrage you felt, and to learn to find a different way to be able to do what you wanted."

In 1965 she and her husband moved to the midwest where he did residency training at the University of Michigan. Goodman had published some freelance articles in the *Patriot Ledger* and with those clips she "walked in" to the *Detroit Free Press.* Managing editor Neil Shine, who was city editor at that time, recalled the meeting: "We usually didn't interview or hire walkins, but I said I'd talk with her, so we went to the coffee shop and I looked at her clips. She had really good stuff, with a fine sense of composition." She was hired as a general assignment reporter, but she had little patience with day-to-day hard news. "She was definitely a feature writer," said Shine.

Shine was sorry to lose his discovery after two years. He later joked that he wished her marriage had broken up in Michigan so he could have kept her on staff. By 1967 the Goodmans were back in Boston, and she had a job as a feature writer for the *Boston Globe*'s women's department. The next year, her only child, Katie, was born, and six weeks later Goodman was back at work. She was living a model existence for a 1960s woman—that is, until 1971 when her marriage ended and she started to examine more carefully her life and the lives of other women. In *Turning Points,* she wrote, "I went from high school to college to marriage to motherhood as if it were all a contract I'd signed. Through my twenties I defended the predictable life with security plans for the present and insurance programs for the future. I drew up more Five Year Plans than the Kremlin."

By 1974 she felt she needed some perspective on the changes she was experiencing, so she drafted a proposal for the study of social change in America and received a Nieman Fellowship at Harvard. Out of that year came the material for *Turning Points*, which was based on interviews with some 150 men and women from twenty to fifty years old. She wrote the book, she said, so that others could learn more about themselves, and in the process her columns became more "thoughtful and compassionate." Doris Grumbach, reviewing *Turning Points* in the *New York Times*, called it one of the many source books "from which the full social history of these revolutionary times will be written."

"It's a great feeling of satisfaction to tackle a problem and come out on the other side with it solved," Goodman said, referring to the writing of *Turning Points*. After her Harvard stint, she returned to the *Globe* and continued her problem-solving for the Living Pages. In 1971, the *Globe* had opened up the Op-Ed pages to in-house columns, and she published a few there, but she had remained a regular columnist in the feature section. Then, in 1975, her columns were brought to the attention of William B. Dickinson, general manager/editorial director of the Washington Post Writers Group. At that time, according to Dickinson, he had a policy of not syndicating any columns unless they were used by the *Post*. He brought Goodman's columns around to the lifestyle editor, who turned them down because they were already overloaded with columnists, and then to the editorial-page editor, who agreed to run a few and see what happened.

Women were not strangers to the editorial pages. Mary McGrory, for one, had been writing for years on politics, but Goodman was the first woman to write directly for and about women. As a result, she started to attract a new readership to the editorial page. In 1976 she was signed up for syndication with twenty-five papers. She stayed on the *Post*'s Op-Ed pages, but the *Globe* waited until 1978 to move her permanently to that spot from the Living Pages. By 1985 she was running in 388 papers, including every major urban outlet except New York. "We caught just the right moment with Ellen," said Dickinson. "At first the column sold by word of mouth. It was the kind of thing women would clip out and put on the refrigerator. Sure it was read by men, but it was taken to heart by women."

Goodman has done guest appearances on TV and radio but prefers writing. "Journalism is always work in progress," she said. "You're only as good as your next column." She calls herself a "picky" writer who is always reordering and nudging words around on her video display terminal. She has to write to space, which means a tight 75 lines on the VDT—and every word counts. After all her reporting and research is done and the idea formulated, it takes her about six hours to write and polish each column. The importance of words was underscored for her when she appeared for a while in

1979, along with George Will and others, on NBC's *Today* show. It amused her that people would write in and ask for transcripts of her commentary. "If I feel that my columns are wrapping the fish the next day," she once said, "imagine—in broadcasting, someone's got the water on in the bathroom!"

Outside of the office, Ellen Goodman lives the good life. She and her second husband, who has two grown children, had known each other for sixteen years as colleagues before they married. They enjoy growing and cooking food, with each one preparing a different course for dinner parties. She plays squash and collects old magazine covers. On weekends, they retreat to a Maine cottage, where Goodman relaxes by picking raspberries. In a 1983 column, she wrote: "I have a sense of well-being here that is rare in my urban world . . . There are times when it seems peculiar that we have to travel to special preserves—parks, islands, countrysides, bushes—just to recover a sense of belonging."

That's the contemplative columnist, but Goodman can also range to a high-squeal, as in a 1979 column on zucchini:

As a rule I resist sharing the details of my most intimate problems, especially the kinky ones, but we all have to break a rule now and then in the public interest and for the private therapeutic value of confession. Therefore, here goes:

My zucchini are sterile.

That is not a piece of graffito. It is a sad tale of infertility. Let me put it another way: I finally have to admit to lavishing time, money, attention and great expectations on four of the only all-male zucchini plants to exist in the memory of my county Agricultural Extension Service. Even though the nice man there told me not to take it personally, this is a toughy.

False pregnancy upon false pregnancy, a veritable plague is occurring in my garden even as we write. Large yellow fruitless (not to mention vegetableless) blossoms come and go in the Whip Inflation Now strip farm that eats fertilizer and brings in a crop at a rough cost of 25 cents per cherry tomato. This godless tenth-acre has broken the local record for nonproducing squash.

In previous years my crop runneth over. And over. And over. It was the sorcerer's apprentice of vegetables . . .

That's Ellen Goodman talking to people at her witty best, one reason why a *Los Angeles Times* editor called her "the thinking woman's Erma Bombeck." Goodman still resents this label being thrown at her, and when she first heard it she wrote a note to Bombeck saying, "You are 'the thinking woman's Erma Bombeck.' "

Columnists, she observed in the introduction to *Close to Home*, "need the egocentric confidence that your view of the world is important enough to be read. Then you need the pacing of a long-distance runner to write day after day, week after week, year after year. One journalist who dropped out of this endurance contest with a sigh of relief said that writing a column was like being married to a nymphomaniac: every time you think you're through, you have to start over again. This was an unenlightened, but fairly accurate, analogy." Nobody can say it better than Ellen Goodman.

Ellen Goodman's columns are as varied as her feelings, her views of life and trends, or today's news. Each touches readers differently. Her column on a Sixties kid, from the work that brought her a 1980 Pulitzer Prize for commentary, reveals the columnist as a muser on change. Her column on the New Bedford gang rape shows Goodman as a social and political commentator.

From a dropout of the Sixties
to a burnout in the Seventies

By ELLEN GOODMAN

The Boston Globe, January 23, 1979

She spied him right away as he jaywalked across Harvard Square. It was 26 degrees out and he was only wearing an old green army jacket and jeans. His shoes were soaked by the snow and his hands were stuffed into pockets instead of gloves.

That was Jack. He was thirty years old, six feet tall, skinny, scruffy, and he refused to dress for the weather. He looked like a boy who still had to be told to put on his boots. Perhaps he was afraid that if he wore a hat, he'd be mistaken as a serious applicant for adulthood.

She ran into him like this when he came into town occasionally to make some money or have his car fixed. Once or twice a year they ended up having coffee together.

The two had met briefly in the late sixties on some story about campus unrest. He was involved; she was reporting. At the time Jack had been a sophomore and she was already a mother. Then he dropped out—not only from college but from growing up—and the gap between their ages had widened.

Now it occurred to her, as they slid into the restaurant booth and ordered coffee, that somebody was always writing about the Sixties Kids. They wrote about the former radicals who were running things like government bureaucracies or businesses—the ones wearing ties and paying Social Security. They wrote about the ones who had moved to communes and stayed on to raise kids, who lived in country towns where the natives regarded them as neighbors now rather than hippies. But very few wrote about the burn-outs. Very few wrote about those who had suffered some psychic disease, a permanent loss of will. Like Jack.

Slowly, Jack told her about the past year. He talked as if he were reading a shopping list of events in no particular order of importance: His car was still working. He still had no furniture, no wife, and no children. He'd had a dog for a while, but no more. He was still painting houses for bread money— outside in the summer, inside in the winter.

Then, from the pockets of his green jacket, he emptied the more serious lint of his life. There was the quarterly letter from his parents pleading with him to go back to school. His unfinished childhood seemed to keep them in a state of painfully incomplete parenting. Behind the letter was a picture of the woman he had lived with last summer, and under that were some fuzzy directions to the house where he planned to spend the winter with friends. Only he couldn't remember whether the house was in Vermont or New Hampshire.

For some reason he irritated her. Thirty years old and he didn't know whether he was headed for Vermont or New Hampshire? States, statistics, plans, slipped through his mind as if through a sieve. She began badgering him. What were his goals now? "I'd like to keep my car running through the winter." Why are you still drifting? "I'm not drifting, I'm living my life."

The woman sipped her coffee. He wasn't the only Sixties Kid she knew. Others, like Jack, had lost the conviction that "it" made any difference; that "they" could make a difference. The distinctions between friends, ideals, politics, jobs, seemed no more important to them at this point than the choice of drinking black coffee or regular.

They did not seem to regard *anomie* as a disease of the spirit, but as a truth. They embraced their lack of purpose as if it were a benign response to a harsh world. They regarded struggle as foolish, differences as illusions. She knew this.

But suddenly she wanted to shake this Jack hard until something rattled out of him, a piece of engagement or anger. She wanted to squeeze his passivity out until it oozed through his damp shoes.

Why was she so mad? Because he had committed the sin of *accidie*—not becoming what he might have? Or because she felt in her gut that it was cowardly of him to quit in this way?

She had never been especially impressed by the heroics of the people convinced that they are about to change the world. She was more awed by the heroism of those who are willing to struggle to make one small difference after another. And he had attacked her heroes.

The two walked back out of the restaurant, onto the brick sidewalk. It had started snowing again. There were windchill factors being read on radios in the cars that drove by them. She wanted to say something important to Jack. As he turned to say goodbye, he stuffed his bare hands in his pockets, and she blurted out, "For Gawd's sakes, get some mittens!"

Horror Show in a Tavern

By ELLEN GOODMAN

The Boston Globe, March 17, 1983

It could have happened anywhere, I'm told. But this time it was in New Bedford.

It could have been any one of a hundred bars, a thousand bars scattered across the country, I'm told. But this time it was Big Dan's.

The facts by now may be familiar to you. At 10 P.M., on Sunday, March 6, a 21-year-old woman was held down on a pool table in Big Dan's and raped repeatedly by four men.

Of course, if the story were as routinely grisly as that, it would have barely made the local papers. It would have never made the network news or the list of causes.

But this rape occurred in the presence of at least a dozen other men, maybe 15 men, maybe 20. We are told that these men did nothing to help the woman. We are told that these men watched. These men cheered. For two and a half hours.

This idea of a cheering squad, a front-row spectator section, is what made this crime leap off the police blotter. The mental image of male voyeurs and the echo of their encouragements won't fade.

We have had to confront the idea that all the men in this bar regarded rape as a show—Sunday Night Live—an X-rated center-ring performance for the regulars. Maybe they even felt lucky to be there.

Over time, I know we have gotten used to the idea that bystanders can ignore a crime. In March 1964, in a Queens neighborhood in New York, 38 people heard Kitty Genovese screaming for a half-hour while she was being murdered, and not one called the police. They didn't want to get involved.

But in March of 1983, in a New Bedford bar, more than a dozen men watched a woman assaulted and not one of them called the police. Because it appears they were involved, enjoying the show. This, we are not used to. Not yet.

It is what sticks in the mind of any woman who reads this story. It is what makes her skin crawl. It is what made 3,000 women—women from the ladies' auxiliary of the Veterans of Foreign Wars and women from Women Against Pornography and women from college campuses—appear at a candlelight parade in New Bedford Monday night.

It is what made them carry placards that read: "Rape is Hate," "Rape is Violence," and "Rape is Not a Spectator Sport."

These men, rooting and approving rapists, forced us to experience gang rape, not as a grotesque brutal aberration but as an approved sexual event.

Inevitably it recalled the most extreme lines and most extreme emotions from Susan Brownmiller's book "Against Our Will": ". . . Men who commit rape have served in effect as frontline masculine shock troops, terrorist guerrillas in the longest sustained battle the world has ever known."

In the days since the rape—days during which four suspects were arrested, the bar was closed, and outrage was expressed by all the right people from Governor Dukakis to Gloria Steinem—we have learned that rape is a crime but there is no law likely to convict a cheering squad. The victim, Jane Doe, can file criminal charges against the rapists and a $10 million civil suit against the bar and bartender who did nothing to stop this assault.

But we have also watched people try to explain how such things could happen. They try to explain away the human horror by pushing it from people like us to "Men like that," "A woman like that."

Weren't the rapists from another country, another culture, I was asked? Isn't New Bedford an economically depressed place? Didn't the bartender try to get someone to call the police? Weren't some of the men perhaps afraid to intervene?

And what of the victim? What was she doing in that bar, anyway? Didn't someone say she knew the men? Inevitably, a spectator told a reporter, "She wanted it. She asked for it."

But it won't do to cubbyhole this crime away. In real life, rape is an ordinary event. In real life, even gang rape is not uncommon.

It occurs at the brutal outer edge of our world, but it is recognizably our world. There aren't that many steps to the ringside seats at Big Dan's. It is a thin line that separates audience from participant.

Few of these men would have watched while a victim was burned with cigarettes. Gang rape, in a New Bedford bar, a college campus, or a.Vietnam hamlet goes on only as long as rape is regarded as another team sport: Men performing for each other. And rape goes on as long as people, including judges and juries and barroom customers, regard this as just another sex act: Sunday Night Live in a bar in New Bedford.

24

Madeleine Blais
(1947–   )

WHILE MADELEINE BLAIS was a suburban correspondent for the *Boston Globe,* she covered the monthly selectmen meetings where proceedings were precise and often interminable. One evening when she returned to the newsroom to write up a story, she remarked to an editor how the bored selectmen consumed endless breath mints and digestive aids. "Is that all you found enthralling, young lady?" he demanded. "What about the vote?" At that point in her career, Blais recalled, "my problem was that I was always forgetting about the vote. It did not compel me. It was not a true unburdening."

Shortly after this rebuke she went to interview the teen-age hockey groupies who hang around Boston Garden, and asked one girl if her dedication to hockey had ever had any beneficial results. Had it, for example, helped her with her school work? "Her answer entranced me," Blais said. "She told me that she had been assigned an English composition on 'What I would most like to be,' and she wrote that she wanted to be hockey ice. I then asked the world's most elementary question: 'Why?' 'Because,' she replied, 'the players would skate on top of me and they would always think about me even when they were away.' I loved her answer: It was so simply, shamelessly amok. It was the beginning of an unburdening," Blais recalled. At that point she decided what she wanted from journalism.

Since then unburdenings have held a fascination for Madeleine Blais, and she has recorded, most recently for the *Miami Herald's Tropic* magazine, stories familiar from popular ballads, stories of love and death, which are told with the exhaustive detail peculiar to gossip. Her magazine articles often run 6,000 words, and she can spend three or four months reporting and writing one. There is a certain tabloid sensibility about her topics, which she usually chooses: the babysitter who kills her charges, the story of amnesia victim Jane Doe, people who struggle with mental illness or live each day with cancer. She sought out Tennessee Williams shortly after he was mugged, his home burglarized, and his gardener murdered.

Violent reality has always intrigued her. As a child growing up in a small Massachusetts town, she saw newspapers as "the true agents of reality." In newspapers, she recalled, "emotions were always running amok; only newspapers exposed the burdens of the heart." The language of newspapers was a wonderful code, with a special vocabulary that suggested the "steamy and forbidden." From the 1950s she still remembered that a woman who shot her husband was always "clad" in something flimsy, and terrible events were always "melees."

Colleagues point to Blais as someone who knew all along what she wanted from journalism, and that meant feature writing, which at age thirty-two earned her a Pulitzer Prize (1980). Issue stories she sees as a challenge and a responsibility, but admits that she has trouble with them, preferring "to begin with the human dilemma."

Her articles are notable for their special point of view. She can write about her wedding or her pregnancy, personal topics that have been tackled before and are often a big yawn, but she brings to her stories a universality that makes them readable and memorable. She likes to write about herself, to make her experiences part of the record, to live her life out in print. "Madeleine has a particular and unusual view of the world," said Megan Rosenfeld, a *Washington Post* reporter, with whom Blais shared an apartment in the 1970s. "She's a very practical person, but she has a strong affinity to the shadowy dark stories of life. She sees violence and danger lurking everywhere. She sees shadows where others don't." Rosenfeld maintained that it was no accident that Blais' Tennessee Williams story was so perceptive. "She really understood the strange world of the artist and his slightly skewed picture of reality."

Blais credits Florida, in part, for helping her build a reputation. "The foliage is so lush there," she said. "The stories seem to exist in the same kind of lushness, just waiting to be picked." More often than not she picks the stories that have weird twists to them, ones with the potential for an unburdening. Her writing style is rich: she has a novelist's eye and a love of words stemming from her Catholic schooling, which she described as "nuns, nuns,

nuns and Latin, Latin, Latin." "Sometimes my writing is very ornate," she explained, "but I try to anticipate the style and form and write plainly also." The structure of the Williams story, written as a one-act play in three scenes, suggested itself during the interviewing process when it occurred to her that the playwright was acting like one of his heroines.

Getting to Williams was initially hard. She went to his Key West home at the appointed interview time of 3 P.M., only to be informed by a guest that he was asleep and she should return in two hours. At that point, Blais said, she was panicked because she didn't know whether he would see her. But he did and the interviewing process continued over three days, including dinners out, seeing a play together, and all the while, Williams talking, talking. "He was on automatic pilot," she recalled. "It was really an easy interview, partly because he had not had that much attention paid to him recently by journalists."

The Williams profile, Blais said, is a good example of the unburdening of a life. Another one she enjoyed was on Private Edward Zepp, a World War I conscientious objector who decided to fight back years later to have his dishonorable discharge erased. This was her lead:

All his life Edward Zepp has wanted nothing so much as to go to the next world with a clean conscience. So on Sept. 11 the old man, carrying a borrowed briefcase filled with papers, boarded an Amtrak train in Deerfield Beach and headed north on the Silver Meteor to our nation's capital. As the porter showed him to his roomette, Ed Zepp kept saying, "I'm 83 years old. Eighty-three."

At 9 A.M. the next day, Zepp was to appear at the Pentagon for a hearing before the Board for Correction of Military Records. "This was," he said, "the supreme effort, the final fight" in the private battle of Private Zepp, Company D, 323rd Machine Gun Battalion, veteran of World War I, discharged on Nov. 9, 1919—with dishonor.

Something happens to people after a certain age, and the distinctions of youth disappear. The wrinkles conquer, like an army. In his old age, Zepp is bald. He wears fragile glasses. The shoulders are rounded. His pace is stooped and slow. It is hard, in a way, to remove 60 years, and picture him tall, lanky, a rebel.

In another story she described her mother, Maureen (Shea) Blais, as one who had "accumulated adages the way others acquire wrinkles or wealth." Her French-Canadian father, Raymond Joseph Blais, a dentist, died of cancer in 1952, leaving Blais at age five the eldest of five children, and his wife pregnant with a sixth. Born on August 25, 1947, in Holyoke, Massachusetts, Madeleine grew up in an 11-room house in Granby, Massachusetts, that had Currier and Ives prints on the wall, a red carpet on the staircase, a huge fieldstone fireplace, a linen closet large enough to hide in, and a five-acre yard.

Amid the serenity of New England, she went to church, crouched in the school cellar during Civil Defense drills, and read the newspapers. She and her siblings were cared for by "an exhausted phalanx of adults," she recalled, "relatives, nannies, nanas and hired help." That life she described as "ad hoc: the pattern was to meet one incontrovertible childish demand after another." A neighbor's child once tried to explain to her mother the absence of order in the Blais household: "They seem to be very nice people, but the toilets never work and they don't even have a pencil sharpener."

Always organized, however, were the children's scrapbooks, containing the art work, compositions and class photos of six children. Her mother, a teacher from a long line of women who had ruled classrooms, considered it her "ancestral mandate to honor language. She is Irish, from a heritage which has always, often tragically, emphasized talk over action," Blais said proudly. The preservation of Blais' words in a scrapbook let her know that she had something worth saying. "It is obvious now that the efforts themselves could hardly have been the point of the encouragement."

Her father's death created in her what she termed a "permanent distance from certain kinds of innocence. I was the outsider, at the primordial door, left out, excellent training for someone whose profession requires precisely that stance: always viewing, never on view, except in tidy print." Her mother decided that the children were too young to attend the funeral, and Blais now wonders whether this deprivation could be connected to her urge—so common to journalists—to "visit places where there is no true invitation, from coronations to back alleys." Moreover, she sometimes feels that her father's early death was responsible for what author Graham Greene called " 'the icicle at the heart of all writers,' a coldness at the center that steadies the knife while performing surgery on one's innermost thoughts: I lived, he didn't." That her childhood was rich despite this loss is clear from her desire to write so often of her own experience, to recreate the past as she did in her *Tropic* story on "The Last Christmas."

Following her mother's adage that "life does go on," Maddy, as she is often called, went through grammar school in Granby, then to Springfield, Massachusetts, for high school at Ursuline Academy, and to the College of New Rochelle, where she majored in Latin and English. By the time she was in college she knew that she had writing talent and, heeding her mother's advice that women should have something to fall back on, "not because they were superior, but because men weren't reliable and might konk out on you," she entered Columbia's Graduate School of Journalism in the class of 1970. It was a time of student unrest and change on the Columbia campus, and at the J-school students were demanding a voice in the educational process and calling for such changes as the return to a pass-fail grading system, which has prevailed for 16 years.

Madeleine Blais

At Columbia, professors noted her lack of enthusiasm for anything except writing, and she nearly flunked a newspaper workshop course because she ignored the production side. But her magazine writing instructor, Paul Brodeur of the *New Yorker*, praised her "style and imagination" and predicted a brilliant career. "I graduated with humility," she said, "but didn't get a job on the *New York Times*, which is what I thought you got after Columbia," she joked. For the next few years she taped interviews for a Boston radio show, free-lanced for underground papers like the *Phoenix*, was fired after five weeks at Hearst's *Record American*, and finally after many applications became a free-lance suburban reporter for the *Boston Globe*, a job that stressed accuracy but not writing. Impatient that the *Globe* would not take her on staff, she moved on—but not upward—to the Boston bureau of *Women's Wear Daily*.

If covering the selectmen's meetings was a bore, the *Women's Wear* job was, in Blais' words, "awful." She recalled it: "It was so out of character for me—some business and some fashion. It was all pretty light-weight. For instance, one day the phone rang, and a woman whose voice was truly filled with desperation wanted to know beyond a doubt what the top three colors would be for the fall." Looking back on this experience, Blais said, "I did a very undistinguished job and was fired in a somewhat genteel fashion."

She moved next to the *Trenton Times*, where she met her future husband and learned that people didn't have to be rich and famous to be interesting and worth writing about. It was 1974 and the *Washington Post* had bought the New Jersey paper in what Blais called a "first act of post-Watergate colonialism," with plans to take some of the New York market. That never happened, and the paper was sold in 1982 to the Allbritton Newspaper Group.

Joel Garreau, now with the *Washington Post's* "Outlook" section, was sent to Trenton to organize the back-of-the-book features. He recalled that "everything that was wrong with an American paper was wrong with the *Times*." But with the *Post* as new owner there was no lack of talent, and he sifted through 100 job applications a week. Interviewing Madeleine Blais, he read over her clips and picked out the hockey ice story. "It had flash and flair," he said, "just the kind of writing I wanted in my section." One of the new ideas Garreau introduced was called "Gazette," a kind of *New Yorker* "Talk of the Town" column for which Blais wrote "tone poems" on Polish women making sausages, the black debutante ball, Knights of Columbus activities, and other local events.

"What I learned very quickly," she said, "was that there were a lot of people with a lot of stories to tell who weren't part of the fashionable WW society and weren't part of the boring local politicians." Garreau recalled, too, that Blais was not only a marvelous writer but a gutsy, tenacious reporter,

and the paper awarded a weekly "Maddy Blais award for balls" to other reporters. "Maddy would always go where angels fear to tread," he said, rec-
ollecting an instance when she insisted on pursuing a story on a politician
and, even though she hated to fly, accompanied him on a trip to get the
information she needed.

Sally Lane of the *Trenton Times*, now a columnist, was an assistant managing editor and edited Blais' copy, which she said was often self-indulgent
in length. She added, though, that Blais could write "with a perception about
delicate social situations without offense to the people quoted."

"Maddy is a very complex person, more so than she appears," said Garreau, remembering that she had a verbal tic he had noticed before only in
Sally Quinn of the *Washington Post*. "In casual conversation, Maddy would
be trying out leads and kickers on you, writing in her head. It was very
strange."

After two years in Trenton, Blais decided to take a break and write a book,
They Say You Can't Have a Baby (1979). It was a topic that interested her,
but one that didn't personally apply. She and Megan Rosenfeld shared an
apartment in Washington, entertaining for the first time as single women,
wanting to have their own "salon," but being able to afford only pot-luck
suppers, which did have the elegance of matching wine glasses and starched
tablecloths. Rosenfeld, later a bridesmaid at Blais' wedding, said she has always admired her friend's sense of what was right for her as a journalist. She
said that the *Washington Post* considered hiring Blais, but didn't, and it was
probably the best thing that could have happened. "At the *Post* they would
have edited her copy and forced it into a mold," said Rosenfeld, "whereas
at *Tropic* they print what she writes."

During two years in Washington, she free-lanced, and the *Miami Herald's Tropic* magazine was a major outlet for her work. In 1980 she joined
the staff and one of her first stories was called "Notes of a Mature Bride."
On the *Tropic* cover of June 22, 1980, she beams from under a wide-brimmed
straw hat, fringy blond bangs dusting her eyebrows, emphasizing her most
dramatic feature: large, dark searching eyes. The story was about her own
marriage to John Katzenbach, journalist and son of former United States
attorney general Nicholas Katzenbach. Her husband, who had been working
at the *Miami News*, moved over to the *Herald* as a general assignment reporter, and when their son was born in 1981 they approached the paper with
a plan for job sharing: Blais would stay home with young Nicholas the first
six months, and her husband would switch from the cityroom to the magazine the next six months. At first, Blais said, she felt "a little bit like a social
experiment." She bought a word processor to work on at home, but after six
months she was "really energized about getting back."

Madeleine Blais sees herself someday as a *New Yorker* writer, and her husband, author of two books, *In the Heat of the Summer* and *First Born*, muses about being a writer in residence at some university. In 1984, Blais and Katzenbach taped a Public Broadcasting Service program on how reporters work. "I often get the feeling that I have appropriated the material," Blais said of the reporting process, "that I am somehow in charge of it, have made it part of myself, have become an expert. It's a different kind of satisfaction than covering a news event, and the one that I know I prefer."

This story on Tennessee Williams was among the articles that earned Madeleine Blais a Pulitzer Prize for feature writing in 1980. Williams died on February 25, 1983. The cause of death was listed as asphyxia resulting from an obstruction in the opening of the larynx; he had choked to death on a plastic bottle cap.

THREE SCENES FROM THE LIFE
OF A TORMENTED PLAYWRIGHT
At wit's end at land's end

By MADELEINE BLAIS

The Miami Herald, April 1, 1979

The scene: Tennessee Williams' house on Duncan Street in Key West, a small, simple, white-frame house with red shutters and a picket fence. The time is late February, day's end. The living room is dominated by books and art. Out back is a studio where Williams works every day, seven days a week, waking up about 5 in the morning and sometimes using a Bloody Mary, if need be, "to overcome the initial timidity." He has often said, "I work everywhere, but I work best here." Under a skylight, surrounded by empty wine bottles and paint-caked brushes, seated before a manual typewriter, he awaits sunrise and inspiration. On Key West, there is a great ethic of sunset, but the playwright stalks the dawn.

Williams is sitting on the patio adjoining the house. He has arisen late from an afternoon nap and his face is still puffy with sleep. In a few hours, he will attend the opening of one of his plays at a local theater. From where he sits, there is a view of the backyard, which is dominated by a swimming pool, strangled weeds and trampled plants. Williams glances with dismay at the untended growth snaking toward the pool.

"My gardener was shot, you know."

Tennessee Williams' life now on Key West in a way resembles the plot of one of his plays: an injured innocent in a honky tonk town pitted against unprovoked malice, deliberate cruelty. Since January, his gardener has been murdered, his house ransacked twice. He has been mugged twice on the street, once reported, once not. His dog has disappeared. One winter evening some kids stood outside his house and threw beer cans on the porch, yelling at America's greatest playwright, "Come on out, faggot." The only person home at the time was a houseguest, writer Dotson Rader, and when the kids set off some firecrackers, Rader remembers thinking: "This is it. They've resorted to guns."

Yet Williams has reacted with the resilliency of one of his heroines, dismissing it all as "ridiculous." He uses the same cliche to explain it away as does the Key West Police Department: "There is violence everywhere." What has happened is enough to "shatter faith in essential human goodness," as Williams himself once put it, but he has insisted on a brave front, as if through "enduring the devil, he will earn, if nothing else, its respect." After the first reported mugging on Duval Street, he told the local newspaper: "I've been here since '49, longer than they have. I'll be back." He joked about the incident, as though through humor he can defeat it: "Maybe they weren't punks at all, but instead New York drama critics." "The mugging," said Williams, sounding almost jealous, "received better and more extensive publicity than anything I ever wrote."

Williams may sound cavalier, but the problems on Key West are of increasing concern to natives and tourists alike. For years the island has had a substantial gay population, and there has always been a certain amount of hot, tropical tension between the gays, rich tourists, leftover hippies, local teenagers, the drifters and the druggies. In the winter the population jumps from 32,000 to 45,000. The visitors range from rich Northerners who arrive by private jet and pay $125 a night for a suite at the newly renovated Casa Marina on South Beach to homeless men arriving by Greyhound from Miami with cardboard cartons as luggage, or, sometimes, green garbage bags. In season, there are 400 robberies a month in Key West. This year, the frequency of attacks on gays has accelerated, and as a result Police Chief Winston "Jimmy" James has dispatched a squad of men to Duval Street late each evening, rounding up the transients on charges such as sleeping in the street, possession of illegal drugs, failure to wear a shirt in public. Still, the attacks continue, and by midnight it is no longer safe to walk the Old Town area.

Chief James says the troubles began in 1912 "when they put in the railroad and we got deprived of being an island."

Dick Chapman, managing editor of the Key West Citizen, believes "winter's got a lot to do with it."

Mayor Charles "Sonny" McCoy says there used to be problems "between the sailors and teenagers after World War II. Now it's gays and teenagers."

It is not as if Williams alone has been singled out for attack. But as the island's most prominent artist in winter residence and most prominent homosexual, the attacks against him are symbolic of something gone terribly awry in this otherwise peaceful fishing village: life is no longer a breeze anywhere, even in the Florida Keys.

Tennessee Williams at age 68 is not in repose on Key West, island paradise at the southernmost tip of this country, the place where the United States runs out of East Coast, known as The Last Resort. Williams has been on

the road ever since, as a young man, he quit his job at the same shoe warehouse where his father was employed (Red Goose shoes, Buster Brown's chief
competitor). He has been a stranger passing through the world's most glit-
tering places. Yet when a New Orleans cardiologist advised him to retire to
Key West and live like an old crocodile 30 years ago, Williams bought his
house on Duncan Street and despite his gypsy nature, it has served as home
base ever since. This season he no longer walks alone on the island at night.
He dismisses it as merely "unfortunate," and says it will pass in a year or
two.

On January 5, Frankie Fontis, a 49-year-old landscape architect, was gunned
down. The curator of the Key West Railroad Museum, Fontis, for almost a
decade, had been Williams' gardener and the caretaker of his property
whenever the playwright was out of town. The police officer dispatched to
the scene of the murder filed this report:

"I walked inside the door and observed the victim, naked [except for a pair
of white socks]. Victim was lying on his back just inside the doorway, a small
hole above right ear, and another small hole below left side of neck. A large
amount of blood was coming out of the victim's nose, also victim was lying
in a large pool of blood which was partially coagulated. Upon checking victim's pulse and breathing I found he was already dead."

Three weeks later, on January 28, Williams and Rader were walking down
Duval Street at one in the morning, a little high, singing hymns:

> He walks with me
> And He talks with me,
> And He tells me I am his own.

From the Key West police blotter, 1/28/79: "Mr. Williams and friend,
Mr. Dotson Rader were accosted by four or five white males in the 500 block
of Duval Street. The attackers advised they knew who Mr. Williams was. At
this point the attackers punched Mr. Dotson Rader in the jaw. Mr. Williams advised that he was thrown on the ground. Mr. Dotson Rader and
Mr. Williams were then kicked at by the attackers. I could not see any evident injury to Mr. Rader or Mr. Williams. Neither wanted to get any medical treatment. The only description available was that the attackers were between the ages of 18 and 25, two had beards and the one who struck Mr.
Rader was blonde-headed, had a darker beard, and wore a turtleneck sweater.
Mr. Williams and Mr. Rader took a cab and went to Mr. Williams' house."

One of the attackers told the playwright: "We know who you are." Does
Williams think the muggers were the same people responsible for the Fontis
murder? "Oh, no," says Williams, "They were just punks. It happened quickly.
There was no injury sustained. A lens fell out of my glasses. The publicity
is ridiculous." Nevertheless, doesn't it bother him? "Of course not."

Why not? He seems surprised by the question, and his answer is delivered regally, in his best Southern drawl, cadenced, liquid, honeyed. "Because, baby, I don't allow it to."

The effect is eerie. Throughout Williams' work there has been one underlying definition of gallantry: "the grace with which one survives appalling experiences." It is remarkable: Williams in his life is imitating his own art.

The playwright steps across the patio through the doors leading to the living room. It is 6 P.M. on opening night. *Suddenly, Last Summer,* one of Williams' more violent plays, will be presented, the second production of the Tennessee Williams Repertory Company's inaugural season. *The Glass Menagerie* opened on January 30. Williams did not attend; he had left town.

He pours a glass of Gallo red wine into a plain kitchen glass. "When they ransacked the house, for some reason, they broke all the wine glasses." It is unclear which burglary he is talking about, the one that occurred January 8 when both Williams' and Fontis' house was broken into and torn apart or the one that occurred at Williams' place about a week later. From the police blotter, 1/14/79: "Entry was gained by tearing a screen and breaking a side window. The entire house was ransacked."

Williams sits on the couch, nursing the wine, waiting for the 6:30 news, a ritual which daily prompts him to wonder whether the planet can make it through 1979 without another world war. Williams at 68 is almost an old man, yet his face retains an atmosphere of lush, full-featured alertness, especially in profile. He calls himself the "most promising playwright on Key West" and he cringes whenever anyone refers to him as the world's greatest living playwright. "I don't like that phrase. It has a way, don't you think, of implying the opposite."

He is gracious, instinctively courtly, even when he is in a bad mood, as he is on this evening. He admits to "always being crazy on opening nights." But that may not be the reason he missed the opening of *The Glass Menagerie.* The rumor among the repertory troupe was that he was afraid his appearance might cause commotion, even violence. There was talk in some circles that he was going to sell his house and move away from Key West. But rumor on Key West is said to grow like a jungle fungus, and Williams dismisses this speculation as so much fungus.

"I am not in the habit of retreat." There is a long silence. "The fact is, I had been planning to be out of town anyway and I don't much care to see *The Glass Menagerie* anymore." Another thoughtful pause: "It reminds me rather painfully of my mother."

He holds the glass of wine in front of him, examining the blood red in the muted twilight. "She never understood how much of her was Amanda," he says, almost to himself, referring to the domineering mother of *The Glass*

Menagerie. Amanda is a woman of false airs and true spirit who insists on arranging for a gentleman caller for her painfully shy daughter, Laura, a character based on Williams' sister, Rose. Tom, Laura's brother, a secret poet known as "Shakespeare" at the warehouse where he works, is forced by his mother to provide a suitable caller.

"My mother is 94 years old," says Williams. "Longevity is a family disease." He punctuates this statement, nervously, with a "little breathless laugh," reminiscent of Alma, the spinster in *Summer and Smoke*.

Williams is joined for the evening news by his two houseguests, writer Richard Zoerink and Rader. The two young men fulfill many roles: sons, valets, chauffeurs, audience, companions. After the news, Williams disappears into his bedroom off the living room to dress for the theater. Dotson Rader talks about the recent fear and loathing:

"It has been terrible, Tenn won't talk about it, but it has been really frightening what's happening in Key West, and what's happening in this house. The worst was the night they stood outside the front porch throwing beer cans and shouting, 'Come on out, faggot.' When they set off the firecrackers, I remember thinking, 'God, this is it. We're under attack; they've started shooting.' I refuse to go out alone at night. I don't need to have my head bashed in with a lead pipe on Duval Street.

"When they broke into the house, they were obviously looking for something. The screens on the windows were slashed, and things were stolen, weird things that don't make any sense: lawn chairs, the toaster. Wine glasses were broken and the rose bushes out back trampled. I am more frightened here than I am in New York. I lock the door of my bedroom at night and I've already decided that if they come back again, I'll jump out the window. They slashed the screens. Go look: it's upstairs.

"The police don't have the manpower to protect Williams as they should. I have been with celebrities doing stories in small towns all over the United States. In most small towns, they realize that if a famous person is hurt there, there are worldwide repercussions: your town gets known as the place where so and so was hurt."

Rader is not sure why Williams has been singled out for attack but he has three theories. "These people are anti-gay, despite the substantial gay population on Key West. They are xenophobes: they don't like strangers, and no matter how many years Williams has been here, the natives don't really accept him. And they hate celebrity, fame.

"Tennessee Williams is one of the great tourist attractions in Key West. You would think the county or city would see that he is comfortable here, safe here, can work here."

Why, in the face of all this violence, has Williams affected an air of unconcern, like Blanche Dubois in A *Streetcar Named Desire,* calculatedly blinding himself to the unpleasantness?

"Oh, he won't say anything. He has to live here. This is, for better or for worse his home."

Williams returns to the living room, dressed for the theater, worried about a hole in his shirt: "Oh well, the shirt is clean, anyway. It's a good idea to look poor. Otherwise you have too many indigent people on your trail."

Williams applies the final sartorial touch before his night on the town: a black Greek sailor's cap of which he is extremely fond. "It makes me look like a mean son of a bitch, don't you think," he says to no one in particular. It doesn't: the cap is festive, nautical, jaunty.

Thus suited, Williams leaves the house with Richard, who drives him to dinner at the Rose Tattoo, a restaurant named in honor of one of his plays. After dinner, Williams walks down Duval Street, past Smokey Joe's with its big lettering: "Hemingway's favorite bar."

Williams points out the Hotel La Concha, where he wrote what is widely considered his best play, A *Streetcar Named Desire.* Key West's greatest tourist attraction is recognized by the polite, early evening crowd of tourists on Duval. Williams refrains from the singing of hymns. Richard asks whether the cast is aware he will be in the audience this evening.

"I hope so, baby," Williams says, sounding cantankerous. He draws a deep breath. "Maybe it will make them act better."

The verandah of a large tourist hotel, later the same evening. Royal palms move with the soft, hot breeze, and an older man, wearing a Greek sailor's cap, sipping piña coladas, is surrounded by young people like a patriarch. They are toasting him with champagne and the music of their laughter. It is the cast party for *Suddenly, Last Summer* and the author is ebullient: Tennessee Williams loved the production, thought it was wonderful, the acting just marvelous. As a gift to the troupe, he offers to sing the hymn that caused so much commotion on Duval Street a few weeks earlier.

The autobiographical nature of the play sets off a stream of reminiscences in the playwright. As in much of Williams' work, the theme of *Suddenly, Last Summer* is incest, this time about a young girl who has just returned from a trip to Europe where she was used by her male cousin as a pawn, procuring young boys as his sexual partners. Eventually, he is destroyed, devoured, cannibalized by a band of berserk urchins. The girl's aunt, Mrs. Venable, wants Catherine put away, punished, lobotomized when she persists in recounting the sordid story of the summer. Mrs. Venable, to a doctor from the local asylum: "Cut this hideous story out of her brain."

Williams speaks with compelling intimacy, alternately referring to the young woman as Catherine and "Miss Rose," his sister, who underwent one of the first lobotomies in the nation. In 1934, an operation to remove a portion of the brain was considered fashionable, almost chic: the latest in putting the deranged out of their misery. This is the central sorrow of Williams' life and for years he has paid her bills at the New York sanitarium where she is confined. In his *Memoirs*, the playwright wrote that taking care of Miss Rose was "probably the best thing I have done with my life besides a few bits of work."

An important thing to know about Williams is that he has two families, this one—the cast, his admiring public—and the one he was born into in Columbus, Miss., the family that moved to St. Louis when he was 8 years old: mother (ill), father (dead), sister Rose (institutionalized), brother Dakin (lawyer in Illinois). It is this second family which dominates his art, and when he is in an expansive mood, his conversation.

Sitting at a large round table on the deck of the Pier House, Williams is besieged by autograph seekers. At one point, a middle-aged woman of substantial girth stands a few feet from the table, theater program in hand, trying to work up the nerve ("You never know whether it pleases a famous person or it turns them off.") to ask him for an autograph. "Well, here's "E" for effort," she says, barging ahead. When she bends over to hand him the program, a wooden pendant she is wearing crashes into his face.

"Oh, excuse me! My husband made that," she says. "He's 82 years old." The woman begins to talk about her husband, but Williams cuts her off. "My mother is 94," he says. The woman looks abashed. "She's dying, you know." The autograph seeker now has the wide-eyed look of somebody who has been told more than she wants to know. "She thinks there is a horse in her living room." The woman flees. Williams keeps talking:

"I used to be kind, gentle. Now I hear terrible things and I don't care. Oh, objectively I care, but I can't feel anything. Here's a story. I was in California recently and a friend of mine had a stroke. He is paralyzed on the right side and he has brain cancer. Someone asked me how he was doing and I explained all this and the person said, 'But otherwise is he all right?' I said, 'What do you want? A coroner's report?' I never used to react harshly, but I feel continually assaulted by tragedy. I cannot go past the fact of the tragedy; I cannot comprehend these things emotionally. I can't understand my friend who is sick in California and who loved life so much he is willing to live it on any terms.

"Sometimes I dream about getting away from things, recovering myself from the continual shocks. People are dying all around you and I feel almost anesthetized, feel like a zombie. I fear an induration of the heart and the heart is, after all, part of your instrument as a writer. If your heart fails you, you begin to write cynically, harshly. I would like to get away to some quiet place with some nice person and recover my goodness. I cannot, for instance, feel anything about my mother. I dream about her, but I can't feel anything. All my dreams concern earlier parts of my life. The other night I dreamt my father told me I could go on the road selling shoes. Back then that's what I wanted to do: go on the road. We remain children in our unconscious. I am happy my mother dreams there is a horse in her living room. Her father would never let her ride a horse, so it is a happy dream. I won't answer the phone on Key West. Every time it rings I am sure it is somebody telling me my mother is dead. I won't answer it myself.

"Right now, my brother Dakin lives near her and checks in on her. My brother gave her a copy of the *Memoirs*. He neen't have, you know." Williams discussed his homosexuality in his autobiography, but the potentially disturbing memoirs didn't bother his mother, "because she thought I'd made them up." Again, the nervous little laugh. "Still it was insensitive of him. He was my father's favorite, but he isn't like anyone else in the family. We've often wondered about that. He keeps running for public offices he can't win. He has threatened to change his name to Illinois Williams. Rather a bad idea, don't you think?

"I would like to invite my sister Rose down to Key West for a visit. I was in psychoanalysis once for about nine months, and the psychiatrist told me to quit writing and to break up with someone. I did neither. But the one thing that analysis showed me was that my father was a victim, too, and mother was the strong one. She is the one who approved the lobotomy. My sister had been away at a school for girls, All Saints School, and when she came home she talked about how the girls stole candles from the chapel and committed self-abuse. My mother wanted her to stop saying all those terrible things, just like Mrs. Venable, the aunt in *Suddenly, Last Summer*. My mother wanted this hideous story cut from her brain. My mother was so puritanical. I was away from home at the time of the lobotomy; I never would have permitted it. I never thought it was right. Mother could not bear the idea of anything sexual. Everytime she had sexual intercourse with my father she would scream. Rose and I would hear her and we would run out of the house, screaming, off to a neighbor's. My mother had three children, so I imagine she was raped rather frequently."

At midnight, Williams and Richard are the first to leave the party, the better for the playwright to greet the next sunrise. As they walk to the parking lot, they realize, suddenly, that a young man is following them. He opens his jacket, revealing a shining gun strapped to his chest and announces: "I'm security, from the Pier House." Williams would later joke that he was more frightened of this guard than the mean streets, but to the armed stranger he says, "We can take care of ourselves, baby."

Noon, the following day. The world's greatest not-yet-dead playwright has survived to greet another dawn: "Mornings," he once wrote. "I love them so much. . . . Their great triumph over night." He is dressed informally, wearing only a bathrobe, having just left his studio where he is working on a play, *Clothes for a Summer Hotel,* about Scott and Zelda Fitzgerald. He has celebrated his session at the typewriter with a swim in his pool. Ordinarily, Williams moves like an old lion, full of slow ceremony. But twice a day he does spirited laps back and forth for 20 minutes, displaying the vitality of a man much younger.

This is to be a session of photographs and the playwright very carefully composes the setting. He arranges himself in his bedroom, next to what he calls "the shrine." Above him on the wall is a portrait Williams painted of his long-time lover, Frank Merlo, who died in the early 60s, heralding for Williams a period of depression that lasted seven years: his own grim battle with the "unlighted side" of his nature. Once, in describing this interval of drugs, booze, insomnia and conversion to Catholicism, since abandoned, he told Gore Vidal, "I slept through the 60s." Vidal responded, "You didn't miss anything."

The shrine honors Miss Rose. There is a tall structure, like a dripping candelabra, an Indian symbol called the tree of life. There are votive candles and, when the rose bushes are in bloom, freshly cut flowers. In the center, is a Madonna, veiled to convey spirituality. It is like the shrine in *The Rose Tattoo* which the author says should not "inspire ridicule, but rather respect for the religious yearning" it represents. There is a small booklet that says "St. Jude's Shrine."

Why a shrine named for the patron saint of lost causes? "Well," Williams says, "what could be more of a lost cause than someone who has had a lobotomy?" He set the shrine in 1970. "I think at that time I had a greater appreciation of Miss Rose's tragedy. I was just out of the bin myself."

Is it true his mother and his sister are the only pure women he has ever met? "Oh, no. My grandmother, too. It shocks me when women are coarse. Women should preserve grace and femininity. Those are the things that attract me to women. Of course, a woman has to let it down during moments of desire in private; she can't always be the reserved lady. I proposed marriage twice in my life, once to a childhood sweetheart and once to a nymphomaniac. I am so glad I didn't get married. I would have no freedom, saddled with a family. Now I have nothing to tie me down, nothing except my sister Rose."

He changes the subject, pointing to the painting of Frank Merlo: "I had many more friends on Key West when he was alive. He was very popular. They say he could have been mayor of Key West. I've often wondered, if I concentrated on it, if I could become a great painter. I trained myself as a writer, in a way, learning stagecraft. But I never had any training as a painter. It comes from the same creative impulse. Sometimes I think of retiring to the Hotel de Cap on Cap D'Antibes in the south of France. It is the most beautiful place I have ever been. I imagine setting an easel out there on the lawn. Monet painted well into his 80's, you know. I'd like to live until I am 75 unless I learn to paint very well. It's ridiculous to deny that the creative powers don't ebb with age, and I don't delude myself that I will surpass my earlier writing because I don't think that's in the cards."

Are these thoughts of death, this desire to get away, a reaction to the troubles on Key West? "Oh, no. It really doesn't concern me. I do sleep with the door to my room locked at night. But there is violence everywhere. I was mugged once in New York City on my way back to my hotel on Madison and 54th. A drunk black suddenly appeared alongside me and grabbed my right arm, saying, 'Give me your wallet.' I said I would as soon as he freed my arm so I could get it. He let go and I seized the moment to rush away from him. I'm lucky, you see."

How does he feel about the band of urchins yelling obscenities on his front porch? "Kids amuse themselves that way, you know."

What about Fontis? Isn't he worried the same people who murdered the gardener are after him? "It's peculiar the way they ransacked the two houses on the same night. They were obviously looking for something. Dope, probably. At least that was the first theory. I don't think there have been any alternative theories. The police called earlier today and told me that they had just opened the safe at the museum (the Railroad Museum where Fontis was curator) and found a stack of manuscripts this high." His gesture is as big as the tree of life. "He was a peculiar man. I guess he supposed the manuscripts would be worth a great deal some day and that he would outlive me." Alma's laugh. "He'd been systematically stealing papers over the course of the nine years he took care of my house. I never noticed any of them missing. It's very difficult to find somebody to occupy your house. He could be so freakish. He was a great, tall man, very burly, and I remember one day I heard a terrible shriek in the garden, somebody wailing, 'I am a sick woman.' I called an ambulance, but the next time he started shouting like that, I didn't call one."

And again, perhaps to himself, Williams says, "I am not in the habit of retreat."

From *The Night of the Iguana:* "When the Mexican painter Siqueiros did his portrait of the American poet Hart Crane, he had to paint him with his eyes closed because he couldn't paint him with his eyes open—there was too much suffering in them and he couldn't paint it."

Tennessee Williams has fallen silent. Wearing only the robe, seated next to the shrine and the portrait of his dead lover who stares straight ahead, there is a nakedness about the playwright, except for one detail. He is wearing sunglasses in the dim room, as if, to reveal his eyes, particularly in the final scene, is to reveal too much, to demand too little of his audience. Still silent, the playwright studies the shrine.

Miss Rose has been punished for her madness, diagnosed as lunacy. He has been honored for his, recognized as genius. Has he escaped?

"Oh, no," he says in that cadenced voice, "I have been punished, too, by her punishment, and by difficulties of my own."

BIBLIOGRAPHY

GENERAL

Beasley, Maurine and Sheila Gibbons. *Women in Media: A Documentary Source Book*. Washington, D.C.: Women's Institute for Freedom of the Press, 1977; second printing, 1979.

Bessie, Simon Michael. *Jazz Journalism: The Story of the Tabloid Newspaper*. New York: Dutton, 1938.

Churchill, Allen. *Park Row*. New York: Rinehart, 1958.

Collins, Jean E. *She Was There*. New York: Julian Messner, 1980.

Drewry, John E., ed. *More Post Biographies*. Athens: University of Georgia Press, 1947.

Emery, Edwin and Michael Emery. *The Press and America: An Interpretative History of the Mass Media*. Fourth Edition. Englewood Cliffs, N.J.: Prentice-Hall, 1978.

Gauvreau, Emile. *Hot News*. New York: Macaulay, 1931.

Green, Carol Hurd and Ilene Kantrov, Barbara Sicherman, Harriette Walker, eds. *Notable American Women, the Modern Period: A Biographical Dictionary*. Cambridge, Mass.: Belknap Press of Harvard University Press, 1980.

Hohenberg, John. *Foreign Correspondence: The Great Reporters and Their Times*. New York and London: Columbia University Press, 1964.

—— *The Pulitzer Prizes*. New York and London: Columbia University Press, 1974.

Hohenberg, John, ed. *The Pulitzer Prize Story*. New York: Columbia University Press, 1959.

Hughes, Helen MacGill. *News and The Human Interest Story*. New York: Greenwood Press, 1968.

James, Edward T., ed. *Notable American Women, 1607–1950: A Biographical Dictionary*. 3 vols. Cambridge, Mass: Belknap Press of Harvard University Press, 1971.

Marzolf, Marion. *Up From the Footnote: A History of Women Journalists*. New York: Hastings House, 1977.

Ross, Ishbel. *Ladies of the Press: The Story of Women in Journalism by an Insider*. New York: Harper, 1936.

Schilpp, Madelon Golden and Sharon M. Murphy. *Great Women of the Press*. Carbondale and Edwardsville, Ill.: Southern Illinois University Press, 1983.

Snyder, Louis L. and Richard B. Morris, eds. *A Treasury of Great Reporting*. New York: Simon and Schuster, 1962.

Spensley, Sarah Amelia. "Pioneer Women Newspaper Writers in the United States." Bachelor of Arts thesis, University of Wisconsin, 1918.

Stein, M. L. *Under Fire: The Story of American War Correspondents.* New York: Julian Messner, 1968.
Walker, Stanley. *City Editor.* New York: Frederick A. Stokes, 1934.
Willard, Frances E. and Mary A. Livermore. *A Woman of the Century.* Buffalo, N.Y.: Moulton, 1893.

MARGARET FULLER

Anthony, Katherine. *Margaret Fuller, a Psychological Biography.* New York: Harcourt, Brace & Howe, 1920.
Bell, Margaret. *Margaret Fuller.* Introduction by Mrs. Franklin D. Roosevelt. New York: Boni, 1930.
Brown, Arthur W. *Margaret Fuller.* New York: Twayne, 1964.
Chevigny, Bell Gale. *The Woman and the Myth: Margaret Fuller's Life and Writings.* Old Westbury, N.Y.: Feminist Press, 1977.
Deiss, Joseph Jay. *The Roman Years of Margaret Fuller.* New York: Crowell, 1969.
Emerson, Ralph Waldo and Forbes Waldo Emerson. *Journals of Ralph Waldo Emerson.* Boston: Houghton Mifflin, 1910.
Emerson, R. W., W. H. Channing, and J. F. Clarke. *Memoirs of Margaret Fuller.* Boston: Roberts, 1884.
Greeley, Horace. *Recollections of a Busy Life.* New York: Arno, 1868; reprinted, 1970.
Howe, Julia Ward. *Margaret Fuller (Marchesa Ossoli).* Boston: Roberts, 1883.
Hudspeth, Robert N., ed. *The Letters of Margaret Fuller.* Ithaca, N.Y.: Cornell University Press, 1983.
Madison, Charles A. *Critics and Crusaders.* New York: Henry Holt, 1947.
Miller, Perry, ed. *Margaret Fuller: American Romantic.* Garden City, N.Y.: Doubleday, 1963.
Ossoli, Sarah Margaret (Fuller). *Summer on the Lakes, in 1843.* Boston: C. C. Little and James Brown, 1844.
—— *Woman in the Nineteenth Century.* New York: Tribune Press, 1845.
—— *Papers on Literature and Art.* New York: Wiley and Putnam, 1846.
—— *At Home and Abroad.* Arthur B. Fuller, ed. Boston: Crosby, Nichols, 1856.
—— *Life Without and Life Within.* Boston: Brown, Taggard and Chase, 1859.
—— *Love-Letters of Margaret Fuller, 1845–1846.* Introduction by Julia Ward Howe. New York: Appleton, 1903.
Wade, Mason. *Margaret Fuller, Whetstone of Genius.* New York: Viking, 1940.
Wade, Mason, ed. *The Writings of Margaret Fuller.* New York: Viking, 1941.

JANE GREY SWISSHELM

Larsen, Arthur J., ed. *Crusader and Feminist.* St. Paul: Minnesota Historical Society, 1934.
Swisshelm, Jane Grey. *Letters to Country Girls.* New York: Riker, 1853.
—— *Half a Century.* Chicago: Jansen, McClurg, 1880.
Thorp, Margaret Farrand. *Female Persuasion: Six Strong-Minded Women.* New Haven: Yale University Press, 1949.
Tyler, Alice. *Freedom's Ferment.* New York: Harper and Row, 1944.
Woodward, Helen Beal. *The Bold Women.* New York: Farrar, Straus and Young, 1953.

JANE CUNNINGHAM CROLY
"JENNIE JUNE"

Croly, Jane C. *Jennie Juneiana: Talks on Women's Topics.* Boston: Lee and Shepard, 1864.
—— *History of the Women's Club Movement in America.* New York: Allen, 1898.
Irwin, Inez Haynes. *Angels and Amazons.* New York: Doubleday, Doran, 1934.

Forcey, Charles. *Crossroads of Liberalism*. New York: Oxford University Press, 1961.
Morse, Caroline M., ed. *Memories of Jane Cunningham Croly "Jennie June."* New York and London: Putnam, Knickerbocker Press, 1904.

LEONEL CAMPBELL O'BRYAN
"POLLY PRY"

Fowler, Gene. *Timber Line: A Story of Bonfils and Tammen*. New York: Covici-Friede, 1933.
Hosokawa, Bill. *Thunder in the Rockies*. New York: William Morrow, 1976.
Smith, H. Allen. *The Life and Legend of Gene Fowler*. New York: William Morrow, 1977.

ELIZABETH MERIWETHER GILMER
"DOROTHY DIX"

Dix, Dorothy. *Mirandy*. New York: Hearst's International Library, 1914.
—— *Her Book: Every-day Help for Every-day People*. New York and London: Funk and Wagnalls, 1926.
—— *How to Win and Hold a Husband*. New York: Doubleday, Doran, 1939.
Drewry, John E., ed. *Post Biographies of Famous Journalists*. "Dorothy Dix Talks," by Hermann B. Deutsch. Athens: University of Georgia Press, 1936.
Kane, Harnett T., with Ella Bentley Arthur. *Dear Dorothy Dix: The Story of a Compassionate Woman*. Garden City, N.Y.: Doubleday, 1952.

IDA BELL WELLS-BARNETT

Lerner, Gerda, ed. *Black Women in White America: A Documentary History*. New York: Vintage, 1973.
Loewenberg, Bert James and Ruth Bogin, eds. *Black Women in Nineteenth-Century American Life*. University Park and London: Pennsylvania State University Press, 1978.
Majors, Monroe A. *Noted Negro Women: Their Triumphs and Activities*. Chicago: Donohue & Henneberry, 1893; reprinted 1971.
Penn, I. Garland. *The Afro-American Press and Its Editors*. New York: Arno Press and the New York Times, 1969.
Wells, Ida B. *The Reason Why The Colored American Is Not in the World's Columbian Exposition*. Chicago: Ida B. Wells, 128 S. Clark Street, 1893.
—— *Crusade for Justice: The Autobiography of Ida B. Wells*. Alfreda M. Duster, ed. Chicago and London: University of Chicago Press, 1970; second printing, 1972.
Wolseley, Roland E. *The Black Press, U.S.A.* Ames: Iowa State University Press, 1971.

WINIFRED BLACK BONFILS
"ANNIE LAURIE"

Black, Winifred Sweet. *Dope: The Story of the Living Dead*. New York: Star, 1928.
—— *The Life and Personality of Phoebe Apperson Hearst*. San Francisco: J. H. Nash, 1928.
Bonfils, W. B. *Roses and Rain*. San Francisco: Walter N. Brunt, 1920.
Green, Ward, ed. *Star Reporters and 34 of Their Stories*. New York: Random House, 1948.
Older, Fremont, Mrs. *William Randolph Hearst: American*. New York: Appleton-Century, 1936.
Swanberg, W. A. *Citizen Hearst*. New York: Scribner's, 1961.
Tebbel, John. *The Life and Good Times of William Randolph Hearst*. New York: Dutton, 1952.
Winkler, John K. *W. R. Hearst, An American Phenomenon*. New York: Simon and Schuster, 1928.
—— *William Randolph Hearst: A New Appraisal*. New York: Hastings House, 1955.

ELIZABETH COCHRANE SEAMAN
"NELLIE BLY"

Barrett, James Wyman. *The World, the Flesh and Messrs Pulitzer*. New York: Vanguard, 1931.
—— *Joseph Pulitzer and His World*. New York: Vanguard, 1941.
Cochrane, Elizabeth. *Ten Days in a Mad-House*. New York: Munro, 1887.
—— *Six Months in Mexico*. New York: J. W. Lovell, 1888.
—— *Nellie Bly's Book: Around the World in 72 Days*. New York: Pictorial Weeklies, 1890.
1890.
Mott, Frank Luther, ed. *Headlining America*, 1937. "Nellie Bly of Central Park," by Mabel
Greene. Cambridge, Mass.: Riverside, 1937.
Noble, Iris. *First Woman Reporter*. New York: Julian Messner, 1956.
—— *Joseph Pulitzer: Front-Page Pioneer*. New York: Julian Messner, 1957.
Ravitch, Irene. "Nellie Bly." Masters thesis, Columbia University Graduate School of Jour-
nalism, 1931.
Rittenhouse, Mignon. *The Amazing Nellie Bly*. New York: Dutton, 1956.
Ross, Ishbel. *Charmers and Cranks*. New York: Harper and Row, 1965.
Swanberg, W. A. *Pulitzer*. New York: Scribner's, 1967.

ELIZABETH GARVER JORDAN

Jordan, Elizabeth G. *Tales of the City Room*. New York: Scribner's, 1898.
—— *Three Rousing Cheers*. New York and London: Appleton-Century, 1938.

ANNE O'HARE McCORMICK

Sheehan, Marion T. *Vatican Journal*, 1921–1954. Introduction by Clare Booth Luce. New
York: Farrar, Straus and Cudahy, 1957.
Sheehan, Marion T., ed. *The Spiritual Woman—Trustee of the Future*. New York: Harper,
1955.
—— *The World at Home: Selections from the Writings of Anne O'Hare McCormick*. Intro-
duction by James B. Reston. New York: Knopf, 1956.
Sulzberger, C. L. *A Long Row of Candles: Memoirs and Diaries*, 1934–1954. New York: Mac-
millan, 1969.

EMMA BUGBEE

Breslin, James. *The World of Jimmy Breslin*. Annotated by James G. Bellows and Richard C.
Wald. New York: Viking, 1967.
Bugbee, Emma. *Peggy Covers the News*. New York: Dodd, Mead, 1936.
Collins, Jean E. *She Was There*. New York: Julian Messner, 1980.
Furman, Bess. *Washington By-Line: A Personal History of a Newspaperwoman*. New York: Knopf,
1949.

HENRIETTA GOODNOUGH HULL
"PEGGY HULL"

Benjamin, Robert Spiers. *Eye Witness*. "Open Grave in Shanghai," by Peggy Hull. New York:
Alliance Book, 1940.
—— *The Inside Story*. "Twenty Died at Dawn," by Peggy Hull. New York: Prentice-Hall, 1940.
Crozier, Emmet. *American Reporters on the Western Front*. 1914–1918. New York: Oxford
University Press, 1959.
Jones, David Len. "And Peggy Hull Was There." Master thesis, University of Texas at Austin,
1980.

Knightley, Phillip. *The First Casualty*. New York and London: Harcourt Brace Jovanovich, 1975.

Kuhn, Irene. *Assigned to Adventure*. Philadelphia: Lippincott, 1938.

SIGRID SCHULTZ

Brown, David and W. Richard Bruner, eds. *I Can Tell It Now*. "The Final Hours of Adolf Hitler," by Sigrid Schultz. New York: Dutton, 1964.

—— *How I Got That Story*. "Herman Göring's 'Dragon from Chicago,' " by Sigrid Schultz. New York: Dutton, 1967.

Givner, Joan. *Katherine Anne Porter: A Life*. New York: Simon and Schuster, 1982.

Schultz, Sigrid. *Germany Will Try It Again*. New York: Reynal and Hitchcock, 1944.

Schultz, Sigrid, ed. *Overseas Press Club Cookbook*. Garden City, N.Y.: Doubleday, 1962.

Shirer, William L. *Berlin Diary: The Journal of a Foreign Correspondent, 1934–1941*. New York: Knopf, 1947.

—— *20th Century Journey: The Nightmare Years, 1930–1940*. Boston: Little Brown, 1984.

Wendt, Lloyd. *Chicago Tribune: The Rise of a Great Newspaper*. Chicago: Rand McNally, 1979.

DOROTHY THOMPSON

Sanders, Marion K. *Dorothy Thompson: A Legend in Her Time*. Boston: Houghton Mifflin, 1973.

Sheean, Vincent. *Dorothy and Red*. Boston: Houghton Mifflin, 1963.

Thompson, Dorothy. *The New Russia*. New York: Holt, 1928.

—— *I Saw Hitler*. New York: Farrar, Straus and Cudahy, 1932.

—— *Let the Record Speak*. Boston: Houghton Mifflin, 1939.

ISHBEL ROSS

Ross, Ishbel. *Ladies of the Press: The Story of Women in Journalism by an Insider*. Foreword by Stanley Walker. New York: Harper, 1936.

—— *Fifty Years a Woman*. New York and London: Harper, 1938.

—— *An American Family: The Tafts, 1678 to 1964*. Cleveland, Ohio: World, 1964.

—— *The Expatriates*. New York: Crowell, 1970.

Walker, Stanley. *City Editor*. New York: Frederick A. Stokes, 1934.

MILDRED GILMAN

Collins, Jean E. *She Was There*. New York: Julian Messner, 1980.

Gilman, Mildred. *Headlines*. New York: Liveright, 1928.

—— *Sob Sister*. New York: Jonathan Cape and Harrison Smith, 1931.

DORIS FLEESON

Casey, Ralph D. *The Press in Perspective*. Baton Rouge: Louisiana State University Press, 1983.

Chapman, John Arthur. *Tell It to Sweeney*. Garden City, N.Y.: Doubleday, 1961.

McGivena, Leo E. *The News*. New York: News Syndicate, 1969.

MARY McGRORY

Hohenberg, John. *The New Front Page*. New York and London: Columbia University Press, 1966.

Wicker, Tom. *On Press*. New York: Viking Press, 1978.

MARGUERITE HIGGINS

Beech, Keyes. *Tokyo and Points East*. Garden City, N.Y.: Doubleday, 1954.
Higgins, Marguerite. *War in Korea*. Garden City, N.Y.: Doubleday, 1951.
—— *News Is a Singular Thing*. Garden City, N.Y.: Doubleday, 1955.
—— *Red Plush and Black Bread*. Garden City, N.Y.: Doubleday, 1955.
—— *Our Vietnam Nightmare*. New York: Harper and Row, 1965.
Howard, Toni. *Shriek with Pleasure*. New York: Prentice Hall, 1950.
Lanham, Edwin. *The Iron Maiden*. New York: Harcourt, Brace, 1954.
Lewis, Kathleen Kearney. "Maggie Higgins," Masters thesis, University of Maryland, 1973.
May, Antoinette. *Witness to War: A Biography of Marguerite Higgins*. New York and Toronto: Beaufort Books, 1983.

ADA LOUISE HUXTABLE

Huxtable, Ada Louise. *Four Walking Tours of Modern Architecture in New York City*. Garden City, N.Y.: Doubleday, 1961.
—— *The Architecture of New York*. Garden City, N.Y.: Anchor Books, 1964.
—— *Will They Ever Finish Bruckner Boulevard?* New York: Macmillan, 1970.
—— *Kicked a Building Lately?* New York: Quadrangle, 1976.
Wodehouse, Lawrence. *Ada Louise Huxtable: An Annotated Bibliography*. New York: Garland, 1981.

JUDITH CRIST

Collins, Jean E. *She Was There*. New York: Julian Messner, 1980.
Crist, Judith. *The Private Eye, the Cowboy, and the Very Naked Girl: Movies from Cleo to Clyde*. Chicago: Holt, Rinehart and Winston, 1968.
—— *TV Guide to the Movies*. Toronto: Popular Library, 1974.
McCreadie, Marsha. *Women on Film: The Critical Eye*. New York: Praeger, 1983.

GEORGIE ANNE GEYER

Geyer, Georgie Anne. *The New Latins*. Garden City, N.Y.: Doubleday, 1970.
—— *The Young Russians*. Homewood, Ill.: ETC, 1975.
—— *Buying the Night Flight*. New York: Delacorte, 1983.

ELLEN GOODMAN

Goodman, Ellen. *Turning Points*. Garden City, N.Y.: Doubleday, 1979.
—— *Close to Home*. New York: Simon and Schuster, 1979.
—— *At Large*. New York: Summit Books, 1981.
Grauer, Neil. *Wits and Sages*. Baltimore, Md.: Johns Hopkins University Press, 1984.

Index